WAR
AND
SOCIETY

WAR
AND
SOCIETY

Historical essays in honour and memory of
J. R. WESTERN 1928–1971

Edited by
M. R. D. FOOT

BOOKS
10 East 53d St., New York 10022
(a division of Harper & Row Publishers, Inc.)

Published in the U.S.A. 1973 by
Harper & Row Publishers, Inc.
Barnes & Noble Import Division

First published 1973 in Great Britain by
Elek Books Limited, London

Copyright © 1973 by Kirsten Western

ISBN 06 492140 9

Printed in Great Britain

Contents

Editor's Preface

John Western spent his life, which was tragically short, in learning, in teaching, and in writing history, and in sustaining his family and his friends. Several of his friends have joined in compiling this book, which they offer to his wife and children as a token – however slight and inadequate – of their respect, their affection, and their continued caring.

John Randle Western was born on the north-eastern outskirts of London on 28 October 1928; close to the mid-point between the end of what his father's generation called the Great War of 1914–18, and the start of the next great international catastrophe of 1939–45. He was the mildest and gentlest of men; but the world he was born into, and the world he grew up in, and the world in which his grown-up life was lived, were all necessarily coloured and distorted by war. He never served in a combatant unit himself – he was only a schoolboy when Hitler's war ended, and was exempt from national service. Wars horrified him, as they horrify anyone sensitive; a former Edinburgh colleague could still remember, over twenty years later, the profound impression made on him by a film of Remarque's, *All Quiet on the Western Front.* Yet he appreciated also the central part wars have played in history, and spent much time and trouble in elucidating their causes, course, and consequences. He taught for his last three years at Manchester a subject of his own devising on the influence of war on society, and this seemed a suitable theme on which to collect memorial essays from his friends; many more of whom would have joined in this tribute had they had anything to say bearing on this topic, or had they had more time, or had the topic been different, or the publisher's indulgence still larger.

John Western won a history scholarship from Merchant Taylor's School to St John's College, Oxford, where he was taught by Lane Poole and W. C. Costin; and in 1949 he was placed in the first class in the final honours school. He took his next degree at Edinburgh, under the direction of the great Richard Pares, with whom he quickly developed a close friendship. His doctoral thesis – never published – dealt with the recruitment of the land forces in Great Britain in 1793–99, during the war against revolutionary France. It explained, with unobtrusive dexterity, the system – if system it could be called, so unsystematic were many of its parts – for manning the regular army, the militia, and the volunteers. With splendid impartiality, Western noticed the difficulties of a conservative régime in a revolutionary age. Arms, for instance, were in no circumstances to be readily available to the urban working classes; while the more docile peasantry could be armed and organised through their landlords.

He stayed on in Edinburgh to teach for a year after graduating there in 1953; and then joined the history department at Manchester, where he spent the rest of his working life. He spent much time on his *magnum opus*, a book arising out of his thesis, *The English Militia in the Eighteenth Century*, published by Routledge and Kegan Paul in 1964. This was an early item in the series 'Studies in Political History' edited by Michael Hurst, also of St John's. Like a pointilliste painting, this book built up a broad view by a myriad of minute touches of colour, explaining in detail the working of English eighteenth-century politics at the critical level of the county. No more need be said of it than the remark of a highly qualified historian, who found it more illuminating about English politics in that age than anything else he had read except Namier.

Soon after he reached Manchester, John Western married a Danish friend, Kirsten Pedersen, who bore him two children, Colin and Isobel. They formed a close-knit family square, bound together in deep affection; settled at Mellor, on the edge of the Derbyshire moors. Dozens of his pupils will remember his hospitality with gratitude, for, never a man to shirk anything, he took on an exceptionally heavy teaching load, even for a Manchester modernist. He ran for many years a special subject on Anglo-German relations from 1898 to 1912, which called for close attention to diplomatic history, and did much general teaching as well.

When Albert Goodwin, who had recommended his appointment, retired in 1969, he was an obvious candidate for the vacant chair of modern history. As professor, he displayed for all too short a time an unusual gift among academic, or any other, committee men. He could sit silent, and apparently abstracted, while colleagues wrangled round him; and when they seemed to have reached an impasse, he would quietly propose a formula that would reconcile all their differences. With his help, the modern historians began a total revision of their way of teaching history; but that is a story for another place. They remember him as a man whom it was impossible not to like a great deal, and who can surely never have made an enemy in his life.

He wrote two other books : *The End of European Primacy*, a textbook on 1870–1945 (Blandford Press 1965, 1971), invaluable to intelligent sixth-formers and first-year undergraduates who want to know about the recent roots of the world they live in; and *Monarchy and Revolution* (same press, 1972), a study of William III's succession to James II which was widely acclaimed when it was published posthumously. For he had just sent off the text to the printer when, in June 1971, he fell gravely ill. His condition was found to be inoperable, and he died on 26 November.

He is buried in Mellor churchyard.

As Denys Hay, one of his Edinburgh friends and colleagues, puts it,

It seems absurd to write about war when one thinks of John Western. As a colleague in Edinburgh from 1950 to 1954, I see him as a young man of peace – gentle, rather dreamy, an immediate friend, and this to many besides his close colleagues and his pupils. But he was interested in the history of war, perhaps because he had lived a sizeable portion of his life through one and thus came to realise how important are the moral and cultural, as well as the economic and purely military, consequences of war. With others of my own contemporaries I certainly found myself in the years after 1945 still preoccupied with aspects of warfare in other times (in my case the later Middle Ages) which would not, I believe, have caught my attention if I had not experienced life between 1939 and 1945.

Hence this collection of papers on the historical connections between war and social organisation; a subject, more and more popular in schools and universities in recent years, of which Western was one of the pioneers.

No one can hope for a single strong connecting thread to tie all these papers together, beyond the insistence in almost all of them on the impact that wars make on society, and societies make on war. All the authors are dons, as Western was; and all knew him, though with varying degrees of closeness. Some helped appoint him, some were appointed by him. Some had known and worked with him and been fond of him for many years; some had hardly met him, but were so struck with him, even at a glancing meeting, that they wanted to join in this act of academic homage. Western abhorred dullness. One of his Edinburgh friends refers to a 'happy vein of quizzicality' in him; he had a strong sense of history's irony, and thought *homo sapiens*, or *homo sentiens*, viewed collectively, on the whole an odd lot. Some of this may come out below.

For the reader's convenience, the chapters are arranged roughly in chronological order; the most recent, probably the most familiar, items are placed first.

Three essays deal with the most recent world war. Alastair Parker looks in detail at the circumstances of the British and French entry into it; and uses unpublished material to establish important new conclusions. Peter Lowe follows, also working largely from the cabinet papers, with an analysis of how the British came to be involved in Japan's east Asian war in 1941. The involvement disastrously overstretched Great Britain's economic resources; Lowe shows it was inescapable. Denys Hay, writing from inside knowledge, shows how government departments were encouraged during the war to record their difficulties, and how they got round them; thus, in the cabinet secretary's phrase, 'funding our war-time experience for future use'.

Five papers follow on the great war of 1914–18 and its aftermath. The editor sketches the permanent principles of subversion that underlay Michael Collins's successful guerrilla in Ireland in 1919–21, and seeks to show how the Irish provided an exemplar for later colonial revolt. They also, unintentionally, provided the inspiration for SOE, of which the first idea germinated on the banks of the Liffey. Michael Rose investigates the origins and growth of the drink control board, which was set up in June 1915, is famous for having kept our pubs closed in the afternoon till the present day, and did much hitherto unnoticed useful work as well; such as stimulating the spread of works canteens. Judith Brown examines the political and social foundations of British rule in India, and discusses how far they were affected by the war. She centres her discussion on the Montagu declaration of 1917, which was, she believes, intended to buttress the existing system; but it began a process of adaptation that led to India's independence. Simon Katzenellenbogen, in a parallel essay on war and the colonial relationship, discusses the war's impact in southern Africa: both in exacerbated Boer–British relations in the south, in Chilembwe's Nyasaland rising that forebode much trouble to come, and in the still troubled field of racial tension in mining areas. Lastly of these five, Peter Fraser explains how the British ran the war : through an efficient cabinet secretariat, a reorganisation of departments, and a dwindling of ministers' personal position *vis-à-vis* the head of the government.

Victor Kiernan breaks quite new ground, in a trenchant and controversial account of the purpose of the conscription system in continental Europe. In his view, it was an adjunct of capitalism in its take-off phase; a device for turning individuals, with ideas of their own, into ordered automata who would carry over to the factory floor the habits of disciplined obedience learned with the colours. Harry Hanham provides an English foil to this continental survey, by investigating – primarily through the parliamentary papers – the national and religious composition of the British army in the second half of the nineteenth century. Like Kiernan, he is sharply aware of the importance of class in society, and provides plenty of food for thought. John Bromley, in an essay particularly closely tied to John Western's work on the militia, indicates from mid-nineteenth-century sources where thoughtful British naval officers believed they might find, in the event of another great war, a reliable alternative to the press gang for assembling reserve crews.

Two essays consider the French revolution, one in general and one through a highly personal case. Norman Hampson, for many years a close Manchester colleague of Western's, examines the impact of revolution and war on what virtuous republicans thought right conduct was. And Albert Goodwin explains what happened to a banker who lent George III's sons money, set out to make a second pile out of transport for the revolutionary armies, and turned out to have had a former royal coachman on his strength.

Penry Williams uses English history in the sixteenth and seventeenth centuries to investigate the problem, currently the subject of so much argument, of when rebellions turn into revolutions; and demonstrates an essential difference between risings against the Tudors and the revolutionary struggle that beheaded a Stuart.

And finally, three members of the Manchester department with interests in ancient history show that there is no great gulf fixed between ancient and modern. Alister Jackson's account of privateering in the Peloponnesian, Alexandrine and Punic wars contains incidents and characters that would have been perfectly in place in the central Europe of the 1630s or indeed of the 1930s, and discussion of modes of right conduct that would have been fashionable in Paris in 1790 or Bloomsbury in 1925. John Graham's article, more close-knit in texture and much more concentrated in time, analyses the motives of the high command of the Roman imperial army at the end of the second century AD in terms that are perfectly intelligible to the modern reader, even if the reader can hardly tell the difference between a centurion and a retiarius : motives do not change as fast as techniques. And Barri Jones's account of the settling of legionary veterans in Etruria, late in the first century BC and early in the present era, is both a prime example of the interaction of war and society, and a study of current topical interest in a distracted and war-torn world.

These papers serve to show the diversity and the unity of history, and to justify the profession of the man in whose memory his friends have written them.

28 February 1973   M.R.D.F.

Notes on Contributors

J. S. BROMLEY, professor of modern history at Southampton since 1960, formerly taught at Liverpool and at Keble College, Oxford. He has edited *inter alia* vol. vi of the *New Cambridge Modern History*, and is at present editing a collection of manning pamphlets for the Navy Records Society.

DR JUDITH M. BROWN, now lecturer in history at Manchester, wrote while a fellow of Girton College, Cambridge, *Gandhi's Rise to Power: Indian Politics 1915–22* (1972), the first part of a political study of the Mahatma.

M. R. D. FOOT, the author of *SOE in France* (1966) and editor of the first two volumes of the *Gladstone Diaries* (1968), was professor of modern history at Manchester from 1967 to 1973. He is now director of studies at the European Discussion Centre (Foreign Office).

PETER FRASER, author of biographical studies of Joseph Chamberlain (1966) and Lord Esher (1973), was long a lecturer in history at Manchester; he is now professor of history at Dalhousie University, Nova Scotia.

DR A. J. GRAHAM, senior lecturer in history at Manchester, has taught ancient history there for many years and is the author of *Colony and Mother City in Ancient Greece*, and has contributed to the *Journal of Hellenic Studies*, *Journal of Roman Studies* and other learned periodicals.

ALBERT GOODWIN, historian of the French Revolution, succeeded L. B. Namier as professor of modern history at Manchester (1953–69). He edited vol. viii of the *New Cambridge Modern History*.

NORMAN HAMPSON wrote *La Marine de l'an II* (1959) and *A Social History of the French Revolution* (1965) while he was lecturer in French history at Manchester; he has been professor of modern history at Newcastle-upon-Tyne since 1967 and has also written the volume on the Enlightenment (1968) in the Pelican *History of European Thought.*

H. J. HANHAM, the authority on the nineteenth-century constitution, belonged to the Manchester government department when he wrote *Elections and Party Management: Politics in the Age of Disraeli and Gladstone* (1959). He has since been professor successively of politics at Edinburgh and of history at Harvard, and is now at the Massachusetts Institute of Technology.

DENYS HAY, professor of medieval history at Edinburgh since 1954, is one of the leading historians of the origins of the Renaissance.

DR A. H. JACKSON joined the Manchester history department as a lecturer in 1968.

G. D. B. JONES, professor of archaeology at Manchester since 1972 and currently head of the history department, has directed excavations in several countries and become, at an unusually early age, one of the leading figures in his subject.

DR S. E. KATZENELLENBOGEN, who took his first degree at Ann Arbor, Michigan, and his doctorate at Oxford, has been a lecturer in economic history at Manchester since 1970.

V. G. KIERNAN, professor of history at Edinburgh since 1970, is the author of *The Lords of Human Kind* (1969), a study of race relations in the epoch of imperialism.

DR PETER LOWE, who has taught history at Manchester since 1965, is a diplomatic and political historian; his works include *Great Britain and Japan 1911–15* (1969).

R. A. C. PARKER, fellow of The Queen's College, Oxford, is the author of *Europe from 1919 to 1945* (1970).

DR M. E. ROSE, lecturer in economic history at Manchester and chairman of the history departmental board, is the editor of a source book, *The English Poor Law 1780–1930* (1971), and author of *The Relief of Poverty 1834–1914* (1972).

DR PENRY WILLIAMS was a lecturer in history at Manchester before he was elected fellow of New College, Oxford; he has written (*inter alia*) on the Welsh marches under Elizabeth I.

1

The British Government and the Coming of
War with Germany, 1939

R. A. C. PARKER

On 31 March 1939 Mr Chamberlain made public a British pledge
to support Poland at once if the Polish government were to use the
national forces to resist a clear threat to Polish independence. On
25 August the pledge was embodied and made reciprocal in an
Anglo-Polish treaty. Early on 1 September 1939 Germany invaded
Poland. At 9 a.m. on 3 September the British ambassador delivered
an ultimatum in Berlin which expired at 11 a.m. when the United
Kingdom went to war with Germany. Why was there this delay?
At the time, some of those who had felt uneasy about Mr Chamberlain's acquiescence in the Munich agreement suspected that Chamberlain himself, probably Lord Halifax as well, and possibly the
most senior ministers or even the majority of the Cabinet had been,
and were still, hoping to evade the fulfilment of the Polish guarantee. It was believed that this evasion had been prevented only by
the threat of a last-minute revolt of back-benchers in the House of
Commons. Either this revolt helped those in the Cabinet who
wished Britain to declare war to coerce Chamberlain and his associates, or it coerced the Cabinet itself into accepting war.

Many people still think the same. It is a view which has the
powerful support of Mr A. J. P. Taylor, the ablest historian of the
period. He has given this view wide publicity in two books, *The
Origins of the Second World War* and *English History 1914–1945*.
Britain would not have gone to war unless MPs had been 'resolute'
– 'the Government tailed regretfully after the House of Commons.'
On 1 September the Polish appeal 'met with a cool response. The
Cabinet decided that if Germany would suspend hostilities and
withdraw her troops, a solution without war would still be possible.'

1

On 2 September, according to Mr Taylor, the Cabinet was now resolute and 'lost patience'. But 'Halifax had new resources . . . the French generals . . . wished to complete mobilisation before declaring war. This gave an excuse for postponement.' In spite of the Cabinet decision of the afternoon of 2 September 'Halifax went on negotiating for a conference with no time limit attached for the withdrawal of German troops. Chamberlain feared to act ahead of the French and was not sorry . . . to be held back by them.' In the evening Chamberlain 'entertained' the Commons 'with prospects of a conference: if the Germans agreed to withdraw their forces (which was not the same as actually withdrawing them), the British government would forget everything that had happened and diplomacy could start again.' Thus angry MPs pushed the Cabinet into pushing Chamberlain and Halifax into war. Mr Taylor's footnote reads: 'It later became the agreed version that Chamberlain was merely covering up for the French and himself had no hope of a peaceful settlement. This is not what appears from the contemporary record.' In his latest book Mr Taylor writes simply: 'On 2 September . . . the house of commons revolted and forced war on a reluctant government.'[1] I hope to show that it is, at least, more complicated than that: that the furthest one can go is to postulate a brief hesitation on the part of Chamberlain and Halifax on the afternoon of 2 September, a hesitation induced by French pressure. No member of the government directly suggesting dishonouring the pledge to Poland. The only issue was this: should the government accept delay while attempts at a negotiated settlement of German–Polish issues were made? If so, should German troops first withdraw from Poland? The nearest anyone in the government came to contemplating 'letting the Poles down' was to hesitate for a moment when faced with arguments in favour of delay to enable Germany to consider negotiating. No one in the Cabinet, however, thought of negotiating while German troops remained in Poland. They must withdraw, and Hitler must call off his assault, before negotiations could start. In any case it was not this hesitation that delayed the British declaration of war: it was, in fact, the French.

Early in the morning of Friday 1 September 1939 a message arrived at 10 Downing Street. It was taken down in pencil: 'German wireless has just stated that Polish troops have crossed frontier in 3 or 4 places.' Soon after, a telegram came from Reuters, handed in at 7.48 a.m.: 'Berlin wireless issued following announcement at 5.40 this morning: Führer issued following proclamation to army.

Polish state has refused peaceful settlement of relations which I desired and has appealed to arms.'[2]

At 10.30 a.m. the Polish ambassador, Count Raczynski, called on Lord Halifax, the British Foreign Secretary, and reported the German attack. Lord Halifax noted that 'His Excellency said that he had few words to add, except that it was a plain case as provided for by the treaty. I said that I had no doubt on the facts as he had reported them that we should take the same view.'[3]

The Cabinet met at 11 a.m. on 1 September. Here is how the record begins: 'The Prime Minister said that the Cabinet met under the gravest possible conditions. The event against which we had fought so long and so earnestly had come upon us. But our consciences were clear, and there should be no possible question now where our duty lay.' Apparently Chamberlain meant war, unless he was showing startling hypocrisy. After a recital of events by Halifax, the Cabinet turned to a discussion of 'the terms of the communication to be sent to the German Government'. It was a question of whether or not to send an ultimatum to Berlin. Halifax, having used extracts from the speech Hitler was making, which showed that Germany really was invading Poland, proposed that the German government should be notified that it must give 'satisfactory assurances that aggression against Poland has been stopped and that the German troops will be promptly withdrawn from Poland' or else Britain 'will without hesitation fulfil their obligations to Poland'. This was approved. At that moment the Cabinet heard the first news of the French desire for delay.

The Foreign Secretary added that he had received a communication from the French Government to the effect that they wished to declare war before we did. The reason given for this was said to be public opinion in France, since the French Government were anxious not to appear to be dragged into war by us. It was agreed that while the French might reasonably claim that we should not declare war before they did, the right course would be that the French and ourselves should declare war at the same time.

Later, the question was raised again whether there should be a time-limit in the message to Berlin, i.e. whether it should be an ultimatum. The report reads: 'It was pointed out that it was important to ascertain the French attitude in regard to this matter. . . . The real question at issue was when the draft telegram should be despatched. On this we should act in consultation with the French Government.'[4]

The instructions to give the warning, as a joint Anglo-French communication, to the Germans were sent in two telegrams to the British ambassador in Berlin, at 4.45 p.m. and 5.45 p.m. on the afternoon of 1 September. Henderson was told that the next stage 'will be either an ultimatum with a time limit or an immediate declaration of war'.[5]

At 9.35 a.m. on the next morning, 2 September, the British ambassador in Paris telephoned to London :

Every hour gained to enable the French general mobilisation to proceed unhindered is precious. It is therefore essential that Sir N. Henderson [British ambassador in Berlin] should not act in advance of the French ambassador. . . . I have no doubt of the final result of to-day's debate here, but attempt on the part of the French Government to curtail it . . . would be resented by public opinion.

Some days before it had already been argued by the British ambassador in Paris that from the point of view of French opinion the British government should not declare war in advance of the French.[6]

In the Foreign Office there soon began to be felt 'a good deal of anxiety over French attitude and their apparently delaying tactics'.[7] At 11.55 a.m. a message was telephoned to Paris for the British ambassador : 'Delays in Paris and attitude of the French Government are causing some misgiving here. We shall be grateful for anything you can do to infuse courage and determination into M. Bonnet.' Bonnet was the French Minister for Foreign Affairs. The British Foreign Office rightly suspected him of willingness to do anything to avoid war. Sir Eric Phipps, the British ambassador in Paris, replied, however, expressing his belief that the reason for the attitude of the French government really was what they said it to be : to make it possible for the evacuation of big towns, and general mobilisation, to take place unhindered by air attack.[8]

A 12.30 p.m. another telephone message to Paris asked for the French government's concurrence in a statement the Prime Minister intended to make to Parliament at 3 p.m. The critical passages in the draft were these :

It is impossible to wait for more than a very limited time before resolving the present situation, and His Majesty's Government do not intend to do so. It is however highly desirable that the action of His Majesty's Government and that of the French Government should be simultaneous and identical, and the French Government are entirely in accord on this point. . . . His Majesty's Government was accordingly awaiting the meeting of the French Parliament, and the two Governments had agreed that, so soon as the requirements of the French constitution had been met, they would jointly make their final communication to the German Government.

The French Parliament was due to meet at 3 p.m.; the British had been told that the French government could not declare war in advance of parliamentary authority. The French at once agreed to Chamberlain's statement.[9] An hour later, however, another message came from Paris. This agreed to the despatch of identical ultimata to Germany after the sitting of the French Chamber. They should be in the terms agreed on by the two governments before the German invasion – a demand that the 'German Government should halt their troops and express their readiness to enter into negotiation, failing which His Majesty's Government would have to take all steps necessary to fulfil their obligations.' The French added a plea for a time limit of forty-eight hours from the presentation of the note. That would delay the British and French declarations of war until late on 4 September, at the soonest.[10]

The real drama of 2 September 1939 in London began, though, at 2.30 p.m. when Count Ciano, the Italian Foreign Minister, telephoned from Rome to Lord Halifax. He said that he still thought it might be possible to call a conference of representatives of France, Great Britain, Germany and Poland. It was an attempt to organise a new Munich. The plan had already exposed Anglo-French divergences, or at least divergences between Bonnet and the British government. On 31 August, at 12.50 p.m., Ciano had telephoned to Halifax suggesting that Mussolini should call a conference to meet on 5 September to revise 'the clauses of the Treaty of Versailles which are the cause of the present grave troubles in the life of Europe.' Chamberlain's first reaction was 'that it was impossible to agree to a conference under the threat of mobilised armies, and he felt that a preliminary condition in any case would have to be a measure of demobilisation.' However, Chamberlain and Halifax asked Corbin, the French ambassador in London, to find out what the French government thought.[11] Daladier, the French Prime Minister, who was increasingly given to violent utterances of defiance which contrasted sharply with Bonnet's smooth evasions, told Phipps in Paris 'that he would rather resign than accept' an invitation to a second Munich.[12] That evening, though, Bonnet persuaded the French Cabinet that 'it would not

be possible to decline [the] Italian proposal offhand' and promised
a draft reply the next morning (1 September) accepting the idea of
the conference. The German attack intervened. The British Foreign
Office therefore telephoned to Rome at 11.20 a.m. thanking Mussolini and adding 'that the action of the German Government has
now rendered it impossible to proceed along those lines.'[13] At the
Cabinet meeting a few minutes later Halifax noted that the Italian
suggestion had been 'overtaken by the course of events' and no
further reference to the plan was recorded at this meeting.[14]

The French reply to the Italian suggestion of 31 August was
different. The reply agreed by the French Cabinet that evening
was shown to Cadogan, the Permanent Under-Secretary at the
Foreign Office, at about 10.15 a.m. on 1 September. It appeared,
as Oliver Harvey, Lord Halifax's private secretary, noted, that 'the
French Government are very anxious to send this reply at once to
the Italian démarche for a conference, even though it is now
academic.'[15] The British evinced no great interest. In fact, Bonnet
contrived to secure the approval of his government to the despatch
of the reply to Rome and sent it to the French ambassador there
without any hint of its 'academic' quality. Thus Bonnet sent a reply
to Ciano which had been drafted before the German invasion of
Poland but which was sent unchanged after the invasion had
begun. It insisted that a conference about Poland must include
Polish representation but gave *'une réponse favorable'* to the projected conference.[16] And on the same day Bonnet sent 'most secret
instructions' to Warsaw to sound the Polish Foreign Minister on
the possibility of a five-power conference. Beck replied that 'it was
time to talk not of conferences but of mutual aid in resistance to
aggression.'[17]

It is not surprising that Ciano told the British ambassador in
Rome soon after 12 noon the same day, 1 September, that he
intended to discuss with Mussolini the possibility of reviving the
proposal for a conference and that 'he seemed to have some indication that the French would not decline.' Next morning, 2 September, Attolico, the Italian ambassador in Berlin, was told to inform
the Germans that a conference could be held in two or three days'
time on the basis of an armistice leaving the armies in their existing
positions. Ciano commented that the idea 'is pursued specially by
France' ['. . . *è ora sollecitata specie dalla Francia*'] and that the
conference would enable Germany to get all her objectives without
war. Ribbentrop conveyed Hitler's reaction to Attolico at 12.30

p.m. He was playing for time. He wanted to know if the British
and French messages of the previous day were ultimata or not and
insisted that the Germans would need a day or two to consider
Mussolini's proposal.[18] Henderson assured Attolico that the British
warning to Berlin had not been an ultimatum, though adding that
he did not believe any conference could be held while German
forces remained on Polish territory. Attolico passed this news to
Ribbentrop at 12.50 p.m. without mentioning Henderson's comment. Ribbentrop asked Attolico to confirm through Rome that no
ultimata had been sent to Germany and told him Hitler would
reply by noon on Sunday 3 September.[19]

At 2 p.m. the British and French ambassadors in Rome were
both called to see Ciano. The latter telephoned to Bonnet who
assured Ciano that the French note had not been an ultimatum and
that in his opinion the French government would agree to giving
time to the Germans to consider the question of the armistice and
the conference. At 2.30 p.m. Ciano telephoned to Halifax.[20]

He told Halifax of the Italian suggestion to Germany. Halifax
said that he thought the British Cabinet would feel that 'the first
step must be the withdrawal of German troops from Polish soil.'
Ciano replied 'that he was afraid that this would be impossible.' It
was after the end of this conversation that the chain of events
began which generated mistrust of Halifax's and Chamberlain's
intentions and the belief that they were plotting a dishonourable
peace. At 2.45 p.m. Sir John Simon, Chancellor of the Exchequer,
was going to make a statement to the House of Commons, deputis-
ing for Chamberlain, who was held back by the continued need to
keep in touch with the discussion with Paris. Simon was to read
the statement drafted that morning with its announcement that the
government did not intend to wait for more than a very limited
time. He was intercepted by Halifax who told him of Ciano's proposal. According to Oliver Harvey, Halifax added to Simon that
'he didn't see how we could contemplate a conference with Germany on Polish soil.' However, as a result of the renewed proposal
from Rome, Simon simply told the House that 'the Prime Minister
will be coming down to the House later in the sitting, and will
himself make a statement which cannot be made at this moment.'[21]

Halifax and Oliver Harvey then went to 10 Downing Street and
Harvey read his record of the Halifax–Ciano interchange to Cham-
berlain. A telephone conversation followed between Halifax and
Bonnet. Halifax reported as his personal opinion that the British

government would insist, as an essential preliminary to any conference, on the withdrawal of German troops from Polish territory. Halifax noted that Ciano had said that Hitler would find this impossible. Bonnet thought the German withdrawal 'desirable'. He added 'that he thought a conference might be contemplated provided that Poland were represented at it. That was the really essential point.' Bonnet then asked again for a time limit of forty-eight hours in the eventual ultimatum – putting off any declaration of war to the evening of 4 September, at the earliest.[22] Bonnet evidently hoped for a weakening of British resolve to fight which he could use to weaken French resolve. He did not get it.

When Chamberlain was told of Ciano's proposal and of the French reaction, he summoned an immediate Cabinet meeting. It began at 4.15 p.m. The most important fact about this meeting is what was *not* said. No suggestion was made by anyone that the proposal made by Ciano, and discreetly supported by Bonnet, should be accepted. No one, that is to say, argued that a conference, or a direct German–Polish negotiation, was acceptable so long as German troops remained on Polish territory. The issue that arose was a much narrower one : whether or not to allow the Germans up to 12 noon on Sunday 3 September or even up to 12 midnight on 3–4 September to think about a conference. Halifax opened the proceedings with an account of the recent conversations with Ciano and Bonnet. Then he set out the conclusions that he and Chamberlain had worked out before the Cabinet met. Simon noted them thus : 'It appeared that the plan which these two provisionally favoured was : (1) An armistice in Poland with the forces on both sides halted *where they were* [Simon's emphasis] in order to give Hitler till noon next day to consider the proposal of a conference. (2) The conference to be entered upon only if Hitler accepted the condition that the German troops must be withdrawn from Poland.' The Cabinet record now reads : 'In the discussion which ensued, it was generally agreed that it would be impossible to have any negotiations with Germany while German troops remained on Polish territory.' Thus was unanimously established the point that Britain was going to war unless Hitler accepted defeat and withdrew from Poland. Discussion then turned to the question of how long Hitler was to have to decide whether or not thus to withdraw. Simon goes on :

My own view was, that it was impossible to concede to Hitler the right to remain on Polish ground merely in order to give him a further period to reflect on the conference proposal. As Malcolm Macdonald said, when Hitler acts, he does not lose any time about it, and when he expects other people to confer, he gives them no time to reflect at all. It was soon clear that the Cabinet view was that no terms could be acceptable which did not involve the immediate withdrawal of German forces. . . . In the end, the Cabinet as a whole adopted the view that we could not countenance any delaying tactics, and that in the absence of a satisfactory undertaking to withdraw, we ought to be at war by midnight. [i.e. that night, 2–3 September.][23]

On this point, then, Halifax and Chamberlain were overruled by the Cabinet. The secretary's record shows that Hoare (Home Secretary), Kingsley Wood (Secretary for Air) and Chatfield (Minister for Co-ordination of Defence), in addition to those who made their opposition clear either then or later in the day, opposed protracted delay. Only Runciman, Maugham, Inskip, Zetland and Stanhope are unaccounted for, and none even of those spoke in support of Halifax's suggestions. The Cabinet agreed : '(1) To despatch a communication to the German Government on the lines indicated in the discussion. (2) Authorise the Prime Minister and Foreign Secretary to settle the terms of the communication, and of the statements to be made in Parliament that afternoon, after consultation with the French Government.'

Cadogan had been summoned to 10 Downing Street at 3.15 p.m. 'Stayed there till 1 a.m.', he recorded in his diary. He was quite clear about the origins of the problems of that day :

Trouble is the French. We can't simply wait longer for a German reply. But the French don't want to present ultimatum till noon tomorrow, with 48 hrs' notice. Found Ciano had been ringing up with proposal for 5 Power Conference. And I think Bonnet has probably committed himself to it too far – trying to wriggle out. . . . Cabinet in afternoon, who wanted ultimatum to expire at midnight tonight. But we couldn't budge the French. Awful evening ringing up Bonnet and Daladier.[24]

The telephoning began immediately after the Cabinet, about 5 p.m., when Cadogan spoke to Bonnet. Cadogan told Bonnet the views of the British government. Bonnet answered that the French Cabinet was going to consider whether they thought the retirement of German troops a necessary condition to their agreement to a conference and that the French insisted 'firmly' on forty-eight hours before embarking on hostilities. Bonnet declared that if the British 'insisted on the midnight ultimatum they would incur a grave responsibility *vis-à-vis* France, because French evacuation is incomplete and will take two days more to complete.' He promised a decision on the final French attitude by 8 or 9 p.m. At 6 p.m. Halifax spoke to the British ambassador in Paris and told him that the French failure to agree on the need for withdrawal of German troops as a pre-condition of any conference and their failure to agree on the time limit to be inserted in the eventual ultimatum were very embarrassing to the British government. Halifax enquired if it were 'impossible to move M. Daladier . . . and persuade him to agree that the ultimatum should expire at midnight tonight?' Apparently, Halifax was loyally carrying out the recent Cabinet decision. At 6.38 p.m. Halifax confirmed to Ciano that the British government insisted on a German withdrawal from Poland before any conference. This caused Ciano to feel that the conference idea was hopeless and, after consulting Mussolini, he dropped it.[25] The British government, by its unanimous decision, had killed the plan. Bonnet's attempt that night to revive it got nowhere. He asked Guariglia, the Italian ambassador in Paris, to tell Ciano that the best way of persuading the British to give up their insistence on the withdrawal of the Germans from Poland would be to persuade the Germans to carry out a limited and symbolic withdrawal.[26] Bonnet knew that unless the British could be persuaded to join in a stand for peace, his efforts to restrain the Daladier government from going to war would be defeated.

It was impossible for Chamberlain to go on postponing any statement to the House of Commons. At 7.44 p.m. on 2 September he made a set of remarks which were more effectively designed for French and Italian and even German consumption than for a House of Commons nearly all of whose members expected an announcement that war would soon begin. Daladier's agreement to a statement that Britain would insist on a withdrawal of German troops was passed to London only at 7.10 p.m. and Daladier refused to agree to an ultimatum expiring at midnight without consulting his Cabinet.[27] Chamberlain gave his statement in these words :

Sir Nevile Henderson was received by Herr von Ribbentrop at half-past nine last night, and he delivered the warning message which was read to the House yesterday. Herr von Ribbentrop replied that he must submit the communication to the German Chancellor. Our Ambassador declared his readiness to receive the Chancellor's reply. Up to the present no reply has been received.

It may be that the delay is caused by consideration of a proposal which, meanwhile, had been put forward by the Italian Government, that hostilities should cease and that there should then immediately be a conference between the Five Powers, Great Britain, France, Poland, Germany and Italy. While appreciating the efforts of the Italian Government, His Majesty's Government, for their part, would find it impossible to take part in a conference while Poland is being subjected to invasion, her towns are under bombardment and Danzig is being made the subject of a unilateral settlement by force. His Majesty's Government will, as stated yesterday, be bound to take action unless the German forces are withdrawn from Polish territory. They are in communication with the French Government as to the limit of time within which it would be necessary for the British and French Governments to know whether the German Government were prepared to effect such a withdrawal. If the German Government should agree to withdraw their forces then His Majesty's Government would be willing to regard the position as being the same as it was before the German forces crossed the Polish frontier. That is to say, the way would be open for discussion between the German and Polish Governments on the matters at issue between them, on the understanding that the settlement arrived at was one that safeguarded the vital interests of Poland and was secured by an international guarantee. If the German and Polish Governments wished that other Powers should be associated with them in the discussion, His Majesty's Government for their part would be willing to agree.[28]

It was this statement that precipitated the cry from a Conservative addressed to Arthur Greenwood as he rose to speak for the Labour Opposition: 'Speak for England!' Simon commented: 'The reaction of surprise and disapproval at what seemed to be a dilatory process with no definite end was extreme. . . . I have never seen such a sudden reversion of feeling in my thirty years' experience in the House.' Chamberlain himself told Inskip later that evening that 'the House had been very restless.'[29]

What is more, many members of the Cabinet were very surprised and angry. They had expected that the decision of the afternoon Cabinet would be put into effect and that war would begin at midnight. Simon's diary makes it possible to explain what happened next with more clarity than has been possible until now.

The House adjourned just after 8 o'clock, and there was a swirl of disappointed and excited Members into the lobby. This was not the end of this strange day's proceedings. About twelve Members of the Cabinet came into my room behind the Chair, and they one and all expressed their surprise that the statement made differed fundamentally from the Cabinet decision, and yet had been announced without another Cabinet being called. They felt that this was putting them in a false position, and, moreover, they were consumed with the fear that the announcement just made would throw the Poles into dejection, and be exploited by the Germans as a proof that Poland was too sanguine if she expected prompt British support. The language and feelings of some of my colleagues were so strong and deep that I thought it right at once to inform the Prime Minister, who was still in his room at the House. He asked me to bring in the protesting and disappointed Ministers, and invited me to state the difficulty. I did so very briefly and moderately. . . . At the same time I said that I shared the feelings of the others that it was surprising to have so grave a variation adopted and publicly announced when the Cabinet had decided otherwise.[30]

After this, Chamberlain returned to Downing Street, where he met Inskip, who had called on a different mission. To quote Inskip:

We heard no time limit had been put into the P.M.'s statement in H. of C., as the French want longer than midnight. I went over to Downing Street to try and see Horace Wilson, with a view to getting the time limit made long enough ahead to give the Germans time to consider it. Everyone was out, but as I was coming away the P.M. met me. . . . When the House had risen he found a number of Members of the Cabinet had been meeting, & complaining that the statement was not what we agreed, & they were in a state of semi-revolt. He sent for them : they came in looking very sullen, & Simon made their point clear. The P.M. told them the French wouldn't agree, & he had to make some statement. The P.M. seemed a little rattled, & his face was deeply lined. I felt sorry for him. . . . The P.M. *is* a man of peace. He spoke to me tonight about the hundreds of thousands of children in France that would be killed, if war came. I told him not to be too much upset by all this.[31]

On this evidence Chamberlain was not in the temper of an ardent warrior. He viewed with understandable dismay the prospect of years of violence and suffering; but he does not seem to have been involved in any plot to desert Poland and settle with Hitler – at worst he was paying too much attention to Bonnet's lugubrious warnings.

Simon's group reassembled in his room after their interview with Chamberlain. Simon wrote a letter to Chamberlain on behalf of the protesting ministers stating 'that our own view was that in no circumstances should the expiry of the ultimatum go beyond 12 noon to-morrow, and even this extension of twelve hours beyond the Cabinet's earlier decision would only be acceptable if it was the necessary price of French co-operation.' At 10 p.m. a message came asking Simon to go to 10 Downing Street. Simon promised 'that I should not agree to a greater latitude of time than that indicated without pressing that they should be further consulted.' At No. 10, Simon, who was accompanied by Sir John Anderson, found Corbin, the French ambassador, and Chamberlain let Simon and Corbin argue. Simon 'observed that 12 noon was the time fixed for the meeting of Parliament next day, and that it was absolutely essential that the Prime Minister, at the commencement of business, should then have a definite announcement to make, either that Hitler had agreed to withdraw, or that a state of war had begun.' Simon heard 'a great deal of telephoning to Paris in the next room, in which I took no part.' About the time Simon arrived in Downing Street, Chamberlain telephoned to Daladier.

The situation here [he is reported to have told the French Prime Minister] was very grave. There had been an angry scene in the House of Commons. . . . His colleagues in the Cabinet were also disturbed because at the Cabinet meeting in the afternoon it had been decided that the time-limit was to expire at midnight tonight. But in the absence of French concurrence it had been impossible for him to say that in the House. If the French Government were to insist on a time-limit of forty-eight hours to run from midday tomorrow, it would be impossible for the Government to hold the situation here.

Chamberlain proposed an ultimatum to be delivered at 8 a.m. next morning, 3 September, and to expire at noon. Daladier quoted Ciano as saying that there was still a chance of German agreement to withdraw from Poland if the delivery of any ultimatum was postponed till 12 noon. (This was not what Ciano had been saying; it is probable that Bonnet had provided a fictitious pretext for delaying matters, still hoping that something might turn up.)[32]

At 10.30 p.m. Halifax telephoned Bonnet and told him that the British decision was that an ultimatum should be presented at 8 a.m. to expire at 12 noon; if the French did not agree, they should deliver their ultimatum separately, provided they acted within twenty-four hours. Bonnet urged waiting to deliver the ultimatum until 12 noon; Halifax replied that it was impossible.[33]

Simon and his associates, fortified by the attitude of the House of Commons, had prevented Chamberlain and Halifax from deferring to the French demands for delay. They were a majority of the

Cabinet: Simon (Exchequer), Anderson (Privy Seal), MacDonald (Colonies), Morrison (Chancellor of the Duchy), Hore-Belisha (War), Colville (Scotland), Stanley (Board of Trade), De La Warr (Education), Elliott (Health), Brown (Labour), Burgin (Supply), Dorman-Smith (Agriculture), Wallace (Transport) – 13 out of 23.[34] Simon's motives are disputed. He himself concluded his account of 2 September with these words: 'The real credit of the conclusion rests with Chamberlain, whose patience under almost unbelievably trying conditions is a marvel, and who never for a moment misunderstood the differences expressed by his colleagues as anything but genuine efforts to help him. And so they were.' Henry Channon MP wrote in his diary of 'the War Party, suddenly strengthened by John Simon, who, I suppose, saw his chance of becoming P.M.'[35] It seems more likely that Simon, whom Chamberlain had not kept fully informed, shared the suspicions of the majority of the Cabinet that Halifax and Chamberlain were somehow working for a way to evade British obligations to Poland and objected to any such evasion.

After the telephoning to Paris, Chamberlain, urged on by Simon, called another Cabinet. The dissentient group assembled promptly, at 11.30 p.m., with Chatfield also there; the others arrived one by one later on. Zetland, for instance, had gone to bed. He had been told, after Halifax had made the same statement as Chamberlain in the House of Lords, that it was unlikely that there would be another Cabinet that evening.[36] The proceedings were amicable enough; there was no confrontation. Chatfield, putting forward the views of the chiefs of staff, urged a short time between delivery of the ultimatum and its expiry, since the Germans might launch a surprise attack in this period, but, on the other hand, stressed the need to avoid offending the French by going to war significantly earlier than them – this led to the suggestion of a 9 a.m. delivery of an ultimatum expiring at 12 noon. Simon suggested expiry at 11 a.m. so that Chamberlain would have something definite for the Commons at 12 noon. Others urged an earlier time to catch the Sunday papers, but Chamberlain's objection to getting too far out of line with the French, 'who after all would bear the main part of the burden', prevailed. The Cabinet agreed that Henderson should deliver an ultimatum at 9 a.m. which should expire at 11 a.m.[37]

Mr Taylor puts in a parting shot at Halifax. He 'delayed once more and put off the ultimatum until the next morning – presumably from habit, not with any hope of escape.'[38] The truth is duller.

There is much to dislike in Halifax, not least his supercilious contemporary comment on the attitude of the Commons on 2 September : 'The general feeling . . . was that the French were trying to
run out of their engagement to Poland and were taking us with
them. For this . . . there had never been the least ground. . . . The
whole thing, to my mind, showed democratic assemblies at their
worst.'[39] But his laziness did not stretch that far. A telephone call to
Berlin was made shortly after midnight to alert Henderson that he
was to go to see Ribbentrop at 9 a.m. The telephoning of the terms
of the ultimatum was delayed until 5 a.m. only because the British
chiefs of staff did not want the Germans to know of it until the last
possible moment.

From the records, it does not appear that Chamberlain planned
any surrender to Hitler; on the contrary, his error was in snatching
at a delusive hope that *Hitler* might still surrender even after he
had launched his attack on Poland or that someone in Germany
might compel him to do so. He wanted, for a moment in the afternoon of 2 September, to follow Bonnet and give the Germans
longer to think about beating a retreat from Poland. This, after all,
was what the policy of the guarantee had meant; British firmness
was to prevent war. Chamberlain was not reverting to 'appeasement'; he was only rather timidly and hesitantly trying to give
firmness a little longer to produce the promised result – peace. Certainly he contemplated war with distaste and reluctance and feared
its possible futility; that does not mean that he intended, in September 1939, to substitute surrender. The rest of the Cabinet, except
perhaps for those politically waning figures Inskip and Hoare, plus
Kingsley Wood and a few silent nonentities, were more eager to get
on with the heavy task of overthrowing Nazism by force. The
significance of this belligerent zeal was mainly to frustrate Bonnet's
attempts to win his colleagues in France for peace (and the free
hand for Hitler in the east). In 1938 he had used British promptings
to hold back the French government. In 1939 the British Cabinet
prevented him from bamboozling Chamberlain into a delay which
could then have been presented to the French Cabinet as British
readiness to accept Mussolini's insidious plan. Perhaps it was France
that the British Cabinet's 'revolt' drove to war rather than Britain.

2

Great Britain and the Outbreak of War with Japan, 1941

PETER LOWE

Winston Churchill has recorded his immediate reactions of delight at the news of Pearl Harbor and the realisation that the United States was at last fully at war as an ally of Great Britain.[1] Yet a little over two months later, on 15 February 1942, Singapore surrendered to the numerically inferior forces of General Yamashita, the greatest surrender in the history of the British Empire, and Churchill faced a motion of censure in the House of Commons as confidence in his leadership wavered. The aim of this essay is to examine British policy towards Japan in 1941 in the context both of the Anglo-American relationship and of the broader origins of the Pacific war; to attempt to answer the questions why war came when it did and whether it might have been avoided. In particular, attention will be focussed on the final months preceding the outbreak of war.

It is instructive to reflect briefly on the contrast between the circumstances in which Japan entered the two world wars, in 1914 and 1941. In 1914 Japan was an ally of Great Britain, developing rapidly in military and economic terms, but lacking the means as yet to achieve effective domination of the Far East. She entered the war in part because of a British request for naval assistance, but more imperatively because of her determination to seize the opportunity for consolidating her position in east Asia while the occidental powers were preoccupied in Europe. While some fighting occurred in the German concessions in China and in the German island possessions in the Pacific, the Far East was essentially a backwater completely overshadowed by the bloody carnage in Europe. In 1941 Japan was a truly formidable power, imbued with a fierce

17

nationalistic ideology and convinced of her imperial mission to construct her 'new order' and 'Greater East Asia Co-Prosperity Sphere'; her weakness lay in paucity of raw materials and concomitant reliance on crucial imports, especially of oil. She was linked with Germany and Italy in the tripartite pact of September 1940 and shared a broadly similar outlook with the two European nations; nevertheless, Japan regarded Germany with some suspicion, the legacy of Hitler's racialism and of his failure to consult Japan before embarking on major policy initiatives.[2] Japan was determined to exclude occidental intervention from her huge sphere of interest, if possible by persuasion but if necessary by force. When the Pacific war began, in December 1941, it was a massive conflict raging from the borders of India to northern Australia and involving countless Pacific islands; it was not subordinate to the European struggle, as had been the case in 1914–18. Historians have tended to underestimate the scale and significance of the Pacific war, though not in the most recent general survey.[3] The 'Second World War' was a conflict of world-wide dimensions; but the term is misleading in some respects, for it comprised two separate wars, turning on events in Europe and the Far East respectively.

In 1941 Great Britain was desperately involved, with the dominions, in building up her resources at home to resist a possible German attempt at invasion at some future date and in defending her position in the Middle East, which hinged on retention of Egypt and on the defence of her essential oil supplies in the region. The United States of America was extending increasing aid to Great Britain, exemplified in the passage of the Lend-Lease bill in March 1941 and in the growing help received from the American navy in combating the German U-boats in the Atlantic. However, there was no immediate likelihood of the United States entering into the war; isolationism was vocal, illustrated in the campaign of the 'America First' organisation, and President Roosevelt preferred a combination of stealth and intermittently decisive leadership to the alternative of an overtly sustained attempt to convert American opinion rapidly to the necessity of complete American commitment to defeat Germany.[4] With regard to Japan, Roosevelt wished to oppose further Japanese expansion but did not want to go to war with Japan. He agreed with Churchill that the European war was of primary importance and that Japan should be kept out of war for as long as possible. Where Churchill and Roosevelt differed was on the best method of attaining this objective. Churchill favoured

a tough approach, believing that Japan could be coerced by American might provided that the United States pursued a consistent
policy, impressing Japan with her tenacity, while Roosevelt was
reluctant to proceed this far for fear of provoking the isolationists
and, perhaps, inviting a premature Japanese attack. When the two
leaders met at Placentia Bay, Newfoundland, in August 1941, the
President bowed to Churchill's insistent pressure that he issue a
blunt warning to Japan that further expansion, after her advance
into southern Indo-China the previous month, would result in war
with the United States.[5] Upon returning to Washington and discussing the matter with the Secretary of State, Cordell Hull, Roosevelt issued a much vaguer warning, lessening the sharp impact
which Churchill deemed necessary. The talks between the United
States and Japan, started in March 1941 to discover if sufficient
common ground existed to reach a peaceful settlement in the Far
East and Pacific, had been temporarily suspended but not broken
off. Roosevelt wished to delay the conflict for as long as possible
and had some understanding of the evolution of Japanese policy,
since the Japanese codes had been broken.[6]

British policy-makers in 1941 faced a singularly unpleasant
dilemma in the Far East. Even before the First World War it had
been manifest that Britain lacked the resources to defend her considerable territorial and economic interests; the Anglo-Japanese
alliance was important in this context, as an example of seeking to
defend British interests through partnership with the only powerful
indigenous nation in the area. With the end of the Anglo-Japanese
alliance in 1921–3, a new policy had to be devised. It rested on the
development of Singapore as the combined fortress and great naval
base which would house the British fleet when it was required to
meet a crisis in the Far East. The development of the base had
been extremely slow and it was not adequately appreciated that in
order to hold Singapore it would be necessary to hold the whole of
Malaya.[7] This fact was grasped by the chiefs of staff in the summer
of 1940; it is doubtful whether it was ever appreciated by Churchill
before the war broke out.[8] Owing to the prior demands of the war
in Europe and in the Middle East, it was impossible to send adequate forces to Malaya. The dilemma was put in pathetically plain-
tive words by the chiefs of staff in a reappraisal of the far eastern
situation in July 1940 :

In the absence of a Fleet our policy should be to rely primarily on air
power. The air forces required to implement that policy, however,

cannot be provided for some time to come. Until they can be made available we shall require substantial additional land forces in Malaya, which cannot in present circumstances be found from British or Indian resources.[9]

The chiefs of staff maintained that every effort must be made to avert war with Japan while simultaneously doing whatever was feasible to improve defences in case of a surprise Japanese attack. Consultations with the American and Dutch authorities took place, but fully effective co-operation was hampered by the view of the chiefs of staff that no promise of British military support could be given to the Netherlands East Indies until Britain herself had received a guarantee of support from the United States; no American promise was forthcoming until shortly before the start of the Pacific war. Within the narrowly British sphere, preparations were handicapped by the number of different authorities concerned and the problem of securing swift co-ordination.[10] The Foreign Office believed that any appeasement of Japan should be eschewed : in the grave situation which had faced her after the collapse of France, in July 1940, Britain had temporarily closed the Burma road to placate the Japanese, but the move had antagonised the United States and China and it could not be repeated. The Foreign Office, as revealed in the minutes of the permanent officials, felt that the chiefs of staff were too supine and that British policy should be more resolute than before. At the same time they appreciated clearly enough Great Britain's inability to take on Japan single-handed. A display of British resolution could inspire more determination in the United States, but it could not be overdone in case the Americans resorted to their habitual fear that the devious British were ensnaring them for their own purposes. Historically, Great Britain had been the principal power in the Far East. She had played the leading role in opening up China to foreign trade and influence, and British material interests had always been greater than American interests. Now the burden of protecting those interests fell primarily on the shoulders of the United States.

In July 1941 the United States had taken a forthright stand in the decision to freeze Japanese assets and impose extremely drastic restrictions on trade with Japan. The importance of the decision was obvious enough but it was far less clear how these measures would be applied and whether they would be fully effective. There was confusion and uncertainty for at least two months after the measures were introduced, one reason being that the American

officials who devised the orders were themselves unsure exactly what
Roosevelt desired, and also because of the muddled communications between the British and American governments.[11] Lord Halifax, the British ambassador in Washington, urged at the start that
care be taken on the British side not to put undue pressure on the
Americans :

While we should avoid, on the one hand, giving the impression that
the United States Government has taken the lead as a result of pressure from His Majesty's Government and, on the other hand, that
His Majesty's Government are not likely to back the United States up,
we should, I think, take the line that it is only natural that the two
Governments should have reacted in a very similar fashion to the
Japanese move in view of the fact that the interests of both are equally
affected by Japanese action.[12]

In any case, Great Britain had to follow suit because of the need
to foster growing identification in Anglo-American policies whatever form this took. It was hoped and, on the whole, believed that
Japan would modify her policies of expansion, but it was simultaneously realised that the reverse might well be true – that Japan
might be stimulated into further expansion as a means of averting
gradual economic strangulation.[13] During August 1941 the British
freezing measures were prepared and enforced by the Treasury and
Ministry of Economic Warfare; according to a memorandum prepared by the latter ministry on 7 September, the measures were
being applied with full rigour : magnesium was the only indispensable import from Japan, no fresh licences were being granted to
Japan in the United Kingdom and all exports from Britain, India
and Burma were being subjected to licence.[14] Uncertainty continued as to long-term American intentions. On 12 September it
was reported from Washington that Cordell Hull had given instructions that there was to be absolutely no weakening on the economic
front *vis-à-vis* Japan; there must, however, be no public statement
on the thoroughness of the freezing policy. Hull wished the British
and Dutch to maintain strong pressure.[15] When Eden met Van
Kleffens, the Netherlands Foreign Minister, a few days later, Van
Kleffens protested at the difficulty of obtaining any clear indication
from Washington on trade with Japan. American officials declined
to comment when asked formally, while in their private houses it
was only after the third cocktail that they became communicative.
Eden commiserated but remarked on the positive side : 'I said that
it was quite true that the United States Government had not given

us much time or opportunity to co-ordinate their policy with ours, but, in fact, they had virtually stopped all their trade with Japan, and this was the most important factor in the situation. We were seeking to do the same.'[16] Dean Acheson, who was intimately involved in implementing the American freezing restrictions for the State Department, demonstrated his concern by drafting a memorandum requesting clarification of high policy by the President and Secretary of State, pointing out that the British and Dutch, far from being behind the United States, were in reality ahead.[17] However, the freezing measures were there to stay and their full extent was clear by October 1941. Whatever consequences ensued, a firm stand had been taken against Japan. It was widely realised that the choice facing Japanese leaders lay, more and more starkly, between radical changes in policy and a retreat from expansion on the one hand, and, on the other, advance into war with the United States, Great Britain and the Netherlands East Indies.

The American decision to act in introducing the freezing restrictions seemed at the end of July to denote a new willingness to pursue a firm policy in Washington and the Foreign Office was anxious to pursue it further. Anthony Eden reviewed the situation in an important minute to guide Churchill at his coming meeting with Roosevelt:

Our main purpose in the Far East is to keep Japan out of the war. The best way to ensure this is by means of a warning from the United States, the Dutch and ourselves of the consequences of further acts of aggression by Japan. This warning will probably be most effective if delivered privately but this is a matter which can be discussed. The United States have always been reluctant to take joint action. The warning would be as effective if the representations were parallel instead of joint. The most probable next victim is Thailand whose Government has already appealed to us to know what help we could give. . . .

The Dominions, especially Australia, are concerned by the fact that though we have acted with the United States in freezing Japanese assets, the United States has not given us any assurance of help should any part of the Empire or the Dutch in consequence become embroiled with Japan. . . .

The difficulty of the President's position is that he can give no undertaking to come to the help of any foreign power without the authority of Congress. At the same time, it is most desirable to secure some assistance in the interests of ourselves and the Dominions.[18]

Halifax favoured discussion with the United States but emphasised that caution was necessary; Sterndale Bennett, head of the far eastern department in the Foreign Office, minuted that it was important to bear in mind the need for American approval if it was decided to forestall a Japanese advance into Malaya by seizing the Kra isthmus.[19] The danger of a Japanese move into Thailand and subsequent occupation of the key strategic point of the Kra isthmus preoccupied British officials in early August. The joint planning staff, who prepared papers for the chiefs of staff, were opposed to any British military initiative in the Kra isthmus to anticipate a Japanese advance unless assured of American support and underlined once again the extreme caution of the defence chiefs; even if the Japanese took over the Kra isthmus, it was held that this would not necessarily result in war. Sterndale Bennett commented that it was an 'ostrich-like' reaction. 'The occupation of the Kra isthmus may not by itself be an attack on our vital interests, but if it can only be acquired for the purpose of a subsequent attack on Singapore, surely it is wisest to oppose it rather than to allow it to develop into a really serious threat to our vital interests. The policy of letting one position after another go suggests our policy towards Germany before the war. . . .'[20] It was eventually decided that the Commander-in-Chief, Far East, could undertake an advance into the Kra isthmus to anticipate Japanese occupation, but only after receiving authorisation from London.

Churchill was at first elated, at his meeting with Roosevelt in Placentia Bay, when the President agreed to warn Japan in unmistakable terms against further expansion. The elation gave way to philosophic resignation when the warning was watered down. To emphasise British feelings, and perhaps as a gentle rebuke to Roosevelt, the Prime Minister made a radio broadcast on 24 August in which he censured Japanese policy and stated that if war occurred between the United States and Japan, Britain would at once support the United States.[21] Churchill's belief apparently was that Japan would respect tough words, but if the desired effect was not achieved then the Japanese could be contained, the principal role in the containment being played by the United States navy and the British forces in Malaya. Churchill was later to vacillate somewhat, but in the main he adhered to this approach towards Japan. In late August the government contemplated a renewed approach to the United States for another, more explicit warning to Japan. A salutary note of reservation was sounded by General Smuts in a telegram sent on 29 August. Smuts felt that it was

essential to possess sufficient strength before threatening Japan with
the dire consequences of her actions and he doubted whether either
the United States or Great Britain possessed such strength :

Question arises whether, if war with Japan does come, we shall not
have to bear brunt of it and this at a time when we may be most
heavily committed in both Europe and Africa.

What really is position of United States of America? How far is
she in fact prepared for war and in particular for first class war in
South Pacific? In spite of much propaganda about American production and preparedness we have little definite information to go on and
provocative ultimatum to Japan may have to be made good by us
while United States of American takes further months of preparation
and organisation for war. Even now American declaration to Japan
is tempered with further discussions and negotiations. And question
arises whether we should not hold our hand until finality in these
exchanges has been reached.

Is it not possible to leave matter for present where American
declaration has placed it and avoid language which may touch face
of Japan and provoke conflict for which America is perhaps not yet
ready.[22]

The United States opposed the idea of a further warning to
Japan at this time, largely because American defence chiefs were
urging the necessity of gaining time to strengthen defences in the
Philippines and because Japan had suggested that a summit meeting be held between Roosevelt and the Japanese Prime Minister,
Prince Konoye Fumimaro, in an attempt to reach a settlement. The
talks between the United States and Japan had been proceeding
intermittently and repetitively since March 1941 in the form of
conversations between Cordell Hull and Admiral Nomura, with
occasional intervention by Roosevelt; Roosevelt, however, preferred to concentrate on the European war and domestic politics
and was usually content to leave Hull to handle the Far East. Great
Britain was not a party to the talks and the Foreign Office found
it irksome and frustrating when Hull supplied limited information
from time to time and made it very clear that he was conducting
the talks independently. Gradually he became more communicative,
but it was only in the last month before war broke out that Hull
proved expansive. The talks stood little chance of success, since the
gulf between the two powers was so great. The United States
wanted Japan to renounce her new order and accept Hull's
cherished four principles. Japan wished the United States to accept

the new order in its essentials and to lift the freezing measures. It was in the American interest to prolong the talks for as long as possible, since this would afford valuable time to strengthen defences while simultaneously depleting the Japanese reserves of oil. The reverse applied to Japan. Time was all-important; when it became obvious that the United States was unlikely to meet Japanese demands, military and naval opinion in Japan applied pressure for terminating negotiations and embarking on war. At an imperial conference in Tokyo on 6 September, the decision to go to war within a month if no settlement was reached was ratified.[23] Konoye acquiesced in the decision, probably because he still hoped he would be able to meet Roosevelt and reach an agreement which could be imposed on the armed forces through the authority of the emperor. The Roosevelt–Konoye meeting failed to materialise owing to Japan's inability to meet Hull's insistence on prior concessions.[24] Concern was voiced in the British Foreign Office at the fact that so little was known of the progress of the talks. In discussion with Halifax on 8 September, Hull said that he presumed that Britain would welcome a settlement if it could be reached on acceptable terms. 'He went on to say, however, that his conversations had not approached the point where they would justify consultations with His Majesty's Government and by a friendly reference . . . hinted that you need not be anxious.'[25] Sterndale Bennett minuted some days later that, while there was now reason to feel some confidence in American policy, 'it is impossible not to have serious misgivings about the whole business.'[26] His misgivings were shared by Eden, who commented that he would discuss the subject with Halifax the following day.

Sir Robert Craigie, the ambassador in Tokyo, had a surprisingly frank conversation with Ohta, head of the European and west Asiatic bureau of the *Gaimusho*. Craigie wondered how long the American–Japanese talks would continue; Ohta said that the internal situation in Japan would prevent them lasting for more than one month and that war was the alternative.[27] Hull still regarded the talks as exploratory, designed to ascertain whether there was sufficient justification for transforming them into formal negotiations. When he saw Halifax on 4 October, he reviewed the course of events :

He said what United States Government had been concerned to do was to try and gain time. He did not conceive that he had been as yet engaged upon negotiations, but rather upon exploratory talks to see whether later negotiations would or would not be profitable. Should this situation develop, he had made it plain to Japanese that Chinese, Dutch and ourselves would have to be brought in.

In exploratory conversations he had consistently taken the line that Japanese policy was a wrong road, and that while United States would do their best to assist Japan in economic field if the Japanese policy got back on the right road, the United States had nothing to offer unless and until essential principles were recognised and put into force. By this he meant, and had made plain to the Japanese, that they should withdraw their troops from China, give up their expansionist policy to the south, recognise the open door in China, and, in short, accept everything for which American policy had stood in China.

Although he had not told the Japanese so, and would deny it if any public suggestion to this effect was made at this stage, his own mind was in favour of distinguishing between the assertion of the above principles in regard to China and position existing in Manchukuo, which traced from earlier date. The implication was that if by any chance United States could get settlement on the lines they deemed acceptable for China, they would not quarrel about Manchukuo.[28]

Thus Hull showed some willingness to move away from the sharp moral disapproval of Manchukuo, which had governed the policies of the Hoover and Roosevelt administrations since 1932; what his colleague Stimson would have thought had this become a serious possibility can be gauged from his reactions to the suggested *modus vivendi* the following month. In the latter part of the interview with Halifax, Hull commented that it was difficult to determine accurately the manner in which Japanese policy would move, but he thought it would be much influenced by the course of the fighting in Russia and in the Middle East.[29] The Foreign Office minutes betrayed some anxiety at Hull's thinking; his remarks on Manchukuo appeared to hint at appeasement of Japan on the lines of the reviled Munich agreement. The Permanent Under-Secretary, Sir Alexander Cadogan, observed : 'We are committed to letting the Americans conduct these "exploratory talks". Mr. Roosevelt obtained the P.M.'s consent to them, and said at the time – as Mr. Hull says now – that he didn't expect to gain much except time from them.'[30]

The next significant development was the resignation of Konoye as Japanese Prime Minister and the formation of a new government headed by a general on the active list, Tojo Hideki. The reaction in London and Washington was one of alarm in the belief that Tojo's emergence might presage an imminent Japanese advance, either against Russia or southward against British, Dutch or American possessions.[31] Joseph C. Grew, the American ambassador in Tokyo, tried as usual to see a ray of sunshine in the new situation, since Tojo, as an active general and a renowned disciplinarian, should prove able to control the army.[32] However, the pessimists were essentially correct. Tojo was willing to make one more bid to reach a settlement with the United States, but this time it would be truly final. War was fast looming on the horizon. Great Britain decided to consult the United States urgently. A telegram was sent to Washington on 18 October stating that the far eastern situation had to be examined in the light of the German successes in Russia and of the growing economic strangulation of Japan resulting from the application of the freezing measures.[33] While Japan might move south, the reverses experienced by Russia and the departure of the government from Moscow might encourage a Japanese attack on Siberia. It was essential to support Russia if such an attack materialised and Japan must not be led to think that she could pick off her opponents 'one by one'. However, Hull did not consider matters to be quite so menacing and pondered the question that always haunted relations with Japan between 1931 and 1941 : how could the 'moderates' in Japan be encouraged? Hull contemplated an isolated barter exchange comprising, for example, a limited quantity of American cotton against Japanese silk. Halifax tactfully observed that Eden would attach great importance to preserving a common front.[34] As Halifax had anticipated, the Foreign Office regarded Hull's suggestion with hostility and the Prime Minister addressed a succinct minute to Eden : '*Foreign Secretary*. This is the thin end of the appeasement wedge.'[35] A reply was sent to Washington casting doubt on any measures savouring of appeasement. At the same time the composition of the Tojo government was less extreme than had been feared at first and it might be best to see how the position evolved. 'Pending this our own inclination is to believe that there is greater hope of inducing a reasonable frame of mind in the Japanese by keeping up the pressure rather than in relaxing even in so small a measure.'[36] Halifax saw Hull again on 22 October to discuss the contingency of a Japanese attack on Russia. Hull stated that the administration had not decided how to meet this situation if it occurred; he himself believed that little could be done beyond strengthening allied defences in the Far East, as was currently happening in the Philippines. He did not consider an imminent Japanese move to be probable and was waiting to hear if they wished to resume the talks. He somewhat mysteriously expressed a preference for a naval blockade against Japan if action proved necessary.[37]

On 1 November Craigie sent a telegram from Tokyo deploring the lack of close and effective consultation between Great Britain and the United States. Craigie doubted whether the Americans comprehended Japanese psychology : the worst mistake that could be made was to underestimate Japanese resolution.[38] Craigie was right in concluding that what Britain wanted was the United States wholly in the war on her side with Japan wholly neutral; he was less helpful in suggesting how the dual aim could be accomplished. Craigie did not seem to realise that Britain was in no position to take command of American policy; rather, she was the junior partner and had to play a waiting game. The Foreign Office officials held that there was a choice between strengthening the united anti-Japanese front, as far as could be achieved, and pursuing appeasement. The former involved the risk of war but with a strong chance of American participation, while the latter could not guarantee avoidance of war. There was no genuine alternative to the existing policy.[39] Cadogan commented :

I agree. The Japanese announcement of M. Kurusu's mission to Washington must bring things to a head soon. That mission must either secure terms acceptable to Japan, or there must be confessed failure of the negotiations. The former is, to me, inconceivable. That means that the process of "gaining time" is nearing its limit. And this would not be a good moment to come into the negotiations.[40]

The conclusion was cogent : the crisis was nearing its climax and the United States had to handle it as best she could. Great Britain would have to accept the consequences. Craigie was informed accordingly and instructed to emphasise to Togo, the Foreign Minister, that Britain desired a just settlement between Japan and the United States.[41] The lesson was publicly driven home by Churchill in his annual address at Guildhall on 10 November when he spoke candidly of the extremely hazardous nature, from Japan's viewpoint, of embarking upon full-scale war in the Pacific; if war resulted between the United States and Japan, 'the British declaration will follow within the hour.'[42]

The crunch had indeed come and the interest lies in the last futile attempts to reach a temporary agreement. In the second half of November both Japan and the United States considered alternative proposals for a *modus vivendi*. The Japanese offered limited

concessions, principally the withdrawal of troops from southern
Indo-China, in return for the lifting of the freezing measures.[43] This
was unacceptable as presented; however, following from the vocal
advocacy by the American chiefs of staff of gaining still more time
to complete defence preparations, Hull suggested to Great Britain,
the Netherlands government-in-exile and China a *modus vivendi*
to last for three months involving the withdrawal of Japanese forces
from southern Indo-China and a reduction in the number of troops
in northern Indo-China in return for the modification of the freezing measures.[44] Initial British reactions to news of the Japanese
approach were cautiously favourable while recognising that it would
take some time to reach an agreement; Cadogan was more pessimistic.[45] Upon further consideration of the Japanese proposal and
of Hull's contemplated rejoinder, the Foreign Office decided that
neither was satisfactory. The Japanese proposal could not be
accepted, as it would involve abandoning the freezing measures.
On the other hand, Hull's proposal did not go far enough in securing concrete commitments from Japan on withdrawal of her forces
from Indo-China; in Britain's view, complete Japanese withdrawal
from Indo-China was axiomatic.[46] British response to Hull's suggestion was, therefore, unenthusiastic but it was positively effusive
when compared with the acrid denunciation uttered by Chiang
Kai-shek. Chiang, who had long been hoping for war between the
United States and Japan as the most efficacious means of removing
Japanese pressure from China and simultaneously permitting him
to settle accounts with his domestic communist foes, regarded the
proposed *modus vivendi* as treachery and as an attempt to achieve
a far eastern Munich with China cast in the role of Czechoslovakia.
The fears were greatly exaggerated, probably deliberately so, but
were nevertheless effective when launched as propaganda in London and Washington. British policy towards China since the beginning of the Undeclared war in July 1937 had been based on moral
support for China and on the extension of the small amount of
material aid which she felt could be spared from the prior claims
of the European crisis. Whatever happened, it was essential to keep
China in the war, if only because she tied down large numbers of
Japanese troops who might otherwise be employed in south-east
Asia or in Siberia.[47] Chiang Kai-shek appealed to Churchill for
support. The Prime Minister had at first modified his customary
preference for an unyielding approach to Japan in a minute sent
to Eden on 23 November, on the grounds that Britain already had

enough war to contend with.[48] Upon hearing from Chiang, Churchill sent one of his personal messages to Roosevelt sympathising with Chiang and referring to the 'thin diet' he was being offered.[49] Chiang also bombarded members of the American Cabinet, other than Hull, with appeals for support, and this action stimulated Secretary of War Henry L. Stimson's affection for China and antagonism to Japan; he voiced his opposition to the *modus vivendi.* Instead Hull put forward a lengthy statement of American principles, calling for a categorical reversal of Japanese policy in all respects.[50] It was regarded by Japan as an ultimatum terminating the talks. Hull viewed it in a similar way : he felt that it completed the record of the long and tedious discussions and the active role now passed from the field of diplomacy to the field of war. Halifax saw Hull on 29 November and reported the views of the Secretary of State :

He said that the situation had not changed, but he thought it was pretty well inevitable that Japanese would take some early action under what he felt certain must now be the increased pressure of the military extremists. He had been impressing on the United States Service Departments that they should prepare themselves for all eventualities. He did not expect that the Japanese would make any reply to the communication the President had given Chargé d'Affaires, and saw no hope of reviving modus vivendi plan.

In a post-mortem of what had passed he spoke with considerable bitterness of the part played by T. V. Soong, both in unbalanced advice given to Chiang Kai-shek and also for breach of confidence with the press.

This had had the immediate effect of swinging Stimson, who had been forward in pressing to gain time, on to the other tack of supporting the Chinese view. He did not reproach His Majesty's Government, but said that they too had been unduly impressed by what he continued to feel unreasoned and unreasonable attitude of Chiang Kai-shek reached on partial information and picture supplied by T. V. Soong. . . .

The plain answer to all this of course is that the Secretary of State had not brought us into consultation at an early enough stage, and I told him that I thought many of these difficulties had arisen because of the extreme rapidity with which things had moved after he had pointed out a stage when he thought he could bring us in.[51]

Halifax pointed out that Britain had been prepared to accept an interim agreement. Hull concurred but left Halifax with the feeling that Churchill's message had played a part in dissuading him from persevering with the *modus vivendi*. Hull added that 'Chiang Kai-shek obviously had always wanted to get us embroiled with Japan and that he looked like being successful.'[52] Hull had not given Britain a copy of the full statement handed to Japan, a further indication of the poor consultation between the two governments, and Halifax requested one; Hull rummaged through the papers on his desk without success. Halifax then referred to the need for co-ordination of defence policies to meet a Japanese attack :

. . . I told him that while it was no doubt quite possible for our staffs to get together in regard to hypothetical developments, it would be necessary, before any general action could be taken, for our two Governments to be absolutely together on policy, and I again asked him what would be the United States attitude in the event of a Japanese attack on Thailand (Siam). To this, however, he would make no direct reply, saying in effect that as Stimson had played a considerable part in busting his diplomatic effort, the situation was no longer one for diplomatic treatment.[53]

At the end of the interview Hull reiterated the importance of the two governments co-operating and not allowing their policy to be determined by China. As Halifax aptly remarked, '. . . he showed no signs of appreciating, and, what in the circumstances, would have been unprofitable to rub in to him, is that a good deal of this might have been avoided if he had been willing to give us longer opportunity of discussion in advance. . . .'[54]

With war becoming more and more certain, renewed debate occurred among the diplomats and strategists in London concerning a British advance into the Kra isthmus to forestall Japan. The subject had been discussed on a number of occasions previously; the Commander-in-Chief, Far East, Air Chief Marshal Sir Robert Brooke-Popham, wished to move if he judged the action to be necessary, but the chiefs of staff had always emphasised that prior authorisation must be given in London. At a meeting of the chiefs of staff on 29 November, the ritual of again stating the desirability of averting war in the Far East was performed; however, it was decided to inform the United States that Britain was prepared, in the event of Japanese aggression in Thailand, to occupy the Kra isthmus if an assurance of American support was forthcoming should the move be followed by armed conflict.[55] A telegram was at once despatched and Halifax reported that nothing could be determined until the President returned to Washington the following day.[56] Halifax was confident that the United States would support

Britain even if Roosevelt declined to give an affirmative answer immediately. In addition, Churchill sent a personal message to Roosevelt revealing that the Prime Minister had reverted to his advocacy of a blunt warning to Japan, as he had urged at the Placentia Bay meeting :

I realise your constitutional difficulties, but it would be tragic if Japan drifted into war by encroachment without having before her fairly and squarely the dire character of a further aggressive step. . . . We would of course make a similar declaration or share in a joint declaration and in any case arrangements are being made to synchronize our action with yours. Forgive me my dear friend for presuming to press such a course upon you, but I am convinced that it might make all the difference and prevent melancholy extension of the war.[57]

On 1 December in Tokyo and Washington decisions of crucial importance were reached. At an imperial conference Japanese leaders finally determined to go to war within a week.[58] In Washington, Roosevelt spoke at length to Halifax and gave the assurance of definite support for Great Britain in the event either of a direct Japanese attack on British possessions or of war resulting from a British advance into the Kra isthmus. Roosevelt said it would be preferable for Thailand to invite British forces in 'but we must clearly do what strategical necessity dictated anyhow.' However, 'we could certainly count on their support, though it might take a short time, he spoke of a few days, to get things into political shape here.'[59] Roosevelt indicated that he was considering a direct appeal to the emperor in an attempt to prevent war but he had not yet decided to proceed with it. In his somewhat casual method of doing business, Roosevelt had at last given Great Britain the promise of full support against Japan which she had striven to secure for so long, indeed which had first been seriously adumbrated by Sir Robert Vansittart in the Shanghai crisis of 1932.[60] The news was greeted with delight in London and a warm telegram of appreciation was sent in reply.[61]

Insight into Churchill's thinking is provided in a minute sent to Eden on 2 December. He believed that a Japanese attack on Malaya was unlikely for several months, presumably stemming in part from his misguided confidence in the salutary effect on Japan of the arrival of the *Prince of Wales* and *Repulse* in far eastern waters. Churchill felt that an attack on the Netherlands East Indies was probable at any time and the United States would then have to reach its decision on going to war with Japan.[62] Halifax saw

Roosevelt again on 4 December to answer certain hypothetical questions raised by the President at their previous meeting. Roosevelt confirmed his promise of support 'as meaning armed support' and approved the implementation of the operation to take over the Kra isthmus if considered necessary. Halifax mentioned the possibility of issuing a warning to Japan coming from the United States, Great Britain and the Netherlands; Roosevelt felt this needed further reflection.[63] Britain envisaged the warning applying to a Japanese attack on Thailand, Malaya, the Netherlands East Indies and on the Burma road from Indo-China. When Roosevelt spoke to Halifax again on 5 December, he opposed the warning applying to the Burma road on the grounds that this concerned the Sino-Japanese war, an old example of Japanese aggression rather than a new one. Possibly Roosevelt shared Hull's animosity at Chiang Kai-shek's recent propaganda campaign, but there was also the political aspect of selling his policy of resisting new Japanese aggression to the American people. In all other aspects Roosevelt was most amenable:

. . . he agrees to warning covering any attack by Japan on Thailand (Siam), Malaya or Netherlands East Indies. He thinks that if the warning is given by the United States, ourselves and the Dutch, we should act independently all within 24 hours, using different language to mean the same thing. . . . He would prefer the United States to get in first. On account of political considerations here, it was important that their action should be based on independent necessities of United States defence and not appear to follow on ourselves. He assumed that you would be concerting with the Dutch.[64]

Roosevelt added that he had heard indirectly from Kurusu, the special Japanese emissary in Washington, that matters were not hopeless and he was, therefore, considering an appeal to the emperor. He proposed that delivery of the warning be suspended until he had finally decided whether to proceed with the appeal to Hirohito. With regard to the Kra isthmus, he repeated his support for the operation but favoured an assurance to Thailand that, even if Thai sovereignty was temporarily destroyed, Britain and the allies would subsequently restore it. Roosevelt sent his appeal to Hirohito on 6 December: it was deliberately held up in Tokyo and did not reach the emperor.[65]

Thus, with Great Britain and the United States preparing for an ultimate warning to Japan and tensing themselves for a Japanese attack somewhere in south-east Asia, the blow of Pearl Harbor fell.

Half an hour before the attack on Pearl Harbor began, Japanese troops landed in northern Malaya; Brooke-Popham had been given permission to launch Operation 'Matador' if he considered a Japanese attack to be imminent, but hesitated when faced with news of the approaching Japanese convoys and it was then too late to move effectively into the Kra isthmus.[66] Rapid Japanese attacks on the Philippines and the Netherlands East Indies followed. The first phase of the Pacific war had begun and witnessed astonishing success for Japan, but she had embarked on a vast adventure which she could not win. Much would depend on developments in Europe; Hitler committed a major blunder, from his viewpoint, in declaring war on the United States shortly after Pearl Harbor. Japan's best hope of success lay in swiftly eliminating the American navy in the Pacific as a serious force and trusting that the war in Europe would go badly for the allies to such an extent that the United States would agree to recognise the 'Greater East Asia Co-Prosperity Sphere' and withdraw from the Far East and western Pacific. The hope perhaps possessed partial justification, but was always an immense gamble and the gamble was lost.

To Great Britain the outbreak of war with Japan appeared almost as an anti-climax after the long period of strained relations between the two countries resulting from the manifest incompatibility in their respective positions; Great Britain was clinging on to her far eastern empire tenuously, while Japan was gradually expanding into what she deemed her rightful sphere of interest. As has been observed, Pearl Harbor and the beginning of the Pacific war may be seen in historical retrospect as another milestone in the one hundred years' war between the occidental and oriental powers.[67] Britain was so burdened in Europe and the Middle East that the Far East came a poor third in defence priorities. When war broke out, naval strength was extremely inadequate; the *Prince of Wales* and *Repulse* were dangerously exposed, although it was in part a matter of ill-luck that they were so swiftly sunk at the start. Air strength was barely half of what had been recognised as essential by the chiefs of staff and far less than was advocated by the Commander-in-Chief, Far East. Military strength had been increased substantially in the course of 1941 but was in no sense adequately prepared for the efficient Japanese onslaught. Undoubtedly the muddle and inadequacy inherent in British defence policy in the interwar years was fundamentally responsible for the fall of Singapore. However, equally significant was the widespread failure of British leaders and officials to comprehend how dangerous Japan was to prove : few anticipated the brilliantly successful campaigns launched on 7 December 1941. The feeling was common that, while it was in Britain's interest to prevent war with Japan if this could be accomplished without any real surrender of principle, if war nevertheless resulted the Japanese could be contained. Eden wrote to Churchill, in September 1941, that Japan was 'an over-valued' military power and the Prime Minister agreed.[68] By the time he met Stalin in Moscow in December 1941, Eden was beginning to realise his error : he told Stalin that Japanese prowess in the air had come as a shock and he seemed willing to accept Stalin's suggestion that German pilots might be serving with the Japanese forces.[69] Churchill was personally shocked deeply at the loss of the *Prince of Wales* and *Repulse*, which had dealt such a cruel blow to his obstinate confidence in the deterrent value of the two capital ships. He was to be further shocked by the disintegration of the British defensive in Malaya and by the act of surrender on 15 February 1942. Japan had been underestimated for a combination of reasons : a feeling of innate racial superiority, ignorance of the fanaticism, tenacity and dedication of the Japanese forces and of the high performance of certain of their aircraft, and a belief that, because Japan had not defeated China completely, she did not constitute such a deadly threat. Many chickens came home to roost between December 1941 and February 1942.

Fundamentally, Great Britain relied heavily on the United States and the responsibility for meeting the Pacific crisis was primarily America's. Relations with the United States had to be handled with great tact and a delicately balanced appreciation of the dangers of trying to persuade her to do more than was politically wise for American leaders at a particular moment. The United States did not consult Britain at all closely on the far eastern situation until the final phase of the crisis in late November and early December 1941. Cordell Hull was largely left in command of the American–Japanese talks by Roosevelt. Hull was a self-righteous, rather irascible old-fashioned Democratic party politician, 'a dreadful old man', as Cadogan was later to describe him.[70] He personified the moral values which were so prominent a feature of American foreign policy. He was determined not to give way significantly to the unjustified Japanese expansion. Hull would not preside over anything smacking of a far eastern Munich, hence his successful opposition to the suggested Roosevelt–Konoye meeting. Equally, however, the United States should not identify herself too closely with Great Britain, hence his opposition to the blunt warning to Japan urged by Churchill and at first accepted by Roosevelt at the Placentia Bay meeting. By the end of November it was clear that the position was very grave and deteriorating. Roosevelt at last took control himself and gave Britain an assurance of firm support. While this was a considerable diplomatic advance, it had come too late in the day for fully effective co-ordination of defence between Great Britain, the United States and the Netherlands East Indies. The Americans had participated in defence talks concerning the Far East and Pacific previously, but had felt unable to commit themselves far for political reasons. The time had now passed and the consequence was the hurried and unsatisfactory establishment of the ABDA command, during the Anglo-American talks in Washington in December 1941–January 1942, leaving the unfortunate Wavell holding twins rather than the baby.

The role played by economic sanctions in the approach of the war confronted Japan with the choice of modifying her policies markedly, of abandoning her new order and Pan-Asiatic ambitions, or of accepting the challenge and advancing her designs by proceeding to war more swiftly. Policy-makers in London believed that there was at least a reasonable chance of Japanese leaders pausing at the brink and drawing back.[71] Officials in the Foreign Office frequently remarked that while Japan was a bellicose power, she was also a cautious power and would not take unwise risks. Such views revealed a poor appreciation of the ferocity and ruthlessness which Japanese nationalism had by this time assumed and also ignored the element of fatalism so important in the Japanese character.[72] Foreign observers in Tokyo, like Sir Robert Craigie and Joseph C. Grew, were correct in warning that Japan would probably strike suddenly and dramatically. Does this mean that the freezing measures were responsible for the outbreak of war? If adopting tough measures against Japan failed to prevent war, would a policy of appeasement have done so? It would appear undeniable that economic action hastened the approach of conflict. In this sense the freezing measures offered Japan no real choice and those who thought they did were mistaken. However, the measures were not responsible for any major change in Japanese foreign policy. For a decade before 1941 and, in a longer perspective, since the Meiji restoration, Japan's aim had been to expand her role in the Far East and western Pacific and secure a diminution in the occidental presence. The proclamation of Manchukuo in 1932 and the development of the Undeclared war in 1937 were milestones along this path. In south-east Asia there were areas rich for the picking, which could help Japan to achieve her aim of political and economic dominance. It was impossible to retreat, particularly as the United States and Britain were supporting China and thwarting Japanese ambitions. Economic sanctions therefore affected the *timing* of war and brought it sooner than would otherwise have been the case, but they did not cause the conflict. War could only have been averted had the western powers been prepared to accept Japanese hegemony and wash their hands of China. Such action would not only have affronted public opinion in Great Britain and the United States, but might, as the situation in China appeared in 1941, have resulted in the fall of Chiang Kai-shek, a peace settlement between Japan and China dictated by Japan, and the subsequent availability of larger numbers of Japanese troops for southward expansion. The price was too high to pay. After their experiences in the 1930s, British leaders felt that appeasement did not pay and they had to bear the claims of Australia and New Zealand in mind. It was politically impossible for Roosevelt to make great concessions to Japan; had he attempted to do so, his domestic position would have been undermined with grave effects on his policy of opposing Germany more and more. For Japanese leaders, there could be no retreat. Shinto nationalism had reached its climax and it was believed that Japan had to press ahead inexorably with her mission. Despite her links with Germany, Japan did not think of herself as entering the Second World War; rather she was pursuing her east Asian war, which happened to coincide with war in Europe and the Middle East. While it might have been possible to have postponed the outbreak of war with Japan in 1941, it is unlikely that it could have been averted completely, since the political realities in the United States and Japan rendered retreat impossible. As for Great Britain, she had largely ceased to count as a genuinely independent factor, as her embarrassing role on the sidelines in the American–Japanese talks emphasised. Her fate lay squarely in the hands of the United States. From the British viewpoint, war with Japan was very much an integral part of the Second World War. What shocks Japan had in store had to be endured until Germany was defeated : it was simply that when Japan administered the shocks they were considerably more painful and humiliating than had been envisaged beforehand.

3

British Historians and the Beginnings of the Civil History of the Second World War

DENYS HAY

It seems absurd to try to cover in a few pages the large and absorbing subject which is indicated in the title of this paper. Some thirty volumes of Civil Histories have been published[1] and scholars are still working on some of the drafts and other materials accumulated but not published by their predecessors. Yet the subject is undeniably of interest to many people other than the handful of us who were actively engaged in it. 'War Studies' or 'Strategic Studies' are now pursued seriously in universities, as they were not before the Second World War, and the interest of the services and the administrators in all countries is aroused by the analysis of their problems in the recent past. To this interest the Civil Histories in Britain have contributed; they have also benefited from it in a measurable way. Surprising as it seems to those who ground them out (while trying to resume normal peacetime work), the volumes sell. Many have had to be reprinted. In the austere terms of Stationery Office economics the Civil Histories have more than paid their way. It was estimated in the mid-fifties that total expenditure on the men and women who, over some fifteen years, actually wrote the twenty-eight volumes then more or less completed averaged just over £830 per department per annum.[2] So the Civil Histories were a sound investment.

The ultimate origins of the whole civil enterprise have to be traced back in the end to the acceptance of official military history, a consequence of that reluctant acquisition of 'a thinking army', with a general staff which 'needed a memory'.[3] Nothing, however, was done until the Committee for Imperial Defence (1904) put the hitherto *ad hoc* efforts to chronicle campaigns on a more regular

39

footing by the creation (September 1906) of an Historical Section.
A well-known historian of the American Civil War became its head
in 1919. The man appointed was Brigadier J. E. Edmonds RE.
He had been born in 1861; as Sir James Edmonds he remained
in charge of the military history of the First World War until the
last volumes came out in 1949.[4] He died in 1956, in his ninety-
fourth year. Sixteen years earlier he played a crucial role in the
story of the Civil Histories simply because his was the only active
historical unit in central government, the narratives of the Navy
and the RAF in the 1914–18 war having been more or less wound
up by 1938, although some volumes were even then still being
revised. In 1939, on the outbreak of war, the Committee for
Imperial Defence (hereafter abbreviated CID) was merged into the
Offices of what then became the War Cabinet, and with the CID
went General Edmonds and his small staff of officers, still digesting
the battles of an earlier generation, still producing large-scale campaign histories which were largely unread by the public and proved
of small use to the Staff Colleges, though senior officers still were
obsessed with trench warfare and hostile to mechanised warfare.[5]

It is usual nowadays to dismiss Edmonds as a fuddy-duddy, a
stick-in-the-Flanders-mud. And there is no doubt that as he grew
older he became less critical as a historian, more reverent of the
heroes of the past, more inclined to gloss over or ignore senseless
carnage and incompetence in high places.[6] But he had in many
ways remarkable talents. The earlier volumes of the military histories of the first war concentrate, it is true, on the description of
battle orders, on troop deployment down to regimental levels, on
the minutiae of local actions, depicted in the remarkable battle
maps with which the series was lavishly provided. But Edmonds
was far from being unaware of the background of politics and
industrial supply, of manpower problems and labour relations. Such
matters are subordinate to his accounts of the fighting, but they
often preface the narrative. For example, *France and Belgium 1914*
has an introduction which contains twenty pages devoted to control
of war policy and munitions; *France and Belgium 1915* has a central
chapter entitled 'Munitions, Recruiting and Manpower in 1915'.[7]
There was obviously something slightly grotesque about a group of
men, however small, still dealing with 1917–18 battles in 1939–40,
when the pre-First World War assumptions about equipment and
strategy were being jettisoned. The Historical Section was not
occupying valuable Whitehall space, it is true. 'Edmonds' men,

what are they doing at St Anne's on Sea?' asked a waggish journalist in the *News Chronicle* on 4 December 1940. 'Why, bless your innocence, they are writing a history of the last war.' In fact they had by then had a hand in starting the history of strategy and tactics for the new war, though that is not the subject of this paper. What is germane is the connection of Edmonds and the Historical Section with the steps which were to result in the Civil Histories.

Between the wars the supervision of the War Histories lay with a sub-committee of the CID, the Committee for the Control of Official Histories (COH). The chairman of this committee was normally the President of the Board of Education. The Secretary of the Cabinet was a member and there were also present senior members of the Treasury and the three service ministries. To this body Sir James Edmonds, the Naval Branch and the Air Historical Branch reported. When the CID merged with the War Cabinet the COH became a Cabinet committee and Edmonds likewise became a member of the staff of Cabinet Office. It proved an important move. At the very start of the war, Lord Hankey, formerly Secretary of the CID and then of the Cabinet, and soon himself to be a member of the War Cabinet, supported a proposal that the Historical Section should be immediately instructed to compile a confidential war diary. He also felt that a Cabinet instruction should be sent to all departments to furnish the Historical Section with material relevant to the production of War Histories; in addition to the service ministries, such instructions would also be sent to the Department of Overseas Trade, the Privy Council, the Board of Trade, the Ministry of Economic Warfare (MEW) and the Ministry of Supply.[8] This initiative was followed by a meeting between the Secretary of the War Cabinet, Sir Edward Bridges, and General Edmonds on 14 September 1939, ten days after the start of the war, when Edmonds urged that civil departments should be requested to keep materials for future historical use. It was agreed that the work of the Historical Section should continue, but it was also accepted that 'no new ground on the writing of histories should be broken.'[9] On 21 September 1939 Bridges wrote to all departments (twenty-four of them) in terms which are worth quoting, since in some ways they were to condition the development of the Civil Histories for the rest of the war :

At the moment, your Department, in common with others is, I am sure, far more concerned with the steps to be taken to win the War than with thinking about the record of the War. It may, indeed, seem a little incongruous to start thinking about the History of the War, but I suppose we must assume that in course of time an Official History of the War will be written.

If no steps are taken now to make sure that the essential material for a History of the War is collected and preserved in convenient form, Departments will be put to a great deal of trouble later on. The object of this letter is, therefore, to suggest certain simple arrangements which it is hoped will not involve any appreciable trouble, and may, indeed, be of convenience to Departments for their own purposes.

I assume that most Departments are arranging, or will arrange, to keep a simple diary of the most important events. This diary, which will no doubt often be a catalogue of the principal happenings on each day, with references to the documents in which those events are chronicled or set out, would alone go a long way to providing the groundwork of an Official History. The suggestion is that copies of all such diaries, together with copies of all important announcements, orders to Commanders, summaries of operations or situation reports, *communiqués* made to the public, and so forth, should be set aside day by day, with a view to their being handed over later on, in such manner as may be agreed with Departments, to the Historians appointed to write the History of the War.

If an arrangement on these lines commends itself to your Department, I should be glad if the person who is deputed to take charge of your diary and to select the documents to be preserved with it, would be good enough to get into touch with Brigadier-General Sir James Edmonds, who will be very glad to see him at any time.[10]

It may be noted that Bridges' assumptions were : that an official history of the war would be written; that, since this was the case, departments would be saved time and trouble later if documents were collected at once; and that the form was to be a 'diary' with supporting documents. There is a hint, hardly more, that such compilations might have a current use. There was no doubt that the diary form was based on Edmonds' familiarity with this type of material.

It is pretty evident that Bridges' letter had little immediate effect outside the offices of the War Cabinet themselves.[11] When the COH met in April 1940 under the President of the Board of Trade, it heard the sort of reports which might have come to any inter-war meeting. Reference was made to the instruction of 21 September 1939 and the Committee was told that it was being observed. At the same time, however, 'it was felt that an inspection should be made to ensure that the work was being carried out on the right lines.' It was stated that Sir James Rae, a distinguished former

Treasury civil servant, would be willing to undertake the inspection. This suggests the need for some coercion, and the COH authorised the action.[12] But, in the event, Sir James Rae found other things to occupy him.

There is another long uncharted interval and the matter does not seem to have been considered again until January 1941, when it was agreed by the COH that 'two officers from the Historical Section should be appointed to visit departments to see that the material for the history of the present War was being collated [*sic*] on the right lines.' One of these officers was to be Lieutenant-Colonel J. S. Yule,[13] who had been lent by the Historical Section to the War Cabinet Secretariat, and the other was to be nominated by General Edmonds. The most interesting feature of this meeting (at which, incidentally, Bridges could not be present) was that the idea was put forward by the Treasury representative 'that historians themselves are the only persons able to carry out the inspection.'[14] It is not by any means clear whether the COH, in drawing attention to the 'two distinct sides of the work to be inspected, i.e. military and civil (including economic)', contemplated the possibility that the latter task might fall to a civilian historian, though that in the event was what was to happen.

Bridges himself sent Yule on his tour round departments in February. He was to begin with the three service ministries, starting with Admiralty and Air Ministry 'where we believe a good deal has been done', and, 'thus fortified', Yule 'would proceed to the War Office'. In retrospect it seems astonishing that Bridges and Yule could not pick up a phone or pin a colleague in a corner of one of the clubs where, doubtless, this sort of business was transacted then as now. But physical inspection was evidently regarded as essential, and one can only infer that Bridges and his staff believed that, at any rate by this time, the war diaries were completely forgotten or neglected, whatever comforting or evasive noises might be made by departments. Bridges' minute to Yule confirmed that he was to go to civilian ministries, accompanied by someone from Cabinet Office 'familiar with . . . the main spheres of Civil Activity connected with the War', and suggested that this should be D. H. F. Rickett. Special attention was to be given to those departments or branches which exist in war but not in peace : e.g. Shipping, MEW, Supply and Food. These departments, wrote the Secretary, 'will in due course be wound up and their records dumped by the ton in some unforgiveable place.'[15] At the same

time Bridges invited Edmonds' views, which were communicated
in a long memorandum of 3 March 1941. This, while arguing
mainly the need of the service histories to deal with the 1939 war
more expeditiously than they had with 1914–18, also envisaged a
large-scale narration of aspects of 'Home and Economic' matters
'in many divisions'. There was something here of what was going
to happen, although Edmonds regarded his 'definite scheme of production' as lying far in the future; and Bridges had earlier hinted
to Yule that he considered Edmonds' lists of civil departments
unrealistically elaborate.[16]

Real action finally resulted from the 'inspection' carried out by
Yule and Rickett. The three service ministries, MEW, Home
Security and Health were visited and so was Sir Stephen Gaselee
at the Foreign Office, though merely for advice on modern techniques for recording data. Yule reported on 12 March 1941 that
the Air Ministry 'has its historical records in the best state in every
way', though the Ministry of Aircraft Production had hived off.
The Admiralty, with a captain RN and a staff of seventeen (including three 'narrators'), was more grudgingly approved: 'somewhat elaborate'. But the War Office were 'behind hand' and many
curious allocations of record material seem to have occurred. As for
civil ministries, Colonel Yule's report reads:

. . . Mr. Rickett and I can only give an indication of the way we are
thinking. Considering the three which I have visited as samples, we
can say that certain broad problems appear to be common to them
all: the form and number of the diaries; the housing in a place of
safety of the diaries and documents collected, away from the originals;
the indexing of such material; the provision, or not, of a narrator who
will start at once on the war story . . .

Of the three Ministries visited only the Ministry of Health is keeping a diary in the form suggested by Sir James Edmonds.

Yule then listed some reasons for proceeding at once to the appointment of 'narrators'. The story would be written near the events and
with relatively complete documentation; the narrator would notice
and have filled gaps in documentation and advise on improvements
in the preservation of records. Certain desirable side-effects were
indicated: economy of expenditure, current use in day-to-day
administration, the provision of a stream of men able to 'hand on
the method for compiling a history evolved by Sir James Edmonds.'
Yule concluded that the Army Council needed a prod, that the

Public Record Office needed more space, and, among other things, argued that narrators should be appointed to write 'first narratives', adding that they would be more useful on the military than on the civil side. When on 14 March Yule and Rickett reported verbally to Bridges, it was agreed that pressure would have to be put on civil departments 'and that the time has come to recommend putting an officer in supervisory charge of the work being done by the Civil Departments.' The COH should be asked to back both the provision of narrators for military, air force and civil histories and, for the latter, the appointment of a supervisor.[17]

Who took the important decision not to appoint as supervisor any of General Edmonds' men or an official from the Office of the War Cabinet? Presumably Bridges, though the record seems to be silent. Who decided to seek the advice of Dr E. A. Benians, Master of St John's College, Vice-Chancellor of Cambridge, a historian, and known to be a very helpful man? Yule saw him on 12 April 1941 and returned with a long list of possibles, among whom – starred, so to speak – was W. K. Hancock (Birmingham), 'an Australian, an Imperial Historian who would be acceptable to the Dominions.'[18] There then followed a long discussion on 21 April 1941 between Bridges, Edmonds and Yule which resulted in three important decisions. Edmonds agreed with Bridges that 'the time had come to have friendly talks with historians of standing at the universities on the subject of the civil history so as to get advice on the manner in which the history should be presented.' Edmonds also expressed the opinion that 'someone of standing' should supervise 'the collection of the material for the civil side.' And Bridges was persuaded that 'Civil Departments with a major interest in the War should employ narrators.' Other informal discussions also took place; Richard Pares, then at the Board of Trade, and E. L. Woodward (Foreign Office) were both consulted. As a result it was decided to put those points to the Committee for the Control of Official Histories, together with a request for the requisite financial approval.[19]

When things got moving in this way it may be surmised that Bridges realised that the COH now had as its ex-officio chairman a new President of the Board of Education, R. A. Butler, who would be prepared to push the project with vigour. Butler was in fact in the chair when the COH met on 30 July 1941.[20] Bridges had prepared a paper covering all aspects of war history.[21] The objects of official history of the war were stated to be :

(a) to record the course of the War as completely as possible for the benefit of posterity, and of the professional student;

(b) to record the organisations set up and found necessary (or unnecessary) for the various aspects of the War effort;

(c) to educate public opinion in the meaning and conduct of the War.

His proposals for the Civil Histories were as follows:

The Civil Histories will describe the war effort as it affected the national life at home and in the Empire. The Histories of Departments of State will record the organisations necessary for a war effort. It is particularly important to do this in the case of the wartime Ministries which will cease to exist in peace.

The Military and Civil Histories should be as full as time and funds will permit. It will have to be decided what can be published, what is to remain confidential and what secret.

To interest and educate statesmen, and the public, certain volumes in broad outline are essential. Above all these must be readable. They will serve, too, as an introduction to Military History and to the study of national effort in war for professional officers, both civil and military.

To achieve these purposes the War Histories will follow a plan such as is sketched out below.

Outline Plan for the Official Histories of the War
1. *Conduct of War*
    (a) These will be general or key volumes and will record the policy of the War Cabinet; the information and reasons for the adoption of this policy; the diplomatic, imperial, strategical, economic and domestic action taken to carry out the Cabinet policy.
    (b) An abridged form of (a) for the general reader. . . .
4. *Civil Histories*
    (a) Key volumes outlining the civil side of the war effort and shewing its effect on the national life at home and in the Empire.
    (b) Histories of the Departments of State shewing the organisations set up and how they worked out in practice.
5. *Unified Histories*
    These will be on certain subjects which affect both Civil Departments of State and the Services. The Medical History is one which it has already been agreed shall be written on these lines. Other subjects which will admit of similar treatment are transportation; communications, including cable, wireless and postal censorship; propaganda. These would include portions of the Histories of 4(b) above, and, in certain cases, might take the place of them.

Here we can see the germ of what were later termed 'synoptic volumes' and a stress on the usefulness of the work to the professional officer, 'both civil and military'. The COH agreed to appoint an advisory committee of historians (whose consent had been previously sought) and it referred Bridges' paper to this professional body. Butler rightly saw that Churchill would be sympathetic. A revision of Bridges' scheme was to be sent to him before being considered by the Advisory Committee.

When the Advisory Historical Committee under the chairmanship of Benians met for the first time in December 1941, the 'supervisor' had in fact been appointed.[22] On 29 August R. A. Butler wrote to Benians inviting him to become chairman and then added that there was 'another matter . . . I should like to mention. The Committee for the Control of Official Histories has had under consideration the appointment of a Historian to act as supervisor. . . . I have seen Professor Hancock, and think he would be a very suitable person to fill this appointment. He is anxious to accept it, but it is necessary to make him an offer fairly soon.' If the consultative committee had existed, the President added, it would have been a matter for its consideration; but time did not allow for this. A month later the President minuted the Prime Minister, explaining what had been done: that 'first narratives' were to be compiled, that Hancock had been appointed and that an 'informal' Advisory Committee of university historians had been constituted. The paper came back: 'Good. W.S.C.'[23]

In his attractive autobiography Hancock has himself alluded to these events. After explaining that he had occasionally met Bridges at All Souls, he goes on :

It was another All Souls man, Denis Rickett, who had told me about June 1941 that Bridges had it in mind to launch a new historical venture in War Cabinet Offices and was wondering whether I might be the man for the job? I had by then already decided that my work in Birmingham was yielding diminishing returns and had discovered the insatiable appetite of government departments for men of my training, for I was receiving letters from my friends in the Ministry of Food or the Board of Trade or somewhere else summoning me to this job or that. But I decided first to talk with Bridges. Was there any use or point, I asked him, in starting to write the history of war before we had won it? He replied that I would find ways of making myself useful in short term but I must also think in long term of the continuity of the State and the advantage of funding our war-time experience for future use – I think this phrase, which later on I often used in my reports and prefaces, was originally his. He told me about the Historical Section, which hitherto had confined itself to military history; but the armed forces nowadays were no more than the cutting edge of the nation at war and their history had no higher importance than that of munition making and agriculture, of shipping, land transport, mining and all the other civilian activities. There was my job if I would consent to take it on. I consented.[24]

Clearly, if Hancock was to make arrangements with Birmingham University towards the end of July (he must, I think, have been wrong about the time being June), then he needed to clarify his position rapidly. Hence the necessity to decide on his appointment promptly and in advance of the meeting of the Advisory Committee.

That body assembled for the first time on 9 December 1941. R. A. Butler inaugurated the proceedings by stressing the need for 'a volume surveying the social questions that had arisen in the country due to the War', and then left the chair for Benians. There was some deliberation on questions of overlap, e.g. how nutrition was to be divided between the Medical Histories (which, it had been earlier settled, were to be unified for all services and for the story of domestic medicine) and the Civil Histories, especially that of the Ministry of Food.[25] But the bulk of the meeting was devoted to the discussion and in general the approval of a paper submitted by Hancock, who had been at work since 1 October. It cannot be said the learned professors were especially well equipped to deal with the administrative and economic problems of the twentieth century; of those present none, save perhaps Maud, could have been described as a very modern social historian. But what Hancock needed was the support of recognised scholars and this he certainly got. Moreover, they were able to suggest names of historians to Hancock, who was having great difficulty in obtaining suitable men and women, most of whom were either committed to war itself, to administration or to teaching in depleted university departments. The most valuable contribution of the Advisory Committee on this occasion was undoubtedly the suggestion of possible narrators. On the other hand, Hancock's paper was itself a remarkably prescient survey of problems and possible solutions.

Hancock's 'Tentative Plan for the Civil Histories of the Present War, and the proposed scheme of work for Narrators in Ministries'[26] is too long to quote in full. Yet, while the published volumes and the numerous unpublished memoranda conform to it and thus afford evidence of good planning, certain basic concepts deserve to be highlighted in his own words. Emphasising how tentative his proposals were, he explained that he was soon convinced that 'my first task would be to find collaborators – called in the memorandum "Narrators" – and establish them in the civil departments', beginning with those likely to be dispersed after the war. He decided to save his own time and other people's by finding out about the grouping of departments 'in relation to some of the more salient objectives of War policy.' He went on :

These investigations have given me my first tentative ideas about the arrangement of the series of civil histories. Food policy offers a simple illustration. The Ministry of Food occupies a central position : on one side of it the Agricultural Departments are responsible for home supplies; on the other side of it the Ministry of War Transport is the agency for delivering imported supplies. It surely cannot be right to split the history of food policy into the separate histories of the Ministries of Food, War Transport, Agriculture and Fisheries, the Agricultural Department of the Scottish Office, and the Home Office as representing Northern Ireland's agriculture. The history should have a unity, in consonance with the unity of plan in which all these departments co-operate; and if investigation should show that the plan has been uncertain and the co-operation defective, this too should be part of the history. Similarly the history of civil defence ought not to be split into the separate departmental histories of Home Security and the Home Office; the Ministries of War Transport, Food, Works and Buildings, and all the others which in greater or less degree are associated for the purpose of civil defence. The greater part of the research will be in the departments; but the research must be co-ordinated above the departments. The same principal holds true of the three departments whose business it is to produce weapons of war. The co-ordination of the historical research undertaken in these Departments will not be satisfactory unless it is based upon a thorough study and understanding of war-time economic policy as a whole.

After discussing the problem of the frontiers of the civil and military sides in, for example, shipping, the scheme that follows is set out :

My first tentative conception of the volumes dealing with the civilian side of the war is as follows :
1. Civil Defence (possibly widely interpreted, to include health, etc.)
2. Food Policy
3. War Production
These heads represent three immediate objectives of policy. There are other heads which represent instrumentalities so fundamental to the

whole war effort that they will demand special treatment in separate
volumes. For example :
4.   War Transport
5.   Labour
In addition there will be a need for volumes dealing with the higher
co-ordination of policy. For example :
6.   Economic Policy (including economic warfare?)
7.   War Administration and the Political Background
I do not envisage a scheme which would simply allot a single volume
to each of these subjects. It will certainly take a number of volumes
to cover adequately the subject of war production. Again, there will
probably be a series of volumes under the heading of civil defence :
public opinion and home propaganda may possibly fit in here. It is
far too soon to sketch a design of publication in any detail.

Hancock then reflected briefly on security, hoping that little
would need to be held back on grounds of political prudence; and
he welcomed the idea of 'a single book recording the essentials of
the nation's war history'.

But there are limits to the material which can be compressed into a
"unified" history. There is a host of interesting and important topics
which cannot be adequately treated even in the main series of volumes,
if these are to be kept within a reasonable length. For example, the
study of price control as an essential part of food policy ramifies into
separate studies of the controls adopted in a dozen different trades.
Here is material for the writers of monographs. There will be room
for monographs by the score. If they are to be sound documentary
studies, their writers will need official facilities, but they need not
necessarily form a part of the official series of war histories.

He proceeded under 'Departmental material' to explain that he had
been warmly welcomed in the ministries he had visited. He criticised
the diary (. . . 'in no sense real historical work; nor is it a primary
historical material'); and in the war-time ministries archival or
registry work 'fell far below peace time standards.' But the historian
had a life-line : to remember to concentrate not on antiquarian
detail but on general policy and the way it was implemented :

But it is obvious that the historian will have to do most of his work on
more generalised material – the periodical surveys of different kinds.
He must begin his investigations at a high level in the Ministry, diving
down from time to time into the complex individual detail as he feels
the need. If he were to begin at a low level in one of the divisions, he
would never come to the surface, and never understand the organisation and functions of the Ministry as a whole.

His concluding section dealt with the pay and duties of the 'narrators'. Their pay was to correspond to university salaries, estimated (in my judgment generously for 1941) at £600–800 for men of lecturer grade; the need for good-quality appointments was emphasised. Hancock also envisaged the appointment of someone who would act as co-ordinator of the war-production side of the history. The Treasury had authorised ten narrators and he hoped to have some at work by the New Year of 1942. The memorandum was dated 14 November 1941. When he reported to the Advisory Committee on 9 December he had only secured the services of four historians, three of whom were to become pillars of the War Histories: Medlicott, Titmuss and Hammond.

In the plan two points stand out: the need for *problems* to be written about, not *departments*; and the conception of general volumes as well as monographs. These two decisions, which Hancock arrived at, it seems, more or less on his own, after his energetic foraging into some sample ministries, were to stand the test of time, as was the impression he created in the departments where narrators as they arrived and set to work were treated kindly, even if officials lower than permanent secretaries sometimes found their activities rather curious. But the connection with the Offices of the War Cabinet was an immense help. One might be in an office in the Ministry of Supply (as I was), but for pay and rations (and, more helpfully sometimes, notepaper) one belonged or seemed to belong to the heart of the matter.

Equally perceptive was Hancock's recipe for dealing with the colossal quantities of record: to go to high policy, then to the application of it, then back to the top, or even higher. In a later draft (1 April 1942)[27] he wrote:

A process of selection is operating continuously in the work of administration itself, and to this process the work of the historian can naturally and profitably conform. The innumerable individual questions which are dealt with every day in the lower levels of administration are from time to time reported upwards as questions of principle; similarly, the decisions on policy which are taken in the highest levels of a Ministry (and higher than that, in Committees of the War Cabinet or the War Cabinet itself) work themselves out in innumerable individual transactions carried through at the lower levels of administration. Much of this activity leaves its deposit of documentary record. If the historian begins his work on the high-level documents of a Ministry, the development of its main policies will before long become clear to him. Then he will feel the need to examine

these policies as they operate in practice – an examination which will
take him into the mass of low-level documents. There he will find the
concrete detail which must be grappled with in all good historical
work. However, he must have the self-restraint to handle this detail
illustratively not exhaustively. Instead of sinking deep into this
great Serbonian bog, he must climb back to the higher level of
Departmental documentation, where the general tendencies of policy
are recorded. Sometimes, indeed, his investigations will lead not down
but up, into the memoranda of War Cabinet committees where the
policies of different Ministries are adjusted, and into the conclusions
of the War Cabinet, which record the final decisions.

And he then proceeded to indicate why departments were sympathetic: they could see that the history might be useful if there were
another war; that it would simplify the transition to peace; that it
might be 'an immediate contribution to the present war effort'.[28]

Hancock's considered plans along these lines were approved by
the Advisory Committee on 28 April 1942. By this time Hancock
had recruited Professor M. M. Postan, from the Ministry of Economic Warfare, who took over responsibility for the production
ministries. By the late summer of 1942 there were in all some
fifteen historians at various levels and of various kinds at work
under Hancock's general direction. There had been some press
publicity earlier.[29] Perhaps the smell of victory lured historians from
class-rooms, administrative posts and uniform to the one war job
for which they had some training. Not all the fifteen of 1942 saw
the job through; but others took their places. At its highest point,
a year or two after the war, Hancocks team was to number about
thirty men and women.[30]

To leave the story at the end of 1942 is, of course, to end before
the decision was made to publish. That decision envisaged the three
'synoptic' volumes by Hancock and Mrs Margaret Gowing (*British
War Economy*), Postan (*British War Production*) and R. M. Titmuss (*Problems of Social Policy*). In their wake came the more
specialised studies. And with publication came the problem of
clashes between public policy and professional standards. The
dilemma was once or twice a real one: that the 'official' side of
official history would compromise or frustrate the 'history' side.
Drafts were always submitted to departments for criticism, which
could be sharp enough (the author recalls the reaction of the old
Ordnance Board to some of his callow animadversions on what he
regarded as a somewhat outdated survival from a distant past). But

it was only in a few cases that a whole volume came in for such violent and high-level attack that its future was in jeopardy. Hancock made it plain that 'he was prepared to withhold a volume on real grounds of security; he was not prepared to emasculate it.'[31] In his memoirs Hancock is very discreet in his references to the possibility of major collisions.[32] In fact the authority of senior ministers did have to be invoked two or three times to overcome departmental obstruction. This was partly because of the atmosphere in which administrators had been trained. When I wrote for publication a brief piece on the 'Official History of the Ministry of Munitions' in the 1914–18 war for the *Economic History Review*[33] it had to run the gauntlet of severe and high-level scrutiny in Cabinet Office. Since then a lot of cobwebs have been blown away, and I cannot believe that this present piece will encounter resistance.

Perhaps a few concluding words may be allowed of a more subjective kind, reflections on the value of the exercise to country, to scholarship, to the members of the team.

Of the three aims which the Civil Histories had – digesting experience against a future emergency, helping in the change to a peace organisation, and offering immediate help during the war – which was most adequately fulfilled? It is much to be doubted whether solutions found for any emergency are much use ten or twenty years later. This seems especially true of the experiences of the winning side. The efforts of the War Office to learn from 1914–18 experience were pathetic in all respects: the Second World War was utterly unlike the First World War, partly because defeat had produced new military thinking in Germany. Yet when Dr Robert Oppenheimer told Hancock after the Second World War that 'nobody ever again would produce a series of histories' such as the British civil series, he meant that atomic warfare would obliterate traditional organisation for war.[34] In fact, for the last precarious twenty-eight years the world has had dozens of wars, some pretty formidable, of a conventionally revolting kind. If war experience is relevant, then its relevance is not necessarily diminished by the possibility of the ultimate destruction of civilisation.

The relevance of the official histories in the transition from war economy and organisation to peace, and to the organisation of government in normal times, are matters which deserve a detailed examination not possible here. In a number of fields of domestic social policy the official histories threw up material, ideas, practices – statistical and historical, central and regional – which had simply

not been conceived before 1939. And it was certainly the case that
other aspects of public policy in the late forties and in the fifties
were enlightened by the monographs, published and unpublished,
which war historians had built up and which had been sifted by
administrators. For instance, Cabinet Ministers taking over new
departments could have a dispassionate and critical picture of their
domains which would not have been otherwise available.

This last point leads on directly to the services afforded by the
Civil Historians to the war effort after they got into their stride in
1942. There is no doubt that this was sometimes important. Postan
was regularly consulted by ministers when he was at the Ministry
of Supply and the Ministry of Aircraft Production; Hurstfield's
work on conservation of raw materials formed the basis of joint
Anglo-American action; Medlicott's retrospective report on the
Ministry of Economic Warfare was circulated as a Cabinet paper.
Examples of this sort of thing could be multiplied. Perhaps the best
evidence of the awareness of reciprocal benefit is the decision to
have official history in time of peace. I am thinking, for instance, of
the official volumes on the history of the Atomic Energy Authority.[35]

Last, what effect did the history have on those of us who were in
it? It gave all of us, I believe, an insight into government at the
highest policy-making points of power which would have been hard
to acquire in any other way. It also warned one that there were
gaps in records, that memories were unreliable. A file would often
begin : 'A to B. We spoke. We decided . . .' When one could consult A and B, they were sometimes unable to give any background
to their conversation; or, when they claimed to remember, their
accounts did not tally; sometimes A, when asked in 1944 about
events in 1941, gave a completely different account from that he
had given in 1943.

Above all, and here I speak in an entirely personal capacity, the
official history offered training of a very high order in honest history
and sensible techniques of research. Hancock and Postan were both
remarkable organisers in their different ways and in particular I
owe much to the critical and imaginative commentaries on my own
work by Professor Postan, to whom I would like to express my
thanks. At the time I found it hard to be told, as Postan slapped
the table sharply with the back of his hand, that my first effort (on
the design and development of the 25 pdr gun) was 'Hamlet without the prince of Denmark'. But I suppose that the *dramatis
personae* were more evident in later work and have perhaps sur-

vived into other and remoter fields than those I associate with the blacked-out London of the last years of war and the first years of teaching at Edinburgh, when a large filing cabinet full of my War History notes used to glare reproachfully at me as I kept a couple of lectures ahead of my classes.[36]

4

The IRA and the Origins of SOE*

M. R. D. FOOT

It is hard to make any sense at all of the history of Ireland's relations with England without going back to Strongbow; but we must here omit the Anglo-Norman invasions, the creation of the Pale, the Tudors' and the Stuarts' colonial ventures and Irish wars, punctuated by a burst of Cromwellian severity of which incidents are still recounted as if they had happened last week. The action on the Boyne on 12 July 1690 brought a comparatively long spell – over a century – of uneasy peace and unquestionable English dominion. But eighteenth-century penal laws were ineffectual barriers against the spread of Rousseaunian doctrines; and the great revolutionary war brought trouble to Ireland again.

* This paper originated as a talk, entitled 'Michael Collins and irregular warfare', delivered in Dublin on 9 January 1969 to the Irish Military Historical Society; to which body the writer is indebted, alike for the original invitation, for the trouble the Society and the Irish army took to provide a transcript from tape, and for leave to reproduce some parts of the material used. An alarmingly large number of former participants were present, including Collins's chief of staff in the Troubles, subsequently commander-in-chief of the Irish army (see the obituary of General Richard Mulcahy in *The Times*, 17 December 1971), three silent survivors of the 'Twelve Apostles', his personal bodyguard; and two former members of the detective division in Dublin Castle, who had doubled their official task by acting among his leading intelligence agents. The final arrangements were in the hands of a dark-haired, keen-eyed, courteous captain in the Irish intelligence branch.

The talk was given, of course, as it is here refurbished, from an entirely independent, non-political, unofficial, historian's viewpoint; no government or university bears any responsibility for it. It was simply prepared as an attempt to set both the Irish effort and Collins's work in their historical context, and to reveal a sequel.

1798 is still a magical combination of figures in that island, for
reasons which even an Englishman can appreciate. Yet the rising
of 1798 was put down promptly from London, as it had to be, given
the context of the war against France which the British were fighting at the time. They could not contemplate a hostile presence on
their west coast while they were fighting their mortal enemy to the
south. It is now clear, from Dr Bolton's and other recent researches
on the Union with Ireland,[1] that there was no deliberate British
provocation of the rising in 1798, as some Irish historians have
wanted to believe; but there was really little hope for the rising,
because the Irish were up against a far heavier weight of metal
than they could then overthrow. The effort in 1848 was more hopeless still, less widespread, less well organised, much less well armed,
and only less tragic in its results because fewer people came out to
be repressed. There was a third effort in the late 1860s by the
Fenian Brotherhood that had been founded on St Patrick's Day
1858; this again quite rapidly dwindled away. In the 1880s there
were further violent Irish attempts to overthrow the British occupation, including that disaster in Phoenix Park on 6 May 1882
when the Irish secretary was deliberately murdered by a body of
wild men from the slums of Dublin armed with knives, an act that
set back the advance to freedom for forty years. It has lately been
shown by Tom Corfe[2] that they deliberately set out to kill Lord
Frederick Cavendish because he was Irish secretary, and were not
simply out to kill Burke, the permanent head of the Irish office,
whom they slew with him. To spare the feelings of his uncle,
Mr Gladstone, it was said at the time that Cavendish had been
killed by accident because he tried to defend his friend; it is now
clear that he was killed on purpose, a blow from which his uncle
never recovered – but that is a different story.

The Phoenix Park murders were followed independently by a
series of more or less bloody disasters, known by the sufferers as the
'dynamite outrages', in London and other cities. For a generation
various statesmen, British and Irish, tried to arrive at a political
solution of the Anglo-Irish difficulties; this went by the name of
Home Rule. Mr Gladstone and Mr Parnell tried to put forward
from their different points of view a system of Home Rule which
would be acceptable to the British and the Irish electorate alike.
This did not quite come off; Irishmen and Irishwomen today are
glad it did not, for if they were offered now the extremely limited
degree of sovereignty provided by either of Mr Gladstone's Home

Rule bills, they would for intelligible reasons refuse it, as something far less than what the Irish wish for national independence deserves. Mr Asquith and Mr Redmond tried again, once more from different angles of approach, to arrive at a suitable Home Rule settlement in 1912–14. These attempts at a political solution led to dire trouble in north-eastern Ireland, where the Ulster loyalists prepared to revolt, if necessary, against Crown authority as a demonstration of their determination to remain under the Crown in London and never to be governed from Dublin.

Troubles in Ulster brought the United Kingdom to the verge of civil war. Indeed the telegram declaring civil war had been written out by the Protestants' leader, Sir Edward Carson, who was on his way to despatch it when he was intercepted by a note from Asquith which said : 'My dear Sir Edward, I think I ought to let you know that war between this country and Germany can now be delayed only by a matter of hours'; whereupon Carson tore up the telegram.[3] The kingdom had come that near to an explosion over Home Rule and Ulster's objection to it in the summer of 1914. This period is better remembered in southern Ireland for Erskine Childers's gun-running at Howth and the ensuing catastrophe in Bachelor's Walk. Next morning, 29 July, *The Times* said in a leading article : 'there can no longer be the slightest doubt that the country is now confronted with one of the greatest crises in the history of the British race.'

Anyone can see in retrospect that the remark in *The Times* was quite true. The European civil war had just begun, with the Austro-Hungarian declaration of war on Serbia : the war in which four great empires fell and a whole stable system of ordering society with them; the first successful communist revolution took place; and twenty-five million men were killed. But the leader in *The Times* did not refer to the great war at all : in Printing House Square, as late as 29 July, the Irish was still the cardinal question. A week later, *The Times* saw things differently; everyone on the English side of the Irish Sea was busy with the war. During that war over a quarter of the entire British male population enlisted, one in eight of those who put on uniform were killed, and the ruling class suffered casualties from which it never recovered.[4]

On the Irish side, the nationalist parliamentarians supported the war, which they saw as one in defence of small nations like their own, Serbian and Belgian, against Habsburg and Hohenzollern imperialism. The sterner Irish nationalists in the inner circle of the

Irish Republican Brotherhood thought otherwise. 'England's difficulty, Ireland's opportunity', the old motto for the age-long cause, was motto enough for them. They stuck to the ideals they had learned from their predecessors in the land war of the eighties, or the Fenian risings of the sixties, of 1848, 1798, 1689 and 1641, and earlier still. A few of the most fanatical of them instigated the Easter Rising of 1916 – which was where Michael Collins came in.

His own work during the rising was subaltern : enough to secure him internment in Frongoch afterwards, but not enough to attract any special notice from his captors. Indeed, so well did he hide in the ruck of ordinary IRA prisoners that no one bothered to take and file a photograph of him (an omission the British later had cause to regret).[5] He remained alert to what was happening round him and sharpened by practical experience his own apprehension of the nature and methods of clandestine war. For he was one of those rare people who could see what the essentials of irregular warfare are, and how they could be applied to his country in his time.

The historian who seeks precise knowledge about how any clandestine personality worked, without having taken part in the same struggle himself, is unlikely to find all he is looking for, because there will be few if any sources for him to consult. If you start a clandestine war, you seldom write down either the fact or the method; one of your first working principles has to be not to multiply evidence which a hostile police force can deploy against you. The ideal clandestine is quite prepared to pretend, if need be, that he is illiterate. If he (or she) must write something down – the business of ciphering or deciphering a message is not so simple that it can be done in your head – the moment he has finished with the piece of paper he sets a match to it, burns every shred, and then breaks up the ash with the match stub. Simple messages pass by word of mouth, perhaps in a simple code unknown to the messenger; complicated messages are, as a rule, better not sent at all.

Now Collins, as an exceptionally able clandestine operator, was a thoroughly practical man as well; he knew the Royal Irish Constabulary and the Dublin Metropolitan Police, his principal opponents in the early stages of the civil war he waged; and he decided to commit a good deal to paper. Part of what he wrote down was too complicated to be entrusted to verbal messages; part, as the war went on and his side gained adherents, arose from the routine business of running a state. For as the struggle developed, the Irish leaders gradually set up, in quasi-clandestinity, the organs of a normal state; the western peasantry learned, for example, to take their lawsuits to republican judges who met behind screens of IRA guards in suitable impromptu courthouses.

Collins's first share in this was to run the army, particularly its intelligence side. From a shifting headquarters in Dublin, he conducted a lengthy and detailed correspondence, in clear, on a typewriter, with various brigades of Irish volunteers all over the country; he kept carbon copies of every letter he sent and hid the copies (and the carbon paper) here and there, varying the hiding places from time to time and never storing everything together.[6] Where all the originals, and all the carbon copies, went is a question of interest, as is the question whether enough of them survive to compose a body of evidence from which an historian could construct a comprehensive military history of the Troubles. Those questions can safely be left to Irish historians to answer, while we turn to more general ones: what were the principles on which Collins worked? What are the essentials for a successful movement against an occupying power?

English readers may be reluctant to follow the suggestion that Ireland from 1916 to 1921 was in a position in any way comparable to that of, say, France or Holland or Yugoslavia during part at least of the war of 1939–45; or that the Irish movement for national independence was comparable to the recent struggles of the French, the Dutch, the Yugoslavs, the Norwegians, the Poles, and so on. (Brigadier W. F. K. Thompson, of *The Daily Telegraph*, heir to the unionist *Morning Post*, has dissented sharply from the view that the current difficulties in Ulster have anything in common with wartime resistance. This shows how closely historical questions about subversion can be tied up with current politics.[7]) The object of this essay is to suggest that there were in fact similarities, sometimes close ones, between what Collins was doing and what – to take three disparate resisters to Hitler – Tito, Jean Moulin, and Bor-Komorowski were trying to do, and even to indicate that Collins's efforts and methods had some indirect influence on those who came later. By looking into the essential elements from which a successful resistance movement can be put together, we may be able to perceive some of the similarities between the Irish case and others.

Five essential elements can be picked out, without which a resistance movement has no chance of success: intelligence, security, arms, hope, and leadership. Perhaps we should add a sixth: luck.

Let us glance at the five in context; Collins was master of all.

Intelligence about what the enemy is up to is, of course, the foundation of all successful military action. Collins's first high post in the IRA was as director of intelligence, and he used with skill and effect the knowledge of how the general post office worked that he had acquired in England as a young man. The years he had spent as a post office clerk in London, learning Irish and making friends in his spare time, brought him a reward. He had a thorough comprehension of the British methods of handling mail; he knew at what points documents might be interceptible, and for how long; and he secured friends who would do the intercepting for him. It did not cross the minds of British policemen or British commanders that the post was anything but safe; they used it a lot and Collins used it too, to emasculate the forces they were beginning to deploy against him.

Beyond getting massive intelligence from postal sources, he embarked on a more traditional and equally effective device : spies in the enemy's camp. Two detective sergeants in D division, the counter-espionage branch at Dublin Castle, doubled that exacting task with the still more exacting one of supplying Collins with precise information about British counter-terrorist tactics.[8] Part of the tactical side was covered with equal aplomb by the senior Castle typist, a respectable lady who, because she had the longest service in her grade, typed all the really secret documents of the intelligence staff, such as the list compiled about noon each day of the houses in Dublin to be raided that night. She left the Castle on the stroke of half-past five every evening; no one ever thought of searching her handbag, in which she carried away an extra copy of everything she had typed during the day. It took about an hour for her extra copies to reach Collins; raids began between eight and nine at night. No wonder they so seldom caught anybody.

This leads to the importance, to both sides, of security; which has of course, interconnections with intelligence. Through his Castle sources, Collins could spot traitors in his own camp and eliminate them; he could often guard also against efforts made to penetrate the IRA, because he was forewarned of them. Such an ideal degree of knowledge is rare and precious; it was particularly precious in Ireland. The Irish are seldom behind the rest of us in one of the commonest of human failings, often fatal to resisters : people *will* *talk*. Once a resistance movement has picked up some momentum, people start boasting of having something to do with it; their boasts are overheard, they are followed and, in the end, somebody is likely to get hurt. The British security authorities in Ireland during the civil war were competent enough to pursue numerous reports of careless talk; hence, in part, the vehemence of the 'walls have ears' and 'careless talk costs lives' propaganda in the war against Hitler.

There is little anyone can do about this except pick taciturn friends if he wants to go policeman-shooting and encourage all his acquaintances to remember that talking is fatal. Collins's best agents and closest friends were people whom he trusted and who returned his trust; as one of them once said, 'It's not asking that's the critical point. If he didn't want to tell me, that was enough for me.'[9] That agent's task had been straightforward. He was a clerk in the Dublin telegraph office. From Easter 1916 he took a copy of every cipher telegram the British sent through there and passed it to the Irish Republican intelligence branch, who seldom had much trouble in making out the sense of the message. Observe how the elements of a successful clandestine organisation support each other : the Irish agents inside Dublin Castle could usually supply the cipher, and the telegraph clerk supplied the uses made of it. The British made the task of reading their secret messages even simpler, both by using an unsophisticated cipher and by sending out in one month's cipher – well on in the month, when one way or another the Irish had broken it – what the next month's cipher was to be.[10]

But our main business for the moment is with security, on which one or two more things need to be said. If necessary, an example has to be made of someone who has talked too much, *pour encourager les autres.* This was a step Collins was prepared to take, when he had to. He had a small, competent execution squad, who carried out such killings as he after due inquiry thought just. The squad's members were themselves so secure that none of them was ever arrested by the British who provided their main targets;[11] and Collins's hold on them was firm enough to protect them from the standing danger of their trade – that killing becomes habit-forming. The later history of Ireland, both in the Irish civil war of 1922–3, when too many gunmen ran riot (and in the process the great bulk of the record evidence for the medieval history of the island was burnt in the Four Courts), and in the Ulster troubles of 1969–73 when gangs of both main persuasions went in for meaningless atrocities,[12] is painfully filled with this tendency of strong men to go on using strong-arm tactics from force of habit. Strategically, they often defeat their own ends by doing so; but wild men like the sight and smell of blood.[13]

More arms have been available recently for wild men than were to be had in the early 1920s, even in the aftermath of a world war. With no weapons at all, a resistance movement is usually powerless, though not always: in Norway, during the German occupation, there was a striking example of the impact that perfectly passive resistance can exert on an occupying power, when the history schoolteachers, as a body, refused to accept the Gestapo's instructions about how history-teaching was to be slanted, and in the end carried their point.[14] This sort of technique had been applied with some success, on Parnell's and Davitt's advice, during the land war of the early eighties, in circumstances that added to the language the name of Lord Erne's agent, the unfortunate Captain Boycott.[15] The time for boycotting passed, at latest, with the gun-running at Larne.[16] Thereafter the connection between political power and physical force reigned in all its starkness.

Phyical force is most sharply asserted, in twentieth-century cities, by firearms. Firearms have to come from abroad, or to be stolen or made on the spot. Abroad is the most promising source, but is likely to involve help from an outside power. The original *francs-tireurs et partisans* of the Franco-Prussian war of 1870–1, after whom the communist-inspired resistance movement of 1941–4 was named, had so little success and were so nearly helpless, because there was no organised power outside France ready to help them with weapons. Collins's IRA was little better placed. Unlike the successor to its name, it had no (or virtually no) contacts with revolutionary trouble-makers in Russia, who in any case had troubles enough of their own at the time. Irish sympathisers in America were his most likely external source for arms, but his enemies held the sea. Some of the rifles landed by Erskine Childers at Howth were still to be had and he was able to raise a miscellany of weapons, ranging from shotguns to an armoured car, by searching and stealing. As the communist proverb of the early 1940s put it, 'Any household has a knife; if you have a knife you can get a pistol; if you have a pistol you can get a rifle; if you have a rifle you can get a machine-gun; arm yourselves!' Collins's men acquired some of their arms in this cumulative fashion. Some others they could make. They had several grenade factories, one of which in Dublin (observe again how all parts of a sound clandestine body hang together) was once raided by the British, who never discovered what it was because the security was so good.

Security needed to be good, for the weapons were painfully scarce. It is said that when the treaty of December 1921 was signed[17] and the British troops were withdrawn, the new Irish Free State government announced that anyone who had carried arms against the British would receive a pension; and that nearly 90,000 applications for these pensions were made. The point was referred to the chairman of the Provisional government, General Collins, shortly before he was assassinated. He commented that he knew there had never been more than 2,800 weapons available.[18]

It showed real economy of force, and real power of clandestine command, to get rid of British forces numbering about 60,000 through the leverage of forces wielding less than a twentieth of their weapons. It also showed unusual political capacity on the part of his colleague, Arthur Griffith, as much as on Collins's own, to apply pressures nicely calculated to make the British change their mind, without forfeiting significant sympathy abroad or endangering the forces at home by attacking on too wide a front. The political victory of the Irish was won on the English side of the sea : the occupying government changed its mind, in response to a change of mind among those who had voted it into power.

Friendship for J. L. Hammond allows me to name him here. As one of the *Manchester Guardian*'s correspondents in Ireland during the Troubles, he took a leading part in bringing home to the British electorate the consequences of the policy of counter-terror their government adopted : the policy guyed in Parliament in the phrase 'There have been no reprisals and they have done a great deal of good.' The counter-terror of the Black and Tans and of the less notorious, but more deadly, Auxiliaries was applied against frankly terrorist tactics used by Collins to deal with the uniformed forces of the Crown. His military tactics combined with Griffith's political ones neatly enough, to provide the Irish with the fourth necessary constituent : hope. With some hope of eventual success, a resistance movement can start. Years, even decades, of preparation may be needed – a political and propaganda task of great complexity. Then, given some change in the grip of the occupying power, such as the distraction of a long war, it may be possible to move over from purely political to military action and to score one or two successful coups. As the movement accumulates successes, it accumulates support; ideally, it soon reaches the stage when it seems likely to win,

and everyone who wants to be on the winning side joins it, unless
atrocious methods are used against it. When some nineteen people
out of every twenty have decided in its favour, nothing short of
atrocity is going to stop it, as the Hungarians found in 1956.

The last essential point for a successful movement of resistance is
really daring leadership: men and women, or *a man* at least, who
will lead from in front. Whatever else Collins was, he was a man
who led from in front: not for him the salon revolutionary's cry
'*Je suis leur chef, il faut que je les suive.*' When there was any really
dangerous job to be done, he took part himself whenever he could,
at the most dangerous point. This of course became known among
the people who worked with him, and made his orders all the more
easy to obey. So the Irish resistance movement, with him in the
lead, escaped from the closed cycle of disaster, betrayal, defeat, new
disaster, new betrayal, *e da capo*. There was no more need for such
counter-productive coups as the murders in Phoenix Park. There
was no more chance for such people as the man who called himself
Henri Le Caron, who was chief of staff of the Clan na Gael – the
Irish revolutionary organisation in America – for some twenty years
and who, during that time, kept the British Home Office fully
informed of its activities.[19] Bloody Sunday, 21 November 1920,
made it clear enough that such opportunities would not be open to
the British any more.

The Irish in fact provided a paradigm of what Mr Gladstone
once called, in quite a different connection, a 'people struggling,
and struggling rightly, to be free';[20] and the force of their example
is the most interesting and historically the most productive thing
they did. They not only saved themselves: they showed a great
many other people how to save themselves. Lenin noted at the time
of the Easter Rising, when he was himself a little-known and almost
penniless exile in Zurich, that if the British, of all empires, had
started to crumble so close to its core, then there was hope for
anti-imperialists the world over.[21] Sure enough, other empires
tumbled soon, with a ruin more complete than has been visited (so
far at least) upon the British. No suggestion is made that the Irish
example had any notable impact, or indeed any impact at all, on
the four great imperial collapses of 1918. Someone strongly hostile
to the Irish might even try to argue that the Easter Rising had done
a tiny bit to prolong the dominion of the Hohenzollerns, but the
case is not a good one. Indeed a more powerful opposite argument
can be urged, that the Rising helped to fell Asquith who, with all

his virtues, was an indecisive leader in war. Certainly, by a freak
of fate, the Rising preserved the life of Asquith's successor. David
Lloyd George was to have sailed to Russia in HMS *Hampshire*,
and would have gone down with her as Kitchener did, had he not
been detained in London by the Rising's aftermath. When a little
of the dust had settled, other groups of people in comparable fixes
to the Irish were able to take heart from their example. The Indian
case is discussed in some detail elsewhere;[22] we need only note here
that Indian nationalist leaders were aware of the Irish struggle, were
encouraged by its result, and were prepared to adopt some of its
methods, though a Gandhian philosophy of non-violent action was
far from the thoughts of Collins's gunmen.

There was a rough similarity in the proportions of Protestants to
Catholics in Ireland in 1921, and of Moslems to non-Moslems in
India in 1947; a further analogy between the two cases is suggested
by the fissiparous tendencies in politics shown in many of the old
imperial territories after the British had left. A more exact analogy
in population figures can be observed in the proportion of Turks to
Greeks in Cyprus in the late 1950s. In India, in Cyprus, and in
many other countries where their colonial rule was threatened from
within, the British followed the course they had set for themselves
in Ireland : unless the circumstances were exceptionally odd, sooner
than stand and fight they went away. The Dutch followed the same
sensible plan in Indonesia. The French in Algeria, notoriously, did
not; but, having once learned their Algerian lesson, they applied it
elsewhere. The Portuguese, refusing to think the plan sensible,
would appear to have current troubles on their hands. Ireland has
in fact become a world model of how to conduct a successful insurrection against an occupying colonial power.

In conclusion it is worth noting that the British drew an offensive
as well as a defensive lesson from the Irish difficulties, learning how
to stimulate resistance to an occupying army when engaged in
another kind of anti-imperialist struggle themselves.

One might have expected that this lesson would be drawn primarily from the goings-on in Ulster in 1913–14; as Stewart described them much later, they were just the sort of thing a first-class
subversive organiser would have run. Consider for a moment the
set-piece on the night of 25–26 April 1914. A leak to the RIC had
hinted that there would be something to look out for and at dusk
a collier, the *Balmerino*, was sighted behaving suspiciously off Bel-
fast. Customs and police spent the night searching her (she was

fully laden – with coal), while, a few miles up the coast at Larne, 25,000 rifles were run ashore from the *Mountjoy*, without inter- ference from the police. A couple of policemen went down to the quay; a dozen Ulstermen simply stood round them, in a tight circle, to make sure they saw and did nothing.

Curiously enough nobody (so far as I am aware) involved in these Ulster operations had anything to do with subversive British activity in the war of 1939; but what Collins did in Dublin had a noticeable impact, in the end, on British secret service method. This impact was made through two of his junior but intelligent opponents, J. C. F. Holland and C. McV. Gubbins. Both were young regular majors (they had known each other at Woolwich) who had distinguished themselves in the 1914–18 war, Gubbins as a gunner on the western front and Holland, more oddly, as an airman working with Lawrence's irregulars in Arabia, where he won a DFC. Both were profoundly impressed with the powerless- ness of regular troops against resolute gunmen who could rely on the local population not to give them away; both had seen enough of the massed slaughter of Flanders to be sick of it; both saw the advantages, in economy of life and effectiveness of effort, of the Irish guerrilla they could not stem. And both determined that next time, if there had to be a next time, guerrilla should be used by the British instead of against them.

Seventeen years after the Anglo-Irish treaty, both were still majors. Holland, who was due to command an engineer battalion, was in poor health and was offered a two-year posting at the War Office instead, to research into any subject he chose. He chose irregular warfare, a subject which, by the summer of 1938, was of such interest to the general staff that he was offered a second GSO II to help him, and secured Gubbins.[23]

In the autumn of 1940, Holland was at last able to take up a senior army engineer's appointment.[24] Meanwhile, this extraordi- narily creative and unselfish character had set up the commandos, the escape service, and the deception service; he had done much towards developing SOE, the Special Operations Executive, and had prepared Gubbins to act as its mainspring.[25] SOE's task was to support resistance to the Nazis wherever it existed and, wherever it did not, to stimulate it. SOE provided most of the arms and the communications, and much of the leadership, for the resistance movements of northern, western, and southern Europe, and in parts of south-east Asia as well. The Irish can thus claim that their resistance provided an originating impulse for resistance to tyrannies worse than any they had had to endure themselves. And Irish resistance, as Collins led it, showed the rest of the world an economical way to fight wars, the only sane way they can be fought in the age of the nuclear bomb.

5

The Success of Social Reform?
The Central Control Board (Liquor
Traffic) 1915-21*

MICHAEL E. ROSE

'It would be hard to say why historians have not rated the effect of
strong drink as the significant factor in nineteenth-century history
that it undoubtedly was', remarked Professor Kitson Clark in his
Ford Lectures of 1960.[1] With the publication of Brian Harrison's
book, this defect has been remedied for the first three-quarters of
that century.[2] Kitson Clark's verdict holds, however, for the late
Victorian and Edwardian period, and to some extent for the period
of the 1914–18 war.[3] It is the aim of this essay to examine briefly
some aspects of the attempt to control the consumption of strong
drink during the latter period.

'War means whisky', pronounced a Senior Fellow of All Souls
in 1914, and ordered a hogshead of the stuff. 'More war means
more whisky', he decided in 1915, purchasing a puncheon. He
died in 1916, a richer if not a more sober man.[4] It was not, however the drinking habits of Oxbridge dons which aroused concern
during the 1914–18 war, but those of the working classes. With the
increased employment and earning power that the war brought, it
was feared that the extra money would find its way from the
worker's pocket, or his wife's purse, into the publican's till.[5] The
result would be increased drunkenness, leading to indiscipline

* I would like to thank my colleagues at the University of Manchester,
together with the staff of the University and City Libraries in Manchester and
of the British Museum and Colindale Newspaper Libraries who have aided my
researches. I owe a particular debt of gratitude to the members of the Manchester University Historical Society's field trip to Carlisle in March 1972.
Their enthusiastic investigation of 'State pubs' provided the initial inspiration
for this essay.

71

amongst the armed forces and lost production in vital war industries. By the early months of 1915, the drink question was causing
as much virulent controversy as it had in 1908 during the struggles
over the Liberal government's abortive Licensing Bill.[6] On 28
February 1915, Lloyd George proclaimed in a speech at Bangor
that drink was doing more damage than 'all the German sub-
marines put together.'[7] A month later, he told a delegation of ship-
building employers, who had called on him to urge the enactment
of prohibition as an answer to bad timekeeping in their industry,
that the nation was fighting 'Germany, Austria and Drink; and as
far as I can see the greatest of these deadly foes is Drink.'[8]

Encouraged by the Chancellor of the Exchequer's rhetoric, those
temperance reformers who believed in prohibition as the only
weapon against the demon drink campaigned vigorously for an end
to the liquor traffic.[9] They urged the government to follow the
example of France, where the sale of absinthe had been banned,
and of Russia, where vodka and other spirits had been prohibited
for the duration of the war.[10] The licensed trade responded strongly
to this attack upon them and called on their parliamentary friends
in the Unionist party to defend them against any unfair restrictions.[11] In May 1915 they also obtained the support of the Irish
party in attacking and defeating the swingeing taxes which Lloyd
George had attempted to place on alcoholic liquors.[12]

Lloyd George's other, and more ambitious, scheme for restrict-
ing drink consumption, that of a complete State purchase of the
liquor trade, was also withdrawn. This was due, in his opinion, not
to opposition from the brewers or their Unionist allies, but to
resistance from temperance advocates in his own party who feared
that this link between government and alcohol would destroy any
future hope of obtaining prohibition, by means of local option for
example.[13] 'It is neither right nor politic for the State to afford
legal protection and sanction to any traffic or system that tends to
increase crime, to waste the national resources, to corrupt the social
habits and to destroy the health and lives of the people', the President of the United Kingdom Alliance told his assembled members.[14]
Trade unionists and Labour MPs meanwhile responded bitterly to
accusations from middle-class temperance zealots, employers and
government ministers that excessive drinking, rather than overlong
hours, bad working conditions and industrial fatigue, was the major
cause of bad timekeeping and lost production.[15] Class resentment of
this sort was embarrassing to the government which, in the after-

math of the Treasury Agreement of March 1915, desperately needed labour support in order to gain the co-operation of suspicious rank and file trade unionists in the working of 'dilution' and other war production schemes. Any legislation on the drink question which appeared to contain class bias was likely to increase the chances of unofficial strikes and industrial unrest in militant areas like Clydeside.[16]

The drink question was therefore by no means the least of the many problems facing the Liberal government and its Coalition successor in 1915. Hasty legislation or partisan statements on the subject could easily stir up and intensify party and class strife at a time when national unity was imperative to the success of the war effort. It was in these circumstances that the Central Control Board (Liquor Traffic) was set up by an Order in Council of 10 June 1915.[17] Consisting initially of a chairman and eleven members appointed by the Minister of Munitions, the Board was given powers of control over the sale and consumption of alcohol in any area scheduled by Order in Council.[18] The areas scheduled were to be those where excessive drinking was held to be interfering with the war effort. Seaports were the first to be placed under the Board's control, Newhaven being the first area to experience it in July 1916, with Southampton, Liverpool and Bristol following in August. By the autumn, control was being extended to industrial areas inland. The Midlands, the West Riding and the London area were all listed for control in November 1915. Three years later, 95 per cent of the population of England, Wales and Scotland lived in areas under the Board's control.[19]

The main restrictions imposed by the Board on scheduled areas were the limitation of hours for the sale or supply of liquor to two and a half at midday and two or three in the evening. No sale was to take place before 12.30 p.m. or between 2.30 and 6 p.m., although premises could open during these hours for the sale of non-alcoholic drinks. Buying drinks for others ('treating') and credit sales were prohibited, as was the sale of spirits for 'off' consumption in the evenings and on Saturdays. Spirits might, by order of the Board, be diluted below the 25 degrees under proof maximum permitted before the war.[20] In three areas, Invergordon and Cromarty in northern Scotland, Enfield Lock east of London, and Gretna on the Scottish border, the Board, late in 1915, was allowed to purchase licensed premises and take over the running of the liquor business instead of merely controlling it from above.[21]

The Central Control Board has received relatively scant attention from recent historians of the war. The last full-scale study of wartime liquor control was published in 1923.[22] The most familiar aspects of the Board's work are the negative, restrictionist ones, particularly afternoon closing.[23] However, Professor Marwick, in his social history of the war, does point to the positive aspects of the Board's policy and to its advocacy of nationalisation of the drink trade.[24] It is surprising, therefore, that the Central Control Board has not received more attention from the historians of state intervention and reconstructionist planning in wartime Britain.[25] Within the brief scope of this essay, it is hoped that an examination of the more constructive side of the Board's policy will serve to show that, far from being mainly concerned with imposing restrictions to meet particular wartime emergencies, it played a social reforming role designed to remodel the drink trade and drinking habits in Britain.[26]

From the first, the Central Control Board saw its role as being wider than the mere restriction of drinking. 'The Board, however, attach very considerable importance to the constructive side of their work and this side has received their careful consideration', they announced in their first report to the Minister of Munitions.[27] One feature of this constructive work was the conducting of objective enquiries into subjects previously befogged by emotional statements and partisan attitudes. Control was never extended to a new area before a careful local enquiry had been held. The opinions of the military, licensing, and local authorities were heard, together with those of representatives of employers, trade unionists, and the licensed trade. Religious and temperance organisations were not invited to give evidence, but they were heard separately if they so requested. Presumably the Board felt that such organisations would be likely to make statements of a dogmatic and partisan nature which would be unlikely to serve much purpose.[28]

In addition to these routine local enquiries, the Board also set up special committees to investigate particular aspects of the drink problem in more detail. In October 1915 a Women's Advisory Committee was established to investigate allegations that higher female earnings and the payment of separation allowances to the wives of soldiers were causing increased drinking by women. The Committee found that, whilst there had been some increase amongst those who had frequented public houses before the war, the great majority spent their wages and allowances wisely. A special enquiry in Birmingham in 1916, after allegations in a local newspaper that female drunkenness in the city was increasing alarmingly, reached similar conclusions. Both enquiries strongly deprecated the idea of imposing 'any restrictions dealing specially with women.'[29] Not only did the Board respect this opinion, but they also tried to improve the conditions for female drinking. In their own pubs in Carlisle, they began to provide separate women's bars in order to bring women within the public house instead of confining them to the doorways and passages where they had previously been served. Facilities for the sexes to drink together were also provided at some of the newer houses.[30] The Central Control Board, like the Ministry of Reconstruction, proved sensitive to the pressures of the feminist movement.[31]

Another problem upon which the Board soon found that 'no body of impartial opinion exists which is ready to be guided by scientific enquiry' was the basic one of the effects of alcohol upon the human body.[32] Temperance enthusiasts, equating drink with drunkenness and drunkenness with alcoholism, saw all indulgence as being physically harmful. The licensed trade on the other hand emphasised the health-giving properties of beer.[33] The Board, feeling that 'a sound administrative policy must be based on a full knowledge of the relevant physiological evidence', decided to form an Alcohol Committee in November 1916.[34] Chaired by Lord D'Abernon, the Committee consisted of eight medical experts, pharmacologists, physiologists and psychologists being prominent amongst them. Experiments were conducted and memoranda and papers discussed by the Committee.[35] As a result, the Board produced in 1918 a pamphlet entitled *Alcohol. Its Action on the Human Organism.* This showed that alcoholic drinks had only limited nutritional value and that their action was narcotic rather than stimulant. On the other hand, it showed that temperate consumption of them was physiologically harmless to normal adults.[36] The Royal Commission on Licensing in 1931 noted the frequency with which this pamphlet was referred to in evidence to it. It 'appears to be accepted on all hands', they remarked, as 'the official and authoritative epitome of the best opinion in the matter.'[37]

One point which the Alcohol Committee was at pains to stress in its pamphlet was that not only should time elapse between periods of drinking, but also that alcohol taken without food might cause injury to the stomach membrane.[38] This association of food and drink consumption was something upon which the Board placed a good deal of emphasis. Its restricted opening hours were physiologically designed to ensure that public houses were open during or just after a period when the customer was likely to have eaten.[39] Early morning opening, which was thought to have been particularly harmful since it encouraged workers to drink on their way to work, often on an empty stomach, was ended. In Scotland, public houses were closed until 4 p.m. on Saturday, which was normally pay day. This regulation was an attempt to encourage men to go home with their wage packets and have a meal before going to the pub.[40]

It was realised, however, that more positive action was required to ensure the proper feeding of workers. Some progressive firms had established canteens in their factories before 1914, but large sections of industry provided no facilities of any sort for the consumption of food during the working day. P. W. Wilson, secretary of the People's Palace Association, wrote to Lord D'Abernon in July 1915, complaining that 150 of the 200 firms his Association had approached had ignored or refused its request to be allowed to establish canteens on their premises. Wilson added that some of the refusals came from 'those which have been most conscious of the drink evil' and he urged that 'a little tactful pressure by the Board would greatly hasten the extension of this work.'[41]

The Board responded with enthusiasm. A Canteens Committee of four members under the chairmanship of Sir George Newman was formed.[42] The Treasury reluctantly agreed to provide up to 50 per cent of the capital required by a voluntary society to establish a works canteen. Employers were allowed to set off the cost of any canteen provision they made against excess profits tax.[43] By 1918, over 900 canteens had been provided, catering for over a million workers at a capital cost to the government of £3½ million.[44]

It was on this question of the finance of the canteen scheme that friction developed. The Canteens Committee, particularly its forceful chairman, Sir George Newman, saw canteen provision as part of a social experiment in industry. The factory canteen would offer a positive counter-attraction to the public house. 'It should be the aim to make the canteen as attractive as possible to the workers, to make them feel that it is their canteen (not a charitable institution), a place where they can expect a good meal at a reasonable price under good conditions and where they can leave the atmosphere of the works behind them', the Committee explained in a pamphlet on the subject.[45] Not only did the Board feel that the canteen was making 'a substantial contribution to the humanisation of industry', but it was also helping to make their restrictive measures more palatable.[46] Thus Sir George Newman regarded some financial deficit in the provision and running of canteens as inevitable and hoped that 'the canteen habit would not be sacrificed to consideration of finance or dictates of mere economic pedantry.' This opinion was not shared by the Finance Department of the Ministry of Munitions whose deputy director, Mr Duckworth, held that canteens, once established, ought to pay their way. In April 1917 a separate Canteens Finance Committee of the Ministry was formed to carry out a close financial scrutiny of canteens in national factories. Whilst this body was intended to work in co-operation with the Board's Committee, it in fact operated 'entirely separately and not without friction.' Newman who had been appointed to the Finance Committee resigned from it when he found that it was not to be subordinate to his own committee.[47]

The Central Control Board also clashed bitterly with the Treasury over canteens policy. In 1918 the Treasury severely reprimanded the Board for establishing five canteens between 1915 and 1917 on their own initiative when they could find no employer or voluntary organisation willing to bear or share the cost. About £12,000 had been spent, it was alleged, without Treasury approval having been sought.[48] Lord D'Abernon indignantly defended his department, maintaining that in two cases prior sanction had been obtained whilst in the others the urgency of the situation precluded any delay.[49]

By this time, however, responsibility for industrial canteens had been vested in a separate department of the Ministry of Munitions.[50] On being informed of this, the Board urged that 'care be taken to see that interests at present in the Board's charge were adequately safeguarded.' In March 1919 they made a bid for the retransfer of canteen administration to their charge, since it was 'an integral factor of their system of liquor control.'[51] Far from regarding canteen provision as a mere emergency measure, the Board saw it as being 'a permanent and essential feature of the modern factory' and one over which they were anxious to re-establish their control.[52]

The aspect of the Central Control Board's work which revealed most clearly the long-term, reforming, reconstructionist ideals which underlay it was the State purchase scheme at Gretna and Carlisle. As with canteen provision, this could be interpreted as a short-term emergency measure which was not dismantled after the war but remained like the rusting hulk of some stranded battleship. The prospect of 10,000 construction workers moving into a thinly populated area of the Western Borders to build a munitions factory; the knowledge that the factory would employ 10,000 workers when operational; the increased demand for licences and the rise in the value of licensed premises in the area – all these served to arouse the fears of those who saw the working man's propensity for strong drink as a threat to war production. By September 1915, when the Board received a detailed report on the Gretna factory from their Scottish assessor, Sir Thomas Munro, the Ministry of Munitions had already taken over five licensed houses within the factory area.[53] These were handed over to the Board, which then decided to purchase public houses in the neighbouring villages.[54]

Given its close proximity and good rail connections, the city of Carlisle was soon affected. Construction workers and factory employees lodged there or visited the city's pubs on a Saturday evening. To the quiet cathedral city this seemed like an invasion of Goths and Vandals as 'men fought like beasts in the streets' and 'every alley was littered with prostrate drunken men.'[55] In such circumstances it was held that the Control Board's ordinary regulations were inadequate, and so, in June 1916, the Board bought control of the drink trade in Carlisle and the surrounding area. By 1918, State purchase covered an area of 500 square miles and a population of about 140,000.[56]

The Board held that they were forced to adopt State purchase when other methods failed, and one of their members, in his history of the Board, attacked 'the fiction that the Board embarked on a large venture in State Purchase and Direct Control solely as an essay or experiment in licensing reform.'[57] Nevertheless, the phrase 'The Carlisle Experiment' soon gained widespread currency. 'It is as a practical test of that theory (nationalisation) that the Carlisle experiment is interesting and will become more interesting as, the war over, men have more time to think of social questions', remarked the *Cumberland News* in June 1916.[58]

Even if the Board was not consciously experimenting, its eagerness to attempt direct control at Gretna before there was any evidence of increased drunkenness or of the ineffectiveness of its ordinary controls, and its rapid decision to undertake a much larger purchase scheme in Carlisle in the face of strong Treasury opposition, would seem to indicate that the idea of nationalisation was prominent in its thinking.[59] Once purchase had been undertaken, there was certainly a conscious attempt to experiment with schemes aimed not merely at reducing drink consumption, but also at changing the conditions under which it was consumed. Edgar Saunders, general manager of the Carlisle scheme, admitted in his fourth report that if the scheme was not 'an intentional experiment . . . a social experiment with far-reaching possibilities emerged.'[60]

The bases of the scheme were the ideas of 'disinterested management' and of the improved public house which had been developed on a small scale by some moderate temperance reformers before the war.[61] Some public houses, particularly the smaller ones in the back streets of Carlisle, were closed down.[62] Other houses were redesigned. Flashy advertisements for liquor were removed, and small bars and snugs demolished to make way for larger rooms which had more seating accommodation and could be more effectively supervised by the publican. Each house was run by a manager, in many cases the former licensee, who was paid a salary by the Board. He was allowed some commission on the sale of food and non-alcoholic drinks but not on the sale of alcohol. Thus he was under no pressure to push drink sales and the maintenance of good order in the house became his main concern.

Food sales in public houses were encouraged and, although these did not increase very rapidly, the Board also opened a number of licensed taverns whose main purpose was the supply of cooked meals at reasonable prices. The best known of these was the Gretna Tavern opened in July 1916 in a former post office which had been acquired by the Board and specially converted. Facilities for recreation were also provided in many houses as a counter-attraction to drink. The redesigned Globe Inn at Longtown had a bowling green, billiard room and institute as well as a refreshment hall, whilst the newly erected Gracie's Banking at Annan boasted a cinema.[63]

Despite the cost of rebuilding and the amounts paid in compensation to owners, tenants and licence-holders, the Carlisle scheme proved financially sound. The closure and sale of smaller, less profitable houses, and the concentration of brewing and bottling which the takeover of rival breweries made possible, enabled substantial economies to be made. The general manager was able to report surpluses of £107,000 in 1917–18, of £96,000 in 1918–19 and of £139,000 in 1919–20. These represented returns of 15, 12 and $16\frac{1}{2}$ per cent respectively on the average capital involved.[64] By 1927 the initial capital advances had been fully recouped and the

State found itself in possession of properties worth about £900,000 and a business yielding an annual profit of £60,000.[65]

Not only was the Board anxious to prove the commercial viability of the Carlisle scheme, it also realised the importance of maintaining close contact with local opinion. In order to facilitate this, local advisory committees were established in the Carlisle and Gretna State purchase areas. These were composed of members of the Board together with representatives of local councils, licensing and watch committees, trades and labour councils, and women's organisations.[66] Their main function was to keep the Board in touch with local reactions to the scheme. Thus complaints about delays in the payment of compensation were passed on by the Carlisle committee to the Board, who were able to persuade a reluctant Treasury to speed up the process.[67] When the committee pointed to the loss which might be sustained by local charities as a result of the ending of donations from the licensed trade, the Board and the Treasury agreed to the committee's subscribing to local charities out of the funds of the scheme.[68]

As far as Carlisle was concerned, the Board was on the whole successful in obtaining the support of local opinion for their policies. Both the Liberal *Carlisle Journal* and the Conservative *Cumberland News* were initially favourable, although the latter remained critical of some aspects of the scheme and by 1921 was demanding its abolition.[69] Local trades unions and other labour organisations supported the scheme and urged its extension, whilst an attempt by the licensed trades to hold a meeting in Carlisle in 1919 to demand the restoration of 'pre war rights and liberties' was a signal failure.[70] The scheme's most violent critics tended to be outsiders, often prohibitionists, who toured the city's pubs asking for food or non-alcoholic drink, counted the number of drunks in the street, and poked their heads into women's bars to be shocked by the obscene suggestions which greeted them. One such, the Reverend Wilson Stuart, a Birmingham Wesleyan minister, set down his findings in a pamphlet which condemned 'State drunkenness in Carlisle under State management.'[71] His allegations brought a sharp reply from a Carlisle Wesleyan minister, the Reverend Bramwell Evens, who dismissed them as partial and biased. Direct control, he claimed, had brought 'the dawning of a new era'.[72]

The majority of visitors to Carlisle did not come in such a hostile spirit. Once the scheme got under way, journalists and delegations from organisations concerned with temperance and drink control came to Carlisle to see the improved public houses, licensed restaurants, and reorganised breweries, and to hear of the improvement in public order as convictions for drunkenness fell from 953 in 1916 to 78 in 1919.[73] The Board and the local advisory committee placed considerable importance on public relations. Visiting delegations were conducted round the main features of the scheme and newspaper articles and other publications favourable to it were noted with satisfaction.[74]

Whatever the Central Control Board's initial motives for embarking on State purchase, they soon came to feel that they were involved in an experiment in social reconstruction.[75] The apparent success of the Gretna and Carlisle scheme led them to consider its extension to other parts of the country. State purchase in the Chepstow area was proposed by the Board in September 1916.[76] Early in 1917 they were considering schemes for Bristol, Glasgow, and Liverpool.[77] In December 1916 they submitted a memorandum to the Cabinet, recommending the adoption of a national policy of State purchase since its efficiency had 'already been proved in four areas.'[78] A few weeks later, the Board appointed a committee to prepare a draft Bill 'containing such provisions as would give effect to a State purchase scheme as a war emergency measure, *together with the outlines of a future permanent scheme.*'[79] [italics mine]

Their advocacy of State purchase did not fall on deaf ears. As has been seen, Lloyd George had favoured State purchase as a solution to the drink problem in 1915.[80] Whilst the proposal had been abandoned 'for the time being', Lloyd George may well have regarded the Central Control Board as an instrument for its fulfilment.[81] As Chancellor of the Exchequer in the dying Liberal government, he had carried the Defence of the Realm (Amendment No. 3) Act giving the government powers 'of selling, supplying or controlling the sale or supply of intoxicating liquor in any prescribed area.'[82] Under the terms of this Act, the Order in Council establishing the Central Control Board was issued. Lloyd George, as Minister of Munitions in the first Coalition government, appointed the Board which was responsible to him. In addition to the work of the Board, an advisory committee under Sir Herbert Samuel had reported in 1916 in favour of State purchase of the liquor trade at an estimated cost of £250 million.[83]

In the face of the Board's memorandum, the War Cabinet at first decided to postpone the question. In March 1917, however, the worsening food situation made reductions in the use of grain and sugar for brewing and distilling imperative. Faced with the likelihood of more stringent liquor controls, the Cabinet gave its blessing to State purchase.[84] Committees were set up to investigate the financial aspects of any such scheme. In 1918 they all reported that they saw no impracticability in, or insurmountable financial obstacle to, its realisation.[85] Thus, despite the initial defeat of 1915, the nationalisation of the liquor industry came very close to being realised in the closing years of the war.

Like so many of the social reform schemes projected and approved under the pressures of war, the State purchase scheme bore no fruit. The Labour party adopted drink nationalisation as part of its programme.[86] Moderate temperance reformers continued to advocate it.[87] Even in government circles, lip service seems to have been paid to the idea.[88] But in August 1920, Lloyd George told Thomas Jones that 'the Labour Party were tepid about it and that he doubted whether 20 per cent of the population wanted anything done.'[89] Political considerations thus blighted its hopes even before the Geddes economies ensured its demise.

The government's failure to extend State purchase made certain the winding up of the Central Control Board. Apart from an extension of the Carlisle direct control area to Maryport, which it obtained in the teeth of the usual Treasury opposition in June 1917, its schemes for direct control in other areas came to nothing.[90] The expert advice it could have given the government in the event of a nationalisation of the drink trade was not required. Once the war emergency ended, the licensed trade strongly urged its dissolution. The Treasury, ever disapproving of its expenditure on canteens and purchase schemes, warned the Board of the need for financial retrenchment.[91] In the face of these pressures, the Board made a 'final bid for supremacy'.[92] In November 1918 general policy was discussed and it was agreed that its main lines should be maintained during the period of the armistice.[93] In March 1919 the Board tried to reassume control of canteen administration.[94] In May, however, the Treasury refused its permission for the purchase of two hotels in Carlisle, 'having regard to the general financial position and to the present state of uncertainty as to the future of the Central Control Board'.[95] This 'state of uncertainty' seems to have undermined the Board's will to survive. After another discussion on general policy, members resolved that 'the Board being essentially a war emergency body, it was desirable that a transfer of powers to a new authority, suitable to peace conditions, should not be unduly delayed.'[96] A few weeks later, Lord D'Abernon was telling deputations from temperance organisations that future policy on drink control was not a matter on which the Board could pronounce.[97]

The Board lingered on for another two years, until pressure from its supporters in the House of Commons forced the government to a decision on liquor control.[98] Under the Licensing Act of 1921, the Central Control Board was dissolved; but the opening hours which it had imposed on the scheduled areas were now extended to the whole country.[99] The State-owned schemes survived, partly no doubt because the government was unwilling to face the problem of unscrambling them and also, in the case of Carlisle at least, because of strong local pressure for their continuance.[100] As State Management Districts, they passed to the control of the Home Office.[101]

Financial stringency, the hostility of older departments of State, the pressures from the trade for a return to 'normalcy' and the failure of the government to press forward with a State purchase scheme, all contributed to the demise of the Central Control Board. Yet it is also arguable that, in a sense, it fell a victim to its own success. By its objective moderate approach to liquor control, it took much of the heat out of the 'drink question'. Its controls were generally accepted even by the working classes on whom they fell most heavily. The Commission on Industrial Unrest found that grievances over drink were concerned more with its short supply and poor quality, matters which were primarily the responsibility of the Food Controller, than with restricted hours or the other regulations of the Central Control Board.[102] Drink consumption and convictions for drunkenness fell sharply. As Arthur Marwick points out, 'the liquor restrictions of the First World War brought about a salutary change in one of the most important social habits of the people of Britain.'[103] By 1919 the drink question was unlikely to rouse such political storms as it had done in the nineteenth century. As Lloyd George saw, there was widespread apathy on, and thus little political mileage in, the subject. In such circumstances there seemed to be little point in embarking upon major schemes for further reform in this area.

It would of course be wrong to imply that the Central Control Board's measures were alone responsible for the change in national drinking habits. The increased price of beer and spirits, and their decreased potency, undoubtedly did much to reduce consumption and public drunkenness. One must also take account of new ways in which people spent their leisure, such as the cinema. By 1936, Mass Observation noted that the pub was playing a smaller part in the life of Worktown than it had ever done. Individualised leisure activities, the cinema, the dance hall and the radio, were taking the place of group activity in the public house.[104] To judge from its findings, indeed, it would seem that the ideal of the reformed public house which the Central Control Board had cherished had not deeply influenced Worktown. If drinking was usually done on a full stomach, it was often done standing in bleak vaults and tap-rooms where food was virtually unobtainable and in little demand.[105]

Yet, despite the fact that its influence either in the short or long run is impossible to assess exactly, a study of the Central Control Board is worthwhile, if only to demonstrate how control of an important and sensitive area of social life in wartime was carried out in a positive, purposeful, and generally acceptable fashion. Of the two survivals of its work, the Carlisle scheme provided a more fitting memorial than did compulsory afternoon abstention. The year which sees the destruction of the last traces of that memorial is a suitable time for a fresh assessment of the Central Control Board (Liquor Traffic).

6

War and the Colonial Relationship: Britain, India and the War of 1914-18

JUDITH M. BROWN

It has become part of the text-book orthodoxy of twentieth-century history that world war has been a powerful solvent of the overseas empires of European states. The Second World War bundled the Dutch out of their Indonesian empire, to take the most extreme case; but it also heralded the end of France's Asian empire, and after it had ended Wavell, as Viceroy of India, believed that the British could no longer hold their position in that subcontinent. Once conceded, Indian independence started the process of un-scrambling Britain's African empire both by example and by its repercussions on the logic of imperial reasoning. The 1914–18 war saw a significant if less dramatic weakening of the imperial bonds which tied Asia and Africa to Europe. It shattered the German empire, but even the victors were less secure than they had been in 1914. In India, though the panoply of empire was still intact, the British had made a critical departure by announcing in August 1917 that their policy was aimed at the 'increasing association of Indians in every branch of the administration, and the gradual development of self-governing institutions, with a view to the pro-gressive realisation of responsible government in India as an integral part of the British Empire.'[1] This meant that colonial self-govern-ment would not henceforth be a constitutional status reserved for white colonies. In other centuries war has served to build rather than to break Europe's overseas empires : the British *raj* in India is a case in point. But the twentieth century's experience suggests the thesis that military conflict on the scale of the two world wars threatens the viability of far-flung empires over traditional and alien societies.

85

War is a challenge to all systems of government. Quite apart from the threat of external intervention and defeat, modern warfare imposes massive strains on the resources of any government, requiring it to make similar demands of its subjects. Its continuance depends both on its technical ability to mobilise the necessary men, materials and money, and on its capacity to create a consensus among its subjects that such an effort is appropriate. Moreover, war may let loose forces of change which alter the locus of power in society and the attitudes towards authority and society on which the governmental system has hitherto depended for its stability. Europe's overseas empires appear particularly vulnerable to this many-sided challenge. Geographical distance from the metropolitan country makes them easy prey for invaders, as the French, Dutch, British and Germans all found to their cost at different times. Imperial governments, as artefacts imposed by superior power, are less likely to be able to attract a consensus in support of war than are governments thrown up by society from the forces at work within it. Moreover, traditional societies will probably experience change as a result of war far more acutely and rapidly than modern societies, and consequently such change may be far more disruptive of governmental stability. Faced with subjects among whom the incidence of power and authority is shifting, whose ideals of polity and society are changing, imperial régimes are prone to be inflexible : their capacity to adapt to changing circumstances is necessarily limited by their *raison d'être* – metropolitan control of and profit from the colony concerned.

To suggest that Europe's overseas empires were vulnerable in war time is easy. To measure their weakness and to document the process whereby imperial authority was eroded is incomparably more difficult. Any colonial relationship is complex and subtle, the long-term result of forces active in Europe and in the colony, which have coincided, dovetailed or clashed, and have modified each other in course of time. It depends in part on the forces of strength deployed by the metropolitan country – men, materials, ideology, and sensitivity to public opinion at home and abroad; and in part on the nature and number of those in the colony who were adverse, acquiescent or active assistants to the imperial enterprise. An attempt to trace the effects of war on a colonial relationship demands investigation of all these areas. It requires the weighing and balancing of intangibles. It also meets the problem of the relative effect of other forces at work which may be unconnected with war. In India's case, for example, a precise assessment of the effect of either world war on the colonial relationship would involve isolating the direct results of war in India and Great Britain and weighing them against long-term change within Indian society, the effects of British policies, the repercussions of world events and ideologies, the death of old leaders and the emergence of new ones, and similar forces at work in British public life.

Whatever the complexities of the colonial relationship, the years of the First World War witnessed a remarkable change in Britain's connection with India. This was registered most obviously in the arena of modern politics, where the tempo of activity and the temper and range of participants were markedly different by the end of the war, and the British increasingly found themselves forced to play the role of canny politician to secure peace and acquiescence for their régime. As more people made greater demands more stridently for place and power within the framework of a modern state, the British realised that they could no longer rest on their laurels as benevolent administrators of a traditional, agrarian society. Acknowledging the changing relationship, one confidential circular for civil servants directed that young Indian Civil Service officers should be encouraged to study political movements, and should be given the opportunity to work where political activity was greatest, for such activity was no longer confined to towns and advanced political ideas were spreading among the landed and agricultural communities.

. . . there is too frequent a tendency to regard politics as the preserve of a small group of *literati*, and to treat it as an interference with the real work of the country. It is necessary to correct this, if the public servant is to take his part . . . in guiding political activity along sober and practical lines.[2]

The most striking evidence of change, however, was the Secretary of State's Declaration of August 1917 and the constitutional reforms which stemmed from it in 1919. By these, one-time imperial autocrats grafted on to the administrative structure of empire enlarged elected legislative councils and devolved considerable power, through the mechanism of dyarchy, to Indians who could command the support of those councils. Caught in the middle of these developments, contemporaries hazarded assessments of the forces behind them. Continually they pointed to war as a motor of change, but the difficulty they experienced in describing the precise link between

the war and the changes around them was symptomatic of the complexity of the problem and the variety of influences at work modifying the colonial relationship. In the words of one Indian, 'the war
has changed us very much. It has changed the angle of vision in
India as well [as] in England. I venture to say that the war has put
the clock of time fifty years forward . . .'[3] Even a post-war Viceroy,
Lord Reading, attempting to assess the effects of the war on Indian
attitudes towards Britain, resorted to generalisations about economic difficulties, the spread of the ideal of self-determination, and
'General unsettlement of ideas and impatience following the war
sown on fertile soil of political immaturity and administrative in-
experience in India.'[4]

   In contrast to such vague fumbling after causal connections, the
1917 Declaration of the goal of British policy in India stands as an
incontrovertible fact; and for several reasons it promises to provide
a definite focus for an investigation of changes in the colonial relationship, particularly the erosion of imperial power, as a result of
the war. In the first place, it not only precipitated change through
the reforms designed to implement it : it also reflected changes in
the relationship between the imperial rulers and their subjects. A
comparison between it and earlier British attitudes is startling.
Whereas Montagu, who made the Declaration as Secretary of
State, spoke of the development of self-governing institutions, only
five years earlier Hardinge as Viceroy had written : 'I need hardly
say that the Government of India have never for a moment thought
that the evolution of this country could be in the sense of Colonial
self-government. The idea is ridiculous and absurd . . .'[5] In the
second place, it is clear from contemporary sources that the Declaration was a direct result of the war. The Viceroy linked discussions
of political advance to the fact of war, and the Government of
India Despatch recommending an announcement of the goal of
political advance was couched in terms of 'the recognition of India's
services during the War'.[6] Consequently, by taking these fixed
points, it may be possible to discuss the effects of war on the colonial
relationship with a degree of precision impossible for contemporaries in their wider-ranging reflections. The aim of this essay is
therefore a limited one : to investigate the social context in India
of the 1917 Declaration; it asks what influence the war had, or
threatened to have, on Indian society under imperial rule, and how
this helped to precipitate such a change of policy. The method
employed is to delimit the foundations of British power within

Indian society, to mark out the bulwarks of imperial authority, and then to see if these were weakened or eroded by war to such an extent that the 1917 Declaration was felt to be necessary.[7] It will not discuss the larger problem of empire's vulnerability in war since it examines only a limited piece of the total jigsaw, and moreover a piece which fits during the early part of the war. But it may serve to underline the complexity of war's effects on society in the context of empire, and its repercussions on the stability of empire during world-wide conflict.

The foundations of British power in Indian society were not uniform throughout the subcontinent. The bounds of the relationship between rulers and ruled imposed by society varied with geography and time because India was so large and its society so diverse. At any one place at a particular point in time the colonial relationship was in a sense unique because it was dependent on and responsive to local conditions and to changes in those conditions. In the Punjab at the turn of the century, for example, the British buttressed their position by a stern tradition of paternalism and alliance with local landholders. In Bengal they had to adapt themselves to the uneasy world of the western educated and the job-hungry, who were fast learning to deal in the currency of modern politics. In cosmopolitan and commercial Bombay they had to establish a harmonious relationship with the powerful mercantile communities who dominated the city and insured its prosperity. But, despite the differences in application demanded by local conditions, there were certain constant features in the social buttresses of the *raj*.

Throughout the subcontinent there was a small European presence which was the core of British administrative and coercive power. In 1922, to an Indian population of 315 million, there were 1,200 British members of the Indian Civil Service – the famous 'steel frame' without which the British felt the fabric of empire would collapse. They were flanked by 700 British Police Officers and 600 British Medical Officers.[8] Behind them was the British Army stationed in India with a strength of 76,953 at the outbreak of war.[9] It was a paltry enough force to hold a subcontinent equivalent in size to Europe without Russia; but British public opinion as voiced in Parliament would not have stood for a more expensive empire. British officials were thoroughly realistic in their assessment of their strength, should they ever have to rely on the European presence alone. In fact, Reading as Viceroy in 1922 bluntly told

War and Society

the Secretary of State that they would probably be driven out of India if they were faced simultaneously with disturbances on the frontier, disloyalty and mutiny in the Indian Army, and civilian outbreaks in several areas, and if reinforcements from outside India were not forthcoming. The *raj*'s 'whole military policy and organisation have always been based on the principle that' it 'must in the last resort look to Great Britain for the assistance necessary to preserve the integrity of the Empire.'[10]

Since the European coercive presence in Indian society was so weak, civil disorder was particularly dangerous for the *raj*, as Reading indicated. The British could cope with local outbreaks but not with widespread, co-ordinated disruption, despite the mobility which modern communications gave them in contrast with 1857. Mass acquiescence was therefore another social buttress with which they sought to secure their rule. In a sense the *raj* was only as strong as it was thought to be; and consequently the British stood jealous guard over their prestige, always considering in any choice of policy what would be the effect on their reputation, whether or not it would be interpreted by Indians as a sign of weakness. Such vigilance and calculation were part of British imperial strategy to insure quiescence under their dominion. In an agrarian economy, rising prices, often following the failure of the rains and bad harvests, were sure danger signals, and for these, too, officials kept a sharp watch. Communal conflicts in a society deeply divided by religion were another likely source of civil commotion. These, with the incidence of local strains such as landlord–tenant relations, might provide fertile ground for any who wished to sow seeds of sedition and turn the distress of the illiterate and inarticulate against the *raj*. The British could and did attempt to relieve and placate mass distress or friction wherever it became apparent, tenancy-protection legislation being an obvious example. Although the comparatively stable conditions and religious neutrality afforded by the empire also helped to secure widespread acquiescence in the colonial relationship, the British were uneasily aware of their ignorance of Indian society. Consequently they looked for allies among men whom considered to be acknowledged leaders in society, to act as nodules of loyalty in return for the favours of the *raj*. The Indian princes were cases of this on a huge scale : but in each area the *raj* sought for stability by attaching to itself local men who wielded varieties of influence and looked as if they could insure the loyalty of their caste or community, their henchmen or their clientele. Precisely who they were varied according to time and place. Consequently society and social change imposed important constraints on the colonial relationship.[11] For other reasons, too, the British needed active allies. Who but Indians could keep the infrastructure of public life going? Empire was impossible without Indian collaboration – in the non-European army, in the administration, at all but the highest levels, in the judicial services, in the modern professions, trade and industry, in the legislative councils set up to remedy British ignorance of Indian opinion, and in the municipalities designed to secure some consensus about the objects and means of local taxation, and to train Indians in some of the arts of modern public life. Indians who actively assisted the *raj* in these spheres gained in return the material rewards of employment. Many also gained access to informal channels of communication with the British which enhanced their local prestige; and they regularly appeared in the honours lists submitted twice yearly by the Viceroy to the Secretary of State – lists which are revealing evidence of the mechanisms by which the British attempted to secure the social foundations of their rule.

If key collaborators, mass acquiescence and a small European presence were the foundations of imperial power, the central problem in relation to the effects of the First World War is whether war worked changes in Indian society which eroded these foundations and made the 1917 Declaration necessary if the *raj* was to continue. Ideally the solution to this problem lies in each local situation, the constraints local society imposed on the colonial relationship, and the way such constraints altered as a result of the war. But analysis in such detail is beyond the scope of any single investigator. Moreover, as far as the 1917 Declaration is concerned, it was the all-India view which mattered. Delhi collected local assessments and reports, boiled them down, and filtered the result back to London where the final decision was made. Thus it was not so much the impact of war on society as how that impact appeared to the Government of India which was the vital link in the reasoning behind Montagu's Declaration.

Superficially Britain's relationship with India seemed as stable as a rock during the First World War. India proved a tremendous asset to the allies, providing men, money, equipment and essential material for the war effort.[12] But behind this outflow of support there lay the reality of an imperial society whose European element was suddenly and drastically reduced. British troops were rushed to

Europe in the first months of the war, to be replaced by territorials who arrived untrained and virtually unarmed. One battalion had 500 rifles which were unserviceable and were marked for drill purposes only. For a few weeks before the arrival of the Territorials the total British garrison in India was less than 15,000.[13] The Viceroy emphasised in November 1914 the risks involved in denuding India of British troops : 'there is no disguising the fact that our position in India is a bit of a gamble at the present time.'[14] He was acutely aware that this was a situation which interested parties could exploit, and if they did so, all he could deploy were Territoral battalions, as the remaining eight regular British battalions could not be moved from the frontier with Afghanistan.[15] The war affected the strength of the civil service as well as the army. ICS men were allowed to join the army and leave for Europe, while in Britain military needs drained off some of those who might otherwise have been recruited to the ICS. Component parts of the 'steel frame' thus had to be extended beyond their original design. But, though the war undermined the *raj*'s European foundation by removing its regular British troops, it would be inaccurate to see difficulties in civilian staffing as a primary factor in the 1917 Declaration, or even as a direct result of war. The weakness of the 'steel frame' only became an urgent problem in the 1920s, when correspondence between successive Viceroys and Secretaries of State was full of it. In 1922 Montagu was writing : 'I am . . . more worried by the dearth of personnel than by anything else . . . I am terribly distressed about the shortage of man-power in India, and I really think that this is one of the most serious situations that I know.'[16] But by then it was clear that strong currents in British society were as much responsible as events in India – the availability of other careers, the relative decline in ICS pay and allowances in a period of inflation, combined with apprehension of the effects of constitutional reform on service careers in India.

The war undoubtedly weakened the European presence in Indian society as a buttress of empire. But the administration went on, the British position held, and they dealt effectively with such local disturbances as occurred. However, in the war years before 1917 they never had to face a major challenge to their physical or administrative strength : Hardinge's fears of 1915 did not materialise. Such a challenge only occurred in 1921–2 in the shape of Non-co-operation. Evidently the lack of widespread, co-ordinated challenge was an essential ingredient in such strength as the British possessed. It points to mass acquiescence as part of the foundations of imperial control, a social phenomenon of critical importance in drawing the parameters of the colonial relationship. Popular, conscious and co-ordinated anti-government agitation was unlikely in a diverse and deeply divided society, large sections of which were backward by the canons of modern politics. The dangers, as rulers of all great agrarian societies have found, were that distress and discontent might precipitate violent and unco-ordinated outbreaks which would place unbearable strains on the resources of order, or that grass-roots hardship and tension might provide forces for others to channel and exploit. To what extent did the war produce such a situation, or how seriously did the British calculate that it might do so?

There is considerable evidence of distress caused by particular local strains at the very roots of Indian society during the early war years. Some of these strains were in no way attributable to the war; as, for example, the difficulties of tenants in the landlord areas of the United Provinces and Bihar, or the troubles of peasants in Champaran, Bihar, who were forced to grow unprofitable indigo crops by European planters. Often, however, they were aggravated by the effects of war. Thus in Champaran war made the plight of the indigo cultivators worse because the district depended on the local railway to export its surplus food and bring in necessities produced elsewhere; and since by 1917 only one-fifth of India's rolling stock was available for ordinary rail traffic, food which should have been taken out of Champaran slumped in price, cutting the producers' profit, while the price of cloth, kerosene and salt soared. In other places local distress was more directly attributable to the war. In the Punjab methods of recruiting and collecting contributions to war loans produced a sour force of resentment; while in one district in Bombay Presidency the local *mamlatdar*'s recruiting methods actually caused a riot.[17] But the discontent and anti-government potential generated by local events were never co-ordinated and the worst of the local eruptions, in the Punjab, Kaira (Gujarat) and United Provinces did not occur until after the 1917 Declaration.

There were, however, forces at work throughout the subcontinent, as a direct result of the war, which threatened to disrupt the public peace and turn popular temper against the *raj*. The most obvious of these was the catastrophic effect of the war on prices.

As early as 1914 evidence of distress as a result of the war was being brought to the notice of the Viceroy; and by 1917–18 the

Prices in India, 1910–20[18]

1910	122	1915	152		
1911	129	1916	184		
1912	137	1917	196	1920	281
1913	143	1918	225		
1914	147	1919	276		

This table is of prices of all articles: 100 = base in 1873.

official report on conditions in India acknowledged that the leap in prices was causing very great hardship. Wholesale food prices were 15 per cent above their level at the beginning of 1917, and 31 per cent above their pre-war level: 'this was sufficient to cause deep distress in India, where the margin of income over bare subsistence is extremely small for the bulk of the population.'[19] Even worse was the rise in prices of imported goods like kerosene and cloth, which were affected by shortage of freight, producing a situation in which speculators could profit and simultaneously increase the distress of the poor. However, the price rise was most rapid *after* the Montagu Declaration: from late 1917 onwards provincial reports sent fortnightly to Delhi were full of bleak accounts of hardship, discontent, rioting and looting of grain shops. Even the appointment of government controllers of prices had little effect and served only to underline the failure of the *raj* to help the distressed. As one Bombay paper commented,

Government have appointed a Controller to satisfy the people. But where do we get kerosene oil, salt, food and such other necessaries of life at the prices fixed by him? Do the shop-keepers care for the fixed prices? Have any delinquents been punished? . . . The war has enriched a few and ruined many. The people are powerless, the Controller is powerless, even Government are powerless, only those who plunder the people on every pretext are powerful.[20]

Yet, even when the pinch of war was sharpest and felt throughout India, the government was never stretched unbearably by outbreaks of disorder and the groundswell of feeling was never channelled and co-ordinated into a single movement capable of breaking up the mass acquiescence on which the strength and stability of the *raj* so largely depended.

To officials scanning the situation from Delhi, religion appeared a potentially more disruptive force than economic hardship, because the war might be expected seriously to disturb those areas with a significant Muslim population. The *raj* was rightly nervous on this

score : although Indian Muslims owed no political allegiance to the
Sultan of Turkey, he still bore the title of *Khalifah*,[21] and war
between *Khalifah* and King-Emperor would at least present Muslims with a distasteful clash of loyalties, and at worst might precipitate *jihad*, rebellion in the name of religion. In September 1914
the Viceroy brooded on the problem : 'the attitude of the Mahom-
edans is quite satisfactory at present, and, as far as I can see, likely
to remain so. . . . If we were at war with Turkey, our anxiety would
be greatly increased . . .' Even in December, when Turkey had
entered the war against Britain, he was satisfied with Muslim attitudes and comforted by the reports that Muslims were being
recruited satisfactorily in the Punjab.[22] Officials calculated that the
real potential for trouble lay in the activities of a group of younger
Muslims, part journalists and part politicians, led by Mohamed
and Shaukat Ali from the United Provinces, who were publicising
the vague ideal of Pan-Islam, the international unity and solidarity
of all Muslims, which the Turkish Sultan had fostered for several
decades. Although a single Muslim polity had for centuries been
a practical impossibility, emotional commitment to the Sultan as
the symbol of world-wide Islamic unity was present among Indian
Muslims and had been strengthened by events which had made it
all too easy for them to feel that the British were sleeping if not
active partners in an international attack on Islam.[23] In such a
delicate situation the widespread publication in Urdu of Pan-
Islamic propaganda threatened to disturb those Muslims who could
be reached via a vernacular press; and early in 1915 the British
decided to anticipate trouble. As Hardinge noted, Muslims were
'undoubtedly sulky' and if the allies suffered any more reverses in
the Dardanelles he feared serious results in India. Consequently the
Ali brothers were interned, 'to take every precaution, and to put
an end to their unwholesome activities'.[24] In the event firm action
combined with divisions of opinion and priority among the Muslim
leadership saved the *raj* from any wide erosion of support in the
Muslim community, but the possibility of such an eventuality
remained, as officialdom clearly recognised. The Lieutenant-
Governor of the UP, the home of the main Pan-Islamists, hinted
at future possibilities. Most Muslims were, in his view, suspicious
of the Christian powers and their treatment of Muslim states,
although they had only marginal affection for the Turkish Sultan
and were content under British rule. But there was a group of professional politicians and ambitious *maulvis* who were willing to

exploit the cry of religion in danger; and such men might well stir up the majority of illiterate and ill-informed Muslims who were generally willing to follow the former, more moderate group.[25] The storm, when it came in the shape of the Khilafat movement, was violent but patchy and its full force hit India after the war when the peace terms were being negotiated.

It would be fair to conclude that the war did not shatter the acquiscence of the vast majority of Indians which helped to make the *raj* viable. War's main effects were only felt by ordinary people after the Montagu Declaration had been considered and made. Nevertheless the Government of India was apprehensive right from the outbreak of war that it might have to cope with widespread disaffection just when its European presence was weak. Early in 1915 the Viceroy put this bluntly: 'the extremists realising our military weakness in India have been actively attempting to stir up trouble and even rebellion. In this they have been helped by Mahomedan unrest due to the war with Turkey, and by discontent with prevailing high prices. And what have we in India to meet this internal situation?'[26] The answer lay in the Indians whom the British could attract to their side, the allies they could count on to keep the country loyal and man the machinery of public life. Though such men were always essential to the *raj*, the British need of them was the more urgent in war time. It remains to investigate whether the war undermined the collaboration network on which the British empire in India rested, whether it so affected Indian society as to change the range of possible and effective collaborators, and thus altered the framework of the colonial relationship.

The princes, rulers of one-third of India, were the most obvious of the *raj*'s allies, and they did not fail the paramount power in the war. They responded to the Viceregal appeal for help with offers of personal service, troops, hospital ships, nurses and money: the Maharaja of Rewah even offered all his personal jewels.[27] It was not until after the war that the British began to feel that these glamorous aristocrats, who had been their 'breakwaters in the storm' in 1857, might well prove to be liabilities rather than staunch and effective allies in a changing India where decisions were made with increasing reference to public opinion. In November 1919 Chelmsford as Viceroy spoke to the Chamber of Princes about the need for progressive reforms within their states – a signal of the *raj*'s changing attitude; and in 1921 came early hints that the British might be seriously embarrassed by their conservative allies

and would certainly be in no position to prop them if they could
not maintain their own strength against internal and external
pressures.[28]

Within British India the *raj*'s Indian employees and troops were
essential for the stability and smooth running of the régime. Indian
soldiers played a significant role in many theatres of the war and
in India itself their loyalty was the more important as British troops
were removed. There were isolated instances of trouble among
them. One company of the 10th Baluchis shot their officer while
embarking for Mesopotamia, and the whole regiment was sent in
disgrace to Rangoon; and there were other signs of unrest in
Muslim regiments. In these circumstances Hardinge gratefully
accepted the offer of 6,000 troops from the Maharaja of Nepal.
They were trained by British officers and kept in hand for any
emergency.[29] The real threat to the loyalty of Indian troops came
in 1921–2 during the Non-co-operation campaign, though even
that had very little effect. The only point at which the British
doubted their ability to hold their Indian Army was during the
final months of their *raj*, when communal strife, not anti-British
sentiment, was the root cause.

During the war the *raj*'s civilian employees worked in conditions
which imposed considerable strains on their dependability. They
might not have to fight, but whereas soldiers were fed, clothed and
paid, minor civil servants and the police had to live with soaring
prices. As one local report noted in 1918, 'There are continued
indications of the almost desperate position to which many of the
lower-paid Government servants in the mofussil are reduced by the
present high prices and of the consequent urgent necessity of granting them relief in the shape of war allowances.'[30] It also indicated
that such men might strike. The British were uncomfortably aware
of the position of their local employees and in some instances gave
war allowances : 50 per cent for the *talatis*, local revenue officials,
of Ratnagiri district, for example, or improved pay, as for Bombay
police constables in 1918–19.[31] But, in company with other Indians,
the *raj*'s servants only felt the pinch acutely after the Montagu
Declaration. It was after that significant modification in the
colonial relationship had been made that the repercussions of the
war were seen in the ranks of these Indian collaborators – in
the 1918 strike of *talatis* in Kaira district of Bombay, for example,
and more dramatically in the *talatis'* strikes which swept Bombay
Presidency in December 1920 in protest against the inadequacy of

the revision of their pay scales. Even then the *raj*'s power to attract men into its service was strong and it had no difficulty in replacing the strikers, while many of them came back to their posts.[32]

Another sector of society on which the British relied, though not in formal terms of employment, was the variety of business groups who kept trade and industry going and supplied essential war stores. After initial transport and market problems, as ships were commandeered for military use and the central European countries' demand for India's raw materials slackened, Indian trade and industry began to boom. In Hardinge's caustic words, 'The commercial classes neither hear nor see anything, and, as far as I am able to judge, are amassing enormous fortunes, cotton, perhaps, being the only exception. Most of these people are simply pursuing their own selfish aims and really don't trouble at all as to what goes on in the country.'[33] Statistics bore him out on profits. In 1916–17 exports increased by 21 per cent and imports by over 13 per cent compared with the previous year, and as Indian industry expanded to meet the allies' demands, the share of manufactured goods in India's exports rose, from less than 24 per cent in 1913–14 to 31 per cent in 1917–18.[34] In Bombay dividends from the cloth mills jumped from 6 per cent in 1914 to over 30 per cent in 1917.[35] However, this euphoric situation did not last long, and India was hit by a post-war recession and currency crisis.

Even before this there had been signs that businessmen were becoming increasingly sensitive to the actions of government, largely because of its intervention in economic affairs. No longer did they 'neither hear nor see anything', untroubled by public affairs. The President of the 1917 Congress spoke of the new interest merchants were taking in politics and listed the war-time controls they had encountered which were prompting them to participate in politics in order to have a voice in the regulation of the economic environment in which they had to operate.[36] Substance was given to such assertions by evidence from Madras, where a Skin and Hide Merchants' Association was founded the same year specifically to lobby the government on the question of war-time restrictions designed to conserve tanning materials. The same concern pushed some of its Muslim members into the politics of the Presidency's Muslim League.[37] In 1919 the editor of *The Times of India* noted that 'the Indian trading community has been made very sore by the various charges on profits' and thought this might work to the advantage of Gandhi's plans for token resistance to the Rowlatt Bills, two security measures the government was contemplating.[38] At the same time a group of Bombay businessmen of impeccable loyalty asked the Government of India to withdraw the Excess Profits Tax Bill which had been announced in December 1918. They complained that war finance had already involved India in higher income tax, super tax, railway surcharges, higher import duty on salt, export duties on jute and tea and controlled rates on a large number of other commodities.[39] These particular manifestations could not of course have affected government deliberations on the Montagu Declaration, but it is unlikely that in the earlier years of the war the government received no indications that some business communities were turning to modern-style politics as a channel for protest and demand as government action increasingly impinged on their occupations.

Despite signs of unrest, businessmen did not fail the *raj* in the development of India's trade and industry. However, there was another aspect to their position as social buttresses of the imperial régime. The British tended to look to influential men in towns to keep the urban populace peaceful. Analysis of the town politics of Allahabad has shown how this type of control could work and how it could break down under the impact of social and economic change.[40] Much investigation is needed before we can say with any certainty how the war affected British allies in urban areas and what repercussions it had on informal networks of urban control. We need, for example, to know whether the men who made profits in war time were able to secure the tranquillity of the urban population, or whether they were eroding the power of older families who had exercised such control in urban society. The available evidence suggests that those who prospered through wartime growth did not manipulate patronage and influence networks which were effective mechanisms of urban control. This was particularly serious at a time when rising prices created hardship and conflict in urban society, and expanding industry attracted recruits to the labour force who were tied to their employers by few traditional bonds of loyalty or deference. In Ahmedabad, to take one case, the owners of the cotton mills did extremely well out of war conditions, but they proved singularly incapable of controlling their work force in 1918. The mill hands in fact responded to no formal or informal leadership until Gandhi took over the direction of their wage claim and strike.[41] In Bombay in 1919 the textile mill owners were similarly unable to control their 140,000 employees and a strike paralysed the entire industry. But it was more like a peasant *jacquerie* than an organised industrial protest: many of the mill hands were peasant migrants, owing no allegiance to the big men in the city and amenable only to the unsophisticated leadership of their jobbers within the factory organisation.[42]

Similar problems confronted the imperial régime in those rural areas where its social buttresses were large landholders, as in Oudh. After the mutiny it had seemed the only sensible course to rely on the landed magnates, the *talukdars* and their like, where they had been manifest leaders in the rural community. But what if their capacity for leadership and control declined as a result of change within society? What if their tenants and clientele became impatient at the relationship of dependence, and other men offering other incentives attempted to assume leadership roles? The cohesion of the great landed estates as social units and their reliability as a base for social control looks, at least in Oudh, less assured the nearer the investigator gets to the mechanics of estate management: the emergence of the anti-landlord peasant movements in Bihar and UP from 1918 onwards is more explicable against the background of such evidence.[43] Yet the peasant movements only erupted after the Montagu Declaration, and even then war was only one of their causes, in that rising prices underlined the precarious economic position of the tenants and aggravated the existing trend for landlords to make their estates pay by exploiting all possible customary dues.

Far more serious for the landlords, and by repercussion for their imperial allies, was a challenge for leadership within rural society which the British themselves helped to precipitate. Western-style education gave other social groups new skills and new avenues of influence, through new professions such as law and through the new political institutions at provincial, district and municipal level which the western educated were well equipped to manipulate. The landlords were acutely sensitive to this challenge. One landlord from UP complained that the Congress politicians were so organised and powerful locally that landholders felt compelled to vote with them in UP Legislative Council proceedings. He therefore wanted the local government to appoint influential landholders as chairmen of district boards, where selection of council candidates took place, so that 'professional politicians' could be kept out. 'Divisional representatives will then be men whose support can be counted upon by Government. The fact that the office of chairman will be in the gift of the Government will prevent influential landholders from going over to the side of disloyal grievance-mongers.'[44] Government officials could hardly fail to realise that the landed were insecure buttresses of empire. The Lieutenant-Governor of UP remarked in 1916 : 'The landed classes seem to me our only standby; they are probably a feeble reed, but they have material interests to protect, and, if we do not go mad with philanthropic schemes for the benefit of the tenants, they must see that their salvation lies with us rather than with the hungry professional mob.'[45] The emergence of 'the hungry professional mob' was of course the result of long-term social change originating in the interaction of Indian society and the new opportunities provided by the imperial régime. Only in the Muslim community was the First World War a particularly critical element in the challenge of the educated to the landed aristocracy. Already before the overt war-time clash of loyalties to *Khalifah* and King-Emperor, Pan-Islamic journalists and politicians had been gaining support among politically conscious Muslims, eroding the assured leadership of the old Muslim aristocrats.[46] The war increased their leverage among their coreligionists, though it split the community politically in the process; as the Pan-Islamists achieved dominance in the Muslim League between 1916 and 1917, the landed tended to retire from the organisation in disgust.[47]

As social change undermined the influence of the landed and decreased their reliability as allies of the *raj*, it became the more urgent for the British to secure the working collaboration of the group they had themselves helped to thrust into public life. In the wider sense of collaboration, the British needed the western educated to man the new professions which were part of the infrastructure of empire, to staff the courts, colleges, schools and hospitals. They needed to secure prominent men as nodules of loyalty, in a society where their own knowledge and power were limited, despite the panoply of empire. In 1858 men like the Oudh *talukdars* had promised to perform this function most efficiently. Now the western educated, increasingly articulate and skilled in the context of a modernising country, appeared as spokesmen and moulders of public opinion, and a reluctant *raj* accepted that they were necessary allies in the imperial enterprise. On a narrower front the British needed the collaboration of those who represented the western educated; increasingly this meant the men who developed a political style which drew heavily for its inspiration on western experience, and who directed their energies towards advancement

in the modern sectors of public life, particularly through more posts
in the administration and more ways of making their voices heard
in the decision-making processes.

The British never felt they could hold the loyalty of all these
overtly modern politicians, or contain and channel all their ambitions. Instead they hoped to attach to themselves those of the
politicians who were willing to co-operate in measured, planned
and orderly advance towards increasing Indian participation in the
higher realms of administration and greater influence in the country's decision-making processes. The hope was practically elevated
to the status of a recognised policy : it cropped up again and again
in government deliberations as the need to encourage or rally those
whom they called the 'Moderates'. In 1910, for example, Hardinge
agreed to receive a Congress deputation in the 'desire to give
encouragement to the moderate section' and he justified his action
in these terms to Curzon, who as Viceroy a decade earlier had
hoped to see Congress into its grave.[48] In 1915 he reflected that a
bonus in interning the Ali brothers was the comfort it would give
to the 'Moderates'; and he replied to a query from the Governor
of Bombay that he probably ought not to receive B. G. Tilak, who
had been convicted for criminal conspiracy, because 'to white-wash
him entirely would have a bad effect upon your Moderates.'[49] The
desire to rally the 'Moderates' was a soft spot in the empire's bulwarks, a point of leverage at which the *raj* was particularly
susceptible. Before the outbreak of the First World War it appeared
to be protected even there : it had what it wanted – western educated Indians to fill the professions and enough of the 'Moderate'
politicians to man the Legislative Councils set up in 1909. In such
a situation the British were secure, and politicians who would have
pressed them to further concessions found themselves in an impasse
from which there seemed to be no escape. They had no source of
leverage against the *raj*. Violence had been proved an unprofitable
and inefficient weapon to which the *raj* merely replied in kind.
Their peaceful demands were brushed aside because the British had
no need of them when they were secure in the collaboration of the
'Moderates'. Had all the politicians been united, or had they been
able to disrupt on a broad front the acquiescence of the majority
of Indians in the *raj*'s existence, they would have had a point of
pressure.

The First World War broke this impasse. It provided both the
impetus and the occasion for pressure on the British at their vulner-

able point, their calculation that they must keep the 'Moderates' with them. The war not only denuded India of European troops, making the British more sensitive to the aspirations of its essential allies within Indian society. It also gave the 'Moderates' the impetus to exploit this situation. Despite their willingness to co-operate in planned political progress they, as much as any Indian politicians, wanted advance towards self-government. During the war allied ideals and propaganda gave them formidable ammunition with which to bombard their British rulers. As one of them put it in 1916, harking back to earlier pledges of equality for all subjects of the British Crown, whatever their race:

We are on the eve of a great reconstruction. The world after the war will not be the same as it was before the war. England and India will participate in that reconstruction. The object of the war is to vindicate the sanctity of treaty obligations, to protect the rights of minor nationalities, to uphold the sacredness of scraps and bits of paper. In the same spirit, I submit, we are entitled to hold that the gracious messages contained in our Charters and Proclamations should be redeemed and upheld, for the moral law does not work by latitudes and longitudes. It is of universal application.[50]

A few months later another politician spoke of 'the promise of freedom for which England has always stood, for which she is striving to-day, and for which both England and India together are striving with one mind and one heart.'[51] This was a war in defence of liberty, self-determination and the sanctity of pledges: in Indian eyes the British in India stood judged by the ideals they and their allies were publicising in Europe. Consequently pressure built up in impeccably 'Moderate' Indian political circles for a declaration of the goal of British policy which would do justice to Indian aspirations for self-government. Sir S. P. Sinha, as President of the 1915 Congress, called for such a declaration; and the 1916 Congress reiterated his call in a resolution on self-government for India. V. S. S. Sastri even made the demand in the exalted surroundings of the Imperial Legislative Council.[52] In 1916 the Lieutenant-Governor of the UP thought it was probably no good even trying to negotiate with the 'Moderates', such was their solidarity behind a demand which would once have been dubbed 'Extremist'; but less than a year later he and his colleague in charge of the Central Provinces pressed for a declaration of Britain's goal in India in view of the nervy impatience of the entire body of the western educated.[53]

The war ended the impasse reached by politicians who wanted to press the British further, partly by creating a situation where the *raj*'s 'Moderate' allies were willing to join forces with them behind a demand for the declaration of self-government as Britain's goal for India. This opened the *raj* to pressure, as it was constantly on the watch lest its allies among the spokesmen of the western educated should turn sour or be swamped by their political opponents. The new-found unity of the politicians was plain for all to see in 1916, when all main shades of political opinion were reflected in the Lucknow Congress which pressed for the announcement of self-government for India at an early date as Britain's goal. The unity was the more dramatic, and the more threatening for the *raj*, because the demand and a scheme of reform to implement it also had the backing of the Muslim League, which was now outside the control of the Muslim aristocracy. Though the politicians' disunity had been one contributory factor in the pre-war political impasse, so had their inability to disturb widespread acceptance of British rule. Even this began to change markedly between 1916 and 1917. Those politicians who wished to push the *raj* furthest and fastest, and increase their own political influence in Congress into the bargain, organised two Home Rule Leagues to mobilise a wide span of public opinion behind their demands. Although they did not reach the illiterate population of town or countryside, or disrupt mass acceptance of the British presence, they made significant inroads into the ranks of English and vernacular literates both in towns and in villages in certain areas, a development which was described fully and with considerable apprehension by local governments in their fortnightly reports to Delhi. It was a particularly ominous sign that, in one part of Madras at least, *New India*, a Home Rule paper, had even in 1916 'a specially large circulation in the lower ranks of Government service.'[54]

Even before the appearance of the Home Rule Leagues the British, worried by the hints of 'Moderate' defection, were weighing up the political situation in the growing conviction that political change was necessary if they were to retain the alliance of a reasonable section of the western educated. At first they contemplated very limited political concessions, and these not until after the war. In 1915 Hardinge believed that, 'With a show of sympathy, and very moderate but justifiable concessions, India will remain peaceful and contented.'[55] 'I am quite sure that concessions must be made at the end of the war, and they must be made gracefully so as to encourage a sentiment of gratitude, and not extorted from us unwillingly.'[56] By mid-1916 in government circles the time scale had altered and a declaration of British intent before the end of the war was being discussed.[57] In November of 1916 Austen Chamberlain, Secretary of State for India, told the Viceroy that he was under pressure from many quarters to make some declaration, and that behind that pressure lay 'the fear that, unless we can throw some plank to them, the Moderates would be swept away in the approaching Congress.'[58] The Government of India had by this time also decided in favour of a declaration, as indicated in their November Despatch to the Secretary of State, and Chelmsford underlined this privately to Chamberlain: 'between ourselves, I think it would be wise now to give an indication of our policy, in view of the prolongation of the war, as early as we can'.[59] As the policy evolved from post-war concessions to immediate declaration of a goal, it was clear that behind the change lay the fear that the *raj*'s 'Moderate' allies were no longer reliable: the declaration was to be a plank thrown to them by which they could return to the imperial bark, bringing as many as possible of the western educated with them. If Chamberlain's assertion is not sufficient proof, the Lieutenant-Governor of the UP, in pressing for a declaration, made the point quite bluntly. 'The vital question for us is, will the Moderates rally to the side of Government and show some political courage and power of resistance, if the Government does disclose a policy which can be weighed, article for article, against the manifestos of the Extremists? Many of my Indian friends think that they will, but that no time should be lost in calling upon them.'[60] In August 1917 the arguments coming out of India had helped to convince the Cabinet: Montagu's Declaration was the result – a calculated gamble for war-time allies which marked change in the colonial relationship and heralded even greater changes to come.

The 1914–18 war left deep and permanent marks in Indian society. This essay has often only hinted at them because its focus is the 1917 Declaration, and the full effects of the war were only apparent after that date. From this enquiry it emerges that the reason for the 1917 policy shift was not that war had undermined all the supports of the *raj*, or so altered the bounds of the colonial relationship in Indian society that the *raj* was unstable without that change in policy which was a crucial point in the subsequent weakening of imperial bonds. The 1917 Declaration was made because war weakened one of the *raj*'s supports in society, the European presence; but more important, because the British calculated that it threatened to shift its other foundations and decided to act before it did, to stabilise the situation and shore up the buttresses of their empire. Confronted with the restiveness of their 'Moderate' allies, the British acted to prevent a united political movement against them which would exploit their military weakness and might gain wide support as a result of the multiplicity of tensions and strains in society which were either visible or predictable as the result of a long war. War highlighted the importance of the 'Moderates' in British eyes, giving them, and through them all Indian politicians, a new degree of leverage in their relations with the *raj*. At this point in time war did not itself create important social change; rather, it gave occasion to forces produced by deep-rooted social changes to show their strength. It demonstrated that the *raj*'s old networks of alliance within Indian society, many of them dating at least as far back as 1858, were becoming outmoded as a result of changes its presence had helped to set in motion.

In retrospect, during the First World War, the colonial relationship appeared to hold firm in India. The Indian empire successfully met the challenge of the war. It defended itself and sent massive supplies overseas to meet the physical threat of Britain's enemies. The *raj* attracted to itself a sufficient consensus to meet the demands made on it by the metropolitan country. It showed itself adaptable in the face of social change when the altering spread and balance of influence in society, though not precipitated by war, began to impinge more forcefully on the British as a result of it, making it clear to the imperial overlords that the social parameters of a viable colonial relationship were changing, constraining it into new patterns and constitutional moulds. However, in responding to the challenge of war, the *raj* started the process of adaptation which finally broke the imperial bonds tying India to Britain. Empire is only adaptable in response to social change to a limited extent: beyond that limit it ceases to be empire and new polities take its place. The Montagu Declaration helped to stabilise the *raj* in 1917, but it pointed the way to an independent subcontinent.

7

Southern Africa and the War of 1914-18*

S. E. KATZENELLENBOGEN

The war of 1914–18 accelerated the growth of nationalist movements in southern Africa, thus weakening the imperial connection,
and hardened the divisions between different groups in society. The
Afrikaner (Boer) community, already seriously divided over the
question of co-operation with the British, was split beyond hope of
reconciliation by strong opposition to South Africa's participation
in the war. This opposition found partial expression in open rebellion and hastened the rise of the National Party to political power.
Black South Africans found that their loyalty to Britain and to the
Union government was of no value to them in their attempts to
secure an equitable share in the benefits of their country's economic
development. They had in fact to face an industrial colour bar
more firmly entrenched after the war than it had been before 1914;
the shortage of skilled white workers, and pressure to meet rising
production costs by employing more black workers, led only to a
temporary relaxation of the barrier to African advancement in
industry beyond the level of manual labourer. War-time restrictions
on shipping space and the difficulty of securing adequate supplies
of manufactured goods from Europe provided the stimulus necessary for South Africa to embark on a process of industrialisation
which was ultimately to give her political independence a firm
economic base.

In the British territories of central Africa, whites and blacks
generally supported the war effort, but in north-eastern Rhodesia
and Nyasaland, which did not share in the general prosperity
engendered by the war, low wages, compulsory carrier work, and

* I wish to express my thanks to Professor Dennis Austin for his helpful
comments on an earlier draft of this essay. Responsibility for what follows is,
of course, entirely my own.

the death of a number of Africans in the opening stages of the East African campaign combined with long-standing grievances against the colonial administration to generate strong disaffection. Millenarian movements gained widespread support and in Nyasaland a Baptist minister, John Chilembwe, led a rebellion intended to publicise African feelings. Though the 'rising' was short-lived and quickly put down, it became the focal point for subsequent nationalist activity throughout central Africa. All the economic, social and political changes involved in these developments were rooted in the pre-war period, but it was the war that gave them the added strength that was to create wide-ranging ramifications for the future.

The rift within the Afrikaner community really began with the Boer War of 1899–1902, when some Boers fought on the British side as National Scouts and Volunteers. In the closing stages of the war a small number, the 'bitter-enders', wanted to fight on when a majority of Boer leaders felt that to do so would be completely futile. The peace terms imposed by Lord Milner were only reluctantly accepted and many Boers went into exile. Many who stayed felt that acceptance of British rule was only a temporary expedient and that the earliest opportunity should be seized to regain their lost independence and secure revenge for the wrongs which they felt, not without justification, they had suffered. The majority of Afrikaners seemed willing to follow the lead given by Louis Botha and Jan Smuts, among others, in co-operating with the British in the task of reconstruction and further development of South Africa. This made it possible to create the Union of South Africa in 1910. As the Union's first Prime Minister, Botha continued his conciliation policy, being firmly convinced that this was the best way to serve South Africa's general interests. Popular support for this view, though strong, was far from unanimous.

In the Free State, under the leadership of General Barry Hertzog, a substantial number of people felt that the conciliation policy was a betrayal of the Afrikaner nation. Hertzog, like Smuts, was born in the Cape, studied law at Stellenbosch, and went on to Europe for further education before returning to South Africa to become involved in politics and the Boer War. In contrast to Smuts, Hertzog studied in Amsterdam, Paris and Bonn rather than at a British university, was a 'bitter-ender' and never faltered in his determination to gain complete Afrikaner independence from Britain, although he did accept the impossibility of doing this by force.

Hertzog was not motivated simply by animosity towards the British, or by a desire to achieve dominance for his own language group, but rather by a deep-felt conviction that South Africa should be ruled by Afrikaners – true South Africans whether of British or Dutch origin – whose primary loyalty was to South Africa. He expounded the view that the two separate cultural streams, English and Dutch, should be absolutely equal in law and allowed to follow their own paths of development. His somewhat tortuous way of expressing himself tended to obscure what he meant and he was widely misinterpreted by the English-speaking community. Appointed Minister of Education in the Free State in 1907, he began to implement his two-stream policy by introducing legislation requiring instruction in the first four years of school to be given in a child's mother tongue, regardless of his parents' wishes. At higher levels, children of one language group had to learn the language of the other. This caused great consternation among many parents who regarded Afrikaans as a useless language and among teachers, many of whom spoke only English. It also strengthened Hertzog's popular support.

Botha had been reluctant to include Hertzog in his Cabinet, but was forced to do so by Hertzog's strong following in the Free State. Hertzog made no secret of his opposition to Botha's policy, constantly attacking government decisions which seemed to put the interests of Britain and the British Empire above those of South Africa. In December 1912 he was forced out of the Cabinet, and in January 1914 formed the National (also referred to as Nationalist) party which was to strive for the realisation of the goals he and his followers espoused. In the face of Hertzog's attacks, Botha maintained that there was no dichotomy between British and South African interests and that he certainly would never do anything he thought would be detrimental to his country. He might have succeeded in reuniting Afrikaners behind his South African party had it not been for the outbreak of war in August 1914. Many saw this as the longed-for, literally heaven-sent opportunity to strike another blow for independence. Attitudes polarised and every South African was forced to decide precisely where his loyalties lay.[1]

When war broke out Botha immediately offered to assume responsibility for the country's defence, freeing the imperial garrison for service in Europe. He was also willing to send a South African expeditionary force into German South-west Africa to seize control of the wireless stations at Windhoek and Swakopmund as

Britain requested; but, realising that some of his Cabinet colleagues would not be in favour of such a move, he waited until the matter could be debated in Parliament before making definite arrangements. There was some feeling that the Union Defence Force should not be used offensively outside the country's own borders in an operation from which it appeared that Great Britain stood to gain significant strategic advantages at little risk, while South Africa stood to lose much and gain nothing. Opposing the motion to send the expedition, Hertzog made one of the few really eloquent speeches of his career. He argued that if the war went in Germany's favour, South Africa could well find itself in the same position as Belgium. If Britain emerged victorious, South-west Africa would 'fall like a ripe fruit into [her] lap'.[2] To run the risk of taking the German territory at the beginning of the conflict was, in his view, the height of folly, particularly as it was most unlikely that the Germans would be able to mount a serious attack on the Union for a considerable time. He concluded with the warning: 'The Government would very speedily find that they had to deal with a population which felt that something was being done which ought not to be done.'[3] Parliament voted overwhelmingly in favour of invading south-west Africa, but Hertzog's prediction soon proved true.

Botha was well aware of the antagonism this decision aroused, particularly in the minds of several Boer generals. He tried to forestall the open rebellion that was being plotted, but to no avail; there is some feeling that he could have done more.[4] On 10 October 1914 Colonel Salomon Maritz, who had earlier defected and joined the German forces, threatened to invade the north-western Cape. Maritz had tried to secure wide-ranging promises from the Governor of South-west Africa, but Dr Seitz and his military adviser did not trust Maritz, being suspicious of his motives. Apparently the only firm promise they gave was to establish a *Vrij Korps* of Afrikaners on German soil under German control. This they did, but it was a far cry from what Maritz had wanted – independence for South Africa and permission to annexe Delagoa Bay if Germany won the war. Maritz's threat was the signal for a series of uprisings in the Free State, the Cape and the Transvaal. Most of the rebels were from the Free State, but there is no evidence that the Nationalist party or Hertzog were directly implicated. Hertzog did, however, give the rebellion tacit support by refusing to make a public statement opposing it. It was more than a month, after all attempts to negotiate a settlement had failed, before Botha led a campaign, using Afrikaner troops almost exclusively, to suppress the rebellion. Organised rapidly in different areas by different leaders, it lacked the close co-ordination necessary for success. By late January 1915 it had been completely quelled and its leaders arrested, except for Maritz who escaped to Angola and thence to Portugal.

With the exception of Maritz, who was very pro-German, the rebels were not motivated by a desire for a German victory over Britain; nor were they, for the most part, rebelling specifically against Britain. They were engaged in an armed protest against a policy decision of the Union government. Armed protests had been a traditional means of expressing such opposition in the Boer republics, and none of the rebels felt they were doing anything wrong, conveniently forgetting that the traditional armed protest did not involve shooting and killing fellow-Afrikaners. The rebellion was essentially a 'family affair' within the Afrikaner community,[5] a community now further divided than it had been, to the point where brother did in fact fight brother, and many congregations of the Dutch Reformed Church had to make provision for rebel and government supporters to worship separately. Punishments were relatively lenient, most of the rank-and-file being sent home, some disenfranchised for a time. The leaders were fined and imprisoned, but all were released before serving their full sentences. Fines were paid by an organisation formed for the purpose, the *Helpmekaar*, which still exists to assist Afrikaners in need and contributes to the support of Afrikaner cultural organisations. Only one man, Jopie Fourie, who had neglected to take the precaution of resigning his commission in the South African Defence Force before joining the rebels and had shot to kill to the last, was executed, becoming an Afrikaner hero. The way was clear for Botha to mount and lead the expedition against South-west Africa which, meeting little effective resistance, was able to accomplish its objective rapidly and with very little loss of life.

Botha and Smuts, convinced they had done what was right, had to face the harsh political reality that many of their followers who had not supported the rebels would never forgive them for having hunted down and killed fellow-Afrikaners merely, it seemed, to oblige the British. Fourie's execution five days before Christmas, for which Smuts was held directly responsible, aroused particular anger. Support for Hertzog and the National party increased. In the elections held in October 1915 they won 27 seats; Botha lost his absolute majority and had to rely on the predominantly British Unionist party to remain in power. During the war a number of decisions made by both the British and Union governments aroused further antagonism. A projected rebellion was nipped in the bud in 1916, but pressure for the establishment of an independent republic increased.[6]

A Nationalist deputation representing the more extreme republican elements in the party went to the Peace Conference to press for the Union's independence, the re-creation of the Boer republics, or independence for the Orange Free State alone. Hertzog did not support the deputation but continued to maintain that South Africa had the right to secede from the Empire at any time. Smuts's attempts to reunify the National and South African parties after the war foundered on the rocks of the Nationalists' unwillingness to modify their position on this point. The first post-war elections in 1920 made the Nationalists the largest single party in Parliament. Smuts, who had become Prime Minister after Botha's death in 1919, was forced to depend on three independent members as well as the Unionists for a slender majority. He found temporary relief in 1921 when, having brought the South African and Unionist parties together, he called another election, securing an ample majority, but at the expense of the Labour party, not the Nationalists.

The Labour and Nationalist parties were able to work together to make Hertzog Prime Minister of a coalition government – the Pact Government – after the 1924 elections, in which Smuts lost his seat. The Labour party still drew most of its support from British workers who did not take kindly to the idea of breaking with the Empire, although the goal of economic independence from British capitalists was attractive to them. The Pact was able to stay together primarily because of the strong stand the two parties took in opposing any relaxation of the barriers to African advancement into job categories traditionally reserved for whites. Smuts was by no means fundamentally opposed to the Pact's 'Native' policy, but several other factors combined to bring about his defeat. These included the economic difficulties in which the Union found itself when the post-war boom collapsed, but more important was Smuts's inability to command the same degree of loyalty as Botha. The two men were of very different character, Smuts being rather more aloof than Botha, who had always maintained a close personal contact with his supporters. The fact that Smuts had studied at Cambridge, his participation in the Imperial War Cabinet, and the feeling after the war that he was more concerned with the Empire and world affairs than with what was happening at home in South Africa, made many Afrikaners distrust him and place their political allegiance elsewhere.

In 1929 Hertzog led the Nationalists to an absolute majority in the Lower House and seemed firmly in power. It soon became clear that he would be under heavy attack from within his own party, and to strengthen his position he formed an alliance with Smuts: the United South African party was founded in December 1934. Some Nationalists would not accept the merger and formed the Purified Nationalist party under the leadership of Dr D. F. Malan. The inter-war years also saw the emergence of organisations formed to promote a greater cultural awareness among Afrikaners and to secure a place for them in the English-dominated worlds of industry and commerce. The feeling grew that English-speakers could not be true South Africans and that a republic should be established as soon as possible. The republican issue remained a vital one in Nationalist politics, though the Nationalists' great success after the Second World War was based primarily on their strong stand on the 'Native Question'.

Prior to and during the war of 1939–45, Afrikaners were once again seriously divided over the question of South Africa's participation in the conflict. There was much greater sympathy for Germany that there had been in 1914, and a large body of opinion in favour of maintaining some form of neutrality. This was the view held by Hertzog, who was forced to resign; he and Malan managed to forestall any repetition of the 1914 rebellion. These two men tried to reach a *rapproachement* over the republican question, but without success. Hertzog resigned from the National party in December 1940 and died in 1942. Some of his followers formed the Afrikaner party, which met with little success and merged with Malan's Nationalists in 1947. The following year Malan became Prime Minister with an absolute majority in both Houses of Parliament. In January 1960 his successor, Dr H. F. Verwoerd, announced the decision to hold a referendum on whether or not South Africa should become a republic. The country was split over the issue: the vote was 850,458 in favour, 775,878 against. On 31 May 1961 South Africa became a republic dominated by Afrikaner nationalists and withdrew from the British Commonwealth.[7]

Unlike the Boers, blacks in South Africa remained for the most part completely loyal to Britain during the 1914 war. Mineworkers pledged themselves to refrain from industrial action and the African National Native Congress ('Native' was later dropped from its name) decided not to criticise the government publicly, while continuing its campaign to secure a fair distribution of land under the terms of the Native Lands Act of 1913. This loyalty was to no avail; the British government refused to intervene on their behalf in any way, either during or after the war. When the war ended and the Congress, along with other African groups, turned its attention more specifically to the question of the Africans' share in the economic expansion of the country, it had to face the industrial colour bar which had withstood the onslaught of economic pressures and had emerged, if anything, stronger and more firmly entrenched than ever before.[8]

The industrial colour bar had its origins in the practical necessities of the early days of mining when skilled and semi-skilled jobs could only be done by experienced miners, who were generally British. As it became possible for Africans to be trained to take over some of these jobs, white miners, no longer able to rely on their own scarcity value, pressed for the application of a colour bar to eliminate competition from lower-paid African workers, even before it began. The situation became more complex after the Boer War when economic conditions forced more and more Afrikaners to leave the land and seek employment in industry. Psychologically incapable of doing the same job as Africans, or of competing with them at any level, Boer employees exerted great pressure on the Chamber of Mines, as representative of all the mining companies, to continue employing blacks only in manual jobs and to limit the ratio of black to white workers. The Chamber was forced to acquiesce; the mines could not be run without white miners, whose union organisation was growing stronger. A general strike in 1913 had led to *de facto* recognition of white unions, although the Chamber only officially recognised the South African Industrial Federation as the miners' negotiating representative in 1915, after a further strike in the Transvaal. The success of the 1913 strike inspired some African mineworkers to strike, largely against the colour bar; but this achieved nothing of lasting importance.

During the war the absence of many white workers and rising production costs led the mining companies to begin using black miners in semi-skilled jobs, such as drill sharpening, which had previously been reserved for whites. The Industrial Federation agreed to this, but by 1918 was alarmed lest the colour bar disappear completely, or the black-to-white ratio go too much against them. The Federation and the Chamber reached an agreement to maintain the *status quo* : nothing further was to be done to alter the ratio. But, after the war, as costs continued rising and lower gold prices seemed inevitable, the companies announced their intention of abandoning the *status quo* agreement and employing a greater number of Africans. Opposition to this came not only from the white miners, but from the Afrikaner community at large. They felt the mining companies were interested solely in maximising profits rather than in the wider issue that Afrikaners considered of prime importance, the maintenance of job security and high wages for whites.

During protracted negotiations the Chamber of Mines proposed a ratio of 10.5 blacks to each white worker. The Industrial Federation countered with a demand for an 8.5:1 ratio to operate not only in the gold mines but throughout industry. In February 1922 a militant Action Group, some members of which were also members of the Third International, armed white miners and set up barricades. A small civil war ensued, the government being forced to use aircraft as well as artillery and infantry to bring it to an end. More people died in this Rand Rebellion than in the South-west African campaign. Singing 'The Red Flag', four of the Action Group's leaders went to the gallows. In the minds of the white miners there was no paradox involved in socialists and communists uniting with other workers to protect their privileged status by keeping another group of workers in a subordinate position. Fear that the mining companies would not continue to respect the colour bar, which had been maintained primarily by custom rather than by law, led to the introduction of legislation designed to ensure its enforcement and which has been modified over the years. Some exceptions to the rules have been made, but, during the seven decades since the Boer War, neither economic pressures nor statutes have had much effect on the colour bar's practical operation.[9]

Generally, all social groups in southern Africa benefited economically from the war. Wages were driven up by the greater shortage of labour caused by the demand for porters and the enlistment of whites and blacks in the armed forces. One cause of resentment among black South Africans was that they were not allowed to serve in any active military capacity. Farmers, both African and European, profited from the increased demand for food, the mining industry in the Union and Southern Rhodesia responded to the increased demand for strategic minerals, and railways and ports handled larger amounts of traffic. Serious problems were to arise after the war, but until then economic prosperity spread. In South Africa high prices for manufactured goods, coupled with the shortage of supplies from Britain, stimulated domestic production and provided the impetus for the country's entry into a new phase of economic growth, its development as an industrial nation.

Some manufacturing industries such as leather, chemicals and food-processing had been carried on for some time, but only on a small scale. The fundamental obstacle to industrial expansion was the fact that mining, while creating essential markets, also absorbed most of the available resources of money, entrepreneurial ability and technical skill. Competition from foreign products was difficult to overcome and much of the industry that did develop was heavily dependent on foreign sources of raw materials. Even the boot-making industry, which had been started by the Dutch in 1652 and was relatively independent, often found it difficult to compete with foreign products as cattle disease often restricted domestic supplies of leather. The war provided some protection, but this had to be re-enforced after 1918 by tariff legislation and other import restrictions. The chemical industry began in the Transvaal in 1892, relying almost entirely on the mines for markets, but until the war made no use of South Africa's abundant sources of the necessary raw materials. Until 1915 there had seemed little practical reason for either private investors or the government to take the great risks involved in changing this situation by expanding domestic manufacturing or developing domestic natural resources. The war demonstrated clearly South Africa's vulnerability to events outside her control and the dangers of excessive reliance on foreign supplies. This, coupled with the erroneous belief that prices for manufactured goods would remain high after the war, convinced both the government and South African businessmen that it was economically and politically feasible, indeed necessary, to expand the country's industrial capacity.

Attention was directed initially towards the iron and steel industry. South Africa had extensive reserves of iron ore in the Transvaal and Natal. There had been some interest in developing them as early as 1860, but it was only in 1901 that a small, ultimately unsuccessful blast-furnace was erected at Pietermaritzburg. Between 1903 and 1914, the greatest interest was shown in the creation of an iron and steel industry based on the use of scrap, of which large stocks had accumulated and to which the mines and railways were constantly adding. Relatively little capital outlay was required for the erection of electric furnaces. It was only during the war that systematic surveys of ore reserves were carried out, and serious attempts, some with government backing, were made to determine whether the native ores could be smelted easily. Pig iron was first produced in 1926 and the industry began to flourish after 1928, when the South African Iron and Steel Corporation (ISCOR) was established. ISCOR's first plant at Pretoria began producing commercially in 1934, and became (with gold mining) the basis of South Africa's industrial strength, promoting the growth of other industries and generating an increasing proportion of the country's national product. While South Africa did not emerge as an infant industrial nation until the 1930s, it was the war of 1914–18 that provided the necessary catalyst for change.[10]

All nationalist movements have goals in common, and a number of parallels between movements in Africa, India, Ireland and elsewhere can easily be seen. Afrikaners would be most unwilling to accept that they had anything in common with black African nationalists,[11] but in addition to the desire to be free to develop their own culture and use their own language, and to eliminate foreign political dominance and economic exploitation, black nationalists in central Africa shared with Afrikaners the experience of the war of 1914–18 as a significant turning-point in their development.

In central Africa reaction to the war varied. In southern and north-western Rhodesia, Africans volunteered to serve in the army and, in contrast to the Africans of South Africa, were allowed to do so in an active military capacity. In north-eastern Rhodesia and parts of Nyasaland, African backing for the war effort was much weaker. Compulsory carrier work and the lack of alternative work kept wages much lower than they were elsewhere, and there was little opportunity for Africans to supplement their incomes by selling surplus food. Millenarian religious cults preaching the imminence of the Second Coming struck a responsive chord : the outbreak of war heralded Armageddon when the colonial powers would be destroyed and the black elect would enter the New Jerusalem. Local prophets emerged and became focal points of opposition to the colonial administration. One of the larger cults, the Jehovah's Witnesses (then known as the Watchtower Bible and Tract Society), was proscribed for advocating passive resistance to the requisitioning of porters, and because the luridly illustrated pamphlets they distributed were considered a threat to morale.[12]

The activities of the Jehovah's Witnesses came as no surprise to the authorities, who were taken rather more unaware by the Nyasaland rising of 1915, led by the Baptist minister, John Chilembwe, who had studied at a Negro seminary in Virginia. Before going to the United States he had been closely associated with Joseph Booth, a freelance missionary who later joined the Jehovah's Witnesses; Booth earned the strong disapproval of his fellow Europeans in Africa by opposing the relative ease of missionary life in comparison with the poverty of most Africans, and by widely preaching a gospel of Africa for the Africans. Chilembwe, on his return to Nyasaland, established the Providence Industrial Mission which set up schools, started farms, became involved in trade, and generally seemed a 'model of respectability'. Outwardly his mission station was a western community, he and his followers wearing Edwardian clothes and emulating Europeans. This hardly seemed a likely place for a rebellion to begin, but Chilembwe became the spokesman for African grievances that had been building up for some time, especially in the Shire Highlands where his mission operated.

Population pressure in the area had been increasing for years; food prices were high because of a drought in 1912 and were kept high by the war. Resentment against Europeans centred round the imposition of hut taxes and the methods sometimes used to collect them. Africans living on European estates had no security of tenure, while the way in which employers treated their workers was often anything but fair. Worst of all, there seemed to be no way in which Africans could gain the ear of officials to press for an improvement in their situation. Particular animosity was directed against the estates of A. Livingstone-Bruce (a son-in-law of the explorer), which were managed by William J. Livingstone (no direct relation), who was known for his harsh treatment of Africans and whose relations with Chilembwe had been deteriorating for some time. These estates and Livingstone himself were the most tangible representation of the system against which Chilembwe acted.

Within six weeks of the declaration of war, the Nyasaland contingent of the King's African Rifles was involved in two days' action against the Germans at Karonga. Of the 60 officers and men killed, wounded, or taken prisoner, 49 were Africans. This fact, added to the increased recruiting of Africans for military service and carrier work, made Chilembwe look for a means of making an effective protest. In a letter to the *Nyasaland Times* he objected to the use of Africans in the war when nothing had been done for them in peace time. 'In time of peace everything for Europeans only. . . . But in time of war it has been found that we are needed to share hardships and shed our blood in equality.'[13] The letter was published on 26 November 1914 but was cut out by the censor after the first run; few people saw it. The government did not see any danger in this, and it is unlikely that, at the time Chilembwe wrote the letter, he had formulated any precise plans for rebellion. The fact that the authorities took no notice of him convinced him that the only way to make an effective protest was to 'strike a blow and die'. On 23 January 1915 William Livingstone's home was attacked: he and two other European men were killed. Women and children were left carefully alone, even when they tried to intervene. The rebels had planned to do much less damage to life and property than they might have, and in fact did much less than they had planned.

Chilembwe's aims are not entirely clear, but it would appear from the available evidence that he was not involved in a widespread conspiracy, as many Europeans feared at the time, and did not intend to become the head of a new Black Kingdom, as some Africans subsequently claimed. He merely wanted to make a gesture which could not be ignored. The rebellion itself was quelled within a few days and Chilembwe was killed on 3 February, while trying to gain refuge in Mozambique. The government immediately took repressive measures to ensure that no further outbreaks of violent dissidence occurred. To a very small extent Chilembwe succeeded; as a result of the rising and the report of the commission that looked into it, the government of Nyasaland began to reconsider proposals, shelved at the outbreak of war, to regularise the position of Africans on European estates. A law passed in 1916, though not as effective as might have been desired, marked the only tangible outcome of the rising and paved the way for future improvements. By and large the rising failed, primarily because it did not have a large, united body of people in arms behind it. It did show Africans that the future could hold more for them than mere acceptance of European rule: the colonial power could be challenged. As Governor Sir George Smith told the Nyasaland Legislative Council, the rising opened 'a new phase in the existence' of the country, a phase of African nationalism in which the legend of Chilembwe, seen as a martyr and model of action, was a most potent force. In death Chilembwe came to play a major role in the nationalist movements throughout central and southern Africa.

A direct result of the war was the acquisition by the Union of a mandate over south-west Africa under the League of Nations. However divided white South Africans may have been over the invasion of that territory, they were virtually unanimous in claiming that it should become part of the Union when Germany lost the war. Apart from obvious geographical connections, South African businessmen had long been involved in south-west Africa's trade and the exploitation of its mineral resources. After the Boer War, some Afrikaners had trekked there to escape British rule, and were joined by others after the 1914 rebellion. By 1919 there was strong pressure for the Union to be allowed to annex the former Germany colony outright. Though unwilling to accept imperial control of their own country, Afrikaners were happy to extend their own power over another. The League of Nations supervision involved in the mandate for the Union to administer south-west Africa as an integral part of its own territory proved irksome at times, but made little practical difference. Pressures on South Africa, particularly with regard to the treatment of Africans, were never strong enough to bring about changes in policy; they are not to this day. The difference between a mandate and complete annexation disappeared almost entirely after the League was dissolved and South Africa refused to recognise the trustee authority of the United Nations.

The granting of the mandate, though it fell far short of what was wanted, made many Afrikaners feel that their stature as a responsible nation had been recognised, a feeling which grew and contributed to South Africa's flaunting of the United Nations. Also of political importance were the Afrikaner emigrants who tended to side with the Nationalists in differences between Smuts and his opponents. South-west Africa's minerals (diamonds, copper, etc.) and livestock (notably sheep) have also made a substantial economic contribution.[14]

This essay has not attempted to consider all aspects of the effect of the war of 1914–18 on southern Africa, but to indicate the more significant ways in which it altered relationships within society there and the relationship between Britain and some of her southern African possessions. Formally the relationship remained the same: South Africa was still a dominion in 1919, Nyasaland a colony. His Majesty's government made no fundamental policy changes regarding Africans and issued no declarations holding out the promise of eventual independence. Yet the nature of the relationships had changed, becoming much looser – imperceptibly, for a time, in Nyasaland, markedly so in South Africa.

By bringing feeling against subservience to Britain once again to the forefront of politics, the war destroyed all possibility of reconciling the white community in South Africa, despite continuing attempts by Smuts and later by Hertzog. In promoting industrialisation the war also furthered the breakdown of the imperial connection by creating the foundation for economic independence. With industrial growth came greater urbanisation and pressure to extend the colour bar to more jobs and to all industries. Economic considerations were not allowed to interfere with the fundamental ideas of racial segregation, propounded most strongly by Afrikaners but shared by most people of English descent. Black South Africans were not allowed to share fully in the benefits of economic expansion; for most of them the war marked the onset of a diminishing standard of living in comparison with whites. In Nyasaland and northern Rhodesia the war exacerbated existing resentment, generated new grievances and began to harden resistance to colonial rule, though the fruits of African national sentiment came only many years later. With the exception of the virtual annexation of South-west Africa, which could hardly have been taken from Germany otherwise, none of these developments were brought about solely by the war. The war strengthened and accelerated forces already existing, being a major turning-point in the ultimate creation of Malawi and, to a lesser extent, Zambia, as independent nations, and the establishment of the Republic of South Africa, officially, if not in all practical respects, outside the British Commonwealth.

8

The Impact of the War of 1914-18 on the British Political System

PETER FRASER

Thanks to the work of the Committee of Imperial Defence, Britain's entry into the war in 1914, which involved complicated naval, military and civil timetables, was smooth and efficient. The CID's 'War Book' proved a great success. But oddly enough the CID had not produced any ideas about the political direction of the war, and the strategic direction was intended to be left to the military and naval staffs, such as they were. The result was a series of improvisations. The cumbrous War Councils, at which military and political counsels were supposed to converge, were a farce. The sudden appointment of Lord Kitchener as Secretary of State for War was, as Asquith admitted, a 'hazardous experiment' and proved a disaster – 'the right man in the wrong place', it was said. Almost equally unfortunate was the re-appointment somewhat later of Admiral 'Jackie' Fisher as First Sea Lord, in spite of a written protest by the King. In default of any other plan Asquith proposed to run the war through the ordinary Cabinet alternated with occasional War Councils advised by the service departments.

Yet the effect of the war on politics was immediate. Scores of MPs enlisted, party opposition ceased, and a blanket of secrecy and censorship descended on the issues of most moment. The public expected the politicians to close their ranks in an *union sacrée*. The expectation of a brief war, and the fact that an election was due in 1915, might have seemed a justification for the Liberals' not offering a coalition, but the main reason was an underrating of the importance attaching to the political direction of the war. The discovery of this was a long process, as the perspectives of the war and the various means by which it had to be waged broadened. As the demands of the war unfolded, the principles and practices of peacetime government were attacked and demolished one by one in political struggles under unfamiliar wartime conditions. Parliament declined in importance, starved of information, robbed of its control over even extraordinary votes of credit, denuded of its serving Members, blighted by a party truce, and kept in existence after 1915 by the impracticability of a wartime election. The press gained in influence and an uninformed public was none the less opinionated even in military matters. Its obstinate attachments to Kitchener, Lloyd George, Robertson and Haig had important consequences. The political direction of the war under Asquith was a matter of informal conferences at Downing Street tempered by a politically divided and ineffective War Committee aided by scores of *ad hoc* committees. But even Asquith's determination to conduct the war on the principles of 'business as usual', *laissez-faire*, voluntary service and departmental responsibility could not prevail against the inexorable demands making for State control and compulsion, supradepartmental government by an inner Cabinet, and the growth of wartime forms of bureaucracy, State socialism, and mercantilism.

The harbingers of the new system of government were the businessmen and experts whom Lloyd George brought into the new Ministry of Munitions, the men on the fringes of government who served Sir Maurice Hankey's innumerable committees, or those who worked on the sub-committees of Asquith's Reconstruction Committee. When Lloyd George became Prime Minister these men, powerfully reinforced by the disciples of Milner who flocked into the new Prime Minister's Secretariat or into Hankey's enlarged CID Secretariat, now assigned to the War Cabinet, began to dominate the regular civil service. The War Cabinet itself was the culmination of a trend which differentiated the inner or directing Cabinet from its periphery of ministers who administered departments. It was justified by the exigencies of war, which demanded a small and all-powerful directorate free from other duties and meeting almost daily. But the chief architects of the new system regarded it as a permanent reform which would survive the peace. Much government planning was done on the assumption that the wartime political structure and the system of State socialism at home and mercantilism abroad which had grown with it would be carried over, albeit suitably modified, into peace. The rapid dismantling of the whole fabric was not expected, and indeed calls for explanation.

R. H. Tawney, writing in the thick of the Second World War, thought that in the previous war 'War collectivism had not been accompanied by any intellectual conversion on the proper relations between the state and economic life, while it did not last long enough to change social habits.' It was therefore vulnerable to counter-attack by the 'interests and ideas' of the pre-war period.[1] Businessmen who gladly waived their high salaries to serve the State in war became stout supporters of free enterprise after 1918. Civil servants who had been outraged by Lloyd George's method of placing new departments, and even old ones, under tycoons representing vested interests, were ready to press for a return to old ways. The Foreign Office, especially, had been largely robbed of its usual powers and pre-eminence by Lloyd George,[2] and there was a movement to place the consular service and economic diplomacy under the Board of Trade through the instrumentality of the Department of Overseas Trade. With Eyre Crowe as its sworn enemy, 'DOT', as it was contemptuously called, did not last long.[3] One sees even the impeccably correct Austen Chamberlain turning against the War Cabinet at the end of the war, when he discovered that as Chancellor of the Exchequer he was not assigned a place on it. Brought into existence without the political participation of the public or the endorsement of the parliamentary parties, the wartime economic controls and the whole fabric of government centred on the War Cabinet passed away unlamented with the peace and the return of Lloyd George from Versailles. The tangible results of the war so far as long-term political development is concerned seem very problematical, though as a war machine the Lloyd George system provided the model for the next war.

The Liberal government's attempt to run the war with the peacetime political machinery is all the more remarkable in view of the 'party truce' which operated from the outset. Party opposition ceased and contests in by-elections were avoided, while about 180 MPs joined the services.[4] The most vital political questions of the moment – recruiting, war supplies, military and naval strategy, Mediterranean and Balkan diplomacy, the blockade, the co-ordination of allied commands, or casualty figures – were shrouded in official secrecy. In these circumstances the Unionists could reasonably have demanded a coalition, but they preferred to bide their time. A general election would normally have been held in 1915, at the latest, and the Unionists were hoping that Asquith's popularity would not survive many months of war. Their rank and file, at a meeting at Lansdowne House in February 1915, expressed 'strong opposition' to the idea of coalition on the ground that public confidence in the Asquith government was waning. On the other hand the party chairman, Sir Arthur Steel-Maitland, felt that the government was still popular, and he feared a 'khaki' election late in the year. He pressed Bonar Law to seek a coalition, but only when there was a 'suitability of occasion', such as an abuse of the press censorship.[5] Following this meeting the party truce was renewed only for a month at a time.[6]

In early March 1915 it was still possible to believe in an Allied victory by the autumn. Great hopes were pinned on the Russian spring offensive. In Gallipoli, after the first naval bombardment of the forts, the marines had landed unopposed, and the War Council was considering the future of Constantinople. On the western front Sir John French was poised for his first large attempt to break the German lines at Neuve Chapelle. In the next two months, however, the prospects in every theatre gravely worsened. In the first weeks of May the Russians were in full retreat for the line of the San, raising a doubt as to the safety of Warsaw. The Anglo-French attempt to force the Straits had failed with the loss of some battleships and the Gallipoli beachheads had stabilised into another deadlock. Here, as in the actions at Neuve Chapelle and Festubert, enormous casualty lists aggravated the disappointment of failure. As the *New Statesman* put it, 'it is undeniable that recent events at Ypres, in Galicia, and in the Baltic provinces of Russia, together with the casualty lists that have been arriving from Flanders and the Dardanelles, have produced a temporary wave of depression in this country. There is a tendency for the prophet in the street to advance his forecast of the end of the war by several months, if not by years . . .'[7] The complacency of the public was also powerfully dispelled by other things that struck its imagination, particularly the use of poison gas by the Germans, and the deliberate sinking of the liner *Lusitania*, supposedly by order of the German government. An honourable peace with the Hohenzollern dynasty or Prussian governing class now seemed impossible. Yet, if the destruction of the 'barbaric' German state became a war aim, what would be the dimensions of the war? One obvious implication of the more formidable outlook was that more men would be needed than the voluntary principle would permit, or rather that compulsion might be necessary to ensure that the most rational use was made of manpower. The army had devoured skilled men indiscriminately, while young loungers were still to be seen in the streets.

The Unionists were united in advocating compulsion and a mobilisation of the nation's industrial resources. If the war lasted beyond 1915 they could be sure of bringing down the Asquith government, provided they were ruthless enough to use their majority in the House of Lords to force a general election. As the country became more zealous in the cause of compulsion, which was opposed chiefly by the Labour movement and the Irish nationalists, so the triumph of the compulsionists in any general election became more certainly acknowledged. On this calculation some Unionists were against accepting Asquith's offer of coalition when it came in mid-May, while Bonar Law represented the patriotic rather than party view in readily accepting a coalition in which the Liberals still held all the important offices, and in which the Labour party and even the Irish nationalists were invited to participate. As it was, the coalition was proffered by Asquith without consulting his Liberal colleagues, after the weekend of 15–16 May on which both Kitchener and Fisher were threatening to resign. Fisher appeared a martyr to civilian interference, while Kitchener appeared as the victim of an intrigue between the entourage of Sir John French and the Northcliffe press, abetted by Churchill, who was known to have visited his headquarters. In its essence the crisis was one of parliamentary confidence. The Commons, however, was now hopelessly unrepresentative and back-bench opposition had ceased to interest the public. The coalition represented a resolve not to hold a wartime election, which indeed presented difficult problems apart from the chief objection that it would impair the unity of the nation and the war effort. For the Commons which was now, with the artificial prolongation of its life and the absence of scores of its Members, becoming like the rump of a Long Parliament, the coalition was a guarantee against the popular revenge of an election.

The introduction of Curzon (Privy Seal), Carson (Attorney-General), Selborne (Board of Agriculture) and Austen Chamberlain (India Office) into the government greatly reinforced the movement in favour of compulsion, the total mobilisation of resources, and a vigorous war directorate. While admiring Asquith's 'imperturbability' Selborne regarded him as 'quite hopeless as a

War P[rime] M[inister].' He had 'no vision, no power or desire of prevision, no ounce of drive . . . not a spark of initiative . . .'[8] Selborne proceeded to implement his own ideas. He appointed Milner as chairman of a strong committee on food production which reported in favour of guaranteed corn prices, minimum agricultural wages, land reclamation and afforestation. To restore land to the plough from pasture, which was relatively less productive, and to overcome the malaise of the pre-war agricultural depression, a firm initiative from the State was called for. Characteristically, Asquith only began to show an interest in Selborne's agricultural policy after the opportunity of the 1916 harvest had been lost.[9]

Meanwhile the battle over compulsion had continued. As soon as the coalition government was finally settled in office, after a week of intense and disgraceful party bickering behind the scenes,[10] Selborne demanded that 'All men . . . from 17 years of age and upwards should be made subject to military law in the sense that the State should be able to order each one of us to perform that service for which he is most competent.' This would require a 'register' of men by age and occupation, and of industries connected with the supply of war material from which 'no man would be allowed to transfer his services . . . without leave.'[11] Through the summer of 1915 the demand for compulsion and also for the control of wages and war profits gathered way. Heartened by public support, the Unionist extremists began to think in terms of blocking the Bill for extending the life of Parliament, which the Cabinet agreed to in June, when it came up to the House of Lords. They demanded a Compulsion Bill to be drawn ready for introduction by 30 November. But they were defeated by the well-known 'Derby canvass', which was the last fling of voluntaryism. As Selborne indignantly recorded, 'We Unionists in the Cabinet would have forced compulsory service in September or October 1915 and we had the P.M. and the anti-compulsionists beaten. It was K[itchener] who beat us by publishing his precious Derby group scheme. It had never even been mentioned in the Cabinet. . . . we could not resign against K[itchener]!'[12] At a heated Cabinet on 15 October Asquith opposed the idea of drawing up a compulsion scheme with the argument that it would 'strangle Lord Derby's scheme in its cradle'. But the compulsionists now had the formidable support of Lloyd George, who at this meeting made what Asquith described as a 'blackmailing speech' threatening a general election when he would 'free himself from all reserve, and go to the country to tell the people the truth.'[13]

The public had, indeed, lost touch with the esoteric game which the politicians, embarrassed by their own divisions, were playing. Kitchener and Lloyd George inspired most public confidence, and yet the former was now thoroughly discredited among his colleagues, who had come to realise that he did not even read the War Office telegrams, far less communicate their import. Relieved progressively of his responsibility for munitions, recruiting, and strategy, 'Lord K' became a mere 'fixed point' of public confidence. Popular confidence in Lloyd George as the first Minister of Munitions was better founded, but the Unionists did not view him as an alternative Prime Minister. '. . . his reckless adoption of new and startling courses on imperfect study and partial evidence', comments Steel-Maitland, 'and his doubtful appreciation of his responsibilities to colleagues would shake the confidence of those who know him in any Government of which he was the head.'[14] As the crisis of compulsion approached, the Unionists were nevertheless obliged to contemplate resignation in support of Lloyd George. The issue of compulsion itself had ceased to be so important for reasons which Austen Chamberlain, representing the Unionists on the Cabinet committee most conversant with the question, made known to his colleagues just before the particular weekend on which Lloyd George had planned to deliver his ultimatum.[15] And indeed Bonar Law, while realising that there would be strong pressure from his party in favour of a general election on compulsion if Asquith did not immediately concede it, at first shrank from the idea of forcing Asquith out of office. A change of government

. . . could not be made in the present House of Commons. There would need to be an election, with all the bitterness which that inevitably creates; and even if we got a large majority the war would have to be carried on in the face of a bitter Opposition in the House of Commons which would, I think, encourage every form of opposition outside. This might mean . . . that something like martial law would have to be established in many parts of the country.[16]

During the weekend, while Asquith was out of town playing golf, his usual mode of encountering a crisis, Lloyd George duly composed his letter of resignation, but on the Monday it seemed to fall flat and only Curzon and Selborne seemed ready to resign with him. Asquith thought he had Kitchener squared, in spite of the awkward demand of the Army Council for 'every available man', but he reckoned without the influence of Lord Esher behind the scenes. Esher convinced Kitchener and Robertson, the CIGS, that they would have to resign in support of their resolution. He also convinced the King's Secretary, Lord Stamfordham, that their resignations could not be accepted and that Asquith's dismissal might be preferable, granted the state of public opinion.[17] Frantic party consultations were held to reach some agreement before Parliament broke up for the Easter recess, but Bonar Law was now being dragged along by the Unionist militants, while Milner, the uncompromising exponent of a wartime election, acted as a bridge between Carson's Unionist War Committee and Lloyd George's Liberal supporters. At the eleventh hour (19 April) the Cabinet could not agree and took the extraordinary decision to appeal to a secret session of both Houses of Parliament. Ostensibly this was to scrutinise the Army Council's figures, but its real purpose was to test the strength of the contending factions.

The crisis of Easter 1916 was itself eclipsed by the Easter Rising in Dublin. Under cover of the latter Asquith was able to escape from his pledges and introduce a Bill for simple compulsion, in which, however, he inserted a clause exempting the Irish. Some, like Lord Robert Cecil, still demanded Asquith's resignation, as a prelude to the formation of a national government whose 'members would be selected not because certain parliamentary interests must be placated' but rather as 'the best persons available'.[18] The bankruptcy of the coalition formed to represent interest groups had been demonstrated by its public announcement that it could not agree on the central problem of the war, and by its appeal to a House of Commons which dared not enforce its real convictions for fear of a popular revenge. While Lloyd George had correctly gauged the state of public feeling on compulsion and the general mode of carrying on the war, Asquith had attempted to conciliate all sections including the Irish and the Labour leaders, and had pleased none.

While there was no national government there could hardly be any vigorous war directorate. Here the same combination of Kitchener's incompetent indecision and Asquith's masterly inactivity, which had delayed compulsion, ensured that there was no effective War Committee to which the Cabinet could delegate the daily direction of the war. The so-called Dardanelles Committee of 1915 and subsequent War Committee were fatally handicapped by having to obtain prior approval from the Cabinet at large for every important departure. Admittedly, the Unionists were divided as to the form the War Committee should take. Austen Chamberlain wanted the War Committee to be also the Cabinet, an idea which he and others forced on Lloyd George later when the War Cabinet was formed. Curzon and Selborne, the two loudest advocates of a firmer direction in the government, made rather tame proposals when consulted by Asquith. Curzon thought a War Committee of five members, as proposed to the Cabinet on 21 September 1915, was too small, while objecting to the Dardanelles Committee of twelve as too large, nor did he ask for daily sittings.[19] Balfour preferred the informal consultations with Asquith which at critical junctures had supplanted both Cabinet and War Committee; but Balfour was regarded by the militant Unionist leaders as a mere tame elephant to Asquith. Writing to Asquith 'something which could not be said even in the privacy of the cabinet', Balfour made Kitchener's unavoidable membership of any War Committee his reason for disapproving of one. 'He detests interference; he detests giving information; when information is squeezed out of him it is not always accurate, and he has no notion of playing the game with all the cards on the table.' Better therefore continue with 'the cabinet system, tempered by occasional, and quite informal conversations, such as you have now and then arranged for in Downing Street.'[20] The real advocate of a small War Committee was Lloyd George, and when he finally succeeded in getting his way he found himself neutralised by Asquith, Kitchener, Balfour, McKenna and Bonar Law.[21] Bonar Law alone represented the Unionist leadership in any real sense, and he would not challenge Asquith's decision to keep the Cabinet as a whole in the paramount place. As Selborne complained, he 'emasculated our influence from the beginning by . . . sticking to the theory that Asquith was indispensable as war Prime Minister . . . and that under no circumstances would he consent to form a War Cabinet.'[22]

The death of Lord Kitchener, drowned on the way to Russia, removed the linch-pin of Asquith's system of wartime government. Kitchener's immense prestige with the public rendered invulnerable both the departmentalism of the War Office and the immunity of the soldiers from serious civilian interference. When Sir William Robertson returned as CIGS late in 1915, he succeeded in obtaining a special 'charter' by letters patent rendering him the sole channel of orders to the armies and giving him the final word in strategic decisions. In Kitchener and Robertson, War

Office departmentalism was doubly ensconced. But Kitchener's opponents in the Cabinet had come near to unseating him late in 1915, and Lloyd George, the arch-enemy of the departmentalism of the War Office, nearly succeeded in getting Robertson's charter rescinded as a condition of assuming the Secretaryship of State for War in June 1916. He failed because the Unionists did not trust him with complete power at the War Office. However, it was not long before Lloyd George started to overrule Robertson by claiming to have one official opinion as War Secretary and another as a member of the War Committee.[23] In the former capacity he knew all about military affairs, and in the latter he could ensure that the War Committee had full information. By late November 1916 the time was ripe for him to press Asquith for a really small War Committee of himself as War Secretary, the First Lord (who would have to be someone other than Balfour) and a third minister without portfolio. Narratives of the crisis which followed have over-emphasised personal rivalries and neglected the main issue, namely that of war direction.[24]

On one side was Asquith, who had promptly countered Lloyd George's demand with a proposal for a second Committee, on National Organisation, both to be under the Cabinet.[25] The inadequate character of this scheme was emphasised by the manifest division in the Cabinet itself between the exponents of what Lloyd George had styled the 'knock out' and those who sympathised with Lansdowne's public move mooting the policy of a negotiated peace. The catastrophic situation in the Balkans, where Rumania was being crushed, and the desperate muddle over manpower, food, shipping, etc., called for swift and vigorous action if the war fortunes of the Allies were to be restored. Bonar Law had to come down off his fence, and the side which his party and the public expected him to take was clearly indicated both by the progress of Carson's back-bench War Committee and the support which Milner was mustering in favour of a National party. Once Lloyd George's demands had been leaked to the press, the Unionists knew they had no option but to support them, though neither they nor Lloyd George himself wanted to displace Asquith from the premiership.[26] Those who opposed Asquith simply wished to give Lloyd George a free hand in the day-to-day running of the war.

The sequel was unexpected. Asquith fell because he hated and distrusted Lloyd George and would not serve under Bonar Law. Consequently the whole fabric of the Lloyd George government was a hasty improvisation. The central idea, that the War Committee and Cabinet should be synonymous, was, as has been seen, dictated by the Unionists. This enabled an increase in the number of departments, whose heads, not being in the Cabinet, were absolved from the collective responsibility of ministers and to a large degree from effective control by the House of Commons. Thus Lloyd George was enabled to oblige the Labour leaders by creating new departments of Labour, Food, Shipping and Pensions, which he promised them before he formed his government.[27] He was also absolved from reliance on established politicians with seats in Parliament and could fill offices with the business tycoons in which he had such faith, with press barons whose support he needed, or with other outsiders like H. A. L. Fisher. The War Cabinet itself was not exactly a national government, for Arthur Henderson sat in it purely to conciliate Labour, while the Unionists necessarily filled the other places. Only Milner could be said to have been chosen for talent and public confidence alone.[28] The really extraordinary feature of the War Cabinet was that its members were relieved from departmental duties. Being without portfolio they became overlords over groups of departments and, not having their own departmental civil servants, they used a separate secretariat, either the Prime Minister's personal one, or the Cabinet secretariat under Sir Maurice Hankey, who had served the former War Committee.

It would seem that at first Lloyd George wanted to expand Hankey's staff – and indeed Hankey, in addition to being Secretary to the CID, had become a general factotum and liaison officer to the Prime Minister. When Stamfordham interviewed Hankey on 4 December he found him strongly opposed to Lloyd George's plan for 'further appointments and a change in status of the Secretary', saying it 'would convert his office into a quasi general staff, and bring him into possible conflict with the CIGS and First Sea Lord.'[29] The subsequent plan of a War Cabinet made an expanded secretariat unavoidable and, while securing Hankey's co-operation, the new Prime Minister set up his own personal secretariat in huts in the garden of 10 Downing Street. The 'brilliant young men' of Milner's 'Kindergarten' were given full scope both here and in Hankey's staff, where L. S. Amery and Mark Sykes became additional 'brains'. The transmutation of Hankey's secretariat and the creation of a Prime Minister's Department represented a very serious incursion into the powers of departments and of the civil service. The Principal Secretary of the 'Garden Suburb', Professor W. G. S. Adams, thought the new department 'should contain the organisation represented by the Junior Lords of the Treasury, the Whips, with the political intelligence department', as well as being 'an administrative intelligence department consisting of liaison officers in touch with' other departments.[30] Under Adams each secretary had assigned to him a group of departments and was free to make suggestions for improving organisation or efficiency, including the creation of new machinery. Departments concerned with the prosecution of the war were required to submit weekly reports to Adams, to establish a surveillance by the Prime Minister. These were later circulated by Hankey to the War Cabinet and the departments ranked as most important.

The new régime was hailed by Amery as a natural evolution. The war had 'only precipitated a change which was already becoming inevitable before it.' The ordinary voter or MP before the war had supported 'not a Cabinet of 20 or more members, but the four or five men who made the policy of the party both in the Cabinet and in the country.' It had therefore been anomalous that 'Every Department was sancrosanct to its colleagues in the Cabinet' and that departmental heads 'were always in the House of Commons taking refuge behind their Cabinet position.'[31] The War Cabinet had indeed broken the tradition of departmental autonomy. Its members, having no particular departmental responsibility, became overlords to groups of departments in the same way as Lloyd George's secretaries were assigned groups of departments, and the first plan was to assign the appropriate secretary to each member of the War Cabinet. The peacetime 'Inner Cabinet' became a body of ministers concerned with policy and not administration, or, as Amery put it, the War Cabinet was 'an expansion of the power and personality of the Prime Minister.'[32] The separation of policy and administration seemed also to meet the needs of the Imperial War Cabinet which, under Lloyd George, became an annual formality, for the Empire Prime Ministers made only general policies. It seemed natural to have an Imperial Cabinet and a Home Cabinet both dealing with higher policy. The ideas of enthusiasts like Amery could not be expected to go down well with the public or with Parliament. The war had already, before Lloyd George's premiership, demoted Parliament to a relatively insignificant position. It was denied the information necessary for effective control of the executive and robbed of its power of checking the government by back-bench revolt or by the monitory trends of by-elections. Under Asquith Parliament was still, however, the mainstay of the Prime Minister's position at the head of the coalition, in the sense that a new Prime Minister would have needed a dissolution. Under Lloyd George, aided by Milner and Curzon, the House of Commons could be slighted and ignored because the Prime Minister had its death warrant in his pocket. Asquith's Whips knew that Lloyd George would have welcomed a pretext for a general election and took care not to give him one.[33] Lloyd George was rarely seen in the Commons and his ministerial appointments seemed to take no notice of parliamentary position.[34] Questions in Parliament, which in any case were screened in war time, were of little effect against a minister who might be an outsider assisted by secretaries who were not regular civil servants. Nor did the criticism of a department or the parliamentary defeat of its head affect the stability of the government under the new régime.[35] Thus the new system of the War Cabinet challenged some of the most sacred constitutional doctrines and was bound to offend the instincts of strong parliamentarians.

For the purposes of the war the War Cabinet system enabled a much wider range of talent and special experience to be placed at the disposal of the government. Lloyd George's willingness to consult anyone and everyone is seen in his choice of the Reconstruction Committee. 'Bring me a list of persons with ideas', he is supposed to have said, and certainly his Committee (later a Ministry) and its sub-committees contained all kinds of outsiders.[36] The Fabians were represented by Beatrice Webb, among others, who as a member of the committee on the Machinery of Government helped to interrogate the permanent heads of departments, parliamentary secretaries and officials of all kinds. Beatrice Webb saw the permanent officials as 'fighting desperately for the control of their departments, against invading "interests" and interloping amateurs.' The guiding principle seemed to be for the new departments to be handed over to the most apposite interest groups. 'The Insurance Commission is controlled by the Shipowners, the Food Controller is a wholesale Grocer; the Ministry of Munitions is largely managed by representatives of the manufacturers . . . while a Duke's land-agent has been placed at the head of the Board of Agriculture . . . a Trade Union official is Minister of Labour . . . and . . . the distinguished University Professor – H. A. L. Fisher – [is] now President of the Board of Education.'[37] The supreme example of

handing over the government to interests came later, when Northcliffe was offered the position of Minister of Information but
declined on the ground that being a member of the government
would prejudice the standing of his newspapers. Thereupon
Beaverbrook took the position, while Northcliffe became Director
of Propaganda to enemy countries.

Wartime changes in the structure and practices of government
were accompanied by equally striking changes in higher policy.
The blockade had originally allowed normal trade to neutrals while
attempting to check the margin which might be supposed to be
destined for Germany. The Board of Trade was primarily concerned with maximising exports, while the Foreign Office occasionally asked for economic sanctions for diplomatic ends. The
lengthening perspectives of the war forced more drastic policies.
At the Economic Conference of the Allies at Paris, in June 1916,
comprehensive plans were agreed for post-war economic co-
operation aimed at diminishing German control over raw materials,
finance and trade on a global scale. This was a long step in the
direction of a new mercantilism.[38] A committee under the erstwhile
Unionist free trader Lord Balfour of Burleigh produced reports
on trade and industry which breathed the very spirit of mercantilism and protection.[39] Wartime revelations of the extent of German
dominance over vital British industries and interests, strategic
materials and international finance were usually spoken of as the
cause of this dramatic change of front. The unexpected duration
of the war and the unexpected importance of economic and financial resources in a war of attrition involved the State in the regulation of prices, wages and profits, the purchase of essential food-
stuffs and materials, the manipulation of foreign credit and the
centralised direction of railway companies, munition factories,
shipping, insurance, and much else. Economists had tended to
agree with Norman Angell's theory that war in modern conditions
of international commerce could not be sustained for more than a
few weeks or months at most.[40] But the striking success of the wartime rationalisation and control disclosed unimagined resources
of economic resilience and endurance through the agency of the
State. War experience also suggested that economic war-power had
to be nurtured in peace, agriculture being an obvious case in point.
Germany was seen as being so well prepared and organised for
economic warfare that it seemed dubious whether the Allies would
be able to enforce any worthwhile peace terms. 'What is really

needed', argued Carson, chairman of the War Cabinet's Economic Offensive Committee, 'is such a complete organisation among the Allies, for their mutual benefit, of all the raw materials and resources of the world, by the time the Peace Conference meets, that there is nothing left for the Germans to get . . .'[41] By the final years of the war the government, through scores of consultative boards and committees, was operating a mercantilist and State-socialist programme with world-wide ramifications.

The new structures of wartime government and the equally extraordinary fabric of State controls, mercantilism and secret diplomacy came into being without parliamentary consent, public discussion or endorsement by the major political parties. They were only dimly understood, and passively accepted *ex post facto*. In so far as they were supported by any particular party groups, these were the Unionist tariff reformers, the Milnerites, and the Fabians. Milner himself, and then Selborne, had chaired the agricultural committees which called for agricultural protection and compulsory powers over the use of land. Before he joined the War Cabinet, Milner had effected a link with the more nationalistic of the Labour leaders on the basis of a programme of State socialism.[42] 'My broad idea', he explained to Steel-Maitland just before the storm over Asquith's domestic policies burst, 'is: The State to cover all risks and pocket all windfalls in the promotion of essential industries . . . I want to bring the community in as a recognised third party in the settlement of this whole Capital and Labour business.' He described the State as 'a controlling and harmonising influence in the relations between capital and labour'.[43] Steel-Maitland had since September 1916 been involved on behalf of the Unionist party in detailed conferences with the Labour group which Milner had been patronising, and by August 1917 a comprehensive programme was finally agreed embodying all the essential features of wartime State socialism, but intended for peacetime. The programme was in harmony with existing practices, with the reports of the Reconstruction Committee, and even of the Unionist Social Reform Committee, and it was approved by Austen Chamberlain and Bonar Law as well as by the Tariff Reform League. It went down well when communicated to some thirty odd of the more progressive Unionist MPs, though it included such items as the State control of key commodities and services, State assistance to essential industries, State control and possible nationalisation of the railways, and the regulation of wages and prices. Industrial

protection, a policy which had been highly contentious before
the war, was thrown in as a mere corollary.[44] As Steel-Maitland
remarked to Bonar Law, the war had 'obliterated many old party
distinctions . . . new questions, new differences of opinion, new
groupings of men may arise . . .'[45]

It must have been almost inconceivable to the wartime reformers
in 1917 that the whole structure would fall to the ground in a
brief post-war boom for lack of political support. It would be far
easier to chronicle the unexpected flight back to the normal and
familiar if outdated practices of the pre-war period than to explain
it. However, the study of wartime politics would suggest some
reasons. The supporters of the new practices were mutually divided.
The Fabians led by the Webbs were keen participants in the Lloyd
George government's early work on the problems of 'Reconstruction', but the alienation of Labour from the government following
Henderson's resignation in 1917 and the wave of pacifism and
syndicalism which swept the Labour movement carried the Webbs
with it. One finds Beatrice Webb describing Milner as the head
of a British 'junker' party, and their manifestoes composed for the
Labour party dropped State socialism in favour of almost utopian
forms of decentralisation.[46] The Russian revolution had indeed
ended the wartime *rapprochement* between capital and labour,
socialism and nationalism. Labour was not prepared to support
the very policies which it carried later. This knocked the bottom
from Milner's design of a national and State-socialist party. Nor
did Lloyd George do anything to explain the constructive political
reforms and social policies of his government to the public. The
election of 1918 was supposed to be a wartime one and the
armistice took the politicians by surprise. Thereafter Lloyd George
was too preoccupied by the problems of peacemaking to keep a
grip on Parliament at home. His régime had slighted Parliament as
well as the hierarchies of Whitehall, and the massive stampede to
normality bears some comparison with the Restoration after the
Cromwellian period.

The results of the wartime interlude in government were more
contingent than direct. The most tangible was the Cabinet secretariat. With written minutes, ministers could no longer conveniently
forget half-baked decisions which proved unfeasible, and their
permanent heads could supply forms of words whose full implications their chiefs need not always understand. Government at the
centre was mechanised and could cope with more complexities, with

the result that it continued to interfere with the technical policies of departments. This was the basis for further developments which would permit the Prime Minister to assume more effective departmental control, usually through 'overlords'. As for the historic departments of State, their position was now compromised and new departments could be created without outraging tradition. The position of individual ministers was likewise subtly transmuted. Before 1914 ministers were never arbitrarily dismissed or changed once in office, and in only the most exceptional cases were they asked to resign. Manipulating ministers in office would have been an affront to Parliament. This tradition did not survive the war. Like the tradition of Liberal *laissez-faire* itself, it became a quaint nicety, dwarfed by wartime paradigms of massive and trenchant improvisation. It was in its destruction of political mythologies that the war had most impact.

9

Conscription and Society in Europe
before the War of 1914-18

V. G. KIERNAN

Between 1870 and 1914 industrial capitalism was establishing itself decisively over major areas of Europe. In the same period military preparations were being based, more widely than ever before, on compulsory service for all citizens, the principle of 'the nation in arms'. There may be good reason to surmise that these two things were not occurring together fortuitously, but that the great transformation could take place so smoothly – with no serious upheaval in any big industrial country like those of 1848 or 1871 in Paris – because the mass armies buttressed society with a firm framework. Like their predecessors they represented a reserve of armed force for maintenance of order; more novel and more important, they counteracted social discontents by 're-educating' youth, year by year, by taking over the strength of the masses and enlisting it on the conservative side. Like the often painful initiation rites of tribal life, or the young Buddhist's term of austere monastic duty, a spell with the colours became the introduction to manhood and membership of the community.

Conscription appears and reappears in world history in Protean forms, and is always a significant index of the society where it is found : to view it solely as a method of conducting wars is to see very little of it. In modern Europe it developed in the eastern lands, after an earlier reliance on foreign mercenary troops, in association with serfdom. In the west the great nation, France, was converted by the patriotic ardour of the Revolutionary wars from professionalism to a general levy of all citizens. Austria emulated the example after its defeat at Austerlitz in 1805, Prussia after Jena in 1806. This country was the hybrid between western and eastern

141

Europe; it was catching the germs of patriotism from the one just
as it began to mark itself off from the other by emancipating its
serfs. Later on it held more steadily to the principle of universal
service than France, which by allowing those who could afford it
to buy themselves off – as Austria ,and most others also did –
reverted in effect during the Second Empire to an army of long-
term professionals. It was this army that was defeated in 1870 by
Germany, now a 'nation in arms' on the Prussian model. Defeat
left the French in a mood to borrow Prussia's system, as Prussia
had once borrowed theirs. Italy followed suit in 1873 and Russia
in 1874, by way of prelude to a war with Turkey two years later.

What was happening was acceptance of a rule in appearance
egalitarian, so that it could seem a concession or accolade to
democracy; but if democracy was being legitimised it was also
being adulterated. These new arrays were very unlike the popular
militias, on the Swiss pattern, advocated by Rousseau[1] and a great
many nineteenth-century progressives (J. S. Mill among them),[2]
as providing for defence without peril to freedom and without
temptation to aggression. When Bismarck, Roon and Moltke were
preparing Prussia for war they thrust the *Landwehr* or militia into
the background and concentrated on the regular army. It was the
same Bismarck who, after his wars, gave the vote to all German
men but took precautions to render it harmless; in the same spirit
Alexander II had lately emancipated the Russian serfs, with due
care to ensure that no great loss was suffered by their masters.
There were some departures from equality in the armies themselves,
apart from the obvious class demarcation between officers and
privates. Avoidance of service by a money payment was abolished
in France in 1872, later than in Germany or Austria, but continued
in Belgium for another generation. Reduction of the term of
service for those with higher education was abolished in France in
1905, but continued in Germany. Everywhere a very large proportion of men liable to the call-up proved physically unfit; here it
was the ill-nourished poor who escaped rather than the better-off.

Subject to these various qualifications, it can correctly be said
that 'Conscription, compulsory education, and the right to vote
formed three pillars of the democratic state.'[3] And though within
the armies anything democratic was firmly ruled out, the hope
could still be indulged that there would be a more cautious and
responsible approach to international relations when a big war
would draw in the manhood of Europe instead of a few regular

soldiers. To a fire-eater like General von Bernhardi, indeed, this seemed so probable that he feared it would lead to decadent think-ing about war as barbarous;[4] the new militarism suffered from sundry inner contradictions like this. There really was a long peace among the great powers, from 1871 to 1914, favourable to the economic expansion in progress, which must have owed a good deal to this factor. As time went on mass involvement came, like atom bombs with us, to be familiar and taken for granted. But there was at first much uncertainty among governments about how their subjects would react to a declaration of war.

There were misgivings among the respectable about the whole plan of training everybody to arms. Their grand watchword, Order, might be said to find its apotheosis in a country's transformation into an armed camp; on the other hand, this meant putting weapons into the hands of the poor, and the shadow of the Com-mune lay for long across respectable Europe. A pessimist in Belgium argued that to let the poor compel the well-off to serve beside them in the forces would be to invite further pressures in the direction of collectivism; to which a War Minister replied that it would be ruinous if the well-off went on buying exceptions and left the forces to be filled with proletarians.[5] One argument of Bloch, the anti-war Polish banker, was that conscription made war too grave a risk : working classes under socialist influence would be mobilised *en masse*, and there would be no knowing how to disband them again at the end – worse cataclysms than the Commune were to be expected.[6] He must have been expressing what many of his class felt when he wrote of 'the long service of the professional soldier' as a safer insurance.[7] Europe was shooting Niagara when it em-barked on this policy, more dramatically than England when it gave votes to Demos.

Yet Bloch felt that, by the 1890s, the opinion had come to prevail everywhere except in Britain 'that great armies are the sup-port of government, that only great armies will deliver the existing order from the perils of anarchism, and that military service acts beneficently on the masses by teaching discipline, obedience and order.'[8] Armies were offering themselves, some more seriously than others, as Europe's teachers and guides, as well as defenders. Need-less to say, the ordinary conservative thought of their teaching as a process of breaking in. Countless men of property must have said to countless young men, as the landowner in Pavese's novel says to the argumentative carpenter's son : 'I'd like to see how you get on when you're called up. They'll knock some of the nonsense out of you in the regiment.'[9] More subtly too, where schools were capable of indoctrination, as in Germany, the army could round off their work; where they were not, it could make up for some of their deficiencies, and also for those of the churches. Britain's industrial, like its 'bourgeois', revolution came very early and could take place under religious auspices. Churches were still powerful in the peasant purlieus of Europe, but even there diminishingly, and in the rapidly swelling industrial areas they were impotent. Mass conscription supplied them with a captive congregation and numerous posts for chaplains, and allowed all the jarring creeds to take their first steps in oecumenism.

Peasants everywhere continued to provide the bulk of recruits; in the industrialising countries, ostensibly because of their better physique, though it may be surmised that there was also at work a preference for rustics as more tractable. They, it could be hoped, would be ready to let themselves be used, if need arose, to overawe mutinous towns. For the peasants, even in darkest Russia, the change from long service for a few to short service for all represented an amelioration. In less benighted lands army service could be seen as a means of civilising the yokel, just as the otherwise abominable conscription of Indians in the Peru of that age could be credited with giving them a sort of introduction to the modern world.[10] Von Papen drew a picture doubtless idealised but not altogether false in his reminiscences of army life at Düsseldorf. 'The families of the Rhenish and Westphalian peasants, who made up most of our strength, were glad to let their sons serve in the Army. They were taught habits of punctuality, good behaviour, cleanliness and a sense of duty, which made them better members of the community.'[11] By this cluster of virtues both their parents and their employers might benefit.

But the critical new force in the developing regions was the working class. Army service may be supposed to have acted as one of its recruiting agents, by helping to shake young men loose from their villages and leading them to settle in the towns, and the experience both of handling modern equipment and of being handled by the drill-sergeant would make them more welcome to industrialists. Likewise, where there was a competently organised military system, the new race of industrial workers might, in spite of their more sophisticated mentality, fit into it more readily than the peasant. They were more accustomed to being away from home. Regiment and factory were each other's counterpart, each with a daily routine based on an exact timetable and a hierarchy of command, in a combination specific to Europe and unapproached by any other civilisation; in America it was being carried further still on the industrial side, with the Ford conveyor-belt running parallel to the Schlieffen Plan. All recruits had the experience of working a couple of years for nothing but their keep, the zero wage that was every employer's ideal standard. After this, very modest pay might look more acceptable. Above all, they were accustomed to obeying orders. For the nervous bourgeoisie, chronically uneasy lest the factory proletariat it was creating should prove a Frankenstein's monster, this was a great reassurance.

Regimentation of the factory on quasi-military lines was a pipe-dream of many philosophers of pessimism, Carlyle, Nietzsche, Spengler, as well as of businessmen like the elder Krupp.[12] Conversely, the more industry grew the more its rationality and organising talent permeated the army. In Germany Bernhardi could assert what could not be said, for instance, in Spain, that army life did wonders for a townsman's health.[13] It was reckoned indeed that two years with the colours could add five years to the German working man's life;[14] on this basis it might even be calculated that conscription did more to prolong the sum of German existence than the Great War to reduce it. Bernhardi wanted the workers fit and well to do their jobs as well as to fight; he was against shorter factory hours, declaring that work is 'the greatest blessing which man knows'.[15] How pervasive was the spirit of the age may be seen, at an opposite pole, in Trotsky's scheme for organising trades unions and labour in Red Russia on military lines.

Thanks to the Revolution the French officer corps was mostly middle-class and professional, with an oil-and-vinegar admixture of aristocracy. In the other big armies the aristocratic contingent still kept the upper hand. In control of the army it had a bastion of class power; for the more earnest-minded a truly national army offered also the satisfaction of regaining a valid social function, of being integrated once more with the nation : a nation refined into the *corpus mysticum* of the army, a partnership, like Burke's State, in every virtue. Universal service by multiplying the number of officers required brought a gradual infiltration of the corps by newcomers from the middle class : in Prussia this was happening from 1860, and in Germany by 1913 reduced the noble share from 65 to 30 per cent.[16] At the same time, however, bourgeois Germany was undergoing the curious 'feudalisation' that has struck historians. There and over most of the Continent the middle classes had abandoned any direct struggle for power and turned to the round-about mode of building a golden bridge, of piling up money. Any social group that allows itself to be turned aside like this from its historical path is denatured and liable to succumb to ideas foreign to it.

It was in great part by coming forward as educator of the masses in respect for order and property that the army was winning the esteem of a bourgeoisie formerly hostile to it. In striving to convert the masses it was aided by its aristocratic outlook, enabling officers to affect, and in some degree to feel, an impartiality between rich and poor. Altogether these new-style national armies could be practical exercises in class collaboration, as champions of universal service seem to have reckoned from the start. In England the ritual of sport performed a similar function : its symbolic figure was Edward VII leading in his own Derby winner, amid applause of high and low. In the more advanced countries on the Continent the classes met under the colours, like well-chaperoned young men and women at a ball. This applies best of all to Germany, the classic land in Europe, as Japan was in Asia, of headlong indus-trialisation contained within a framework bequeathed by a feudal past. Only in these two countries and in France (apart from Switzerland with its militia) did universal service become a truly national institution, an essential part of public life; for eastern Europe it was too modern, for Britain and Scandinavia, as for the USA, too archaic.

'Anybody could rule this country,' said George. '*I* could rule it.' Jerome's three men on their bummel were impressed by the way that, even when back in civil life, the German remained a soldier, looking up to the policeman as his officer and mentor; and they noted how the schoolroom paved the way for the camp by its 'ever-lasting teaching of duty', in other words 'blind obedience to every-thing in buttons'.[17] In 1906 the man who was ruling Germany discoursed lengthily to a British diplomat on 'the advantages of militarism to the youth of the country and on its popularity in Germany'.[18] It sounds as if William appreciated clearly enough that the system was at least as vital for keeping the people quiet as for keeping the frontiers secure. This meant in the first place keep-ing Germany secure for Hohenzollerns and Junkers. Against the corrosions of industrial society, its 'wide-sweeping inanimate agencies and mechanical procedures', an injection of warlike ideas was, as Veblen pointed out, the best safeguard.[19] Francis Joseph instinctively protected himself against modernity by scarcely ever in his long life appearing except in uniform, like a knight of old never laying aside his armour.

In the second place the army had to extend its patronage and protection to the new capitalist class; and it could do so more successfully because it stood, or seemed to stand, outside the realm of capitalist greeds and offered an alternative to them. A concept of the army as a school of national virtue went back to the early nineteenth-century reformers and now, as then, but on a far greater scale, the country was undergoing transformation, amid which the army had a reassuring fixity like Wordsworth's mountain 'familiar with forgotten years'. Nowhere else had civic and private qualities been so closely enmeshed with it as in Prussia, which unlike Rome had no senate as an alternative focus. 'The voice of our national conscience', William's toady Prince Bülow could unctuously write, 'tells us what German militarism really is : the best thing we have achieved in the course of our national development as a State and as a people.'[20]

Nowhere else, correspondingly, did army service and industrialisation fit more closely together, each reinforcing the other. By damping down class tensions the army conferred a gift on the bourgeois Liberals that did at least as much as his unification of Germany to reconcile them to Bismarck, and turned them into National Liberals as socialists were later to be turned into National Socialists. In Prussia serfdom had been abolished from above, by reformist aristocrats, not from below by revolt. Ever since 1525 Germany had known no such fundamental class conflict as France in 1789, 1848, and 1871; and this left open a broad ground for Hohenzollern and Junker to occupy as arbiters. They could in some practical measure fulfil what in England was only a Carlylean or Disraelian fantasy of aristocracy coming forward to befriend and lead a bewildered mass of workers. Conscription and Bismarck's welfare programme were two sides of the same flag : one showed the young man how powerful was the State and how limitless its claim on him, the other showed him how much the State could do for him.

Bülow was drawing a very rosy picture of the officer corps and bestowing heavy flattery on bourgeois self-esteem, when he described it as a meritocracy, 'formed from members of the intellectually superior classes'.[21] But his picture was not altogether fanciful, especially if one looked back at the victors of 1866 and 1870, at a time when their class, the smaller nobility or gentry, was still untouched by the contact with plutocracy which bred Mammon-worship in the army later on. In those days they really were 'a military community of a very unusual kind'.[22] They had some affinities with the Teutonic Knights, Prussia's first crusading founders. A Guards officer of the bluest blood might dine for six-pence and deny himself a penny cup of coffee.[23] Such an army could present itself as a truer version of socialism than any preached by the agitators outside.

'The contact between officers and other ranks was very close', von Papen wrote of his early army life, 'and although discipline was strict, a human relationship was built up that lasted all our lives'.[24] It was only with soldiers, or servants, that his class – like the British in India – could find a 'human relationship' now. Reality was of course often less idyllic, and tyrannical officers of the type common further east were by no means unknown. In 1892 Engels hugged himself over the appearance in the socialist press of a royal corps-commander's condemnation of ill-treatment of privates.[25] On the eve of the Great War the Prussian Minister of War, General von Falkenhayn, had to stress that recent episodes of the same sort had 'brought the Army and its institutions under heavy attack'.[26] Yet there was a sufficient number of more responsible men to give these institutions a strong flavour of paternalism; an attitude still more marked in the Japanese officer caste, and quite absent from a British army whose privates were merely odds and ends from the poorest working class, or from the Irish peasantry, enlisted for pay.

'Belief in a mission of popular education may be ascribed to the German officers' corps as a general conviction.'[27] It was a regular duty, General von Eichhorn reminded officers of his 18th Corps in 1909 in a highly revealing circular, to conduct political instruc-tion, to mould their men into 'loyal subjects'. 'The young soldier's mind', he urged, 'is normally like a piece of wax on which every sort of impression can be made. Many, of course, have already been infected by Social-Democracy before they were called; but they are young, their sickness is only superficial, and their service with the colours must work like a healing spring, and wash the sickness out of their system.' What was paramount, he added, was the need to win their confidence. 'The men must be convinced that the officer is their best friend, and that what he says is true and right.'[28] A quotation from *Hamlet* follows; this commander was far from illiterate, in spite of his mixed metaphors. But here, as in many other ways, the implications of this whole epoch can be seen carried to their grotesquely logical conclusion in National Socialism.

It was the consensus of respectable opinion 'that the habit of obedience to constituted authority acquired in the army . . . formed the best possible guarantee against the undue spread of socialistic doctrine.' In uniform men learned 'the hopelessness of armed resistance', while later they learned 'the substantial advantages that accrued to them personally from their previous connection with the services'. When, during the 1880s, the army intake was allowed to drop, it was found that men who had not been through the ranks were less acceptable to employers, tended to be unemployed, and hence to turn socialist. To remedy this it was decided in 1893 to shorten the term and increase the number.[29] Yet in 1911 Bernhardi was bitterly complaining that only about half the able-bodied men available were being called up and that the big towns were being neglected; universal service was being abandoned to the French. 'Opinion oscillates between the wish to enforce it more or less, and the disinclination to make the required outlay.'[30] Dislike of tax burdens must have been a real obstacle. Some of the wealthier may have been coming to feel by this time, after decades with none of the dreaded workers' outbreaks, that insurance against socialism could be obtained more cheaply. The army's own sense of its educating mission is likely to have been weakened by the dwindling of the aristocratic element, still more of its old Spartan standards. Besides all this there was the fact that nobles, still holding many key posts in the army, were unwilling to have the officer cadre further diluted by middle-class entrants, as would inevitably happen if the army were brought up to full strength. This feudal prejudice may have cost it three corps, and with them perhaps the failure to reach Paris in 1914.[31] Here is another glimpse of the many contradictions besetting the task of turning a class society into an armed nation.

In France the bloodthirsty suppression of the Commune made a rift hard to overcome. It was carried out by the old professional army, whose triumph over the people added to its failure against the Prussians made it so obnoxious that something else had to be put in its place. The new army set up in 1872 was more egalitarian than the German; happily for France, there was nothing paternalistic about it. This was a bourgeois country, dedicated to rugged individualism, yet at the same time one of inadequate industrial development. Barrack conditions were rough and ready; so, when the Great War came, were medical services, as in Napoleon's day. Habits of colonial conquest and of drilling or dragooning native troops helped to fix the army's character; though it was to the more intelligent officers familiar with colonial problems, such as Lyautey, that the thought of the officer as educator was likeliest to occur.

To the young Frenchman, by contrast with the German, his spell with the colours was commonly a mere blank, or interruption of life, a disagreeable duty to be got through as best might be. To the propertied classes the masses remained for long an unknown quantity; at the outset many must have distrusted general military training as much as Thiers did, regarding it as a rebirth of Jacobinism, a desperate expedient forced on them and other ruling classes by the necessity of not seeming less patriotic than the German. Uncertainty about how a swollen factory proletariat would behave may explain in part the sluggish growth of industry, the preference of capital for foreign investment. For straightforward use as an armed police the new army could not be reckoned as reliable as the old one. It was favourite doctrine with the Kaiser that the soldier must be ready to fire on his closest relatives at the word of command. But when, at Fourmies in 1891, French troops were ordered to fire on a crowd in the marketplace, some officers refused to repeat the order, most of the men fired in the air, some did not fire at all: one, Lebon, 'because his mother might have been in the crowd', and his captain upheld him.[32] There was all the more need to make the army a support to order by the other, more oblique means of using it to fill the public with fear and hatred of the national enemy, pride in empire, and thirst for glory.

In nineteenth-century Spain when Liberals were in power a National Militia, where all were supposed to serve, existed side by side with a force of conscripts serving for a fairly long term (eventually eight years). Democrats wanted to abolish this regular army altogether; conservatives when in power suppressed the militia. Selective conscription, with substitution allowed to those who could afford to pay, was restored after the stormy days of the First Republic in 1874. It continued to do well enough for a repressive government as a gendarmerie, but the army could acquire no national appeal because its purpose was too blatantly obvious: except for colonial rebels there was no external enemy in sight. As to shepherding the new working class into the national fold, it faced the special disadvantage that industry was located chiefly in the national minority regions, Basque or Catalan, where conscription was a further goad to regional feeling. It was a special levy of conscripts for Morocco in 1912 that provoked a general strike at Barcelona and Spain's 'Tragic Week'.

When Italy went in for general conscription in 1873, it was by way of a facile substitute for the nation-building programme needed to turn its formal political unification into a living reality; soldiers from different provinces were put together in the same units. In the industrialising north military service could have some of its normative influence; for the most part it was simply one more burden on the peasantry, and the south, to which Piedmontese rule was foreign rule, could not be roused to much indignation against either of the indispensable 'national foes' dangled by turns before it, Austria and France. The rational reluctance of Italians to fight for their rulers in either of the two world wars was foreshadowed by their inclination to evade military training, by desertion or emigration. It required 'superhuman efforts', a senator lamented, to get conscription established in Sicily, and then it was largely undone by so many Sicilians flocking abroad.[33] A law of 1888 sought to prevent men below the age of 32 from leaving Italy; it had little success.

'That the English have no universal military service is one of the shortcomings of English culture,' wrote Treitschke, finding fault with their vulgar addiction to games and athletics instead of to 'noble arms'.[34] There were some demands for conscription from army men, others from conservatives whose motives seemed transparent to one of their critics : 'They do not mention the foe within; but he is in their minds much more than the foe without. A drilled and disciplined proletariat is their hope against an insurgent democracy.'[35] Long after that date, in April 1970, a local survey of opinion reported a majority in favour of a return to conscription, chiefly on the ground that a spell of strict discipline would do young men good. Here the social calculation can be seen long outlasting any argument of military utility.

By imposing conscription on Italians and Germans Napoleon did much to turn Europe against him; when Britain had to adopt conscription in 1916, Irish bitterness was redoubled. In general, if the system helped to counteract socialism in the advanced countries, it helped to worsen one of the gravest problems of the more backward, that of national minorities. In Russia this was displayed on a vaster scale than in Spain and more intensely than in the

Habsburg empire. The Ottoman empire, which counted its subjects
by religion, not nationality, was safer while it adhered to its time-
honoured usage of conscripting only Muslims and making others
pay an extra tax. Backward Turkey was ahead of Europe in treating army duty as a badge of honour instead of a hardship. When
the Young Turks seized power in 1909 and in the name of equality
and fraternity extended the privilege to Christians, they only made
their Christian subjects more eager to see the end of the empire.

Elsewhere in eastern Europe the practice had for a long time
been selective conscription of peasants, for very long terms : in the
Russia of Nicholas I twenty-five years, or virtually for life. The
longer soldiers were kept away from their old homes and ties, the
more blindly obedient they became and the more easily employed on
their chief business, keeping the people down. Where a peasantry
was being reduced to serfdom, or otherwise broken in, conscription
had punitive uses in place of educational. A recalcitrant peasant
would be disposed of by being drafted into the army, in much the
same way as in Russia his lord might have him removed to Siberia.
In Sweden in the seventeenth century the lord's power to rid himself of an individual in this way was a valuable means of subduing
the whole class, by depriving it of leaders.[36] In Denmark, for half
a century from 1735, peasants were chosen for the militia by their
landlords; this was far less onerous, but extremely unpopular nevertheless, so that here again a strong weapon was placed in the landowner's hand. In Austria the government or its local representatives
were empowered to put any suspected trouble-maker on the army
roll without more ado; service was perpetual. Good use was made
of this in 1790 when there was peasant agitation to be dealt with.[37]
So good an idea was sure to strike other masters far away. During
Venezuela's wars of independence we hear of a Negro slave sent
into the army because he was too independent for his owner's
liking.[38]

In Russia links between conscription and the spread of serfdom
were close, and hatred of army enrolment helped to fan peasant
resistance. To the non-Russian peoples of the empire it was a special
grievance, most of all when they did not share the Orthodox
religion which gave the Tsarist army most of its moral cement.
This was especially the case with the Jews, for whose benefit conscription took the highly educational turn of an attempt to
Christianise and Russify them.[39] For a régime so primitive as the
Tsarist, the change to a modern national army was bound to be,

as for Turkey, a hazardous experiment. 'The Russians . . . have adopted a system of universal liability to service for which they are not civilised enough,' wrote Engels.[40] 'And then, where to find officers for so many in a country without a bourgeoisie?'[41]

Russia in fact possessed neither a mature middle class, such as gave the French officer corps its professionalism, nor a genuine aristocracy, such as gave the German its paternalism. With class conflict smouldering in the countryside, landlord officers and peasant recruits were unlikely to meet in brotherly harmony. For winning over or neutralising the discontented workman this army was even less well qualified; high-handed treatment of workmen in the ranks, and in the navy where more of them were required, by their *high-well-born* officers only exasperated them further. One of the Tsar's reasons for proposing a peace conference and reduction of armaments was that more artillery would call for more skilled craftsmen in the army, whose loyalty could not be relied on.[42] This clumsy, inert force could still be massively employed, as the French and probably the German could not, for crushing internal revolt, as in 1905–6; but it was as ill-equipped for anything like 'moral rearmament' as for fighting artillery battles. In 1917 the weakest link at which the chain of Tsarist authority snapped was the army.

Resistance to conscription was everywhere on a small scale. It was proof of the power the modern State had built up that it could enforce what Tolstoy called a condition of slavery with 'a degree of humiliation and submission incomparably worse than any slavery of the ancient world.'[43] Defiance needed the convictions of a group to nerve it; this was nearly always a religious body, and in a series of countries there were small sects whose members refused to serve. In Russia the Doukhobors, spiritual descendants of the old Ana-baptists, did so; the government retaliated brutally.[44] Tolstoy made himself the mouthpiece of protest, and conscription became one of his main indictments against Tsarism. He argued that the way to prevent war was not any artificial device such as an international tribunal, but a simple refusal to put on uniform.[45]

Tolstoy tried to demonstrate that even the physical risks incurred by refusal were smaller than those of army life and war. He may have been right, but it was not an argument that would embolden many individuals to challenge their rulers. For this a strong positive faith was needed. Religion being overwhelmingly on the side of Caesar, the alternative was socialism, which however was not prepared, like some of the religious minorities, for direct action against conscription, but relied on the gradual effect of its anti-war campaigning. Tolstoy and the socialists may each be said to have seen some weaknesses of the other's approach. He taxed the workers with 'participation in murder', because they 'either consent or pay the taxes for the army or become soldiers themselves, regarding such action as quite normal.'[46] The time to oppose general conscription may have been when it was new and unfamiliar. But in Prussia it was much older than socialism, older than the working class itself, which was born inside its prison; and the longer it went on anywhere the more mechanically it came to be identified with patriotism and civic duty.

Socialist inaction early on must be explained partly by illusions about its 'democratic' nature, its resemblances to the 'national militia' type of defence force. It might again be hoped that, by being subjected for only a year or two to army control, the masses would be inflamed by it, not tamed; that the ruling groups of Europe were digging their own graves by teaching their subjects how to fight. At the end of 1888, when Boulanger seemed on the verge of power in France, with no visible programme except a march on Berlin, Paul Lafargue wrote to Engels: 'War today means the people in arms; and that is what Conservatives of every kind dread.'[47] Three months later he added: 'Perhaps the declaration of war will usher in the revolutionary era. War means the people armed. In Paris and in many other towns there will be uprisings.'[48] This looks in retrospect a romantic vision. Yet his expectations must have been nervously shared by many of the bourgeoisie, and may have been less unrealistic then than they were later. If so, Europe's rulers were well advised to postpone their rupture for so long, until another quarter-century of the drill-ground had done its work.

'The army has become the main purpose of the State', Engels wrote in *Anti-Dühring*, 'and an end in itself.'[49] It was not quite this, if we allow for its social utility. But Engels suffered from no illusion about war being a godsend to socialism. Weighing the chances in 1889, the certain horrors 'against what slender hope there is that this ferocious war results in revolution – this is what horrifies me.' And if revolution broke out in France, Russia would join with Germany to crush it.[50] The mass armies stood ready to 'restore order' in other lands, not only in their own, as they were to attempt to do in Russia after 1917. Engels wanted a militia instead of a regular army, quoting with approval a dictum that the Republic in France, or democracy, 'will always be in danger so long as every worker does not have his own Lebel rifle and fifty cartridges'.[51] This became the standard socialist thesis. In 1891 Kautsky and Bernstein, admitting that at present 'the disbanding of standing armies is utterly impossible', proposed 'conversion of the standing armies to citizen armies'.[52] In France Jaurès, ardent advocate of peace as well as – unlike the Marxian socialists – ardent patriot, made himself the spokesman of the idea. In 1907 it was endorsed by international socialism at the Stuttgart congress.

It may not have been altogether beside the point to ask whether citizen armies or militias would really be immune from the infection of chauvinism, as enthusiasts like Jaurès believed.[53] The experiment, in any case, was not tried by any big country. In the meantime, Engels may have set an example of being too hopeful that a rising tide of radicalism would exorcise the spirit that the armies were seeking to instil in their men. Jubilant over some successful demonstrations in France, he wrote: 'These bloodless victories are an excellent way of accustoming the soldier to the supremacy and infallibility of the popular masses.'[54] This was allowing too little for the moral or psychological influence of the drill-ground. Engels was one of curiously few leading socialists, in that militarising age, to have worn uniform himself, but that was long ago and he had been out of personal contact with his countrymen for many years. He was impressed by the more favourable aspect of army training, the methodical habits it helped to impart to the German workers' movement. 'Our organisation is perfect – the admiration and despair of our opponents . . . our military training and discipline is invaluable.'[55] These are qualities any serious movement demands (just as a factory does, and Engels had been a mill-owner as well as a soldier), and he was always critical of inefficiency, of which he observed a great deal in French left-wing activity. Ultimately, however, the beneficiary would be the employer, yearly receiving his contingent of workers ready for factory routine, instead of socialism – not Spartacus but Noske.

Tolstoy had a clearer sense of how young men, 'thanks to artful discipline, elaborated during centuries – are inevitably transformed in one year into submissive tools in the hands of the authorities.'[56] Conscription was, as he said, a form of slavery and shared its *infantilising* impact, most extreme on those of stunted mental growth like the East Prussian or Russian peasantry. 'No man, whatever his political convictions, who is serving in the army, and has been subjected to that hypnotic breaking in, which is called discipline, can, whilst in the ranks, avoid obeying commands, just as an eye cannot avoid winking when a blow is aimed at it.'[57] Training, mostly drilling and marching, had as its cardinal aim the total absorption of the individual in the uniformed mass, a submission akin to the blind faith exacted by religion. Carried over from the past into an epoch when new weapons were rendering it obsolete, it was justified by its social function of licking a whole male population into shape as professional armies had been.

In most recruits, in the more developed countries, there would be a more positive, emotional response as well. It is hard for the individual to go on feeling at odds with the life round him, and the more so when this is as close and all-enveloping as an army's; the most reluctant would be impelled to come to terms with it. He would learn to hug his chains, if they were as decently gilded as they were in Germany, so as not to feel galled by them or go through his term chafing at the drudgery and despotism to which he was subjected. Once he accepted his lot he could let himself be drilled into a warrior, into a collective *raptus*, as the savage dances himself into ardour for the fight or the hunt, or a dervish into a fit of mystic rapture. Mimic battle could take on the quality of a game. Annual manoeuvres in Germany, presided over by the All-Highest and wound up by his favourite *coup de théâtre* of a grand cavalry charge, might be poor preparation for actual warfare, but excellent for the results on participants. One of the young soldiers we meet early on in *All Quiet on the Western Front*, seated on their commodes out in the balmy summer air, is not quite sure whether the Kaiser ever has to visit the lavatory.

If on common days of the week a man suffered from his army boots (which were playing havoc with Europe's feet), his easiest consolation was grumbling at the villainous foreigners whose fault it was that he had to go clumping about in them. Thus army life intensified that diversion of discontents outwards against foreign bogies that was so large a part of Europe's adaptation to this traumatic period of social transition. Altogether, the average individual would come out of it more firmly integrated in the national collective. It would be of interest to know how many socialists whose faith remained militant had, for medical or other reasons, been spared the brainwashing of the barracks. Of those young men who most feared or resented the prospect of service, a good many avoided it by emigrating, as Italians did in such numbers. Emigration, temporary or permanent, was a more engrained habit in Italy than anywhere else, and socialists of Mussolini's generation often turned to it on principle. It was to escape conscription that many of the Russian Jews who poured into England in the late nineteenth century left home.[58] An enquiry among 131 immigrants in the USA showed that 18 of them – 5 Russians and 13 Greeks – had crossed the sea for the same reason.[59] Several states besides Italy sought to prevent this by legislation; but it probably did more to ease the system by providing a safety-valve than to make the men who stayed at home less willing to go through the mill.

'A really national army unites all the citizens of the country', wrote Treitschke.[60] It was a security against class war, that is, but sooner or later the price might have to be a foreign war. When 1914 duly came it was naïve of those who approved of the military system simply for its peacetime benefits to feel astonished and indignant. Lichnowsky accused an irresponsible Hohenzollern of perverting 'militarism, which by rights is an education for the people and an instrument of policy', to purposes of aggression.[61] It always had to have international tension to sustain it; as Tolstoy said, governments could have no wish for their quarrels to end and would invent fresh ones if the old ones vanished, because there was no doing without them as 'a pretext for keeping up the army upon which their power is based.'[62] Those issues, looked back on today, often seem ludicrously trivial; under cover of them aggressive aims, older or newer, were developing which had nothing to do with the basic function of the military system, the preservation of social order.

As Chekov noted, there was a type of officer, common in the home of Russian roulette, who craved for war as a distraction. 'The idle, so-called governing, classes cannot remain long without war. When there is no war they are bored.'[63] To the more earnest type, far commoner in Germany, army life could be fully satisfying in itself. It was a German, Colonel von Schwarzhoff, who undertook the defence of the spiritual values of militarism at the first Hague Conference.[64] Yet any officer corps must be conscious, like Napoleon, of the need to *chauffer la gloire*, to win fresh laurels, from time to time. It ceases to command respect if it never does any fighting, wears no medals earned under fire; to say nothing of the sluggishness of promotion. The peace before 1914 was already embarrassingly long-drawn and made at least sabre-rattling obligatory. Moreover, while the middle class learned to ape the warlike deportment of its superiors, the Junker caste was acquiring a relish for bourgeois fleshpots. Two social elements were mingling in a compound far more combustible than either by itself. With Treitschke's disciples preaching war as the only antidote to national decay, and Bernhardi pressing the views of the more bellicose soldiers, the chimney-barons' imagination – notably but not only in Germany – might well be fired and set them thinking of their own growing strength and that of the army, wondering what windfall gains of markets, materials and empire the two together might not yield.

Ironically, national antagonisms were being fanned in order to justify the existence of armies of a type poorly suited to fight the war they were likely to bring about. There was some half-comprehension of this among professional officers, who were nowhere genuinely eager to have to deal with all the manpower offered them. Their talk of 'nations in arms' was more rhetoric, designed to keep the people in the right frame of mind, than sober planning. In particular the French generals, with their smaller population and greater fear of civilian criticism, were (as Jaurès complained) banking on a short war, to be fought chiefly with the 'barracks army', the troops immediately available, whose term was extended in 1912 to three years.[65] They must have expected these to be more docile, as well as in better trim, than recruits called back after years of exposure to the contagions of civil life. To the extent that the public was aware of this design, universal service would become a far lesser deterrent to war. Each age-group in turn took its risk of war breaking out while it was with the colours : after that it could expect to be well away from the firing-line. When the war turned out to be quite literally a conflict of peoples in arms, in the more modern countries the long decades of drilling proved their worth by leaving the millions ready conditioned to endure the ordeal, if they also dictated in advance its primitiveness. The more worm-eaten political structures collapsed. Capitalism survived and flourished where it was already strong, but its hinterland of eastern Europe was lost.

10

Religion and Nationality in the Mid-Victorian Army

H. J. HANHAM

The British army has always adopted an instrumental view of religion. Religious services, and especially those of the established church, have been valued as a contribution to the morale (and hence the good order) of the army. Prayer has been deemed efficacious in propitiating the God of battles. Church parades have helped to keep the rank and file spick and span. And even chaplains, though accepted reluctantly, have been thought to have their everyday uses – in comforting the sick, in burying the dead, in writing letters for the illiterate, and in keeping the Other Ranks under watchful surveillance.

The army has never been much interested in doctrine, perhaps in reaction against what it has always considered the religious excesses of the Cromwellian army. Its ideal form of service has been the Prayer Book of the Church of England and its ideal sermon a brief morale-building exhortation. Its chaplains have been expected to display the downright no-nonsense attitude towards spiritual matters which is supposed to mark the practical man, and which is sometimes hard to distinguish from worldliness. Many of them have been drawn from families with military traditions and some have been former regular officers. They have not usually been very influential, nor have they usually been effective preachers. For preaching the army has usually looked outside its own ranks, to occasional visitors and to preachers at neighbouring churches. These preachers have, however, always been watched attentively for any sign of unorthodox or seditious views. Indeed, in the course of the 1880s the Queen's Regulations were specially amended to

take account of seditious language preached, the fear being of
Irish nationalists rather than socialists :

Whenever seditious or inflammatory language is made use of during
the service in any place of worship not under military control, the
senior officer present will use his discretion in withdrawing the troops
with as little interruption as possible, and marching them back to their
quarters; or, if circumstances render it desirable, Officers Commanding
will prevent their men from attending divine service if such language
is likely to be used in sermons.[1]

Late in 1850, Lord John Russell, then Prime Minister, launched a
characteristically hasty and ill-judged attack on Roman Catholicism
and Anglo-Catholicism. In a public letter to the Bishop of Durham
he was ostensibly concerned simply to denounce the Vatican
decision to confer English territorial titles on the Roman Catholic
hierarchy already at work in England – the so-called 'Papal aggression'. But he launched out as well into a eulogy of 'the glorious
principles and the immortal martyrs of the Reformation', a reaffirmation of the principle that 'No foreign prince or potentate
[i.e. the Pope] will be permitted to fasten his fetters upon [the]
nation', and a deunciation of 'the mummeries of superstition',
which had been revived by members of the Church of England.[2]
For a brief moment it seemed as though a wave of intolerance
was passing over the country, but the tide of Protestant enthusiasm soon ebbed, leaving Lord John lamely protesting that
he meant no offence to what he insultingly called 'loyal Roman
Catholics'.[3]

The Peelites were particularly affronted by Lord John's outburst,
because it seemed both to have lowered the tone of public debate
and to have been intended as an attack on their High Church
colleague Gladstone. Sir James Graham, writing to Sidney Herbert,
was full of indignation.

Lord John's letter [to the Bishop of Durham] was hasty, intemperate,
and ill-advised. He sought to catch some fleeting popularity at the
expense of the principles of his political life; and in his eagerness to
strike a blow at 'Gladstonism', he forgot that the 'superstitious mummeries' which he enumerates are part of the creed of one-half of the
British Army, and of eight millions of his fellow-subjects [the Irish].[4]

Sir James Graham was a successful administrator, who usually
tried to get his facts right. If he believed that half of the army
consisted of Roman Catholics, and, by implication, of Irishmen,

then others must have done so too. But was Graham right in thinking that the army was so unrepresentative of British society as a whole?

In 1830, when Graham first entered the Cabinet, his description of the army would have done well enough. There were then many more Irishmen in the infantry than there were Englishmen, and the number of English and Irish non-commissioned officers and men in the army as a whole was very much the same. This did not mean that the Irish constituted fifty per cent of the army, because there were Scots to be taken into account, but it did mean that the Irish constituted 42.2 per cent of the army.[5] Given the immense popularity of O'Connell's repeal movement, that was an alarming proportion, because it meant that a substantial section of the army had to be regarded as at least potentially disloyal and unsuited for employment in Ireland. Ten years later, in 1840, the Irish were still as numerous in the infantry as they had been in 1830, but the proportion of Irishmen in the army had declined to 37.2 per cent. There is a gap in the published figures between 1840 and 1868, but when they resume they show a further decline in the Irish share of the army to 30.8 per cent. And from then on the proportion of Irishmen gradually dropped to 12.2 per cent in 1896.[6] The late-Victorian army was always predominantly English.

Army statistics must be viewed with the same sort of caution as other nineteenth-century statistics, but those relating to nationality appear to be in line with all the other evidence. The statistics of religious denominations published after 1861 are entirely consistent with those for nationality down to the 1880s, if it is assumed that Roman Catholics can be identified with Irishmen. During the 1880s and 1890s the number of Catholics was somewhat higher than the number of Irish, but that is presumably to be explained by the fact that the army had begun to recruit a larger number of English-born children of Irish Catholic parentage. The correctness of the regimental returns on which the published statistics were based is also borne out by the reports of the Fenians who infiltrated the army in 1865–7 and the proceedings of courts martial set up to try Fenian soldiers. Certainly, even at their most optimistic, the Fenian leaders never claimed that Irish soldiers constituted one half of the army. All that they wanted was 'a large body of trained fighting men' whose loss would weaken and demoralise the British army.[7]

Though the proportion of Irish and Roman Catholic soldiers steadily declined over the years, Ireland throughout the nineteenth

century supplied more than its share of the army (see table below).
It is not clear, however, that there was anything special about
Ireland that made the Irish particularly keen to enlist. Rather it
seems to be the case that Irish recruiting followed very much the
same trend as English recruiting. Ireland was simply like good
recruiting districts in England, where men were encouraged to
enlist by the want of alternative employment.

	Irish pop. % of UK pop.	Irish % of British army	Roman Catholics % of British army
1830	32.3	42.2	n.a.
1840	30.6	37.2	n.a.
1861	20.0	28.4	28.5
1871	17.5	24.5	24.7
1881	14.8	20.9	23.4
1891	12.5	14.0	18.4

It does not even seem to be the case that the Irish gentry supplied
more than its fair share of officers, as common report had it. George
Meredith no doubt reinforced the notion with a well-known line
of 1885 :

'Tis Ireland gives England her soldiers, her generals too.[8]

But the detailed figures we have for the 1870s show that the
proportion of Irish officers was not much higher than one would
expect from the population of Ireland in 1871 (20.1 per cent) and
was almost exactly proportional to the population (17.5 per cent)
in 1878.[9] Irish officers were only disproportionately numerous in
relation to the size of the Irish Protestant community from which
they were drawn. In terms of number of officers per head the
Church of Ireland, disestablished in 1870, was presumably the most
army-oriented denomination in the British Isles.

Though the reputation of Scottish solders as fighting men was
very high, there were never as many of them in the army as there
were Irishmen. The Irish at their mid-nineteenth-century peak
numbered 55,000, and at their lowest ebb 25,000 : the Scots held
steady at between 13,500 and 17,000 until the South African War,

then rose quickly, only to sink again from 22,500 to 17,250. Scots amounted to about 13.5 per cent of the army in 1830, when Scotland contained 10 per cent of the population of the United Kingdom, a little under 10 per cent in 1870, and about 8 per cent during the rest of the century, when Scotland had about 10.5 per cent of the population of the United Kingdom. Scots were thus over-represented in the early Victorian army and under-represented in the late Victorian army. Scottish recruiting was simply not keeping up with population growth.

Both Irish and Scottish soldiers often seemed more numerous than they were because their presence in the army made the army seem somehow un-English. The army was in fact one of the few institutions in which the notion had ever taken root of the United Kingdom as an entity which constituted something more than an uneasy conjunction of England, Scotland and Ireland.

The army seemed un-English for another reason : it did not have more than a sprinkling of Methodists or Dissenters, though they constituted in many ways the most dynamic section of English society. It is impossible to know how many soldiers had Methodist or Dissenting backgrounds. Recruiting staffs habitually classified any man without well-established chapel-going habits as 'C of E' and, unless there was some strong incentive for him to change, he was normally content to leave things that way. Many officers (and most Anglican chaplains) discouraged their men from subsequently changing their religion, even though a simple declaration of a desire to change it became all that was required after 1860. Those that did change were often alleged to have done so for frivolous reasons.[10] The only information available relates to those who after 1863 formally declared themselves to be 'Other Protestants' or Wesleyans. The 'Other Protestants' constituted about 3 per cent of the army in the 1860s, rose to 4 per cent by 1879 and remained fairly constant until 1881. Absolute numbers rose from 5,280 to 7,334.

Most of the 'Other Protestants' demonstrated, when they were given a chance, that they preferred to be classified as Wesleyans. By the time the statistics had settled down in 1884 there were about 7,000 Wesleyans to 1,050 Other Protestants. The Wesleyan proportion of the army (which presumably included most of those brought up in one of the other Methodist denominations) then gradually rose from 4 to 5 per cent. By the turn of the century there were over 11,000 Wesleyans and under 2,000 Other

Protestants. After the South African War in 1903 there were about 13,500 Wesleyans to about 3,250 Other Protestants, who in the following year were further divided into 2,541 Baptists and Congregationalists and 878 Other Protestants. Wesleyan numbers then slowly diminished to 9,750 in 1913, by which time the Baptists and Congregationalists had just about reached 4,000, and the Other Protestants were once again over 1,500.

The general nonconformist suspicion and disapproval of the Victorian army can only have been reinforced by the fact that it recruited such a tiny number of English nonconformists. It was not that the army did not want nonconformists. It was rather that nonconformists (as distinct from Methodists) were so overwhelmingly middle-class that service in the ranks of the army made little appeal to them. The rank and file of the army was drawn from those sections of the working class where organised religion was represented by the Church of England, Roman Catholics and Methodists rather than by the old Dissenting bodies.

Readers of Evelyn Waugh's *Men at Arms* will recall his portrait of the Halberdiers.

One of the characteristics of the Halberdiers was a tradition of firm churchmanship. Papistry and Dissent were almost unknown among the regulars. Long-service recruits were prepared for Confirmation by the chaplain as part of their elementary training. The parish church of the town was the garrison chapel. For Sunday Mattins the whole back of the nave was reserved for the Halberdiers who marched there from the barracks behind their band.[11]

The Halberdiers, in short, were as English as it was possible to be, and English in a peculiarly Anglican way.

The point Evelyn Waugh was trying to make about the Halberdiers is that they were not like other regiments in 1939. Such Englishness is deeply rooted in the history of a number of regiments, but it has never been common. Most regiments have had to accept the fact that, if they are to keep up the standard of their recruits, they must draw on Scotland and Ireland as well as England. The Household Cavalry and Foot Guards (apart from the Scots Fusilier Guards) seem always to have been more English than the rest of the army.[12] But if one looks at the returns for the 1870s it is apparent that there were also quintessentially English regiments in other parts of the army, a number of them poor-genteel like the Halberdiers. Those regiments with more than 90 per cent of their

NCOs and men Englishmen in 1878 were an interesting lot : the 2nd and 3rd Dragoon Guards, 1st Dragoons, 14th Hussars, 1st, 2nd and 3rd battalions Grenadier Guards, 1st and 3rd battalions Coldstream Guards, 2nd battalion 23rd Foot, 50th Foot, 3rd and 4th battalions 60th Rifles, 2nd, 3rd and 4th battalions Rifle Brigade.

These ultra-English regiments were balanced by a number of essentially non-English regiments. In 1878 twenty-five battalions had a non-English majority. Of these nine were less than 20 per cent English : 2nd battalion 18th Foot (Royal Irish), 27th Foot (Inniskilling), 42nd Foot (Royal Highland), 71st Foot (Highland Light Infantry), 79th Foot (Cameron Highlanders), 86th Foot (Royal County Down), 88th Foot (Connaught Rangers), 92nd Foot (Gordon Highlanders), 93rd Foot (Sutherland Highlanders).

The Scottish and Irish regiments of the army constituted an active and visible minority. Their position in the army was, however, rather different. The Scottish regiments had an excellent record in action, in the Crimea, in India during the Mutiny, and in Egypt, and there was something of a late Victorian popular cult of the Highland soldier. The number of Scottish soldiers, however, was not large enough to supply even the nominally Scottish regiments with the men they needed, and there were very few Scots available for service outside the Scottish regiments.

There were nineteen nominally Scottish regiments in 1878, four of them with two battalions each.[13] Taking each battalion as a unit, one obtains the following figures :

Scots in Nominally Scottish Battalions, 1878

% Scottish	Officers	Men
80–100	1	4
60–79	2	4
40–59	4	2
20–39	6	6
Under 20	10	7

Only three regiments drew 60 per cent of both officers and men from Scotland, the 42nd, 79th and 92nd Foot, all of them Highland regiments. Another four Highland regiments, the 71st, 72nd, 78th and 93rd, drew 40 to 60 per cent of their officers and over 60 per cent of their men from Scotland. At the other end of the scale, five nominally Scottish regiments drew less than 15 per cent of their non-commissioned officers and men from Scotland.[14] These regiments were clearly not Scottish regiments in any meaningful sense of the word. The remainder of the Scottish regiments drew a sufficient number of men from Scotland to give them a Scottish flavour, but were either largely English,[15] or mixed regiments, with less than 50 per cent of their men drawn from any one country.[16] Nor would the picture be different if the figures of 1871 were substituted for those for 1878.

Scottish recruiting was clearly unable to keep up with the demand for Scottish soldiers. Highland regiments did better than Lowland regiments, partly because their traditions were stronger. Even they, however, did not find it as easy to secure recruits as they had once done. The depopulation of much of the eastern and northern Highlands, and the weakening of the feudal ties that had been so important in securing recruits during the Revolutionary and Napoleonic Wars, meant, indeed, a permanent narrowing of the basis for recruiting. In the Lowlands prejudice against military service was strong among the respectable working class, and the army had in any case to compete with industry and American and Canadian emigration agents. When Lowland regiments were brought up to full strength it had normally to be by drafting in additional English and Irish soldiers. The Cameronians (26th Foot), for instance, were proud of their Scottish traditions and had their base at Hamilton in Lanarkshire, on the face of things an excellent centre for recruiting in the Clyde valley. Yet the Scottish traditions of the regiment had to be instilled into a predominantly non-Scottish rank and file : 345 English, 306 Scots, 276 Irish in 1871; 143 English, 190 Scots, 138 Irish in 1878. Moreover, the task had to be entrusted to non-Scottish officers : 27 English, 4 Scots, 11 Irish in 1871; 17 English, 2 Scottish, 5 Irish in 1878.

The Irish role in the army was different. There were proportionately and absolutely many more Irishmen, and Ireland was consciously used as a pool for making up recruits. Irishmen, as a consequence, were widely distributed throughout the infantry regiments, where they accounted for 26.05 per cent of the total in 1878. This made things easier for Fenian recruiters in 1865–6, for they were able to build up a substantial body of supporters in nominally English or Scottish regiments, as well as in the predominantly Irish Royal Irish Fusiliers.[17]

There were only ten nominally Irish regiments by 1878, of which only one had two battalions. In addition there were six formerly Indian regiments which were based in Ireland and recruited there,[18] and three regiments that were substantially Irish in composition, though not in name.[19]

The nominally Irish regiments fall into two groups : five with a clear majority of Irish NCOs and men,[20] and five with a third Irish or less.[21] None of these regiments had a majority of Irish officers, the proportion actually being highest (37.5 per cent) in the case of the regiment with the lowest proportion of Irish NCOs and men, the 1st Dragoon Guards. The normal complement of Irish officers in Irish regiments was 25–30 per cent. Non-Catholic Irishmen formed a significant proportion of the rank and file only in one case, of the Ulster-based 86th Foot, which was 87.4 per cent Irish but only 57.2 per cent Catholic.

It is a striking fact that Irish regiments never attained the celebrity of their Scottish counterparts, or their sense of solidarity. There were so many more Irish in the army than there were Scots that one would have expected the balance to be the other way about. There were actually more distinctively Scottish regiments in 1878 than there were Irish regiments, at least in terms of composition, though Scots constituted only 8.5 per cent of the army and the Irish 26 per cent.

Public concern for the welfare of soldiers first emerged during the Crimean War. The sufferings of the army in the field were brought home so forcefully to the public, and Florence Nightingale became so much a national heroine, that the plight of the common soldier could not be overlooked. The War Office was prodded into taking the first faltering steps towards the creation of an effective system of military hospitals by building that architectural monstrosity, the Royal Victoria Hospital at Netley (1856–63). The supply and medical services of the army were overhauled and there was much talk of further reforms, for which money was never available.

There was strangely little concern with what was to happen day by day to the troops when they returned from the Crimea. Dr Rule's preaching station at Aldershot was one of the few practical Christian gestures to come out of the Crimean War. Another, less effective, perhaps, was a 104-page tract published in 1857 by the Religious Tract Society, styled *Religion in the Ranks: or, Letters from Soldiers in the British Army, with an Introduction by the Chaplain General of the Army.*

Narratives of the war [wrote Chaplain General George R. Gleig] are frequent. Here, for the first time, is offered to our notice the reflection of the inner minds of a faithful few, who, brave as the bravest, and ever ready to dare and to suffer, were in every change of circumstance sustained and comforted by the happy assurance that their peace was made in heaven through faith in our Lord Jesus Christ.[22]

A trickle of lives of those few 'saints' among the officers who had fallen in battle also emerged from the presses, the most effective being the *Memoir of Captain M. M. Hammond, Rifle Brigade* (1858), the biography of a singularly upright man who was killed immediately on his arrival at Balaclava. But there was no great outburst of Christian sympathy.

The Indian Mutiny of 1857 changed that. The Mutiny was seen as an attack on Christianity by the forces of heathenism and savagery. The army found itself overnight committed to the unexpected role of defender of the outposts of Christendom. And it was an army whose leadership was remarkably fitted for that role, for it included more prominent evangelicals than any other army of the century. Lord Shaftesbury, who had condemned the lack of respect accorded to religion by Lord Raglan and his colleagues in the Crimea, was able to join in paeans of praise to those two redoubtable Christian warriors, Lawrence and Havelock.[23] The press was full of tributes to the high principles and devoutness of those who had saved India, both officers and men. Sir Henry Havelock, whose military exploits had made him a popular hero even before his death in the field, became for Protestants of every denomination the martyr hero of the age. A devout evangelical himself, whose chosen friends were the Christian missionaries at Serampore, he had spent his life spreading the Gospel among the soldiers of the Indian army. Tributes to him were paid by all denominations, even though he was known to have been a Baptist convert.[24] For the next fifty years there was to be a steady stream of books on the Mutiny heroes and the Christians who had built the Indian empire as a contribution to God's cause.[25] The dour Havelock had been content to leave the world with the message: 'See how a Christian can die'. But the mood of elation which followed the defeat of the Mutiny is better expressed by Sabine Baring-Gould's words of 1864 :

> Onward, Christian soldiers!
> Marching as to war,
> With the Cross of Jesus
> Going on before.

There was one obvious way in which this new-found enthusiasm for the army could be put to use. At Aldershot, under Prince Albert's watchful eye, a great new centre for the British army had begun in 1854. There were a few permanent buildings, but most of the men in 'the camp' were accommodated in temporary wooden huts or in tents until the authorities finally decided to make Aldershot the army's principal home base in 1892. There was scarcely any town worth speaking of, and the churches were cold, chiefly iron, relics of the first phase of building.[26] Drink and prostitutes were the only amusements regularly available until the Prince Consort donated a library in 1859–60. There was a clear call for club-houses and missions, such as had already been pioneered by philanthropists and evangelicals for civilians in other parts of the country. It was not until 1862, however, that a suitable missioner was found to work at Aldershot.

The movement to create 'soldiers' homes' had been inaugurated at Chatham in 1861, when the Wesleyan Charles Henry Kelly opened a little club-house in a basement, with a reading room, a chapel, and minimal sleeping quarters.[27] Mrs Louisa Daniell, who started the first Aldershot soldiers' home in 1862, was less pressed for money. She had already been working as an evangelical home missionary, and could count on the support of the great evangelical philanthropists, Lord Shaftesbury, Lord Kinnaird, Stevenson Blackwood and Robert Baxter.[28] Her 'Mission Hall and Soldiers' Home and Institute' eventually had a lecture hall seating up to 500 for services, a tea and coffee bar, baths, sleeping quarters, a smoking and games room, a reading room with newspapers and a lending library, and an annex for soldiers' wives. The Wesleyan Soldiers' Home, which followed in 1869, was at first on a more modest scale, but in 1875 moved into larger quarters and became something of a model, with no fewer than four branches in different parts of the camp.[29] A Church of England Soldiers' Institute, founded in 1883, was on an equally substantial scale and boasted a famous billiard room. The Primitive Methodists and the Salvation Army also provided soldiers' homes on a more modest scale in the 1890s.

What happened at Aldershot was repeated elsewhere. The Wesleyans established a chain of soldiers' homes at Chatham, Malta, London, Woolwich, The Curragh, Hong Kong, Colombo, Bangalore, and Salisbury Plain.[30] Mrs Daniell and her daughter, who succeeded her in her work, established branch homes at Weedon, Colchester, Manchester and Chatham. Church of England Soldiers' and Sailors' Institutes spread under the auspices of an association formed in 1896. The Salvation Army and the YMCA also took up mission work among soldiers.

All of the soldiers' homes were regarded by their sponsors as essentially ventures into the mission field. The published accounts of the lives of Mrs Daniell and her daughter are largely concerned with their success in saving souls, rather than with their contribution to social welfare. Yet it was their social function that gave them their significance. The State held back but the churches did not. For many years they provided the few social facilities that were of any account for the common soldier (the officers had their own comfortable officers' club). Many soldiers did not much care for the type of evangelical piety that motivated the sponsors of soldiers' homes, but they were grateful for what they got. It was not until the very end of the nineteenth century that the army itself began to compete with the soldiers' homes. New barracks were built, sports and games were introduced, food was improved, writing rooms, coffee rooms and concert halls provided, and there was also an overall improvement in cleanliness.[31] Officers were encouraged to take an interest in their men, to learn their names, and to get to know them individually. But for respectable soldiers the soldiers' home continued until 1914 to be the centre of much of their social life.

More than that, the homes had a definite educational function. The army attempted after 1846 to raise its educational standards, though it was not until 1890 that it finally adopted a system of written examinations which must be passed by NCOs as well as officers. The proportion of those who could neither read nor write fell from about 19 per cent in 1861 to less than 2 per cent in 1889, of those who could read but not write from 20 per cent to a little over 2 per cent. Correspondingly, those with what the army described as 'superior education', or what the Education Department would have called an elementary education, rose from about 6 per cent in the 1860s to about 85 per cent by the end of the

1880s.[32] By then something like 40 per cent of the NCOs and men had gone to the trouble of taking and passing the examinations for one of the army education certificates.[33] For many soldiers, anxious to overcome deficiencies in their education, the classes held in the soldiers' homes were the only effective ones available. The churches were still doing in the army much of the basic education work for which the board schools established in 1870 had been intended.

The reward for the churches who engaged in army work was a consciousness of having made a definite contribution to the raising of standards of behaviour in the army. It was never clear just how far the undoubted improvement that took place was the consequence of Christian missions, but that there had been a change everyone agreed. There was still too much drunkenness, even at the end of the century, but it was no longer accepted as part of the natural order. Moreover, the churches in 1893 had at last decided to join forces against it and to merge their denominational temperance societies into a single Army Temperance Association. By 1895 there were reported to be 8,641 members : later the number rose to 20,000.[34]

There was a sense of pride well justified in what had been achieved when a Wesleyan chaplain wrote in 1899 :

Too often do we hear people speaking as though our troops were a mere body of drilled scapegraces, whereas this is far from the truth. . . . Our army is one of which we, as Englishmen, have good reason to be proud – its bravery and discipline have never been called into question, and I rejoice to know that its standard of morality becomes higher year by year. Purity and temperance are making headway against the once proverbial evils of military life.[35]

The Indian Mutiny caught the public off guard. For a time it seemed not merely that the Indian empire might be lost, but that the French might choose the time of England's weakness for a display of strength. In 1857–9 there were a series of scares lest war should break out, and a fear of invasion led to a demand for the creation of a new force of volunteers for home defence. Starting at about 100,000 in 1859, the number of volunteers rose to over 200,000 in the 1870s, when there were more volunteers enrolled than there were regulars.

The first wave of volunteers is said to have included a disproportionate number of wealthy and professional men, just as those who first volunteered for service in South Africa in 1899 and in France

in 1914 were disproportionately drawn from those groups. But the
volunteers soon settled down into a different mould. The new citizen
army now consisted largely of the middle-class denizens of suburbia,
clerks and artisans. This meant that the volunteers were able to draw
upon the resources of sections of the community from which the
regular army did not recruit. Though the general tone was somewhat imperialistic, and there was plenty of the Anglican would-be-
aristocratic snobbery that flourished among army officers, the
volunteers were not in any sense a homogeneous body. Promotion
was decided by election, with the consequence that like tended to
consort with like, an Anglican and Tory corps to be balanced by
a nonconformist Liberal one. It was even possible for a Radical,
Unitarian cotton merchant to be elected to command a corps.[36]

The volunteers shared one common belief : that a disciplined
force was required to defeat a disciplined enemy. Though they were
too often casual about their duties, volunteers had a strong belief
in the abstract value of regular military drill and military organisation. They were also, for the most part, active members of churches
or chapels.

From the first there were those who saw the volunteers not
merely as a defence against the French, but as a defence against
the chaos and irreligion that they observed about them in the great
Victorian cities. It was left to a Scottish volunteer officer, William
Alexander Smith, a Glasgow businessman who gradually worked
his way up from private to colonel, to recognise that the volunteers
could become the model for an organisation designed to protect
the young from the moral contamination by which they were
surrounded.[37] From that recognition stemmed the Boys' Brigade,
which rapidly became a great international movement.[38]

The Boys' Brigade began in Glasgow in 1883. The founder was
a member of the Free Church of Scotland, rather than the established church, and the Brigade from the beginning had something
of a nonconformist flavour, though it was ostensibly inter-denomi-
national. Units were developed in association with particular
churches or chapels, and in this way the values of the volunteer
movement secured a considerable degree of church and nonconformist recognition. The price, however, was a series of denominational secessions and rivals : the Church Lads' Brigade (1890), the
Boys' Life Brigade (1899), and the Boy Scouts (1908), all of which
grew out of the Boys' Brigade, and also the Catholic Boys' Brigade
and the Jewish Lads' Brigade which were parallel organisations.

The Boys' Brigade, like the volunteers, adopted army nomenclature, army ranks, and army organisation, undertook extensive
military drill, and was regularly inspected by army officers. The
founder once said that its watchwords were 'Discipline and
Religion'. The declared objects were 'the promotion of habits of
Obedience, Reverence, Discipline, Self-respect, and all that tends
towards a true Christian manliness'.

The Boys' Brigade started a controversy in nonconformity that
is perhaps scarcely dead even now. After 1890 the majority of its
members were Baptists, Congregationalists, Presbyterians and
Methodists, and its membership was steadily growing. A number
of nonconformist ministers saw in the Brigade an attempt to subvert
the principles of English nonconformity and denounced it. They
recognised that it had to a marked degree abandoned the norm of
reference to individual conscience as the guide for action, and that
it had substituted for conscience the conventions of an essentially
conservative social order. The founder of the movement, with his
emphasis on discipline rather than religion, did little to disarm their
fears. Indeed, the Boys' Brigade was perennially reluctant to accept
any departure from the canons of middle-class respectability.
Baden-Powell's *Scouting for Boys* was first published in the *Boys'
Brigade Gazette*, but the Boy Scouts, with their exotic emphasis
on camping in the veldt and their khaki uniforms, found it impossible to confine themselves within the established routines of the
Boys' Brigade.

The Boys' Brigade seems, indeed, to have been almost over-
anxious to emphasise its respectablility. There was never any risk
of its being associated in the public mind with that other body of
admirers of military organisation, the Salvation Army. The Salvation Army took to military uniform quite as much because it was
composed of individualistic eccentrics, who needed to be reminded
that they belonged to the same organisation, as because of any love
of military ways. The object of the Salvation Army was the saving
of souls and the trumpeting of Christ's kingdom, not the discipline
for its own sake of the Boys' Brigade.

The significance of the Boys' Brigade is that it was able to do
what the army had never wanted or tried to do. It succeeded in
instilling into the minds of hundreds of thousands of young nonconformists the idea that the army stood for a system of values
that transcended the men who composed it. By doing so, it not only
prepared the way for the recruiting drives of the First World War.

It helped to undermine the essentially civilian system of values which had guided English nonconformity for two centuries.

Social divisions in Victorian England commonly found expression in religious terms. The Church of England, like the Conservative party, stood for things as they were; nonconformity for the bristling enterprise of business and industry, the demand for equality of opportunity, and activist Liberalism; the Primitive Methodists for the new trade-union movements of the coalfields. The acceptance by the army of religious pluralism, and the acceptance by the churches that the army might provide a model for civilian behaviour, must therefore suggest the question : was there not in late Victorian England a substantial shift in the social function of the army?

This is not the place to explore the question at length. Two points, however, immediately suggest themselves. First, the army had substantially shifted its ground in its attitude to the common soldier. The Duke of Wellington in his more pessimistic moments had been inclined to think of the army as little better than cannon fodder : a mixture of Irish and Scottish mercenaries and the scum of English society. After the Indian Mutiny the common soldier began at last to be regarded as a working man who had undertaken a special type of duty, and increasingly as an Englishman (as distinct from an Irishman or a Scotsman).

The army's recognition of Wesleyanism was more than a gesture in the direction of religious pluralism. It involved the acceptance that common soldiers might legitimately owe a dual allegiance : on the one hand to king and country, on the other to the tenets of an unfashionable religious denomination. The implication was that the army could at last count on the common soldier to accept his allegiance to king and country as his primary obligation, not to be lightly abandoned. Other allegiances, to family, to locality, to religion, could be recognised because they were essentially subordinate. The army in other words had secured sufficient public recognition to enable it to relax its codes and to begin to come to terms with the increasingly plural society from which it recruited.

Secondly, the new flexibility of the army was a consequence of growing civilian recognition that the maintenance of Britain's imperial position depended on the army almost as much as on the navy – a product alike of the acceptance of the need to defend the sea route to India and of the growth of European armies after

1870 – and of a growing sympathy for the common soldier, Kipling's Tommy. But there was more to it than that. With Liberalism in decay at the end of the nineteenth century, there was a fundamental uncertainty as to the way in which a Liberal society should develop. In English nonconformity and English Liberalism this showed itself as a cleavage between those who clung to the old mid-Victorian ideal of a society of autonomous, almost anarchistic individuals, such as was still posited by the Newcastle programme of 1891, and those, among them Joseph Chamberlain and Sidney Webb, who sought a new social order in which there would be a sort of collective guarantee that each man should be secure of his distinctive place, rather than being made the prey of market forces. The Boys' Brigade derived from this second strand of Liberal thought. It sought to temper the economic and religious anarchism of British society by the inculcation of orderly values borrowed from the army. The army was no longer seen as a militaristic threat to individual liberties or an authoritarian anachronism. Rather it seemed to stand for the voluntary acceptance of a common purpose, a common discipline and, if necessary, a common sacrifice. During the South African War the army attracted a degree of popular sympathy out of all proportion to its achievements. The soldiers in the field figured in the press as typical Englishmen, showing characteristic English fortitude in adversity and serving as worthy representatives of their country. The army which came into being after the Haldane reforms was thus able to draw upon a measure of popular sympathy and understanding such as no British army had enjoyed before. The soldier was now a patriot, not a wastrel.

APPENDIX I

Nationalities of Non-Commissioned Officers and Men

Year	English and Welsh N	%	Scots N	%	Irish N	%	Empire N	%	Foreigners etc. N	%	Not Reported	Total
1830	44,329	43.7	13,800	13.6	42,897	42.2	n.a.		n.a.		518	101,544
1840	51,559	46.5	15,239	13.7	41,218	37.2	n.a.		n.a.		2,902	110,918
1868	106,810	58.4	17,011	9.3	55,583	30.4	n.a.		879	0.5	2,507	182,790
1869	103,426	60.1	16,372	9.5	50,331	29.2	n.a.		940	0.5	1,153	172,222
1870	101,909	60.3	16,163	9.6	47,151	27.9	n.a.		849	0.5	2,838	168,910
1871			No Returns									
1872	117,701	65.0	15,885	8.8	44,092	24.4	n.a.		n.a.		3,293	180,971
1873	120,134	67.0	15,254	8.5	42,284	23.6	n.a.		679	0.4	1,032	179,383
1874	118,348	67.5	14,507	8.2	41,124	23.4	n.a.		650	0.4	972	176,101
1875	119,246	67.7	13,915	7.9	40,626	23.1	n.a.		584	0.3	1,646	176,017
1876	118,701	68.3	13,813	7.9	39,360	22.7	n.a.		571	0.3	1,305	173,750
1877	123,467	68.7	14,190	7.9	39,977	22.2	n.a.		622	0.3	1,561	179,817
1878	124,708	69.2	14,235	7.9	39,121	21.7	n.a.		690	0.4	1,421	180,175
1879	121,421	66.8	13,914	7.7	36,871	20.3	n.a.		706	0.4	8,962	181,874
1880	122,774	67.6	14,446	7.9	38,359	21.1	1,770	1.0	297	0.2	4,093	181,739
1881	123,135	68.8	14,415	8.1	36,872	20.6	2,113	1.2	213	0.1	2,270	179,018
1882	124,434	69.3	13,723	7.6	36,945	20.6	2,065	1.2	238	0.1	2,049	179,454
1883	128,531	70.1	14,516	7.9	36,297	19.8	2,124	1.2	208	0.1	1,672	183,348
1884	123,191	71.9	13,432	7.8	31,694	18.5	2,140	1.2	155	0.1	674	171,286
1885	128,021	71.6	13,720	7.7	31,133	17.4	2,272	1.3	157	0.1	3,506	178,809
1886	138,032	72.4	15,495	8.1	31,573	16.6	2,266	1.2	152	0.1	3,234	190,752

Year	English and Welsh		Scots		Irish		Empire		Foreigners etc.		Not Reported	Total
	N	%	N	%	N	%	N	%	N	%		
1887	146,171	73.7	16,446	8.3	32,153	16.2	2,262	1.1	155	0.1	1,020	198,207
1888	149,123	74.3	17,082	8.5	31,335	15.6	2,435	1.2	156	0.1	512	200,643
1889	150,030	74.9	16,834	8.4	30,297	15.1	2,504	1.3	134	0.1	518	200,317
1890	151,289	75.8	16,534	8.3	28,712	14.4	2,584	1.3	129	0.1	225	199,473
1891	151,992	76.2	16,409	8.2	27,782	13.9	2,709	1.4	99	0.1	468	199,459
1892	153,107	76.5	15,990	8.0	26,779	13.4	2,936	1.5	122	0.1	1,082	200,016
1893	156,781	76.7	15,917	7.8	27,143	13.3	3,120	1.5	119	0.1	1,327	204,407
1894	159,611	77.5	16,742	8.1	25,933	12.6	3,125	1.5	134	0.1	370	205,915
1895	162,782	78.0	15,973	7.7	26,200	12.6	2,933	1.4	146	0.1	639	208,673
1896	163,076	78.2	15,800	7.6	25,381	12.2	3,078	1.5	154	0.1	1,072	208,561
1897	159,475	77.0	16,203	7.8	25,664	12.4	2,933	1.4	150	0.1	2,644	207,059
1898	158,648	76.7	16,479	8.0	26,376	12.7	3,027	1.5	141	0.1	2,236	206,907
1899	164,997	76.6	17,280	8.0	28,352	13.2	3,022	1.4	96	0.1	1,580	215,327

Year	English and Welsh[1]		Welsh		Scots		Irish		Empire		Foreigners		Not Reported	Total
	N	%	N	%	N	%	N	%	N	%	N	%		
1903	202,562	75.8	n.a.		22,442	8.4	31,467	11.8	10,461	3.9	155	.1	266	267,353
1904	203,832	76.2	n.a.		21,852	8.2	30,654	11.5	10,143	3.8	145	.1	975	267,601
1905	190,192	74.7	4,553	1.8	20,388	8.0	27,785	10.9	9,271	3.6	557	.2	1,720	254,466
1906	187,235	76.2	4,151	1.7	19,766	8.0	25,397	10.3	8,866	3.6	93	.04	226	245,734
1907	178,240	76.9	3,588	1.5	18,129	7.8	22,836	9.8	9,014	3.9	25	.01	74	231,906
1908	181,496	77.2	3,437	1.5	18,480	7.9	23,158	9.8	8,452	3.6	22	.01	81	235,126
1909	183,702	77.5	3,240	1.4	18,530	7.8	22,955	9.7	8,344	3.5	12	.01	105	236,888
1910	184,054	77.9	3,061	1.3	18,581	7.9	22,237	9.4	8,152	3.5	4		106	236,195
1911	185,666	78.2	3,075	1.3	18,581	7.8	21,860	9.2	8,087	3.4	4		114	237,387
1912	183,891	78.4	3,076	1.3	18,258	7.8	21,421	9.1	7,838	3.3	1		114	234,599
1913	179,237	78.6	3,124	1.4	17,282	7.6	20,780	9.1	7,574	3.3	1		120	228,118

[1] From 1905 English only.

Notes

No statistics were compiled for 1900–2, because of the South African War. From 1903 Colonial corps are included, among them in 1905 512 of the Chinese regiment returned as Foreigners. Indian and African troops were excluded at all times. When the basis of compilation was changed in 1905 to distinguish the Welsh from the English two other changes were made. The simple description, English, Scottish, etc., was changed to read 'Born in England', 'Born in Scotland', etc. A new table was also added for British subjects born abroad. Of these there were in 1905 282, 1906 244, 1907 248, 1908 283, 1909 317, 1910 301, 1911 335, 1912 302, 1913 303. These figures have been omitted from the table. Statistics are for 1 January of each year to January 1903 (except for 1868–70), then from 1 October

Sources

Statistics for 1830 and 1840: HC 307 (1841), XIV, 93. *General Annual Return of the British Army .. 1880* (C.3083) 65. HC (1881), LVIII, 563; *1898* (C.9426) 94. HC (1899), LIII, 428; *1907* (Cd.3798) 91. HC (1908), XI, 99; *1913* (Cd.7252), 92. HC (1914), LII, 358.

APPENDIX II

Religious Denominations of Non-Commissioned Officers and Men

Year	Church of England		Presbyterians		Wesleyans		Other Protestants		Roman Catholics		Not Reported	Total
	N	%	N	%	N	%	N	%	N	%		
1861	124,252	59.3	22,947	10.9	n.a.		n.a.		58,630	28.0	3,840	209,669
1862	119,223	60.0	20,844	10.5	n.a.		n.a.		56,104	28.2	2,544	198,715
1863	116,493	57.0	23,109	11.3	n.a.		3,549	1.7	58,623	28.7	2,431	204,205
1864	110,255	55.7	21,016	10.6	n.a.		5,280	2.7	58,021	29.3	3,413	197,985
1865–67			No returns									
1868	106,135	58.2	17,433	9.6	n.a.		5,669	3.1	51,889	28.4	1,357	182,483
1869	101,373	57.9	18,185	10.4	n.a.		5,962	3.4	47,484	27.1	1,933	174,937
1870	98,754	58.7	16,769	10.0	n.a.		5,751	3.4	43,590	25.9	3,368	168,232
1871	106,221	60.7	16,429	9.4	n.a.		6,111	3.5	42,295	24.2	3,974	175,030
1872			No returns									
1873	115,621	64.5	15,782	8.8	n.a.		5,962	3.3	40,986	22.8	1,032	179,383
1874	114,030	64.8	15,166	8.6	n.a.		6,446	3.7	39,488	22.4	971	176,101
1875	113,614	64.5	14,629	8.3	n.a.		6,401	3.6	39,727	22.6	1,646	176,017
1876	112,876	65.0	14,320	8.2	n.a.		6,224	3.6	38,971	22.4	1,359	173,750
1877	116,585	64.8	14,342	8.0	n.a.		6,737	3.7	40,591	22.6	1,562	179,817
1878	116,223	64.5	14,060	7.8	n.a.		7,033	3.9	41,437	23.0	1,422	180,175

Year	Church of England N	%	Presbyterians N	%	Wesleyans N	%	Other Protestants N	%	Roman Catholics N	%	Not Reported	Total
1879	112,419	61.8	13,662	7.5	n.a.		7,117	3.9	39,713	21.8	8,963	181,874
1880	113,808	62.6	14,019	7.9	n.a.		7,254	4.0	41,911	23.1	4,747	181,739
1881	114,133	63.8	13,947	7.8	n.a.		7,334	4.1	41,335	23.1	2,271	179,020
1882	115,065	64.1	13,472	7.5	6,422	3.6	1,258	0.7	41,091	22.9	2,146	179,454
1883	117,866	64.3	13,973	7.6	6,757	3.7	1,136	0.6	41,943	22.9	1,673	183,348
1884	112,605	65.7	12,619	7.4	7,037	4.1	1,050	0.6	37,300	21.8	675	171,286
1885	116,005	64.9	12,690	7.1	7,517	4.2	1,030	0.6	38,062	21.3	3,505	178,809
1886	124,550	65.3	14,343	7.5	8,422	4.4	1,122	0.6	39,133	20.5	3,182	190,752
1887	131,637	66.4	15,040	7.6	9,133	4.6	1,024	0.5	40,352	20.4	1,021	198,207
1888	133,737	66.7	15,585	7.8	10,066	5.0	1,297	0.6	39,446	19.7	512	200,643
1889	134,247	67.0	15,680	7.8	10,025	5.0	1,167	0.6	38,679	19.3	519	200,317
1890	134,973	67.7	15,444	7.7	10,387	5.2	1,166	0.6	37,278	18.7	225	199,473
1891	135,505	67.9	15,160	7.6	10,495	5.2	1,234	0.6	36,695	18.4	468	199,459
1892	136,512	68.3	14,968	7.5	10,707	5.2	1,445	0.7	35,514	17.8	1,082	200,016
1893	139,442	68.2	14,890	7.3	10,888	5.3	1,511	0.7	36,530	17.9	1,327	204,407
1894	141,567	68.8	15,146	7.4	11,035	5.3	1,554	0.8	36,390	17.7	370	205,915
1895	143,947	69.0	14,824	7.1	11,134	5.3	1,554	0.7	36,674	17.6	639	208,673
1896	144,301	69.2	14,563	7.0	10,950	5.3	1,812	0.9	35,627	17.1	1,123	208,560
1897	140,921	68.1	14,650	7.1	10,835	5.2	2,353	1.1	35,492	17.1	2,693	207,059
1898	140,721	68.0	14,984	7.2	11,170	5.2	1,888	0.9	36,183	17.5	2,296	206,907
1899	145,842	67.7	15,622	7.3			1,958	0.9	39,073	18.1	1,662	215,327

Year	Church of England N	%	Presbyterians N	%	Wesleyans N	%	Baptists and Congregationalists N	%	Other Protestants N	%	Roman Catholics N	%	Jews N	%	Mohammedans, Hindus, etc. N	%	Not Reported	Total
1903	182,963	68.4	20,139	7.5	13,450	5.0	n.a.		3,232	1.2	44,119	16.5	185	0.1	2,999	1.1	266	267,353
1904	182,243	68.1	20,099	7.5	13,200	4.9	2,541	0.9	878	0.3	44,195	16.5	181	0.1	3,296	1.2	968	267,601
1905	174,060	68.3	18,853	7.4	12,912	5.1	2,531	1.0	1,042	0.4	40,632	15.9	178	0.1	2,838	1.1	1,702	254,748
1906	170,690	69.4	18,392	7.5	12,726	5.2	2,723	1.1	861	0.4	38,067	15.5	188	0.1	2,120	0.9	211	245,978
1907	162,754	70.1	17,251	7.4	10,868	4.7	3,047	1.3	1,753	0.8	34,043	14.7	191	0.1	2,231	1.0	16	232,154
1908	165,288	70.2	17,492	7.4	10,749	4.6	3,370	1.4	1,581	0.7	34,542	14.7	219	0.1	2,168	0.9		235,409
1909	166,717	70.3	17,463	7.4	10,630	4.5	3,725	1.6	1,587	0.7	34,677	14.6	221	0.1	2,181	0.9	4	237,205
1910	166,540	70.4	17,512	7.4	10,488	4.4	3,772	1.6	1,472	0.6	34,283	14.5	221	0.1	2,208	0.9		236,496
1911	167,281	70.4	17,433	7.3	10,481	4.4	3,983	1.7	1,546	0.7	34,613	14.6	233	0.1	2,152	0.9		237,722
1912	165,668	70.5	16,918	7.2	10,166	4.3	3,970	1.7	1,586	0.7	34,266	14.6	232	0.1	2,095	0.9		234,901
1913	161,232	70.6	15,971	7.0	9,755	4.3	3,937	1.7	1,589	0.7	33,662	14.7	236	0.1	2,039	0.9		228,421

Notes

No statistics were compiled for 1900–2 because of the South African War. Colonial corps are included, but not Indian and African native troops. Statistics to 1899 are for 1 January, thereafter for 1 October of each year.

Sources

General Annual Return of the British Army . . . 1880 (C. 3083) 66. HC (1881), LVIII, 564; *1898* (C. 9426) 95. HC (1899), LIII, 429; *1907* (Cd. 3798) 93. HC (1908), XI, 101; *1913* (Cd. 9252) 94. HC (1914), LII, 360.

11

In the Shadow of Impressment: Friends of a Naval Militia, 1844-74

J. S. BROMLEY

For all the illuminating local detail which it lavishes on the practical operation of the 'constitutional force', John Western's study of the eighteenth-century militia never fails to extract, from the debates in press and Parliament that periodically made it a high national issue, fundamental conflicts of political philosophy or strategical theory. There was, for instance, especially in the 1790s, a growing desire in government circles for the frank recognition of the home defence force as a nursery for the regular army; yet the Militia Act of 1802, although basically a government measure (unlike its famous predecessor of 1757), 'did not really create a rational defensive system composed of several distinct but complementary and mutually supporting types of force', because it deferred too much to the tradition of 'the militia as a force only occasionally embodied, which civilians could enter without being turned into professional soldiers'.[1] The friends of the militia, in other words, were enemies of a militia reserve. In 1808 Castlereagh's ingenious separation of a local from a regular militia, while it provided Wellington's army with its main source of recruits, was an acknowledgment of the political impossibility of military conscription in Britain; and a century later, it was the refusal of its colonels to merge their historic individuality with the regular army, or even with a new type of territorial force, that led Haldane to destroy the militia altogether.[2]

The strength and structure of militia ideology in Victorian England have yet to receive the attention they deserve. The suspension of training after 1825, and of the militia ballot in 1829, did not strip this 'oppressive farce' of a large permanent staff which

183

included 1,800 corporals and 800 drummers.[3] Plans for its full-scale revival began at latest with Graham and Herbert in 1845 and, of course, positively obsessed Palmerston in the following years; more was involved than the administration of a snub in his tit-for-tat against Russell's bill in February 1852 – all the difference between a local and a regular militia, available for service in all parts of the kingdom. There was controversy about the retention of the ballot in Derby's Act of the following June, the tightening of Crown control in Herbert's measures of 1859 and Cardwell's decisive transfer of this from Home to War Office. The county spirit was still more eroded by the insidious urbanisation of the time and (as some thought) by the Volunteer fever of 1859, following the voluntary expatriation of eleven militia regiments for overseas garrison duty during the Crimean War, when also the newly revived militia furnished the army with 33,000 recruits.[4] Whatever the arguments about its constitution or final end and usefulness, however, the militia provided a standing reminder from 1852 to 1907 of the adult Englishman's contingent obligation to perform military service of a kind, even though recourse to the ultimate sanction of the ballot was never needed.

As a reality the militia was by no means derisory during the decades when British strategic doctrine emphasised passive defence against invasion, when screw-propelled ironclads eclipsed the classical naval doctrine that Britain's maritime frontier was the enemy coast.[5] Partly for this very reason, militia ideas exercised a strong attraction in a quarter where they have been little noticed, among thoughtful naval officers in search of an alternative to impressment. In the land militia, with its familiar and indeed mild connotation, they saw the principle of a conscription that was acceptable because its basis was universal and effective because its execution was rapid.

In general, be it said to their everlasting honour, it was professional officers, not their ever-ready radical critics from Hume to Cobden, who after 1815 multiplied schemes for avoiding ultimate resort to press-gangs in the event of a major maritime war, especially another war against France, with her celebrated *Inscription Maritime*. Whatever doubts uninformed English naval historians may throw on this well-tried institution, the Victorian navy assumed that their old rival could place her fleet on a war footing in a matter of weeks, whereas it took months to commission a British warship even in peacetime – a contrast maddeningly at odds with relative strengths in merchant seamen and liable to make nonsense of any marginal superiority in battleships. The French themselves took this view, in the further knowledge that British strength was scattered over the oceans and that there was often no Channel squadron worth the name.[6] Palmerston's steam-bridge nightmare and his so-called Follies were nurtured on these facts, which indeed impressed military leaders from Wellington to Wolseley.[7] If the Admiralty remained more sceptical, there is no doubt that the manning of even the peace establishment caused it endless anxiety until the Crimean War, after which it committed the folly of losing several thousand prime seamen who had enlisted under the ten-year continuous and general service terms introduced in June 1853.[8] But Admiral Sir William Parker's Manning Committee of 1852–3, the authors of this and other recommendations for endowing the standing navy with 'a permanent constitution' (in place of hire-and-discharge), made only timid proposals towards exorcising the spectre of wartime impressment, which therefore continued to occupy naval pamphleteers. It did so even after the Hardwicke Manning Commission of 1858–9, less fearful of costs, had produced more promising proposals for building up a reserve, for it was many years before the quality of the Royal Naval Reserve was to look convincing at all to eminent authorities, some of whom felt strongly that it was based on false principles. The whole question of wartime manning could still arouse misgivings as late as 1874, when Rear-Admiral Sherard Osborn, a hero of the China wars best known for his promotion of Arctic exploration, produced the last scheme for raising a naval militia.

The prerogative power to conscript all seafaring persons, far from being renounced, had been carefully underwritten by Sir James Graham's manning legislation. A movement to abolish it in the House of Commons – with which Brougham appeared willing to compromise – struck Graham as 'fatal . . . to our naval power' and he resisted it strenuously: the Acts of 1835, introducing seamen's registration and limiting compulsory naval service to five years, were intended to kill it; and Graham later asserted that in these measures Grey's government attached most importance to Parliament's reaffirmation of the sovereign's 'right of demanding compulsory service, and that, too, in terms more distinct than any statute had before used'.[9] In 1853 Graham removed the double bounty awarded in 1835 to those who should volunteer within six days of a call-up by proclamation, because it made such proclamation

expensive, and went on to provide for an extension of the five
years' compulsory service in case of necessity. The Act of 1853
indeed took a step in the direction of French practice by converting
'the general proclamation into one which, at the pleasure of the
Crown, might be restricted to specified ages and classes . . .'; but,
significantly, nothing was said about methods of enforcement if
the necessity arose, as during the Crimean War. In the event it
did not – at the price of sending ships to sea often seriously under-
manned.[10] Admiral of the Fleet Sir Thomas Byam Martin, who had
written a powerful defence of impressment in 1834, was prepared
to call it 'a hateful practice' in 1852, and yet :

The suspending the power of impressment is worthy of any sacrifice,
excepting that of hazarding delay in the equipment of the fleet. . . .
England need be very cautious in dealing with a matter so vitally
affecting all her most precious interests; and much as impressment
is to be deprecated as an offence to the personal rights of Britons, let
us not be unmindful of its past benefits.[11]

It is doubtful whether the old man spoke only for his own generation of officers, survivors from the Napoleonic war for whom
pressing had not acquired the resonance of a satanic myth, who
knew how it had been used to prevent war in 1787 and 1790–1,
and who were shortly to contrast 1854 with 1793. The ugly
problem was simply evaded in the hope that 'urgent necessity'
would in the public eye justify desperate remedies. The 1859
Manning Commission, unlike Admiral Parker's Committee of 1852,
declared openly that impressment would no longer work, but it
nevertheless rejected the advice of Captain Denman, a leading
witness before both bodies, to 'abolish impressment in a general
Act introducing a new system'.[12]

The Honourable Joseph Denman, whose ideas may have been
close to those of the Prince Consort,[13] for he commanded the
Queen's yacht from 1853 until at least 1861, was only the most
eloquent of a number of friends of a naval militia. What characterised this type of manning reformer was that he combined a
keen perception of the obsolescence of pressing with an equally
strong (but rarer) belief in the indispensability of compulsory service.
The illusion of reliance on pressing in the age of reform was itself
never more neatly perforated than by C. H. Pennell, Chief Clerk
at the Admiralty and one of the few civilians to make a serious
contribution to the problem, but not for long a militia enthusiast.

In one of the memoranda he wrote for the 1852 Committee, besides referring to 'the naked facts of the case' – the spread of strong views of the liberty of the subject through all classes and the seamen's proven ability to exploit new techniques of 'combination' or of 'evasion', thanks to steamships and railways and not least the ease of becoming an American – Pennell quietly observes that even a quantitatively successful press would not supply the practised gunners needed in any future war, which would probably be 'a word and a blow'. Was it expedient 'to stake the safety of the country on means . . . which, *if they fail, all else fails*? [Pennell's italics]'[14] The only certain result would be 'the permanent alien-ation of large numbers of our seamen', whose distrust of the navy (and especially of naval discipline), rooted in the tales of their fathers and grandfathers, was the starting-point of the whole man-ning debate. Captain Denman, who had lurid visions of street-rioting and of modern juries bringing in verdicts of justifiable homicide when a press-master was murdered (but of murder when a press-gang took a life), was already convinced in 1852 that only by placing seamen 'on the same footing as other classes' would government enlist public opinion on its side and take away 'all just ground of discontent among the seamen themselves'.[15] Six years later, he admitted that seamen could not in one sense be placed on quite the same footing as their fellow subjects, because 'we should always require from them a more advanced state of preparation', which was a reason why the State, contrary to established practice, should assist in reviving the bankrupt merchant seamen's pension fund. Above all,

. . . I object to impressment, not because it is severe, not because it is unjust, though I believe it to be so in the greatest possible degree; yet in our present condition, if I believed it would serve our purpose, I would urge its continuance until a better system could be adopted; but I would abolish it because the right of the Crown to claim this service in the hour of need would be lost and sacrificed, if impressment were resorted to as the means of enforcing it.[16]

So long as its workings were reasonably predictable, pressing admittedly offered the overwhelming advantage of a rapid and massive mobilisation. It was now of more importance than ever, given the mid-century technological revolution in navies, to perfect this advantage. The answer, thought Denman, lay in what had long ago occurred to military impressment, which had been 'modified and regulated by modern legislation into the form of militia, which is raised on constitutional principles'.[17] Anything less, as was maintained in 1860 by Admiral Sir William Bowles, another steady enthusiast for a naval militia, was mere 'expedients', indeed 'dangerous and delusive experiments'.[18]

The full pedigree of an English sea militia cannot here be traced. On the analogy of the land militia after 1757 – with its provisions for balloting, substitutes, bounties, annual training and limited service – it bears no real resemblance to the comprehensive *Inscription Maritime*. This had been indeed the favourite model for manning reformers in the eighteenth century, but the discordant agitation of the 1740s and 1750s, analysed by John Western, produced at least one proposal for finding sailors as well as soldiers from a 'list of no-property men' in the parishes, under identical militia rules except that the sailor's bounty should be one guinea more. An 'Officer of Rank' in 1791 mentions a similar scheme and also a version of ship-money, each county to finance a ship called after it and man her – 'on no account to be sent upon foreign service, but considered as attached to the British nation, as the land militia are to the island of Great Britain'.[19] Although nothing came of it, a principal object of Graham's Registration Act (framed by Lieutenant J. H. Brown) was to facilitate a naval ballot; and there is a suggestion that the second Viscount Melville, First Lord in Liverpool's Cabinet and 'the finest friend the Navy ever had', had toyed with the idea.[20] It is certain that the mid-century re-activation of interest in the militia, after the Tahiti war scare of 1844, spread within the next six years through naval circles. In October 1851, as First Lord, Sir Francis Baring himself suggested a naval ballot to Russell. A month later *The Times* came out in favour of a great maritime militia. The idea was thoroughly explored by Admiral Parker's committee of naval officers, one of whom, the Hon. R. S. (later Sir Richard) Dundas, produced a 'Rough Sketch of a Scheme for raising Seamen by Ballot' which received the guarded approval of Byam Martin.[21] More impressive than Dundas or Denman, however, because he would have been concerned in operating a ballot, was the Registrar-General of Seamen, John Hoskins Brown, who told the Committee that throughout the changes in registry law he had 'still further shaped the regulations to this end': it needed only an Act of Parliament to set the machinery in motion. Brown apprehended no serious opposition from the seamen; and one of his collaborators, William Hemsley, the shipping master at Sunderland, where 'ignorant prejudices' about the reformed navy died hard, thought that 'a system of ballot is rendered imperative'.[22]

Commander Brown's plans provided for the fundamental difference between 'mariners', migratory but registered, and the large but less precisely known number of resident 'aquatics, being watermen, bargemen, boatmen, fishermen, etc.; in fact, all persons who gain their living, or any portion of their living, by connection with the sea.' Under old legislation a high proportion of the aquatics, in particular, was protected from the impress, while both aquatics and mariners were exempt from liability to militia service – a conjunction of privileges which advocates of a sea militia were quick to spot.[23] There were certainly mixed opinions about the suitability of the aquatics for service afloat. Captain W. L. Sheringham, a distinguished Admiralty surveyor whose boatwork had gained him intimate knowledge of the coastal population, was sceptical about the fishermen :

I must give it as my opinion that, as a body, their peculiar habits of life render them impatient of control . . . that their accurate local knowledge procures them additional means of subsistence as pilots, not to mention other occupations . . . that they are generally possessed of some property, which they would be unwilling to abandon. . . .[24]

This property, 'consisting of boats, nets, lobster and crab pots, and the like, frequently amounting in value to a considerable sum', also deterred a fisherman's son from leaving home; he became useful to his parents at an early age and would inherit the stock in trade. Such reservations did not prevent Captain W. H. (later Sir William) Hall from proposing a marine militia of fishermen, whose numbers after a recent tour of the coasts he estimated at 130,000 : English 21,000, Scottish 41,000, Irish 68,000. Only the Irish, Hall confessed, 'are better fitted for shore defence'; it would be otherwise with the fishermen at least of south-eastern England and of the Scottish north-east and islands. He too would use the ballot if voluntary enlistment failed : fishermen of 19–30 to serve in men-of-war up to five years, those of 30–40 on tug-steamers converted into gunboats for coast defence, the rest as a home guard.[25] Above all, in 1852, Rear-Admiral M. F. F. (later Admiral Sir Maurice) Berkeley, who served on eighteen Admiralty boards and specialised in manning problems, threw the weight of his authority on the side of a sea militia, drawn from residents of the seaboard. Berkeley, however, added a major qualification : militiamen should not be required to serve out of the Channel. With such a guarantee, and the same inducements as were offered to the land service, volunteering would very likely suffice.[26]

Berkeley's purely defensive type of sea militia was simply a salt-water adaptation of the basic concept of the English militia ashore. Two rather detailed schemes of this kind impressed the Parker Committee. The first, which they printed, came from Captain Sir Thomas Hastings, Principal Storekeeper of the Board of Ordnance. Hastings had earlier (1832–45) been the second captain of HMS *Excellent*, the Navy's school for seamen-gunners at Portsmouth, whose foundation had owed much to the efforts of Captain William Bowles, Comptroller of the Coast Guard in 1822–41, MP for Launceston 1844–52, a member of the Earl of Haddington's Admiralty board 1844–6, a vice-admiral and KCB in 1852.[27] Hastings and Bowles sent a joint memorandum to the Admiralty, in July 1852, which includes the suggestion that all the seaports be assessed for quota-men, procured by ballot if necessary and not confined to 'the sedentary part of our maritime population'. With help from his brother-in-law, Palmerston, and the Home Office Solicitor, Bowles was later to develop this idea into the Heads of a Bill[28] modelled on the Militia Act of 1852: it excludes 'Naval Militia Districts' (under Deputy Lieutenants and Admiralty nominees) from the English counties and comprehends all seafarers (a wider term than mariners) once the Privy Council has to order a ballot, in which event the first-class Naval Militia Man (aged 30 or less) becomes liable for 'actual service' anywhere afloat. Before Bowles had converted him to this bolder conception, however, Hastings had himself worked on a detailed plan.

Avowedly shaken by the Tahiti war scare – when 'we were not only without a fleet in the Channel, but it was seen that seamen could not be obtained without resorting to impressment, which could not be done till war had been declared' – Hastings had talked the matter over with Haddington. With the First Lord's encouragement and the aid of the Admiralty Solicitor, his 'Proposal for establishing a Coast Militia' was ready by July 1846.[29] Hastings envisaged a 'coast militia' divided into five classes from 18 to 60 years of age, to be raised by the county magistrates and parish constables for three to five years' service, extendable in wartime but only for service in the Channel, along the coasts or ashore – unless the militiaman was individually 'by custom, liable to be impressed'. Balloting and calling-out would be conducted under regulations modelled on those of the regular militia. Efficient substitutes would be allowed; the Admiralty would determine annual training (a month or six weeks), discipline, arms and accoutrements; and when employed, the militiamen were 'to enjoy all the advantages of pay, provisions, prize-money, pensions, etc., to which the petty officers and seamen of the fleet are entitled.' Disbanded and renewed every fourth or fifth year, this militia should ensure a force of 12,000 to 15,000 'partially trained men . . . ready for instant service'. It would consist of 'fishermen, bargemen, lightermen, watermen, keelmen, and those employed in rivers and canals' – in short, Commander Brown's 'aquatics', though Hastings explicitly embraces 'all persons who gain their living by the construction, equipment, or supply of shipping'. If these did not suffice, all men residing within five miles of the sea might be liable to ballot, an idea that was to form the basis of a draft bill published in 1874 by Sherard Osborn, who considered that few men living within twenty-five miles of the sea would be altogether unacquainted with it.[30]

Hastings, true to the mood of the time, was clearly dominated by the scope for passive defence, even if he feared 'incursive attacks' rather than full-scale invasion : predatory incursions, often experienced in the past from the French corsairs, might be easier in steamships. So the coast militia would be required to man the guardships and forts or batteries ashore, notably around the dockyards. Hastings, in fact, was also an initiator of the experiment of 1845 in 'blockships' – ships of the line converted to steam power for service as mobile batteries at critical points along the coasts.[31] The handling of such ships, of course, would make fewer demands on that exercise aloft which characterised the able seaman, while creating a new demand for stokers and other non-seamen. What Hastings primarily sought for his militiamen was exercise in gunnery, small arms and cutlass, exercise rendered as simple as possible and kindly administered. This last injunction was intended for naval officers, since the coast militia would have no others – a serious flaw in the 'militia analogy', as experience was to show.

Hastings's Proposal, which did not dismiss ultimate resort to pressing, fell far short of such a mobile sea militia as Denman and Bowles were advocating by 1852. His coast militia bore a stronger resemblance to the corps of Sea Fencibles of 1798–1810, except that these had been volunteers and embodied in wartime only. Their name was borrowed, indeed, for the second scheme which is said to have impressed the Parker Committee. It came from Sir

Charles Elliot, RN, governor of Bermuda, who in July 1846 had printed for private circulation *A Proposal in behalf of the Seamen of England*, in which the Royal Navy was presented as merely the military corps of 'the naval array of England' – that is, 'the whole body of the population employed in navigation and the fisheries, to be called the Navy of Great Britain'. Towards the end of 1852, emboldened by the current newspaper debate, Elliot published these nineteen propositions as an Appendix to an elaborate plan for the muster, exercise and reward of 'a powerful Sea Fencible Force, for service on or off the shores of the United Kingdom', computed at a total of 40,000 men costing £450,000 a year.[32] Half this force would consist of 'Moveables', first-class seafarers, aged 18 to 45, liable for service elsewhere than at the places of their enrolment and expected to exercise every ten days

. . . in the service of cannon, the use of small arms, including the cutlass, the service of the fire-engine, the mounting and dismounting of ship and field-guns, the prompt, orderly and silent embarkation and disembarkation of troops, and generally in all the duties incident to flotilla service. . . .

The second half, the 'Reserve Class of Sea Fencibles' (*aet.* 17–50), would serve only at their place of enrolment unless proclaimed moveable 'in a state of actual war'; it might include 'Occasional Men' – temporarily unemployed seamen who could be mustered for three hours daily five days a week. For training purposes, the coasts of England and Scotland were to be divided into eight sections, with a separate organisation for Ireland. The merit of the plan was that it should have familiarised 'the general body of seafarers with the public service by some degree of training near home; and Elliot was probably the originator of the concept of Naval Districts on which Bowles and Osborn were to base their more ambitious plans for a militia-type conscription. Elliot, like Hastings, recognised that success depended on a judicious choice of officers: 'A harassing mode of exercise, regardless of the character and pursuits of the people, could not be too carefully shunned.' Unlike Hastings, he was evidently willing to rely on bounties and pay (increasing when a man was marked 'trained') to attract volunteers. Hardly more than Hastings, however, did Elliot depart from the notion of a militia rooted in home defence. His trained Fencibles were to enjoy the pay and victuals of able seamen in the Royal Navy, with pension rights if they served long enough; but such general service was again a matter of free will.

The recommendation of the Parker Committee was a good deal more modest : five or six thousand 'Royal Naval Coast Volunteers', who would 'enter into a Distinct Engagement to serve afloat' but would 'not be required to proceed to a Distance exceeding Fifty Leagues from the Coasts of the United Kingdom'. The Act constituting the Royal Naval Coast Volunteers, which received the royal assent on 7 July 1853, extended this limit to 100 leagues (for one year) in case of actual or imminent invasion; in 1863 the limit was removed altogether, but only for volunteers entering or re-entering after the passage of the amending statute on 6 March.[33] At no time was there to be even a contingent ballot. From 1853, in fact, the application of the ballot to the regular militia itself was suspended from year to year. It was not needed. In the case of the navy it was felt to be unreliable, and its incidence haphazard and unfair. As the Parker Committe reported,

To confine its exercise to those Classes only which happen to be within the Limits of the United Kingdom on the Occasion of an Emergency would reduce the Number of Seamen liable to Ballot to a very small Proportion of those really effective; the Men thereby obtained would necessarily be drawn from the Classes which, being the most sedentary in their Habits, would be the least efficient for the active Duties of Her Majesty's Ships; and as the Majority of the best Seamen of the Country would, from their Absence abroad, escape its immediate Operation, the Semblance only of Justice would be maintained, with much real Hardship and Inequality upon those subject to its Demand.[34]

In 1859 the Hardwicke Commission reached the same conclusion. The ballot was open to most of the objections to impressment, without promising to produce 'any great number of men on an emergency'. Further, it would select a much larger proportion of those eligible than had the ballot for the regular militia.[35] (Hence the large size of the Naval Militia Districts proposed in 1874 by Sherard Osborn, who contemplated a constituency of several million men, without restriction (to seafarers.)

It must be said that the militia enthusiasts occasionally made the worst of a good case. When a Commons Select Committee went over this ground in 1861, Baring exposed the most obvious flaw in Bowles's militia analogy :

Is it possible for a clodhopper to go away easily, and is it not very easy for a sailor to do that? – I should not expect to get the best seamen by means of the scheme which I propose; it would be rather as a great increase of strength in numbers than that you would get the best seamen in that way.

Bowles admitted that he was relying on 'the sedentary part of our population on the coast', even though he had denounced the Naval Coast Volunteers as the worst possible description of local militia. He was also driven into declaring his ignorance of 'the detail' of ballot machinery.[36] Again, Sir Richard Dundas told the Hardwicke Commission that he had never maturely considered his own 'rough scheme' of 1852, then or since; he spoke of 'some description of ballot' and agreed it could only apply to 'fishermen and men of that description', if volunteering failed during war; it was merely a substitute for impressment.[37]

Denman indeed stood his ground much more convincingly before the Hardwicke Commission, even when cross-examined by Cardwell, who evidently took a major part in these discussions; but his defence of the efficacy of a ballot, and indeed of its equity (since the regular militia managed to recruit without it), depended on a whole series of other measures 'to render the royal navy congenial to the tastes, habits, and inclinations of our seamen as far as possible', to erase the memory of past breaches of faith, and to compensate for an 'earlier . . . and more severe service' than would ever be required of other citizens. Denman was prominent among those who vainly pleaded for a State-aided pension fund for merchant seamen, if only 'as a means of rendering the registration more effectual, and . . . of attaching our seamen to the country, which at present has a very feeble hold upon them, especially considering the position which the United States of America now occupy'.[38] Had such measures been adopted, paradoxically they should have rendered a ballot superfluous, especially as Denman urged it only 'in aid of' existing 'special reserves', notably the Marines and the recently much improved Coast Guard Service, which had come under Admiralty control in 1856 and was incidentally responsible for training the Coast Volunteers.[39] Denman, however, was far too deeply imbued with the 'great principle' of national service to allow the State to trade special concessions like pensions for an individual service obligation – to regard them, in short, as a sort of retainer, a term which exactly describes the 'inducements' proposed by the Hardwicke Commission for joining their new Royal Naval Reserve. Ironically enough, together with a long-term plan for feeding this reserve with boys trained in a much increased number of school-ships, these inducements owed

much to Denman's suggestions for creating confidence in the operation of 'a fair system' of compulsory service.[40]

In facing the dire circumstances which might call for compulsion,
neverthelesss, it must be said that the friends of a naval militia
displayed on honest realism rather fudged by the Commission,
which, having argued against pressing, ended by maintaining the
proclamation clauses of Graham's Act of 1853. They refused to
abolish impressment because their proposed voluntary reserve might
not always suffice, while on the other hand they did not like the
militia analogy. Bowles and Osborn were alone in pressing this
beyond the needs of home defence. Even Denman never proposed
that a naval militia could be asked to do more than man the
Channel fleet. He thought indeed that his militiamen would readily
volunteer for general service, but those who did so would have to
be removed from the Channel fleet. This was not a very convincing
answer to Cardwell's question : 'Still the presence of any one man
on board a ship who was only enlisted for a limited service would
paralyse that ship if it were intended to employ her for general
service?'[41]

Apart from a thoughtful contribution to the impressment debate,
and to the underlying problem of how to bring naval and merchant
services into closer touch and mutual sympathy, the mid-century
campaign for a naval militia resulted only in the twenty-year
experiment of the Coast Volunteers, who last appear in the Naval
Estimates for 1873-4.[42] They received qualified praise from the
Coast Guard captains examined by the Hardwicke Commission.
Very few Volunteers, it was said, had come in from the coasting
trade, and there were dead recruiting areas like Deal and Harwich;
Liverpool families frequently interfered when their men were about
to sign on; in many places recruits were discouraged by having to
travel great distances to enrol or attend their 28 days' annual drill.
Nevertheless, the bounty and wages were attractive. Six thousand
Volunteers had been entered, at a rising annual rate, during the
years 1854-8; as many as 1,470 were to come forward in 1865.[43]
There was general agreement on their aptitude for gun-drill, much
less on their capacity for exercise aloft, a failing that was to keep
many a robust fisherman out of the Second Class Naval Reserve
after this was established in 1871,[44] but not one which the Parker
Committee had cared about. Some Volunteers were part-time
smugglers who did not get on well with their officers from the Coast
Guard – naval men in any case whose manners and modes of

address did not always please. The witnesses all refer to the 'dirty habits' of the Volunteers, likely to cause friction on a man-of-war. But their chief limitation as seamen was that 'they look a great deal to their not being called far from their homes'.[45] They needed continual assurances against a naval trap. If the enrolment figures for 1864 and 1865 scarcely support the notion that the force declined simply because the statutory limit on service afloat was repealed in 1863, it is true that Admiral (later Sir Walter) Tarleton, who was responsible for the decision to phase out the RNCV as soon as the RNR (Second Class) was introduced, later said that the fishermen, unlike the longshore men, 'would not give up their occupations to go on board ship, to live for 30 days amongst people of different habits from their own'.[46] They continued to find an eloquent champion in Thomas Brassey, MP for Hastings and a lifelong yachtsman; but one who had commanded the Coast Volunteers was to describe them as 'the worst stick the country ever attempted to lean upon'.[47]

The sad end of the RNCV underlines a contrast that the friends of a naval militia always overlooked. In a series of articles contributed to *The Nautical Magazine* in 1858, Captain Sheringham, a late convert who wanted the Coast Volunteers to survive, asked whether the regular militia itself would prosper under strict army discipline :

Both officers and men of the Militia, when disembodied, return together into civil life; the latter therefore feel that the former still remain their all-sufficient safeguards . . . ever ready to check any attempt at interference with their prescriptive rights, and the better able to do so as their means and station in life place them beyond the fear of any pressure on the part of the executive.[48]

Perhaps, after all, a Commodore of the Royal Victoria Yacht Club had struck at the root of the matter in suggesting a Marine Militia officered by yacht-owners – 'none but gentlemen in some degree proficient in seamanship . . .'[49] Amateur yachtsmen (and oarsmen) were in fact precisely the class to which Brassey, with Goschen's support, was to look for the Royal Naval Artillery Volunteers whom he inaugurated and led in 1873; but this was explicitly a gentlemen's corps in all ranks and not expected, by Goschen at any rate, 'to have superlatively good sea-legs'.[50] The fishermen and their like, if they volunteered at all, would belong to the second class of Naval Reserve. Besides being divorced in this way, neither class of volunteers in the least answered to the idea of a naval militia as conceived twenty years earlier by the advocates of a fair and reliable substitute for impressment. Two of them at least, Elliot and Denman, were yachting men.[51] And yet, generous and sensible as their schemes might be, they all lost sight of the neighbourly, almost sporting affinities which held the English militia together. They took from it two features that were effectively concealed from sight after its resuscitation in 1852 : the principle of compulsory service and its neglected cushion, the ballot. At least their efforts may remind us of the power of the original militia idea long after the period to which John Western devoted years of profitable study.

12

The French Revolution and the
Nationalisation of Honour

NORMAN HAMPSON

Montesquieu's *De l'Esprit des lois*, which Burke considered to be 'probably the most important book that had ever been written', defined the terms in which Frenchmen were to think about political problems during the second half of the eighteenth century. Montesquieu divided all states into three broad categories, republics, monarchies and despotisms, the last of which he dismissed as the negation of good government. Of the remaining two, he tended to consider republics in terms of ancient Greece and classical Rome. Their principles and history were of academic interest, their ideals perhaps a reproach to the Europe of his own day, but they belonged to a past that had not much contemporary relevance. His main concern was with monarchies, the principles on which they rested and the means by which they might be made more humane and more respectful of the liberty of their subjects. Rousseau, when he published *Du Contrat social* fourteen years later, in 1762, accepted more of Montesquieu's argument than has been generally recognised. He did, however, re-define the word 'republic' to mean, not a type of constitution, but any political society in which government rested on the tacit or explicit consent of the governed. He consequently transferred to contemporary society criteria which Montesquieu had thought relevant only to the distant past and he also developed arguments of his own about the general will which was the collective voice of a particular society. The extent of Rousseau's influence, and in particular the influence of *Du Contrat social*, has been disputed.[1] It was reprinted only once between 1764 and the outbreak of the French Revolution, but there

199

had been thirteen French editions within a year of its publication and although it attracted fewer readers than his philosophical novel, *La Nouvelle Héloïse*, the pamphlets of 1788–9 and the speeches of revolutionary orators show clearly enough that those who were politically active were familiar with its arguments, even if they did not appreciate the metaphysical conundrums posed by his conception of the general will.[2]

Montesquieu's analysis of monarchy was a rationalisation of the mental attitudes which, in fact, underlay *ancien régime* society in France. Rousseau's republican ideology could easily be used as the basis for a repudiation of this society in terms of ideal values. This was to happen during the French Revolution, when a conscious effort was made to use political power to re-shape the machinery of government and the character of the French people into conformity with the ideal standards of the republic. In this process, the honour which Montesquieu had seen as the basis of monarchical society was rejected in favour of republican patriotism, but the attempt to resuscitate the spirit of Sparta in eighteenth-century Europe produced a new ideology: revolutionary nationalism.

For Montesquieu, the sense of honour on which monarchies rested was a feeling natural to the upper classes and confirmed by their education, which impelled them to seek status for themselves and their families, or to affirm the status they already enjoyed, within a hierarchical society. It was 'not so much what we owe to others as what we owe to ourselves . . . not so much what draws us towards our fellow-citizens as to what distinguishes us from them.'[3] 'The nature of honour is to demand preferences and distinctions.'[4] Since the greatest honour was associated with the service of the king, those who lived by the code of honour would spontaneously gravitate towards the royal service, in war, in the exercise of the king's justice or in the royal administration. The satisfaction of family pride not merely staffed the institutions of government but ensured, in theory at least, that office would be discharged with a sense of responsibility. 'Each acts for the common good, while conscious only of following his particular interest.'[5] The 'invisible hand' of eighteenth-century economic liberals was thus invoked by Montesquieu as a kind of providential regulator which allowed society to function on a basis of natural inclination rather than of altruism. He was at some pains to dissociate the working of the system from any objective moral basis, freely admitting that honour was purely a matter of social convention. 'Philosophically speaking, it is a false honour which directs all the parts of the state, but this false honour is just as useful to the public as true honour would be to private individuals.'[6] In practice, therefore, honour provided rulers with cheap but conditional service from their most distinguished subjects. Rewards need cost no more than titles and decorations, but the monarch's power was circumscribed by the fact that a noble's prime allegiance was to himself and to the privileged corporations, such as Provincial Estates and Parlements, that conferred on him a status and dignity which were not derived from the king. It was precisely this tempering of royal power by the existence of autonomous corporate bodies and by the personal code of honour of their members that constituted the difference between monarchy and despotism, and Montesquieu quoted with approval the refusal of a provincial governor to carry out the king's order to massacre the Huguenots in Bayonne, as something not possible.[7]

All of this was in total contrast to the situation assumed to have existed in classical republics. These rested not on honour but on *vertu*, which Montesquieu defined as 'love of the laws and of the *patrie*.'[8] Such public spirit was 'a feeling and not a body of knowledge. The lowest man in the state . . . can experience this feeling as well as the highest.'[9] The purest form of the republic was therefore a democracy. In democratic republics the state rested on a basis of equality which in turn implied universal frugality.[10] As the ambiguous term *vertu* implied, the democratic republic was therefore both a real (if vanished) type of government and an aspiration after the ideal, in which all citizens would subordinate personal to public interest. Unlike a monarchy, the republic did not benefit from any providential identity of what Pope called 'self-love and social' and its continuance depended on 'a renunciation of self, which is always a very arduous thing.'[11] As he had shown in his *Lettres persanes*, Montesquieu considered that a state which required so much self-denial was unlikely to endure for long. As a practically-minded man, he was much more interested in studying his own society in which 'The state exists independently of love of the *patrie*, of the desire for true glory, renunciation of self, sacrifice of one's dearest interests and all those heroic virtues that we find in the classics and which are mere hearsay so far as we ourselves are concerned.'[12]

Whereas Montesquieu wrote as a noble and a former member of one of his beloved *pouvoirs intermédiaires*, the Bordeaux Parlement,

Rousseau, an outsider by deliberate choice, proclaimed in the introduction to *Du Contrat social* that he was 'born a citizen of a free state [Geneva] and a member of the sovereign power.' In his more practical writings he recognised the force of existing social conventions such as the code of honour, but his contemporaries, like subsequent critics, tended to find his political message in *Du Contrat social*. This was planned, not as a socio- logical study like *De l'Esprit des lois,* but to solve the more philo- sophical problem of finding a moral justification for political sovereignty. He began by affirming that all legitimate governments, whatever the form of their constitution, rested on the assent of the general will. In his sense, therefore, 'Every legitimate govern- ment is republican.'[13] Rousseau accepted Montesquieu's conception of the republic as a régime based on *vertu*, but he did not share his predecessor's belief in the existence of moral absolutes. For him, it was the transition from natural to civil society that transformed men into moral beings. Moral values were therefore a social creation and could not transcend the self-interest of the society to which they owed their birth. The general will of a community, as an expression of that self-interest, was therefore not merely politi- cally, but also morally infallible. 'The sovereign, by the mere fact of its existence, is always what it ought to be.'[14] In so far as there was any discrepancy between the moral will of the community and the subjective judgment of a citizen, the individual should there- fore accept the verdict of the general will as binding upon his own conscience. If he resisted, the community should 'force him to be free.'

In a world of morally autonomous sovereign states, international relations could not be subject to any overriding moral law. In theory, Rousseau accepted their equality, but throughout his writings he had a particular affection for Sparta. He disliked eighteenth-century cosmopolitanism and felt that patriotism would be most cohesive when experienced as a state of latent hostility between 'us' and 'them'. Although he did not spell this out explicitly, it followed from his premises that if one state was a genuine re- public, in his sense of the term, and another was not ruled by the general will of its citizens, the former was *ipso facto* ethically superior and any conflict between the two would take on the nature of a moral crusade.

Montesquieu's conception of the spirit of a monarchy explicitly repudiated patriotism. The basis of the noble's service to the king was personal and voluntary, a matter of inclination rather than of duty. 'There is nothing which honour prescribes to the nobility so much as serving the prince in war. . . . But when it imposes this law, honour wishes to remain its arbiter. If it is offended it demands or allows that one retire to one's home. It wills that one should be able either to aspire to employment or to refuse it. It holds this liberty dearer than fortune itself.'[15] Men of honour formed part of an international society, as wide as the civilised world, which lived by the same rules. The democratic republic, on the other hand, egalitarian in essence, could find no place for honour with its distinctions and hierarchy of status. In its place it put the duty of patriotism, which was national and unconditional. The individual had no personal imperative to invoke against the demands of the majority and in cases of disagreement the community was the arbiter of its own quarrel. This antithesis between honour and patriotism was more than an abstract conception of political theory. It was part of the language in which Frenchmen formulated their thoughts, and unless its nature is understood a good deal of their thinking and action will be only partially intelligible.

Montesquieu's theories rested on an idealised but basically accurate analysis of actual French society. Service in the army was badly paid, except for the Court nobility who enjoyed accelerated promotion, but was still eagerly sought by those more interested in status than money. Officers were free to leave when they chose and, if they judged their merit insufficiently rewarded, to enlist in foreign armies. Wars were fought to rule and the fate of officer prisoners of war was regulated by an elaborate and admirably humane system of parole, which rested on the well-justified assumption that the officer would have more regard for his personal honour than for the victory of his country.[16] Governments themselves contributed to this attitude by cashiering officers who broke parole in order to escape.

Civilians also, when they accepted royal disfavour in defence of their corporate privileges, claimed that it was honour that commanded disobedience. Président de Brosses, when he drafted a remonstrance for the Parlement of Burgundy in 1762, wrote that 'Honour is a law which no power can oppose. Over the upright man it exercises the first of all authorities.'[17] In some circles at least, ideas as to what constituted status do not seem to have changed much during the century. The letters patent conferring a dukedom on the Comte de Tavanes, as late as 1786, offer a whole shopping list of honourable characteristics : length of lineage, royal service, extensive estates, 'magnificent' château and 'very good' seigneurial rights.[18] There is certainly nothing here to suggest that anyone was having any doubts about the values of the *ancien régime*.

In Europe as a whole, classical patriotism found few defenders. 'Roman patriotism !' said Goethe, 'heaven preserve us from anything so monstrous.' Perhaps the most thoroughly unpleasant characters in *Tom Jones* and *Peregrine Pickle* are the tutors, Square and Jolter, whose professions of classical *vertu* conceal somewhat different qualities. The point was generally taken that patriotism, with its duty of total self-subordination to the nation-state, could have no place in eighteenth-century society. When the term 'patriot' was introduced it referred, not to a defender of the state against its foreign enemies, but to a revolutionary who aimed to replace the monarchical by the republican concept of government. It was used in this sense in both France and the United Provinces in the 1780s.

How far these aristocratic values were shared by ambitious and educated commoners is far from clear. Certainly the trend of much of the thought of the Enlightenment was towards the tangible and material. In everyday life there was resentment of aristocratic *morgue*, but this rarely prevented the disgruntled from seizing an opportunity of joining the charmed circle themselves. Reformers objected not so much to the code of honour itself as to its restriction to the nobility. They aspired to the sort of society that existed in England, where the gentlemen enjoyed the kind of status that was reserved, in France, for the noble. There were, however, exceptions. Carnot, who had been rejected as a prospective son-in-law by a man in the process of acquiring nobility, denounced both the code of honour and the *philosophes* who had come to terms with it. In a recently discovered speech to the Arras Academy, he asked himself how 'these leaders of philosophy, who pride themselves on rising above the prejudices of the century, come to be, in a different respect, the most abject slaves. Honour, the first of these prejudices, which in fact comprehends all the others . . . is practically the only motive of their conduct.' After a bitter exposition of the conflict between the dictates of honour and human and divine law, he went on to admit that 'It is nevertheless from this honour and the prejudices to which it gives birth that stem almost all the usages and customs to which the different peoples of the earth have enslaved themselves.'[19] But this was in May 1787, when the revolutionary crisis had already begun.

When representatives of the French nobility challenged the reforming absolutism of Calonne in 1787, they claimed to be the heirs of Montesquieu, fighting the good fight against the despotic tendencies inherent in the French monarchy since the days of Louis XIII and Richelieu. As the struggle intensified in 1788, innumerable pamphlets denounced the excesses of 'ministerial despotism'. 'A king ceases to enjoy the rights of kingship as soon as he outrages nature proscribes [*sic* : 'prescribes'?] what is repugnant to honour.'[20] The Parlement of Nancy, protesting against Lamoignon's judicial reforms of 8 May 1788, took up Montesquieu's old argument that social levelling was characteristic of despotism. 'It is thus that the drawing together of social ranks, the abolition of the privileges which distinguish them, the extinction of intermediate bodies and subordinate authorities, gradually undermines the foundations of monarchial government and prepares the way for arbitrary rule.'[21]

There were many, however, who broadened the debate to enlist the support of the *philosophes* as a whole and began to employ republican concepts and terminology. They had, no doubt, been encouraged in this direction by the Parlements themselves which, when it suited them, had for a generation been talking of 'citizens' instead of 'subjects' and of the 'nation' instead of the 'kingdom'. A pamphleteer apostrophised the army officers who were so reluctant to suppress the riots of 1788 : 'Heirs of your ancestors' valour as well as of their names, you have adopted neither their ignorant pride nor their savage disregard of the rights of man : beneficent philosophy softens your habits, enlightens your minds and teaches you to appreciate the value of a citizen.'[22]

By 1789 many of the nobility had convinced themselves that the sacrifice of their fiscal privileges would enable them to make the best of both worlds and to play the republican card while still retaining all the trump cards of a hierarchical society. The Provincial Estates of Artois were so exclusive that they kept out most of the local *nobility* and they had no intention of broadening their membership when they proclaimed, in January 1789, that 'Everything seems to be moving . . . towards that equality, so necessary in a great state, where the members of all the orders of society, finding the same protection, owe each the same aid and the same taxes; yet without harm to the legitimate distinctions which the honour of a name, the brilliance of rank and birth should preserve for those who received them from their ancestors or obtained them by their merit or station.'[23] Those of the nobility who were excluded from the local Estates were rather less satisfied with the situation : 'Thirty years ago, men did not have such a clear idea of the rights of man, considered both as man and as citizen. . . . Are we Frenchmen? Are we subjects of Louis XVI? What is the use of being noble if one is no longer a citizen?'[24] It was these 'citizens' who, three months later, wrote into their *cahier* no less than fourteen articles calling for the retention or extension of the privileges peculiar to the nobility.[25] What was true of Artois seems to have held good for France as a whole and the nobility of the entire country confronted the Estates General with its republican slogans, which were increasingly at variance with its monarchial interests.

During the first phase of the Revolution itself, from the convocation of the Estates General to the fall of the monarchy, there were occasional attempts at a rearguard action in defence of the old principles. It was perhaps appropriate that one of the most bitter of these should concern the navy, many of whose officers were drawn from a Breton nobility scarcely renowned for its enlightenment. The reorganisation of the royal navy in which commoners had, with very few exceptions, been confined to the lowest rank of sub-lieutenant, revealed attitudes that were probably more often felt than publicly expressed. Merchant navy officers, who were all commoners, demanded the right to retain their rank when transferred to fighting ships in war time. The outraged spokesmen of the *Grand Corps* of the noble officers from the royal navy, instead of taking their stand on the specialised knowledge required in the fighting fleet, preferred to imply that commoners would run away. The Chevalier de Coudraye explained to the Assembly that 'The fighting fleet . . . should have glory and the defence of the *patrie* as its only goal. Love of riches makes men insensible to honour.' The Comte de la Galissonnière, supporting him, complained that the proposed reform was 'a system invented by that innovating spirit which is partially responsible for our ills.'[26]

The navy had already provoked a revealing disagreement between Robespierre and the spokesman of the *comité de marine* in the previous year. When Robespierre objected to a penal code that proposed to keel-haul seamen for offences for which officers would merely be cashiered, Defermon explained to him that 'Officers are punished by the loss of their honour, which is what a Frenchman holds most dear.'[27] When one considers that Defermon was one of the more radical members of the committee, it is clear that the old attitudes died hard, at least where the navy was concerned.

From the extreme Left, Robespierre castigated honour in terms reminiscent of those used by Carnot, his former colleague in the Arras Academy: 'That spirit, at once tyrannical and servile, base and arrogant, that feudal extravagance dignified with the name of honour.'[28] 'What is this honour then . . . which supposes neither love of the *patrie* nor respect for humanity nor the faithful discharge of the most sacred duties of the citizen? . . . Honour is the particular patrimony of the officer corps.'[29] When Brissot called for war in the name of French honour, in January 1792, Robespierre countered him wih a republican definition: 'Magnanimity, wisdom, liberty, happiness, *vertu*, that is what constitutes our honour. The honour that you would revive is the friend and supporter of despotism, it is the honour of the aristocracy's heroes, the honour of all the tyrants.'[30]

This rejection of aristocratic in favour of republican values was not confined to Robespierre. Welcoming a deputation of Quakers, as President of the Assembly, on 10 February 1791, Mirabeau told them that their pacifism was no longer justified in a revolutionary France whose wars could only be defensive. In effect, this was to endorse Rousseau's view that the citizen could not appeal to his individual conscience in a state where the general will was effectively sovereign.

The whole question of war and peace had been debated at length in May 1790. Speakers of the Left insisted that revolutionary France would never provoke an aggressive war and an official resolution to this effect was voted. It was, however, the moderate Clermont-Tonnerre who asserted that the Revolution had made France qualitatively different from her neighbours. 'I am aware that enlightened self-interest, universal reason, blessed philosophy could bring about universal peace. But we are the only people constituted on true principles of justice and national equity.' Rather oddly, it was one of the spokesmen of the extreme Right, Cazalès, who, while attacking what he called 'modern philosophy', put forward a Rousseauist conception of exclusive patriotism that was badly received by his fellow-deputies. 'Love of the *patrie* should be the exclusive object of our affection. Love of the *patrie* creates more than men, it creates citizens. . . . As for me, I declare that I do not care for the Russians, the Germans and the English; it is Frenchmen whom I cherish; the blood of a single one of my fellow-citizens is dearer to me than that of all the peoples of the world.'[31]

When revolutionary France actually found itself engaged in what must by definition have been a defensive war, even though it was actually declared by France, the situation was complicated by the fact that the king was hoping for a French defeat. This posed a dilemma, both for the patriot who was also a constitutional monarchist and for the royalist who found that the pursuit of honour and the service of the king pointed in opposite directions. The problems of both were soon solved by the insurrection of 10 August 1792, which swept away the monarchy and resolved the contradiction between republican principles and monarchical institutions.

The French republic gradually came to impose on the population the kind of constraints that Montesquieu and Rousseau had assumed citizens would impose upon themselves. Both authors had treated a republic as the constitutional expression of the innate republicanism of its citizens. The Convention and the Committee of Public Safety found, like Lenin after 1917, that they had to create a kind of society of which they should have been the products. The France of 1793–4 was full of royalists and recalcitrant Catholics who rejected the republic on principle. From the most optimistic point of view, the remainder of the citizenry, who had grown to maturity in the enervating corruption of Talleyrand's *douceur de vivre*, was unlikely to show much spontaneous enthusiasm for the arduous self-discipline of republican *vertu*. The creation of republican *moeurs* therefore called for both the repression of opposition and the indoctrination of the uncommitted. 'If the strength of popular government in peacetime resides in *vertu*, its strength in time of revolution is in both *vertu* and terror; *vertu*, without which terror is fatal, terror, without which *vertu* is impotent.'[32] The policies of *l'an II* therefore owed much of their inspiration to the ideas of the writers of the Enlightenment, but were distorted by an entirely different political context. Many of those responsible for their adoption saw them merely as the temporary response to a military crisis and those who aspired to create a new kind of republican man were never more than a minority of the minority.

Little by little the republican state came to assert, in theory and in practice, the kind of total claim over its citizens that had been denied to the monarchy. In August 1793 the entire population was placed under requisition until French territory should be liberated and men in the 18–25 age-group were called up at once. All kinds of labour were requisitioned as required. Although the right to private property was guaranteed, its exploitation was circumscribed. Wages and the prices of essential commodities were controlled and the state fixed profit margins, requisitioned merchant ships and land transport and imposed punitive taxation on the wealthy. Historians have been tempted to see in the controlled economy of the year II a kind of primitive socialism, but this is an historical anachronism. In practical terms it often amounted to the revival of regulations of the *ancien régime* that had been discarded by the economic liberals of 1789. Ideologically, it all followed from the precepts of egalitarian republicanism as defined by Montesquieu and Rousseau, with the rather important exception that it was imposed from above instead of being volunteered from below. The Paris Commune tried to enforce morality by chasing prostitutes off the streets, while Robespierre and Saint-Just advocated indoctrinating the young in compulsory state boarding-schools where the emphasis would be on *vertu*, frugality and military training rather than on knowledge.

Honour was now explicitly repudiated in favour of republican patriotism. The Minister of War wrote to the Commander-in-Chief on the Ardennes front on 11 April 1794 : 'The word "honour" is entirely out of place in republics. It must be replaced by *vertu*, courage, patriotism, probity.'[33] The Comte de Canclaux understood the new language and, when dismissed from his command, reported to his superiors : 'I am retiring with the submission of a republican who serves his *patrie* only when and as it wants to be served.'[34] Robespierre expounded the basic theory at some length in his speech of 5 February 1794 on the principles of public morality. 'We want an order of things where all the cruel and base passions are chained up and all the beneficent and generous ones stimulated by the laws . . . where distinctions arise only from equality itself. In our country, we wish to substitute morality for egoism, probity for honour, principles for conventions, duties for propriety, the rule of reason for the tyranny of fashion.'[35]

Something that the *Montagnards* did not find in Rousseau was the growing conviction that the Revolution had made France different from and superior to other states. In November 1793 Robespierre declared that the defeat of France would bring back the Dark Ages and by May 1794 he thought France's lead over the rest had increased to two thousand years.[36] In theory, no doubt,

what the French had accomplished could be achieved by any other
nation, but the revolutionaries soon tired of waiting for the rest
to overthrow their 'tyrants' and catch up, and it was gradually
assumed that the regeneration of France was due to qualities
inherent in the country, to which foreigners could not aspire. 'Alone
among the peoples of the world, it is made to re-establish the reign
of liberty on earth.'[37] 'You are, amongst the nations, what Hercules
was amongst the heroes. Nature had made you sturdy and powerful; your strength matches your *vertu* and your cause is that of
the gods themselves.'[38] The invocation of Hercules showed how easy
it was, even for a man like Robespierre, who opposed wars of conquest, to equate *vertu* with power and to descend to vulgar jingo-
ism : 'Today one Frenchman is worth more than ten Prussians.'[39]
Couthon went farther than Robespierre, who had only wanted to
re-establish liberty. 'Since human societies first came into being,
there has only been one land where freedom, equality, *vertu* and
reason could combine in peace and live in the gentle intimacy of
four sisters, created to spread happiness over the earth, and that
land is France.'[40]

A natural consequence of such 'republican' attitudes was that the
war against the European 'tyrants' gradually came to be seen as
a war between peoples. The responsibility for this did not lie wholly
with France. The British government in particular fought with a
brutal disregard for the conventions of international law that it
might not have shown in a war against a monarchy. The naval
blockade was extended to cover supplies of food, a French frigate
was seized in a neutral port and French *assignats* were forged in
England. It was understandable that the Convention should have
voted Pitt 'the enemy of the human race'. Many revolutionaries
wished to encourage the enslaved British to overthrow their 'tyrant',
but they soon lost patience with the lack of response from across
the Channel. The Convention, as usual, saw the dangers of the
direction in which it was moving, and continued to follow it all
the same. On 9 October 1793 Fabre d'Eglantine and Robespierre
persuaded it to vote the arrest of all English civilians living in
France and to confiscate their property. Robespierre, who had
never shared the Anglomania of some of his colleagues, quoted
another deputy as having said that France was at war with the
British government and not with the British people. 'That speech
made me shudder.' A week later, when it was proposed to extend
the measure to the arrest of all enemy aliens, the Committee of

Public Safety was accused of wanting to 'nationalise' the war. This was still sufficiently heretical for the spokesman of the Committee, Saint-Just, to repudiate the charge, but the Bill was passed all the same. In December foreigners were excluded from public exployment and from sitting in the Convention, a reversal of the attitude of the previous year, when French nationality had been offered to Paine and a small group of international celebrities. The culmination of this policy came after an attempt to assassinate one of the members of the Committee of Public Safety which was somewhat hastily attributed to the British government. Barère, whose political mutability reflected whatever happened to be the orthodoxy of the moment, made the most ferocious speech of his career. 'It is time for national hatred to pronounce itself. . . . *Il n'y a que les morts qui ne reviennent pas.*' The docile Convention obediently decreed that no British or Hanoverian prisoners would be taken.[41] That this was not so much a temporary aberration as an indication of a trend was shown on 4 July when Barère – again – called for a war of extermination and secured a vote that all foreign garrisons holding French towns should be executed if they failed to surrender within twenty-four hours.

This was the end of the road, both logically and chronologically. The creation and protection of the ideal republic had come to rest on a policy of unlimited terror at home, as dictated by the ferocious law of 22 *prairial* (10 June) and a war of extermination against foreign enemies. Within a month of Barère's speech, Robespierre was dead and the Convention had stripped the Committee of Public Safety of its dictatorial powers. For better and worse, the Thermidoreans had no use for either *vertu* or terror. With the overthrow of the revolutionary dictatorship, the attempt to create by force the kind of society that Montesquieu and Rousseau had conceived as a natural product and to impose it on a hostile Europe disappeared for ever. Later revolutions would have other objectives. But the Thermidoreans did not repudiate the entire legacy of the year II. What was retained was a new sense of the omnipotence of the state – temporarily concealed by the weakness of the central government – and an assertion of the national superiority of the *Grande Nation*.

The rule of Napoleon was to show that revolutionary patriotism, shorn of its democratic and egalitarian aspects and of its dedication to *vertu*, had assumed some of the characteristics of aristocratic honour and transferred them from the individual to the nation-

state. The most respected members of society were once again the
military men, but their obligations and rewards were dictated by
the Emperor rather than by their own volition. Status, as exemplified by the Legion of Honour and the Imperial nobility, was
determined from above. French society was egalitarian in the sense
that no one could claim privileges on the basis of birth, but the
Emperor, in the name of the nation, granted rank and distinction
in accordance with what he assumed to be social utility. The fact
that the new nobles aped the manners of the old, together with
the traditional association of honour with the martial virtues,
tended to obscure the distinction between those who were made
dukes because they had earned the rank of field-marshal and those
who had formerly sometimes become field-marshals because they
had been born into ducal families. Honour was now national
rather than personal. Obligations were defined and imposed by the
Emperor. The service of the state was something that he demanded
and for which he paid. It was neither the privilege of the seigneur
nor the voluntary tribute of the citizen. In its descent from the ideal
to the actual, patriotism had acquired a more restrictive meaning
and the new nationalism offered neither the aspirations of *vertu*
nor the old safeguards of honour.

13

War Transport and 'Counter-revolution' in France in 1793: the Case of the Winter Company and the Financier Jean-Jacques de Beaune

A. GOODWIN

At the conclusion of a war, are we recompenced for the death of multitudes, and the expense of millions, by contemplating the sudden glories of paymasters and agents, contractors and commissaries, whose equipages shine like meteors, and whose palaces rise like exhalations? These are the men, who, without virtue, labour or hazard, are growing rich as the country is impoverished; they rejoice when obstinacy or ambition adds another year to slaughter and devastation; and laugh from their desks at bravery and science, while they are adding figure to figure, and cypher to cypher, hoping for a new contract from a new armament and computing the profits of a siege or battle.
Dr Johnson, *Falkland Islands*

The case of Jean-Jacques de Beaune and the so-called Winter Company was one of suspected but unconfirmed 'counter-revolutionary' conspiracy on the part of an international financier who was engaged, in the spring of 1793, as a war contractor in the provision of horse-drawn artillery trains for the French republican armies.[1] It was complicated by its association with an ill-fated piece of Anglo-French financial jobbery designed to furnish a temporary relief for the accumulated indebtedness of George Prince of Wales and his brothers, the Dukes of York and Clarence. It is of interest to the historian not only because it helped to strengthen, and may indeed have finally clinched, the argument for the State control of French war transport, but also because it throws a lurid light on the practical difficulties of military administration at a time when

213

the European counter-revolutionary crusade was gaining rapidly in scope and impetus. It illustrates the shifts to which that government was reduced in its defence policy and the extent to which the French war effort was being paralysed in the spring and summer of 1793 by the rivalry between opposing groups of war contractors and by the struggles between political factions in the National Convention. It helps to explain the closure of the Paris Bourse in the summer of the same year and the subsequent campaign to liquidate foreign financiers in the capital. Just as the crisis of 'federalism' precipitated the organisation of the highly centralised system of 'revolutionary government', so the financial scandals and logistic problems involved in this curious and long-forgotten imbroglio facilitated the transition to an unprecedented type of war economy devised by the Jacobin Committee of Public Safety.

Jean-Jacques de Beaune, the chief actor in this tragi-comedy, was a person of uncertain origins, about whom we possess only a few fragmentary biographical details. His commercial rivals and political enemies sought to depict him as a shady and rather unsavoury adventurer of a type familiar in eighteenth-century Europe. At different stages of his picturesque and chequered career, de Beaune described himself, according to the exigencies of his situation, as a member of the Dutch burgher 'aristocracy', as a Frenchman born in Holland, or as an English merchant who had become a nationalised French citizen. Such statements were not irreconcilable or necessarily based on misrepresentation. It seems likely that he was a Dutchman of French parentage and it is certain that he sought and obtained French citizenship in the early stages of the revolution. In 1793, at the age of forty-four, he had behind him a long and unenviable record of financial speculation in various European capitals. Once he had become politically suspect it was not surprising that he should have been denounced, in the revolutionary hyperbole of the time, as a man 'who had littered Europe with his bankruptcies and had spread ruination behind him at Amsterdam, Rotterdam, Hamburg and London.'[2] There is some evidence at all events that in 1786 de Beaune had been to Russia and had had financial dealings with Prince Potemkin, the ablest and most powerful of the favourites of Catherine the Great.[3] In 1787 he had quitted Amsterdam in haste as a bankrupt and had sought refuge in London, at the time of the collapse of French influence in the United Provinces as the result of Prussian military intervention. In doing so, de Beaune had absconded with Bertha, the young, attractive and wealthy wife of one of his friends and whose maiden name was Winter. They were accompanied into exile by Bertha's father, who seems to have accepted the illicit relationship thus established between his daughter and the refugee financier.

Despite his previous financial failures and his probable connections with the pro-French Patriot faction in the United Provinces, de Beaune soon recouped his fortunes in England, no doubt with the assistance of Bertha's father. By 1789 he had established himself as a merchant with an address at Union Court, Broad Street, in the city of London. It was as such that he presented himself to Lord Moira – contact man of the Prince of Wales – as a possible money-lender to the heir to the English throne.[4]

In the winter of 1789, although the prince's liabilities, amounting to over £160,000, had been paid off by Parliament two years previously, and although £10,000 a year had been added to his income from the Civil List, as a result of Fox's explicit denial of the prince's marriage with Mrs Fitzherbert, the extravagant and prodigal eldest son of George III once more found himself overwhelmed by enormous debts.[5] To extricate himself and his brothers from these burdens, the Prince of Wales had availed himself of the services of a confidential agent, Nathaniel Parker Forth, who had been employed on secret diplomatic missions to Maurepas just before France's alliance with the American colonists and who was on intimate terms with the Duke of Orleans.[6] Forth negotiated a series of loans from French creditors amounting to £300,000, secured on the revenues of the Duchy of Cornwall and carrying interest at the rate of five per cent. Under the terms of this agreement the income from the duchy was to be made over by its Receiver General to the banking house of Ransom, Morland and Hammersley of London, which was to remit the interest due to the French creditors at half-yearly intervals. Unfortunately, shortly after this scheme had been promoted and part of the advances transferred to England, the English Crown lawyers ruled that the loans were illegal. Forth had therefore been compelled to return to France in order to repay the money which had been advanced, to prevent the remittance of the remainder, and to cancel the securities.[7]

It was in these circumstances that the Prince's advisers accepted offers of financial assistance from the Duke of Orleans, who was then ostensibly on a diplomatic mission to the Court of St James, and from de Beaune.[8] Each appears to have made separate loans to the royal princes of £100,000. Under the terms of de Beaune's bond, dated 5 June 1790, the three princes bound themselves severally and jointly, in the penalty of £200,000, to pay interest on the loan at the rate of five per cent for the next twenty-five years. Repayment of the principal was to be made by annual instalments of £10,000, starting in 1806 and continuing till 1815. De Beaune was authorised to divide the loans into shares of £100 each and to dispose of them to investors. In order to prevent the shares being issued in excess of the sum borrowed, it was provided that they should be registered by an accredited notary public. The terms specifying the security for the loan and the payment of interest were similar to those incorporated in the French loans negotiated by Forth.[9] The new loan contracts were more strictly drawn and did not involve any immediate recourse to the French money market.

They did not, however, preclude de Beaune from floating the loan abroad at a subsequent date. This is exactly what he did, later in 1790, when he transferred his activities to Paris. He realised, of course, that he held an asset which would appeal to French investors as soon as their confidence in the new paper currency, issued in August 1790, began to sag.[10] The loan offered a fixed and reasonable rate of interest, secured on the hereditary revenues of the Prince of Wales, and was calculated in terms of sterling. Thus, when de Beaune decided, in December 1790, to throw open the loan to French investors, in order to liquidate his holding, he found ready acceptors. The legal formalities for the sub-division of the loan were scrupulously observed and the shares were registered with a notary-public in Paris called Brichard, who also handled the loan made by the Duke of Orleans. A skilful prospectus, outlining the terms of the bond, was put out and soon de Beaune was able to turn these assets, as they were liquidated, to other uses.[11]

Together with his pseudo 'father-in-law', de Beaune then established in Paris a commercial and banking house of a kind familiar in England and Holland, using part of the funds raised by the sale of the bearer-bonds. The control of this so-called Winter Company, with a capital of four and a half million *livres*, was vested in de Beaune. According to the latter, the original purpose of this venture was to encourage French merchants in the provinces to bring their cloth and other manufactured goods to the capital, where there was a scarcity of such commodities, and to make their sale possible at competitive prices.[12] Hardly had this organisation been completed when, at the end of 1792 or beginning of 1793, de Beaune was approached by an associate called Boursault. The latter suggested that the new company might perform a useful public service, at a time when French military commitments were being rapidly extended, and presumably might also expand its own profits, by contracting to supply the government with horses and equipment for its artillery trains.[13]

Throughout the *ancien régime* it had been the practice of the French government to provide its soldiers with nothing except their arms and munitions. Food, camp equipment, stores and means of transport were supplied by private contractors who advanced the necessary funds and were repaid by the royal Treasury at its convenience.[14] This was partly an expedient adopted by a financially embarrassed Treasury, but it may also have been due, as Lefebvre suggested, to the distaste of the nobility in command of the French armies for matters of administrative or technical detail.[15] In time of war this reliance of the State on military contractors became even more pronounced and led to the paradoxical situation in which the government found itself compelled to advance the money to finance contractors. These practices were continued during the revolution and definite contracts were made by successive War Ministers for the supply of essential military services. Among these the transport services were particularly important at a time when the pace of military operations had suddenly increased. Private contractors not only undertook to move rations and all forms of military supplies from the producers or manufacturers to the garrison towns or armies in the field, but also provided the cavalry and artillery with horses, carts and gun-carriages. Such a system lent itself to abuse, and the war contractors of the seventeenth and eighteenth centuries had become as notorious for the illicit fortunes they had acquired at the State's expense as the Farmers-General themselves.

Since the retreat of Prussians after the battle of Valmy in September 1792, the French armies had been everywhere on the offensive, and in November, after Jemmappes, General Dumouriez had overrun Belgium in a few weeks. So swift and unexpected had the advance been that the problems of logistics had become acute. But, simultaneously, complaints against the contracts entered into by the War Minister, Servan, before the fall of the monarchy had

resulted in the establishment, in November 1792, of a government
purchasing commission, which it was hoped would be able to take
over from some of the more prominent war contractors the provision of military stores and supply services as from 1 January
1793.[16] This plan was aimed at the more notorious entrepeneurs,
such as the abbé de'Espagnac, who had secured contracts which
placed huge fortunes in their grasp. For field commanders like
Dumouriez, however, the administrative change-over would have
come at an inconvenient moment and would have resulted immediately in a slowing down rather than in a speeding up of supplies.
Dumouriez was, indeed, so preoccupied with this threat that he
was considering establishing his own supply services and making
direct contracts with financiers such as d'Espagnac, who were only
too anxious to meet his requests. These manoeuvres naturally drew
down on Dumouriez the suspicion of Jacobin politicians such as
Prieur de la Marne and Cambon, who were determined to bring
the army supply services under closer governmental inspection and
control.[17] In other words, the whole system of military supply had,
in the winter months of 1792–3, become a matter of high policy
and an issue which divided the contending political factions in the
Convention.

It was in this confused situation, in which the d'Espagnac
contracts were coming under increasing attack, that de Beaune was
tempted to set up as a rival war contractor. On 22 January 1793,
the very day after the execution of Louis XVI, de Beaune signed
a contract with the War Minister Pache to supply the French
artillery with 5,100 horses, equipped with harness, and to recruit
and clothe a corps of drivers drafted into brigades with a cadre of
officers and a complete staff organisation. Pache undertook to
advance 1,300,000 *livres* to the Winter Company for this purpose
and de Beaune was expected to find financial guarantors for the
capital advanced. Although de Beaune subsequently admitted that
if this contract had been in force for two years, the company would
have made a profit of about a million and a half *livres*, these terms
were, nevertheless, considerably more advantageous to the French
government than the contracts previously entered into between
Servan and the abbé de'Espagnac.[18]

In February and March 1793 the Winter Company thus took
on the character of a para-military organisation. A headquarters
staff was formed at Bercy, on the outskirts of the capital, de Beaune
became director of the enterprise and his artillery trains were

organised into thirty brigades of about sixty drivers each. To each of these brigades were attached one *conducteur en chef*, one *conducteur en second* and two subalterns.[19] The recruitment of the drivers was entrusted to those officers who were given commissions by the company itself.[20] Hundreds of horses were rapidly acquired and pending the completion of the brigades were placed in depots at Vincennes, Bercy and Saint-Cloud, where they were branded as fit for service. De Beaune's offices in the rue de Montmartre in Paris became the scene of feverish activity as the preparations went forward. Late in March 1793, after the revolt in La Vendée had broken out, de Beaune made a verbal agreement with Hassenfratz, a high official in the War Ministry, to provide another 3,454 horses, bringing the total covered by his contracts up to 8,554.[21] Recommendations for commissions in the organisation poured in from deputies to the Convention and were examined and approved by the headquarters staff. Among the latter was Drouet, the famous posting master of Sainte-Menchould who had stopped Louis XVI on his flight to Varennes, and who was now a member of the powerful Committee of General Security.[22]

From the end of March 1793, however, rumours began to circulate in the capital that royalist sympathisers, under cover of false names and with forged identity papers, had obtained commissions from the company and that returned *émigré* nobles had enlisted in de Beaune's artillery trains as ordinary drivers.[23] These suspicions deepened when the official on the staff at Bercy who kept the registers of those to whom commissions had been granted (a certain Antoine Michel) was denounced as a former coachman of Marie-Antoinette.[24] The motive imputed to the alleged royalist officers and drivers in the pay of the company was that, if and when they were detailed to operate in La Vendée, they had planned to desert and to hand over their horses, equipment and gun-carriages to the rebels.[25] The response of the Committee of General Security was, on 12 May 1793, to order the arrest of nine members of de Beaune's organisation, who had been denounced as concerned in the conspiracy.[26] On the same day the recently instituted Committee of Public Safety formally revoked the Winter Company's service contracts with the War Ministry.[27]

In the course of the next week the suspected royalists were carefully interrogated by the president of the Committee of General Security and his colleagues. The examination of the accused and a number of witnesses indicated that the Committee was dealing with a small group of young, shiftless, irresponsible and down-at-heel ex-nobles or adventurers who had enlisted in de Beaune's organisation to escape their creditors, or out of spite against local revolutionary authorities which had confiscated their estates, or simply in order to avoid being drafted into the army. One of them, the *ci-devant* Count Étienne Malet from Excideuil (in the Dordogne), compromised several of his fellow prisoners by admitting that they had told him of their intention to desert to the Vendéen rebels and by confirming that some of them were former nobles who had changed their names.[28] When examined the next day, Jean de Cressac Lubriac, also from the Dordogne area, repudiated the charge of nobility (though Malet's testimony suggested this was perjury) and contended that, for several years, he had been engaged in fitting out ships for the slave trade and had later been a discount and commission agent. He admitted that he had spent several months in jail in Paris, having been released by the mob at the time of the September Massacres, but disclaimed all knowledge of the alleged conspiracy.[29]

One of the prisoners was Charles Salvi, aged thirty, a native of Brescia in the republic of Venice, who said he had come to France in August 1791, but that he had only managed to eke out a hard-won existence in Paris by giving lessons in Italian or selling books. He admitted that in February 1793 he had been given a commission as a *conducteur en chef* with the Winter Company by citizen Wiscowitz, a Polish inspector on de Beaune's headquarters staff. When accused by the president of the Committe of General Security of being in touch with the *émigré* princes and of being a spy in the pay of the British government, Salvi indignantly repudiated the suggestion and urged in self-defence his abject poverty and the fact that he had been obliged to pawn his own clothes. In any case he had recently been obliged to resign his commission with the company.[30] Two other accused were the brothers Cavin. The elder, J.-J. Cavin, was a man of some substance from Montpellier who had been given a commission as a *chef de division*. He admitted having been told that a former coachman of the queen was on the headquarters staff, but denied any knowledge that royalists had infiltrated the company.[31] The younger Cavin seems to have been an incorrigible ne'er-do-well, dissolute, drunken and quarrelsome, who had fallen foul of the company officials and had recently been dismissed for financial malpractices.[32] The other four suspects interrogated were a Breton nobleman, Jean François Marie

Kératry, whose estates had been sequestrated and who had recently been imprisoned on charges of counterfeiting *assignats*, Menissier junior, whose father was alleged to have been fencing master to the princes of Condé, and two other noblemen, Charles de Lamberty and Charles Robert Pressac. The latter's real name was de Tessierès; he could be proved to have joined the army of the *émigré* princes, and he was also in possession of forged identity papers. His estates in the department of the Haute Vienne had been confiscated and he was living in Paris on money remitted by his wife in letters addressed to the wife of Bordas, one of the deputies to the Convention. He denied that he had emigrated, or that he was married, and asserted that he had only joined de Beaune's company as an ordinary driver because he had sprained his foot and wished to serve on horseback with the army of the North.[33]

From these interrogations and the examination of witnesses it was evident that several of the accused had counter-revolutionary connections which they had attempted to conceal by prevarication. Some had not been able to give satisfactory reasons why they had joined the Winter Company as officers or ordinary drivers. All except one, Menissier junior, were therefore remanded into custody on 23 May by the Committee of General Security and ordered to be sent for trial before the Revolutionary Tribunal.[34] Although de Beaune himself and his associates, as well as the prisoners, were subsequently cross-examined by the public prosecutor of the Tribunal, little fresh evidence of the alleged counter-revolutionary conspiracy was forthcoming.[35] Four of the accused – the elder Cavin, Malet, Salvi and Kératry – were released without further delay, while the rest were left to languish in prison till 1794, when Pressac preceded Robespierre to the guillontine by one day; the others were released shortly after Thermidor.[36]

Meanwhile the Winter Company had petitioned the Committee of Public Safety against the revocation of its contracts. It was able to show with documentary support that its operations had been impeded by Pache's successor at the War Ministry, General Beurnonville, who had withheld the stipulated financial advances, even though the necessary guarantees had been forthcoming, until the Convention had forced his hand. The company had, moreover, speedily rectified its initial error of judgement in authorising the granting of commissions by the use of a wooden stamp and in delegating the recruitment of the drivers to the officers. It had been in this way that the ranks of the organisation had been infiltrated by the crypto-royalists now safely in confinement. Early in March strenuous efforts had been made to ensure that all officers had fulfilled their engagements as recruiting agents and to check that they themselves were the holders of properly authenticated *certificats de civisme*. Large numbers of commissions had been recalled on these grounds and finally all those which had not been signed by de Beaune personally were declared null and void. De Beaune was also able to disprove that his company had ever connived at the alleged conspiracy and to explain how the rumours of its complicity had arisen. Initially these had developed early in March 1793, when the company had made a patriotic offer to the Commune of Paris to detach for service against the Vendéen royalists a hundred of its officers who were awaiting their dispatch to Belgium. Though this offer had been accepted by Santerre, the commander of the Parisian national guard, these units had in fact been ordered off to Valenciennes and Metz on the intervention of the War Minister. Loose talk among the drivers had, however, been seized on by the officers whose commissions had been revoked and more particularly by the agents of de Beaune's competitors in the war-contracting business. These had been distorted into allegations that de Beaune's officers intended to hand over their horses and equipment to the royalist armies of the West.[37] These explanations, coupled with advice tendered to it by the committee of General Security, induced the Committee of Public Safety on 23 May to reverse its earlier decision and to renew the Winter Company's contracts.[38] This approval was, nevertheless, accompanied by securities against future malpractices on the part of the company and by instructions to the War Minister to prepare plans for the government itself to take over the war-transport services.[39]

Suspicion of de Beaune's complicity in these alleged treasonable designs, however, smouldered on and in June was revived when Lacoste denounced him to the War Contracts Commission on a number of trumped-up charges of malversation which showed that his enemies were determined on his ruin. Once again, under cross-examination by members of the Commission, de Beaune was able to exculpate both himself and his associates from charges of financial manipulation, non-fulfilment of his contracts and royalist manoeuvres. He was able to show that Michel, the former coachman to Marie-Antoinette, had been dismissed in disgrace from the royal service because of his family relationship to Drouet and that his activities on the Winter Company's headquarters staff had been

above reproach. He also convinced the Commission that the horses
and equipment he had provided for the army of the North had not
been sub-standard, that he had not fallen behind with the services
he had contracted to supply and, finally, that his profits were
moderate, as compared with his rival war contractors.[40]

The mounting campaign against the latter, however, reached its
zenith soon after and the case for the governmental control of the
military supply services was established in detail by an important
report to the Convention made by Dornier on 22 July.[41] On the
basis of Dornier's draft scheme a decree was carried on the 25th,
amalgamating all the different branches of war transport – the
commissariat, stores and hospital services – with the exception of
the artillery trains, into a single organisation in the form of a *régie
intéressée* or quasi-public board administered by seven controllers.
A proper establishment in the way of horse transport for all the
forces in the field and in barracks was created and provision was
made for tighter financial control and regular inspection. It is
significant, however, that artillery transport was not for the time
being made subject to the new *régie*, and that de Beaune's contracts for the provision of horses, although pruned by fifty per cent,
were temporarily continued. Practically all other war contracts
were cancelled as from 1 August 1793.[42] The day of the war contractors was now virtually over : the Winter Company had, it is
true, survived its second crisis, but its future was foreclosed. It
lingered on till 5 January 1794, when a decree of the Convention
finally terminated de Beaune's remaining contracts at the same time
that it streamlined all the war-transport services by absorbing the
administration of the artillery trains into the governmental *régie*
established in the previous July.[43]

Meanwhile de Beaune's own days were now numbered. He had
been again denounced on 17 October 1793, and arrested and
imprisoned on the following day, this time in consequence of a
decree extending to 'Dutch' residents the provisions of earlier legislation directed against the subjects of countries with whom the
republic was at war.[44] It was inevitable, once this had happened,
that de Beaune's earlier operations as sponsor and promoter of the
French loans to the English princes should have been uncovered.
Nor was it likely that he would escape unharmed from the revolutionary judicial process a second time, whatever the merits of his
defence. On 11 January 1794 he was sent for trial before the
Revolutionary Tribunal by the Committee of General Security;

his indictment by Fouquier Tinville was dated 9 February, he was condemned to death along with Brichard and other associates on the 13th and guillotined the next day.[45] The public prosecutor had his own interpretation to place on the Anglo-French loan operations. He contended that de Beaune had been the cat's-paw of the English princes, who had chosen this devious method of financing not themselves but Louis Capet; and that the loans were fictitious. Alternatively, the loans could only have been intended to provide facilities for the French nobility to emigrate to England.[46]

Swindler de Beaune may have been, but the evidence does not support the views of either Fouquier Tinville or M. de l'Estapis that he had been throughout an undercover agent of the counter-revolution.

14

Rebellion and Revolution in Early Modern England

PENRY WILLIAMS

In a recent and stimulating article Professor J. H. Elliott argued that modern historians, accustomed to the paradigm of revolution established in France after 1789, have tried to detect its features in the revolts of the sixteenth and seventeenth centuries. Seeking class-conflict, revolutionary organisation and innovating ideologies, we have usually found them. He goes on to suggest that we may have been too much concerned with doctrines of change and with 'underlying social causes', too little interested in the mortality or minority of princes and in loyalties to a local or national community. Not until the eighteenth century, he implies, did 'rebellion . . . come to assume the characteristics of revolution'.[1] This distinction between rebellion and revolution is an important tool of analysis for the early modern period. Rebellion involves either a protest movement designed, by a display of force and numbers, to remedy specific grievances, or an attempt to seize political power. After successful rebellion particular concessions might be made by the government or a new monarch might occupy the throne; but there would have been no attempt to change the structure of the political system or the balance of power between its parts. Such a change, whether achieved or not, is the mark of revolution. This distinction was put with characteristic lucidity by Aristotle :

. . . hence arise two sorts of changes in governments; the one affecting the constitution, where men seek to change from an existing form into some other . . . the other not affecting the constitution, when, without disturbing the form of government, whether oligarchy, or monarchy, or any other, they try to get the administration into their own hands.[2]

225

The object of this paper is to apply the distinction to early modern England, to suggest that by the mid-seventeenth century revolution had begun to emerge where rebellion alone had been possible before, and to offer some explanations for the change.

The revolts of mid-sixteenth-century England were neither in aim nor in results revolutionary: some were essentially protest movements, designed either to prevent a specific act of policy or to remedy particular abuses; others involved the seizure of power by the removal or assassination of the monarch. The only protest movement of the sixteenth century which was played out through all its acts to a successful conclusion was the mass refusal to contribute to the Amicable Grant in 1525. Following the capture of Francis I at Pavia, Henry VIII planned to invade France and assume the French crown. Commissions were issued demanding a benevolence of one-sixth of the wealth of the laity and one-third of the wealth of the clergy. In spite of bonfires, victory processions and a great deal of Tudor rhetoric, there was a general reluctance to pay in London, Kent, Cambridgeshire, Essex, Norfolk and Suffolk. Wolsey met with obstinate resistance from the citizens of London, who refused to contribute anything. Warham, impressed by protestations of poverty and himself displeased at still awaiting repayment of an earlier loan, was equally unsuccessful in Kent. The Duke of Norfolk managed to persuade the citizens of Norwich to promise money, although his progress was hampered by reports of the resistance in London. But he and his colleague, the Duke of Suffolk, met serious resistance on the Norfolk–Suffolk border. Near Bury they were confronted by a crowd reported to be 4,000 strong; rumours of larger gatherings in Essex and Cambridgeshire alarmed them still further. As news of resistance spread from one area to another, it became increasingly difficult to extract money even from those who had originally agreed to pay. The ringleaders were called into Star Chamber, reprimanded and pardoned; the King called off the tax. Royal policy had been defeated, in part because men like Norfolk and Suffolk had been reluctant to back it against hostility, and in part because the different regions were encouraged by the rumours of resistance elsewhere.[3]

Interestingly enough, there were attempts to repeat this success three years later in the hard spring of 1528, when corn prices were high and a slump in the cloth market had caused unemployment. Protests from cloth workers in East Anglia, Wiltshire and Gloucestershire moved the government to order their employers to keep them at work. But a petition from Kentish yeomen that the King repay the forced loan of some years earlier met with a cold response. Although Archbishop Warham, to whom they first applied, was unwisely sympathetic, the government, supported by local nobles and gentlemen, repressed them sharply. Some of the Kentish men seem at this stage to have concocted a half-baked scheme for capturing Wolsey, taking him out to sea and drowning him. The most significant element in their plan was a plot to get hold of some local gentlemen; this, they thought, would give them some kind of authority. However, the Kentish landowners were firmly on the side of the Crown and the conspirators were convicted by a commission of *oyer et terminer.* Two lessons seem to emerge from the events of 1525 and 1528. Protest might succeed when the government was demanding action from the populace, but was much more difficult when the populace demanded something – in this instance money – from the government. Secondly, success was impossible when the nobles and gentry withheld their support.[4]

The most important and the most complex of the sixteenth-century protests was the Pilgrimage of Grace of 1536–7. Mr Mervyn James has convincingly shown how this fits into the tradition of late-medieval movements of dissent, and it is worth illustrating from the history of the Pilgrimage some of the characteristic features of that tradition.[5]

A basic element of these protest movements, defence of the local community against intrusion and interference from outside, was very evident in the Pilgrimage. At the time of the first outbreak at Louth, three sets of commissioners were operating in the area : a royal commission for dissolving the smaller monasteries; a second royal commission for assessing the subsidy; and an episcopal commission investigating the fitness of the clergy. The rumours circulating in Lincolnshire and the north at this time renewed men's apprehensions. It was said that all church jewels and chalices would be confiscated; that 'there shall be no church within five miles, and that all the rest shall be put down'; that every man should be sworn to a statement of his wealth, and that if he turned out to be worth more the surplus would be confiscated; that no one should eat white bread, goose or capon without paying a tax to the King.[6] Not surprisingly, the pilgrims sought a scapegoat for their fears and found one in Thomas Cromwell. Darcy's outburst against him was typical : 'Cromwell, it is thou that art the very original and chief causer of all this rebellion.'[7] In demanding that the King dismiss Cromwell and his other heretical councillors, the Pilgrims saw themselves, and indeed were, standing very much in the tradition of medieval political dissidence. An anonymous piece of advice to the pilgrims defended their action :

Where it is alleged that we should not take upon us to assign his Grace's Council it is necessary that virtuous men that loveth the commonwealth should be his [council] . . . Who reads the chronicles of Edward II what jeopardy he was in for Piers de Gavestan, Spencers, and such like councillors . . . Richard the II was deposed for following the counsel of such like.[8]

That the Pilgrimage was much more like a demonstration than a true rebellion is shown by the peaceful conduct of its supporters. Admittedly, in the early stages of the Lincolnshire rising the local crowds got out of control : Dr Raynes, the bishop's chancellor, was beaten to death, and Thomas Wolsey, a servant of the late cardinal, was hanged. But thereafter the leaders seem to have established a firm discipline. In Yorkshire there was very little fighting, for Darcy and Aske were careful not to engage the royal troops. In a society marked by petty violence and rioting such restraint is remarkable.

Although the pilgrims were drawn from many different social groups, with varied and even conflicting interests, there was, except in one area, no class antagonism. The exception was the northwest, where the estate management of the Earl of Cumberland had angered his tenants and where economic grievances were in consequence dominant.[9] Elsewhere the peasantry seems to have been ready to follow the lead of nobles and gentry. It would be wrong to see the poorer classes as entirely manipulated by their betters, for they reacted spontaneously and emotionally to the rumours that were going about the north. But it would be still more misleading to accept at face value the claims of the nobles and gentlemen that they were forced into the rising.[10] The landowners gave the leadership which the peasants needed and to which they responded. It is true that the leaders did not always maintain complete harmony with their followers : Lord Darcy told Somerset Herald that, when the pilgrim leaders were conferring with Norfolk on Doncaster Bridge, 'because the lords and we tarried a while about the entreaty our own host would have runned upon us to have killed us, saying that we would betray them.'[11] But it would surely be a mistake to interpret such suspicions as evidence of class conflict. Nor can the collapse of the Pilgrimage be attributed, as some historians have made out, to the social divisions in its ranks. Indeed quite the reverse, for the rank and file of the movement was still sufficiently obedient to its leaders to disperse when commanded; and that dispersal was fatal to the cause.

In many ways so typical of late-medieval protests, the Pilgrimage did however foreshadow later and different conflicts. Although the participants were probably moved in the main by apprehension at the encroachments of royal and episcopal authority upon their property, privileges and traditional ways and, in some cases, by resentment at the loss of power, they were drawn by their own protests to question more fundamental issues of State and Church. It is unprofitable to ask whether they were moved in this more by political, economic or religious factors. Historical matter cannot be neatly sliced into these convenient explanatory segments, for the Church was inextricably enmeshed with social life. Whatever the reason, some of the pilgrims – a few in Lincolnshire and rather more in Yorkshire – came to question the royal supremacy and the structure of ecclesiastical authority.[12] Having done so, they were involved in an ideological problem more difficult to resolve than the specific grievances and fears from which the protest had in the first place sprung.

If the Pilgrimage was, in the main, characteristic of the protest against outside interference, Ket's revolt in 1549 was essentially an appeal to the central government against the abuses of local officials and landlords. Even less than the pilgrims did Ket and his followers intend to seize power for themselves : they simply wanted to ensure that the natural rulers of county society behaved in the proper and traditional way. Nor, in spite of their complaints against the gentry, did they engage in real class conflict. Although the chroniclers of the revolt were hostile to the rebels and determined to condemn them as enemies of ordered society, the worst they could say of the rebels' treatment of the gentry was that

. . . indeed they did press their weapons to kill some of those gentlemen brought to them, which they did of such malice, that one Mr Wharton, being herded with a lane of men on both sides . . . into the city [of Norwich], they pricked him with their spears and other weapons on purpose to kill, had they [the gentry] not had great help to withstand their malice and cruelty.[13]

Wharton in the event survived; and there is no record of any gentleman being killed by the rebels, except in battle; and the

battles were started by the government, not by Ket. The extraordinary mildness of the rebels is also revealed in a story about the
early life of Matthew Parker, who went up to Mousehold Heath
to preach to the throng. Those round about him 'revered' him, but
the rebels in the further ranks grew hostile. To quieten them the
vicar of St Martin's and two or three musicians struck up an
English *Te Deum*,

. . . with solemn music and distinct notes, elegantly set for the delight
of the ear; by the sweetness of which song they being ravished (for
they were unwonted to music) their cruel and raging minds (bewitched
with these unaccustomed delights) by little and little were appeased.[14]

This was not the behaviour of revolutionaries. Nor do their demands reveal any desire to change the social structure. Except for
the vague clause that 'all bond men shall be made free, for God
made all free with his precious blood-shedding', their requests were
all conservative, harking back to conditions as they were in the
early part of the reign of Henry VII, urging the end of abuses by
landlords rather than the destruction of property.[15] In the early
stages of the revolt Ket's men were apparently as respectful of
property as they were of human life. Only after the government
had sent troops against them under the command of Northampton
did Ket find it impossible to restrain some of his followers from
burning and looting in Norwich. The reaction of the Privy Council
turned a fairly pacific and well-disciplined protest into something
like armed revolt.[16]

Protest movements like the Pilgrimage of Grace, Ket's revolt and
the south-western rebellion of 1549 were characterised by formal
articles of grievance presented to the monarch or the Privy
Council.[17] Other movements, like Warwick's *coup d'état* in 1549,
dispensed with such formalities since they were intent upon power.
Wyatt's rebellion in 1554 illustrates the contrast. Although Wyatt
and his friends rejected the proposal by William Thomas for Mary's
assassination, they realised that the Queen would never willingly
give up her project of marrying Philip. They almost certainly
intended to depose her and put Elizabeth and Courtenay on the
throne. This ultimate intention had to be concealed if they were
to gain popular backing, and Wyatt's formal proclamations were
cast in a traditional form : 'we seek no harm to the Queen, but
better counsel and councillors.' But the conventional demand
obscured their real and very different purpose.[18] The revolts and

conspiracies that followed Wyatt generally involved the seizure of power rather than the presentation of grievances. The plans of those muddled and frightened men, the northern earls of 1569, are admittedly far from clear; but it is likely that their recusant advisers, if not the earls themselves, aimed at substituting Mary Stuart for Elizabeth. Essex in 1601 intended the destruction of the Cecils rather than Elizabeth : unlike most of the others he was not concerned with usurping the throne, though he was very much concerned with securing the accession of James. Apart from these open rebels a long line of conspirators, stretching from Sir Henry Dudley in 1555–6 to Guy Fawkes in 1605, aimed at subverting the succession to the throne.[19] Although they were usually discovered before their plans were complete, these conspirators nevertheless aimed at rebellion and must be considered in its context. Their tactics differed from Wyatt's in two important respects. From Dudley onwards they realised the importance of foreign military support; and from Ridolfi onwards they mostly intended the assassination of the monarch as the first step in the seizure of power.

The disturbances of the mid-seventeenth century were different. For the first time genuine revolutionary principles were expressed in the Leveller and Digger pamphlets. Although the Leveller leaders were not entirely united or consistent in their political proposals, some of them advocated democracy. Rainborough's speech in the Putney Debates leaves no doubt of his revolutionary character :

I do not find anything in the Law of God, that a lord shall choose twenty burgesses, and a gentleman but two, or a poor man shall choose none; I find no such thing in the Law of Nature, nor in the Law of Nations.[20]

Leveller proposals for the sovereignty of the representative body, for equality before the law, for the election of all local officers, for the conversion of copyhold into freehold, were demands for radical changes in the structure of society; they contrasted starkly with the conservatism of Ket.[21] Although these men were a small minority and although their cause ultimately failed, their impact on the events of 1646–8 was nevertheless dramatic and resounding.

Can we see anything revolutionary in the more moderate and more successful parliamentarians like Pym? Did they step beyond defensive positions? Were their proposals fundamentally different from traditional demands for good counsel? They were certainly anxious to justify their actions in terms of history and precedent, as indeed were the Levellers; and when they looked for help in the past they generally found it. But there is a difference between the justification for actions and the actions themselves. In impeaching Strafford for acts against the commonwealth rather than against the King, the parliamentary managers were able to use earlier precedents and they may possibly have convinced themselves that they were keeping within the bounds of law and tradition. But the act itself was surely different in kind from anything that had gone before.[22] Again, the demand for ministers acceptable to Parliament could possibly be put into the context of medieval requests for the removal of unpopular councillors. But there is a difference between the removal of royal servants at the demand of rebels and the appointment of men acceptable to a permanent institution. In November 1641 Pym proposed a resolution that

. . . we shall be forced, by Discharge of the Trust which we owe to the state, and to those whom we represent, to resolve upon some such way of defending Ireland . . . as may concur to the securing of ourselves from . . . mischievous Counsels and Designs . . . and to commend those Aids and Contributions which this great Necessity shall regain, to the Custody and Disposing of such Persons of Honour and Fidelity as we have come to confide in.[23]

D'Ewes, who was usually ready to support traditional remedies, thought the resolution 'of very dangerous consequence'. Pym's motion hinted at a distinction between the State and the King which was alarming to conservatives and surely carried revolutionary implications. Sir Edward Dering wrote of the Grand Remonstrance:

When I first heard of a Remonstrance . . . I did not dream that we should remonstrate downwards, tell stories to the people, and talk of the King as of a third person.[24]

The distinction between King and commonwealth made impossible the old stance of dissidence in a context of loyalty; it was a decisive break with the past.[25]

There was, then, a broad change in the nature of protest in early modern England. Movements like the resistance to the Amicable Grant and the Pilgrimage of Grace stemmed from a long medieval tradition of limited opposition, which could sometimes change the policy or the advisers of the Crown. But by the middle of the sixteenth century confessional strife had made this sort of limited protest too dangerous to tolerate. Under the tensions of

Reformation Europe it could no longer be contained within the bounds of loyalty. Ideological or religious conflicts forced upon both the Crown and its opponents a different strategy. The Pilgrimage of Grace marks the transformation : in its beginning very much a movement of limited dissent, it carried more threatening implications of religious civil war.[26] Although protest movements of this sort recurred in 1549, they had no real future except in the isolated sphere of agrarian discontent, and not much future there. But the intrusion of religious dispute did not at once turn rebellion into revolution; at first it merely changed the strategy of rebellion. The plots against Elizabeth, the murder of Moray in Scotland, the assassination of William of Orange in the Netherlands and of Henry III and Henry IV in France, were typical forms of political action in a world which used the medieval weapons of the succession struggle for new ideological ends. In England this strategy was abandoned with the failure of the Gunpowder Plot in 1605. The opposition to Charles I never took the form of a struggle for the succession; no one tried to assassinate him. Instead he was tried for treason; and the step taken from the assassination of a monarch to his trial marks an important stage in the emergence of revolution. But it was not an irrevocable step : the succession struggle could still return to English politics and did so in 1688; it is no coincidence that its return marked the most conservative of political revolutions.

Enduring for at most a few weeks, Tudor protest movements had neither the thrust nor the stamina to achieve, or even to bring near, that collapse of government which was necessary before truly radical action could begin. The causes of their failure and the limitations on their field of action help to explain why they carried no revolutionary implications and remained mere rebellions.

All the Tudor revolts found it difficult to transcend regional boundaries. The Pilgrimage of Grace admittedly spread over five northern counties; but, even so, Lancashire was kept largely loyal to the Crown and southern England was hardly touched by it. Although there was sympathy for the pilgrims in the south, it never turned to action : Marmaduke Neville, brother of Lord Latimer, reproached some Essex men for their inaction with the words, 'we are plain fellows and we showed our mind. Ye southern men thought as much as we, though ye durst not utter your mind.'[27] Ket's revolt was almost entirely confined to Norfolk. In a year during which enclosure riots were exploding over parts of the midlands and the south, the rebels apparently did not try to look beyond their own county and the fringes of Suffolk; nor was there any response to them elsewhere. This cannot be explained by the peculiarities of Norfolk's fold-course system, since this was far from prominent in the grievances of Ket's followers. Although these grievances were shared by peasants in other counties, no general movement ensued. Equally, the religious disquiet of the southwestern rebels had been voiced by others, notably in Oxfordshire. Yet the rebels stayed in Devon and Cornwall, made no effort to recruit support elsewhere, and received none. Wyatt's revolt was of course more carefully planned: risings were intended to break out in the midlands, the south-west, and the Welsh Marches, as well as in Kent. It is not surprising that the revolts in the midlands and the south-west went off at half-cock, before Wyatt's rising had gained impetus; but it is significant that, when Wyatt was seen to be gaining ground and threatening London, he should have received no support from outside his own county. The impression left by all these movements is an overwhelming regionalism, the near impossibilty of achieving a national rising.

The sixteenth-century revolts were also largely rural, for the social grievances of the rebels had little to do with the towns, being concerned with tenant-right, fines on entry and enclosure. The Pilgrimage had some support from towns like Beverley and York, but others, notably the more prosperous like Newcastle and Hull, did their best to stand aloof. There was admittedly an element in Norwich that supported Ket. The leaders of the town co-operated with him at first, perhaps *faute de mieux*; but, from the moment that York Herald dubbed Ket a traitor, the mayor and aldermen did their utmost to dissociate themselves from the rising. Even if one suspects that the contemporary narratives were deliberately playing down the city's support for Ket, the articles of the rebels were overwhelmingly agrarian, in spite of the signature of Mayor Cod at their foot. In the south-west, Exeter, in spite of the conservative religious sympathies of the ruling oligarchy, stayed firmly hostile to the rebels. Above all, Wyatt found no support in London in 1554. Encouraged by the desertion of the City militia to his side, he had good reason to hope that London would let him in. It did nothing of the kind and thus made certain the failure of his enterprise. Almost half-a-century later the Earl of Essex also relied upon the support of London and was disappointed. While the loyalty of the metropolis was perhaps the best guarantee of survival for the dynasty, reliance upon peasant bands was a major weakness of the rebels. For peasants could not act without effective leadership and showed themselves at every crisis reluctant to move far from home.

Many of the protest movements, though not all, were really peasant riots that expanded more or less accidentally into larger movements. In their different ways both Ket's revolt and the south-western rising serve as illustrations. There had been many enclosure riots in Norfolk before 1549 and several earlier protests in the south-west against the government's religious policy. There was no par-ticular reason why the disturbances of 1549 should have made a bigger explosion than their predecessors. But such accidental and spontaneous outbursts were difficult to take much further. The rebels found themselves without any effective strategy and survived as long as they did largely because of the indecision of Somerset. Both groups stayed on their home ground, lost the initiative and waited for the government to strike.

Although Aske and Ket were in their way effective, indeed remarkable leaders, they lacked the standing to gain more wide-spread support. During the Pilgrimage of Grace the major leaders of society stayed loyal to the Crown or at best equivocated. If the Earl of Northumberland wavered, the Earls of Cumberland and Derby played a major part in keeping support for the Crown alive, and the southern magnates rallied without exception to the King. Against men like these, honest Tom Darcy did not count for much.[28] In 1554 the leaders of the conspiracy were all upper gentry, except the Duke of Suffolk. Those magnates who might have been expected to support rebellion were either, like Huntingdon, intent on working their way back into favour or, like Pembroke and Lincoln, waiting upon events. Only the Elizabethan revolts of 1569 and 1601 had real aristocratic leadership. The rising of the northern earls showed that even such hesitant bunglers as Northumberland and Westmorland could find substantial backing in the north. It also demonstrated that they could find none elsewhere. The second Earl of Essex produced the one really aristocratic revolt of the century, graced by the Earls of Southampton, Bedford and Rut-land. Its ignominious failure suggests that the royal Court was by then too strong a magnet for discontented earls to build up a threatening and independent clientele.

Whatever may have happened to the peerage as a whole in the Tudor period, the power of the great magnate was undoubtedly in partial eclipse. By 1485 there were only two surviving Welsh marcher families of real political weight: the Herberts and the Staffords. The Herbert heiress was married to Henry VII's companion-at-arms, Sir Charles Somerset, and the Staffords were relegated to insignificance in 1521. In the north, the midlands and East Anglia the Percies, Dacres, Nevilles, Stanleys, Talbots and Howards were still powerful at the start of the period. By 1570 the Percies, Dacres and Nevilles had been eliminated or subdued. Some families did of course build dynastic power under the Tudors: Charles Brandon, Duke of Suffolk under Henry VIII; the Russells, Herberts, Dudleys and Seymours under Edward VI. Brandon was childless and Seymour's power short-lived. For the others Court life seems to have been more attractive than the creation of a regional affinity. It is significant that the Earls of Pembroke, however influential they may have been in Glamorgan, made Wilton their principal seat and never tried to become a marcher power. More important even than the behaviour of the great nobles was the curious infertility of the Tudor dynasty. This, combined with the destruction of the Yorkist line, deprived the opposition of the leadership of any prince of the blood.[29]

Finally, belief in the propriety of resistance or rebellion was becoming enfeebled in Tudor England. The medieval doctrine of resistance seems still to have been remembered by some in 1536. The anonymous author of a letter to Aske – 'my poor advice to my lord captain' – advocated battle rather than submission.[30] Lord Darcy expressed some relic of this older view when he told Somerset Herald that his honour was more important to him than anything else. Having promised to be true to Aske he would never, he said, betray him: 'for he that promiseth to be true to one, and deceiveth him, may be called a traitor, which shall never be said of me.' Yet even Darcy was determined to rebut accusations of treason against the King: 'it shall never be said that old Tom shall have one traitor's tooth in his head.'[31] Among the rank and file there may have been fewer scruples: when Archbishop Lee preached to the pilgrims and told them that it was unlawful to do battle without the prince's command, the leaders had to protect him from the anger of the congregation.[32] But those leaders showed a marked reluctance to carry dissidence to the point of disloyalty. By the middle of the century the doctrine of obedience was being insistently preached, with little suggestion that resistance could ever be legitimate. Even the most outspoken critics of the landlords told the peasants that rebellion was inexcusable, was indeed the first and worst of all sins.[33] Their view was echoed by Sir Thomas Wyatt's words on the scaffold in 1554 : 'For peruse the chronicles through, and you shall see that never rebellion against their natural prince and country prospered.'[34] In 1569 the Earl of Westmorland, just before he took up arms, voiced serious doubts about rising for the sake of religion : 'those that seem to take that quarrel in other countries are accounted as rebels; and therefore I will never blot my house which hath been this long preserved without staining.'[35] Whatever he thought he was entering upon, it was evidently not rebellion, which he regarded with distaste.

By contrast with the weak and limited rebellions of the sixteenth century, the opposition to the Stuarts showed an unprecedented resilience and strength. Once that opposition had been carried into military resistance, the way was open to more radical political action. Obviously, the hostility aroused by Stuart government accounts in part for the emergence of revolution. A ruler who seemed sympathetic to Rome and the Habsburgs, who exploited every legal ambiguity to his own advantage, who destroyed the consensus of Tudor politics, was not likely to survive for long. His fall was hastened when he presented the English opposition with support from north of the border. In the sixteenth century the foreign ally of dissent, Spain, had never come near to effective action within England. It failed to win the allegiance of more than a few native Catholics and its offers of support made their position more difficult. But while Spanish conspiracy united the political nation behind the Queen, Scottish action, thanks to the ineptitude of Charles, enabled the parliamentary opposition to destroy the independent power of the King, just as in 1688 Dutch intervention allowed the Anglican nobility to achieve the removal of James.[36]

But if widespread grievance and external support were necessary conditions for the emergence of revolution, they were probably not sufficient. Governments could disintegrate under the pressure of overwhelming discontent without the opposition becoming revolutionary. The Fronde, devastating as it was for the French Crown, produced no structural change and, except briefly in Bordeaux, no demand for radical action. The strength of feeling against the Stuarts and the resilience of the parliamentary leadership were not the only elements which distinguished the Civil War from the Tudor rebellions.

Under the Long Parliament a theory of constitutional resistance had emerged from three decades of conflict between Parliaments and monarchs from 1601 to 1629. Where the disputes of the six- teenth century had been occasional and specific, the seventeenth century provided a continuity of argument which allowed a distinctly constitutional position to be defined. By the late 1620s the leaders of the Commons were demanding, not merely the redress of individual grievances, but the surrender of some part of royal power. By 1640 the interest of the monarch had been separated from the interest of the State. Once this ideological separation had been achieved the opponents of the Crown could move beyond the remedy of abuses to constitutional change.[37]

Constitutional theory was buttressed by religious belief. Calvinist doctrine could of course be used to justify obedience as well as resistance, and the Elizabethan Puritans had exalted the power of the Christian magistrate. But Calvinism also sounded a call to build the New Jerusalem, a construction programme which involved preliminary demolition. Charles I was hardly the man to undertake that, and the loyalties propounded by earlier Puritans were dis- solved by his support of Laud and his apparent accommodation with anti-Christ. In 1640 the millenarian hopes of the radical Puritans could only be achieved through political revolution. For the radicals and for their more moderate brethren such action was made easier by the erosion of deference through Calvinist preach- ing. Although most Puritans wanted to preserve *a* social hierarchy, their belief in the sanctification of the elect lowered their respect for the existing order.[38]

In contrast to regional movements like Ket's rebellion and the Pilgrimage of Grace, the Civil War drove across county boundaries, drew reluctant shires into the struggle, and split the political nation in two. It was a national conflict, reflecting the widening political arena of the seventeenth century. Admittedly there was still a very strong sense of community in the seventeenth century and county rivalries played a large part in the divisions of the time. To some extent the county communities may, with the decline of seignorial bonds, have become more tightly cohesive than before;[39] but the local interplay worked either to limit the spread of conflict or to determine the composition of the two sides. War on this scale was made possible by a new sense of national community, which enabled opposition to rally round an institution rather than a prince of the blood : before the seventeenth century this simply does not seem to have been possible except in terms of regional protest. The recent emphasis in Stuart scholarship upon the local elements of the Civil War has usefully corrected the Whig view of a single conflict and greatly enriched our understanding. But concentration upon the grass roots should not be allowed to distract attention from the lawn : comparison with Tudor rebellions shows that the political stage was enlarged in the seventeenth century and that this was crucial to the emergence of revolution. As long as revolt was confined to the defence of local interests or the claims of a candidate for the throne, it had to be basically conservative in posture. Only a national movement could demand changes in structure.

The reasons for the emergence of national politics were many. One was obviously the increasing role of Parliament. Another was a common habit of thought induced in the political nation by its education at the universities and the inns of court. This access to education and the greater literacy of gentry and merchants permitted a response to ideology and propaganda which had been muted before. A third development sprang perhaps from the Elizabethan government's appeal to the patriotic instincts of a Protestant community. The crucial text was Foxe's *Book of Martyrs* which, in spite of its monarchical sentiments, nourished a sense of patriotism, of feeling for country, which was eventually able to stand apart from the Crown.[40]

Perhaps most important of all was the role of London which, as the centre of Court life, the law-courts and commercial activity, drew together the leaders of county society and provided a political impetus that was all its own. From the early decades of the century the Feoffees of St Antholin's had underwritten the movement for a reforming ministry in provincial towns. In the violent days of 1641-2 the city Puritans ensured the success of Strafford's attainder and the safety of the Five Members. Once the parliamentarians had won control of city government the major financial resources of the country could be turned against the King.[41] The role of London makes seventeenth-century politics quite different from the rural and provincial protests of the sixteenth. The apparently unconditional support given by Tudor London to the Crown was no more. Although the city was often on the 'conservative' side after 1642, its active participation in national politics was thereafter established. The London mob and the manipulation of London government were crucial elements in the Exclusion crisis and its aftermath.

This involvement of London coincides with a shift in the literature of social complaint. In the sixteenth century the great weight of the attack had been directed to rural grievances. The sermons of Latimer, *The Discourse of the Commonweal*, the pamphlets of men like Crowley, were preponderantly aimed against the oppression of the peasantry. The misdeeds of merchants and usurers, the hardships of small traders and urban artisans were a secondary concern. The first sign of change appeared with the apprentices' riots in London in the 1590s. In the early years of the next century social criticism was mainly conveyed through the drama. Jonson and others did not entirely ignore the oppressive landlord, but their target was the greedy merchant or financier: the country begins to take on an ideal complexion against the town; and the ills of the country were often attributed to the intrusion of urban ways. No doubt the Jacobean playwrights wrote as they did because their audience was urban and their enemies were the city fathers. But they probably appealed to and stimulated a genuine discontent. More significant than the playwrights were the Levellers. Far from being a coherent or organised party, they had various aims and origins. But by and large they appealed to the townsman of moderate means, the artisan or the small trader. No challenge to the social order could come from peasants, who might try to humiliate the gentleman but scarcely contemplated replacing him. The Levellers by contrast saw him as an intruder into English liberty. The spread of literacy, the appearance of newspapers and the multiplication of political and religious pamphlets had between them created a small but conscious group of urban revolutionaries.[42]

Attempts to account for the outbreak of the Civil War in terms of economic change and social tension have often failed before the evident fact that the two sides were so similiar in their composition. Class divisions or structural imbalance cannot explain why men fought for Parliament or for the King. Much of the explanation for that has to be seen in the immediate context of the reign of Charles I. But I have tried to show here that the question why men fought a war is not the only one to ask. The *nature* of the struggle also needs explanation. The development of ideology, the implications of Puritanism, the appearance of a national politics, the education of the gentry, artisans and shop-keepers, the extension of communications and the response to propaganda, the changing attitudes of London and the emergence of urban protest all help us to understand the transition from rebellion to revolution.

15

Privateers in the Ancient Greek World

A. H. JACKSON

The privateers of modern history were among the many interests of the late Professor Western; a survey of their early counterpart may seem an appropriate contribution, from a colleague studying ancient history, to these essays in his memory.

The privateer, the irregular auxiliary, whether citizen or foreign, who plunders enemy subjects, shipping and property on behalf of a belligerent state, has a very respectable ancestry; possibly as old as war and piracy themselves, certainly going back to Greek antiquity. It is true that there were differences between the irregulars discussed in what follows and what our term privateer calls to mind for many people, namely a sea-borne plunderer with 'letters of marque'. Though some Greek irregulars worked by sea, there was plenty of warfare by land, or on both elements at once, to give employment to others. Indeed, two Greek words often used for such irregulars can each be used both of the land and of the maritime variety.[1] For convenience both are called privateers here. As for 'letters of marque', originally a commission granted by a state to someone injured by a foreign state or its subjects and allowing him to seek compensation by seizure in reprisal of property belonging to that state and its subjects (such commissions being commonly granted without overmuch concern about the truth of allegations of injury when the foreign state happened to be the enemy of the commissioning state),[2] in the pristine simplicity of Greece such formalities were not always necessary. For a long period it gave Greek belligerents no embarrassment merely to invite any who wished to do so to use their harbours and lands as bases for plundering raids against the enemy. These raids and raiders were spoken of in the same terms and described by the same words as those used of random unprovoked freebooters.[3] Behind this lay an original

241

(and in some conservative regions a long-maintained) tolerance, in law and in moral thought, of what we would call piracy and brigandage, a feature of Greek society to be discussed in its place near the end of this essay. But we may still properly speak of Greek privateers.

In the three centuries down to 500 BC there were freebooters enough to have served in its many but ill-documented wars, even though no reliable sightings can be reported of privateers at work in this obscure period.[4] But it would have been no sudden revolution in warfare when Athens planted exiled democrats from her enemy, the island of Aegina, at Sunium to raid their homeland, shortly before 490 BC. Some of the guerrilla raids on the invading Persians in 480 and 479 by refugees on the Parnassus massif may well have been by irregulars, as plunder was their aim.[5] In the following thirty years of Greek hostilities against Persia privateering is untraceable. They are thinly recorded years, but Athens, then suppressing freebooters in the Aegean, may not have encouraged anyone to go privateering against Persian provinces nearby in case her own corn-ships and tribute-yielding allies should also suffer.[6]

But in the century after 431, wars were both frequent and well-recorded; privateers therefore abound. In the Peloponnesian War, Sparta set raiders to prey on merchants bound for Athens past the headlands of south-west Asia Minor, and these same privateers no doubt helped to catch the neutral and enemy seafarers whom Sparta mercilessly slaughtered in 431. When the peace of 421 was breaking down, partly because of raids on Sparta sponsored by Athens, Sparta proclaimed that anyone who pleased on her side could plunder Athenians, though outright war was not yet declared.[7] From 411 to 404 BC Sparta allowed exiles from Athens to use her raiding base at Deceleia to plunder Athenian farms,[8] and in the endless struggles after the Peloponnesian War all kinds of privateers found work enough.[9] Those Sparta invited to use her base at Aegina for raids on Athens in 389 earned a mention among the reasons why, in 386, Athens accepted peace terms dictated by Persia in Sparta's interest.[10] As the fourth century progressed, if that is the right word, Philip II of Macedon who, like Sparta before, lacked a strong navy, sent out privateers who even kidnapped an Athenian in the Olympic truce of 348 (the captive claimed a refund of his ransom-money), while Athens and other enemies of Philip deployed their own against him, Athens' navy being past its best.[11] As Alexander the Great conquered the

Persian empire, Greek officers and rulers on Persia's side unleashed privateers against his Greek sympathisers, as Alexander's enemies in Greece may also have done.[12] After he died in 323 BC, prospects for privateers were again excellent as Alexander's generals and their heirs battled for decades over slices and crumbs of his vast new empire. Thus Antigonus the One-Eyed, his son Demetrius the Besieger and grandson Antigonus Gonatas were leading employers even when their navies ruled the sea. But, besides the Antigonids of Macedon, the other great Hellenistic dynasties, the Ptolemies of Egypt and the Seleucids of Syria, were sometimes so served, as were weaker powers, especially the Aetolian League.[13] When Rome began interfering seriously in the Greek East from 200 BC onwards, privateers disrupted her supply-lines and attacked her Greek friends, who replied with irregulars of their own against their enemies.[14] Later in the second century when, thanks to Roman policy and Greek disunity, the pirates of the mountainous Cilician coast of Asia Minor were no longer held in check, their use as privateers by a rebel in the Seleucid empire is said to have greatly encouraged their rise. In the next century the Cilicians were turned against Rome by Mithridates; given this opportunity for consolidation, they grew into the worst plague of piracy known for many centuries in the Mediterranean till Pompey the Great cured the plague or most of it by some swift bloodletting and by astute resettlement;[15] interestingly, it was his son Sextus Pompey who used pirates, some perhaps retired Cilicians, in the civil wars eventually won by Octavian.[16]

This is only a brief outline of some conspicuous examples of the use of privateers by land and sea; many others will be mentioned in the following pages. But it is clear even from these that privateering was regarded as having considerable nuisance value in the wars of the Greek world, though no war of importance seems to have been decided by it. This nuisance value is easy to explain. Plundering was then, in all kinds of ways and situations, a much more significant tactical and strategic weapon than it has been in much warfare of more recent times, partly because today destruction has become a much easier method of reducing an enemy's morale and strength. Naturally, Greeks at war sometimes had hatred enough to massacre and lay waste whole cities and their territories, to sink and to drown convoys and crews. But it caused the enemy as much damage and terror, and satisfied needs and impulses as strong as hatred, to kidnap and loot for ransom, sale or one's own use and exploitation. Since Greek society was generally slave-owning, captives were more often sold than slaughtered, and thus war could be more humiliating but less violent for the losers and victory could pay for itself more often than is usual today.[17]

For the work of plundering, privateers were very useful, especially when a state could not or would not spare regular forces for it. Thus, when Athens planted the refugees at Sunium to raid Aegina, it was at a time when she needed every warship she could build or borrow to face Aegina's line of battle. Again, Aetolia in the third century had no regular navy and relied for sea power in war not only on allies but on the enthusiasm and expertise of her privateering citizens, the same men whose peacetime raiding (usually unprovoked but disguised under a flimsy pretext of reprisals) helped to give Aetolia influence of a kind over vulnerable Aegean cities.[18] Likewise in 210 BC, when Rome's legionaries facing Hannibal needed any auxiliaries available, a whole Sicilian bandit community was transplanted to her feeble Greek ally Rhegium (Reggio di Calabria) to help annoy Rhegium's neighbours, who were on Hannibal's side.[19] Meanwhile, in the Aegean an outbreak of plundering and extortion led by an Aetolian in 205 or 204 BC was in fact a fund-raising mission in aid of his secret employer, the Antigonid Philip V of Macedon, who had a feeble fleet and needed money to build himself a strong one; when his new fleet was severely battered by his enemies in 201 BC, Philip fell back on privateers again.[20] Of course, a really strong naval or military power like Athens after 482, with her mighty fleet, or such as the Deinomenid despots of Syracuse or Dionysius I, would need all the booty available to finance their costly forces and might not have wanted any privateers to compete with them for it; we hear of no privateers of theirs. Or, like Classical Athens and Hellenistic Rhodes, some might not wish to foster the freebooters they suppressed in peace, as privateers in war. But, even when Athens' sea power was at its strongest, she used them by land where she was weaker.[21]

Besides, privateers' qualifications could be most attractive. Many were expert brigands or sea-raiders, skilled in pouncing on ill-guarded villages or in rowing down slow-sailing merchantmen under cover of a barrage of arrows, and would already have the weapons and galleys for their job.[22] Even exiles like those at Sunium, or the Helot rebels whom Athens turned against their Spartan masters in the Peloponnesian War, would make up what

they lacked in experience and toughness by their local knowledge
and devotion to the task of robbing those who had robbed them
of their homeland. Moreover, all such irregulars were somewhat
more expendable than trained regulars, citizens or mercenary;
hence they were used not only for looting but as 'forlorn hopes' on
occasion, like the ten Aetolian raiders who put up the scaling
ladders for Gonatas' dawn surprise of the fortress of Cassandreia
in 276 BC. When the Sicilians were dispatched from Rhegium in
209 to ravage the fields of Bruttium and storm the walls of Caulonia
nearby on Hannibal's side, it was not only a compliment to their
skill as robbers; they were the bait to draw Hannibal down into
Calabria while Tarentum (Taranto) was betrayed back to Rome.[23]
If your enemy's cavalry killed some of the exiles you harboured
against him, then the rest would make all the more responsive and
dependant puppets when you set them to rule over their beaten
city.[24] Foreign professional raiders would rarely have the political
influence and troublesome claims that allied states might have in
victory. Besides, in peace-time they could be ideal undercover
agents for making difficult the lives of those you were at peace
with but wished to weaken. Thus in 204 BC an Aetolian leading
twenty raiding ships in the Aegean and extorting money from
merchants and cities would have been nothing new in himself and
a great deal of trouble to Rhodes, whose prestige and customs
revenues depended on protecting those merchants and cities.
Rhodes and Philip V were officially friends; Aetolia had only just
lost a war against Philip in 206. Men might not at once suspect
that Philip was the raider's master and that Rhodes' strength and
influence in the Aegean were an awkward obstacle to certain plans
Philip had for expansion in the Aegean and further east.[25]

What is more, privateers seem to have been cheaper auxiliaries
than less expendable trained mercenaries or citizen regulars, so
far as the limited evidence suggests. Naturally, bargains between
host and guest would vary with the bargaining strength of either
party; desperate exiles whose sole hope lay in their country's enemy
would no doubt settle for less than a strong band of independent
professional sea-raiders who could offer their services to the enemy
if he seemed more generous and more likely to win. The Sicilians
had no choice but to raid from Rhegium for rations alone, plus
what they could capture, and rations or ration-money for raiders
are mentioned in Demosthenes' day.[26] Even a dangerous Illyrian
chief with 30 raiding galleys could be hired for what seems to have

been less than regular mercenaries' pay; admittedly, he was an
ally officially, but one not too unlike a stateless raider-captain
turned privateer.[27] After all, unless on a storming party, the
privateer was free to loot and run and could have claimed no
danger money for facing enemy battle-lines. He might need rations
to keep him going, but some may have been expected to capture
even those.[28] As to booty, some, like the Sicilians at Rhegium, could
keep their full takings, but some were actually expected to hand
over a large or small proportion to their hosts; obviously, an
employer who demanded all the catch would advertise in vain for
privateers.[29] Foreign privateers might betray their hosts on occasion,
it is true, and smuggle the enemy inside the gates; and, on more
than one occasion, discontented citizens used irregular plundering
forays as cover for treacherous negotiations.[30] But regulars, whether
mercenary or citizen, could present similar risks at times and, to
judge from their frequent employment, the nuisance value of these
irregular agents, often expendable and cheap compared with
regulars, outweighed their potential dangers in the eyes of many
belligerents.

Just as clearly, service as privateers often seemed worthwhile. Let
us consider now the privateers' point of view. For citizens privateering could be safer and more profitable than a place in the phalanx,
or on the rowing benches of a Greek warship which was generally
a fragile craft. Exiles could try to plunder their homeland from
some base of their own, but they frequently relied, from necessity
or sympathy, on their homeland's enemy for all kinds of help as
well as the provision of bases. Impartial neutrals or stateless professional raiders could find rich booty and ransoms elsewhere than
in a war zone where they would face competition from the
belligerents' regular armies and fleets; or they could dodge about
inside a chaotic theatre of war, plundering both sides and uncommitted to either.[31] But for these, too, service with one side would
have some advantages over making both sides their enemies. Service
would guarantee a friendly base and a convenient fair-sized market
for selling miscellaneous loot and captives; if your host's camp or
city was temporarily glutted with food and slaves after some lucky
capture by his regular forces, at least you could eat well and
cheaply, and anyway next month your host might be blockaded,
starving and glad to pay you the earth for a dozen sheep. It was
worth waiting if the best loot was locked up inside a besieged city's
walls; meanwhile, you could enrich yourself and ingratiate your-

self with the besieger who employed you in time to earn a good place when the city was thrown open to looters, by foraging in its countryside and ambushing its supply convoys.[32] It would be a further attraction if rations or even some sort of pay were offered, while if the host expected a share of the booty it could be child's play for a free-ranging irregular to cheat him; after all, embezzlement by Greek regulars was hard enough to control.[33]

Some prices recorded for captives and booty in war will vividly illustrate how well privateering could pay. The worthwhile catches most commonly encountered were captives who could be returned to their relatives and friends for large ransoms; or, if too poor to pay, they could still be sold to the slave-dealer, even if for less than in settled peace-time trade. Thus, about 400 BC, it could cost one man between 60 and 100 drachmas to stay alive for a year; a single rich Athenian's ransom could be between 2,000 and 3,000 drachmas, a common soldier's or rower's ransom 100 or 200 drachmas.[34] Sold as slaves in war-time, such men might have brought smaller but still worthwhile sums, even if only 20 drachmas a head. In the mid-third century, to stay alive for a year could cost a single man between 90 and 120 drachmas; a recently published inscription reveals that the ransom charged for some Athenian country people kidnapped by raiders in war-time was 120 drachmas each.[35] In 189 BC envoys taken by privateers were asked for 30,000 drachmas (5 talents) each and settled for 18,000 (3 talents).[36] As for other booty, a richly laden merchant ship waylaid in war-time in 355 BC yielded 9½ talents (57,000 drachmas).[37] Commoner and more modest prizes could still repay the dangers of privateering. In peaceable trade of the first half of the fourth century, a good horse could bring a few hundred drachmas, oxen from 25 to 90 a head, and sheep or goats about 12 to 15 each. In a war zone prices would vary wildly if a glut of booty or a famine occurred.[38] But even so, remembering that in a glut a privateer might sometimes be able to take time off to seek a good price for his wares in some calmer region nearby, we can imagine how fortunes could be made by the lucky and a living made at least, if one was careful. Besides, the servitudes and risks of privateering would be less than the soldier's, albeit without his steadier income. As to sharing[39] and spending we can only guess, by analogy with freebooters' and soldiers' habits. If exiles had not lost all their property and other income, they could spend on hiring mercenaries and bribing sentries or politicians.[40] Other varieties of privateer would have caroused or gambled their profits away, confident that there was more where they had come from. More sober spirits would buy a swifter horse or galley, ransom a friend or do some other favour, repay their debts or lend at interest themselves, save for a daughter's dowry or against being ransomed themselves one day, re-stock ravaged estates or retire as comfortable landowners.[41]

Privateering, then, could be an attractive proposition to both parties concerned, and belligerents to employ privateers were common enough. To meet their needs there existed various sources of supply which were sometimes combined, and which can now be considered. For some of these the social and economic ills afflicting the ancient Greek world were largely responsible, for others the nature of social or political life could be the cause. One source was a state's own citizens. Possibly an important source in some Archaic city-states, it was long significant in poorer, less advanced regions like Crete and Aetolia, where open freebooting was a normal pastime till much later.[42] Even after Archaic times, in a sophisticated and settled city under blockade a well-born amateur might go out for booty and excitement, or even a trusted slave could be sent out to loot and kidnap.[43] But in states with regular armies and fleets most able-bodied citizens would often be wanted for these; Classical Athens and Hellenistic Rhodes may even have effectively banned any privateering by citizens.[44]

Another source was friendly or neutral states' subjects; of these Aetolia was a notably impartial supplier in the years around 200 BC and probably since much earlier. Her rapacious citizens were apparently allowed to serve foreign states even against Aetolia's own friends, without any special authorisation by the Aetolian government. Their victims complained of this extra liberty allowed them, which other states did not then allow their subjects at their friends' expense.[45] Exiles from a country could also be enlisted by its enemies, as we have seen; but not all the many exiles generated by the often eventful political life of Greece, and who turned to raiding, confined themselves to plundering their own land.[46] Many joined the numbers of stateless freebooters who were a fourth reservoir of potential privateers, to be found at many times and places whenever no strong power tried to suppress them. Debt, never rare in the Greek world as a whole, and slavery, widespread from at least the sixth century, produced fugitives from time to time who might raid to live.[47] Or mercenaries made redundant when one war ended might live by robbery and turn privateer on occasion.[48] These four main sources of recruits would not all be accessible at all times. But not many belligerents can have advertised in vain if their terms were reasonable.

As to numbers employed, expendable irregulars paid little if at all were perhaps rarely counted by employers, for we hear little on this. Some big concentrations are known; Demetrius the Besieger had several thousand in 302 BC, drawing doubtless on much of Greece, the Aegean and the other large areas he then controlled.[49] The Sicilians at Rhegium, criminals, exiles and fugitive debtors from many cities, numbered 4,000. Perhaps 10,000 Cilicians served Mithridates.[50] But more modest bands could be effective. Sparta's Peloponnesians in 430 BC could have been one or two hundred only, in 332 BC a pro-Persian despot had perhaps not many more, and in 190 BC raiders plundering Chios, a Roman supply-base at the time, could defend themselves against a strong Roman fleet though they numbered perhaps only several hundred in their 15 raiding galleys.[51] Even very small groups had their use. On land and by night a single bold horseman could string together over a score of men, women and children, while rounding up many sheep or cattle would be easy for a skilled man.[52] We hear of a skiff light enough to be loaded on to a cart by its crew, and of another hunting with a 30-oared galley and 40 or so well-armed men aboard.[53] For a small city to invite too many privateers could have been more dangerous to it than to its enemies. But this question cannot be fully answered and other, equally important, questions have even less evidence to permit much investigation.[54]

Lastly, a further question deserves and may reward investigation : why were belligerents so often prepared to use privateers? Their practical advantages, though clear enough, do not entirely account for their use. The answer may lie partly in two facts. First, the majority of Greek public opinion long approved of plundering the enemy in war and supposed that the gods also approved. Even today there can still be seen, at the great sanctuaries of Zeus at Olympia or Apollo at Delphi, monuments dedicated to these gods and paid for out of the proceeds of the shares of booty which the victorious dedicators assigned to the gods in thanks for their help and favour.[55] It was always right to plunder enemy property and for long the sale of Greeks by Greeks into slavery was an accepted part of warfare. Even when the enslavement of Greek captives in war became less reputable from the fifth-century enlightenment onwards, at least in more sophisticated parts, slaves and other property could be looted by regular and irregular forces without embarrassment.[56] Only sacred property and persons such as priests or others with a special individual grant of immunity from the enemy state were immune throughout the whole of Greek history.[57] Thus, what privateers did was quite consistent with sentiment about war.

Secondly, what they were was for long quite respectable, even though today we would regard privateers as criminals under international law and little better than pirates. But, as has been said above, what we call piracy – namely, random unprovoked robbing and kidnapping of foreigners – was for long not regarded as immoral.[58] In the society reflected in Homer's *Iliad* and *Odyssey*, which is thought to be that of the tenth, ninth or eighth centuries BC, at the very beginnings of Greek history, private raids against foreigners were no disgrace in most people's eyes, so long as the raider's state had no relationship with the victim's state.[59] In the *Odyssey* there is one dissenting voice, that of Odysseus' swineherd Eumaeus, himself a victim of kidnappers and strong in the belief that the gods love not evil deeds and send retribution on men of ill-will who plunder foreigners.[60] But Eumaeus accepts that it is Zeus who allows such raiders to capture booty, and he seems in a minority of one amid a general acceptance of raiding as an activity that nobles and kings might freely indulge in. The poet Hesiod, writing around 700 BC, does condemn violent acquisition of riches, but he may have had in mind robbery within the community, not raids against foreigners far away.[61] Later, when Homeric values were being questioned by some advanced minds in the sixth century, raiding was no disgrace in a city like Phocaea (at least not against barbarians), if not quite so honourable against Greeks perhaps.[62] Even in sixth-century Athens the law allowed 'men going after booty' the same freedom to make legally binding contracts as that enjoyed by pious worshippers and peaceful traders. Some have been so alarmed at the thought of Athens, the leader of Greek civilisation, as a nest of pirates that they will have this law mean only privateers or men banding together to take reprisals for wrongs done them by foreigners.[63] But there seems to be no other reason why sixth-century Athenians should not have been allowed to make unprovoked raids on states in no relationship with Athens. Why should anyone care if an Athenian raider plundered and enslaved in the wild West Mediterranean, or even against Lemnos, say, or Mytilene in the Aegean? When Athens suppressed

freebooters in the Aegean from 482 onwards, this was surely more
for practical reasons than from altruism.[64] The peace she imposed
on the sea and the great alliance she constructed against Persia
would have done much to make men used to living without raids,
if they were not so already, and Thucydides assumes that his sophisticated readers regard freebooting as shameful. But at this very
time in Aetolia and its neighbourhood the grand old Homeric view
prevailed,[65] and Plato writes as if there existed in late-fifth-century
Athens clever young men who thought it just for the strong to
plunder the weak.[66] Even in Classical Athens evidence that freebooting was positively illegal under all circumstances, and not
merely immoral, is hard to find,[67] and even in the third century,
when many cities suffered from it, freebooting could be made just
respectable by official pretence that it was plundering in reprisals
for wrongs by the members of the state attacked, a pretence which
Aetolians often exploited.[68] In Aetolia bare-faced raiding may still
not have been totally illegal; there the proper name Laistas, clearly
derived from one common word for 'raider', was quite respectable
even about 200 BC.[69] It may only have been after the Roman
conquest, and perhaps only when Pompey pacified the Cilicians,
that all unprovoked raiding, disguised as reprisals or not, came to
be treated as illegal and not merely as immoral everywhere in the
Greek East.[70] We cannot hope to define Greek views of raiding
precisely in all periods and places, but it seems unlikely that there
was a single, steady and unanimous evolution in laws and moral
theory about it, everywhere following the most enlightened minds
in the most advanced cities, which suffered most obviously from
freebooters.[71]

Thus, not merely the fact that privateers plundered the enemy,
but also what they were – namely, private groups raiding foreigners
(rather like the freebooters just discussed, indeed often those same
freebooters) – were the more easily acceptable. The official phrases
used of privateers seem indeed to reflect contemporary feelings on
plundering in war and on freebooters, if we can trust our evidence.
In the fifth and fourth centuries, privateers were not injured innocents taking reprisals but raiders raiding, described by the same
words as freebooters. Thus, in two later fifth-century treaties,
Athens' partners agree not to harbour raiders or to raid themselves,
among other hostile acts such as helping Athens' enemies : privateering against Athens as well as random freebooting must here be
meant.[72] In 416 and 389 Sparta simply invited those who wished

to do so to raid Athenians and Attica, and such invitations were explicitly banned in a treaty Thasos broke in 341–0 BC.[73]

But later, when freebooting was widely disguised as reprisals for alleged wrongs by those attacked, and when opinion was strong enough to make belligerents cease the profitable practice of enslaving whole Greek cities, at least for a while, there is evidence that some belligerents mobilised privateers by inviting private persons to seek reprisals by plundering for wrongs allegedly done them by the enemy. The result would be the same as that of the simpler Spartan invitation of 389 BC; all professional bandits and sea-raiders not otherwise engaged, and also some amateurs, perhaps, would go forth from the belligerent's land against his enemy, except that for propaganda purposes they were now strong in the wrath of injured innocence, instead of being baldly styled 'raiders' with the same word and title as that given to freebooters like themselves by the majority of public opinion. Perhaps even some genuinely wronged by the enemy state would have hastened to settle old scores quickly in response to the belligerent's proclamation, for states were slower to grant justice to foreign nationals than to their own subjects on the whole. There is evidence for states in the Hellenistic age, who did not mean to go to war, authorising private reprisals by their own aggrieved citizens against foreign powers that had denied them justice.[74] There is also evidence that, in 220 and 219 BC respectively, Achaea and Sparta, concurrently with formal declaration of war, also issued proclamations authorising acts of plunder against their enemies; the phrase used by Polybius (IV, 27, 7 and 36, 6) is closely paralleled in an inscription of the middle of the third century or earlier, where it seems to be equated with the authorisation of acts of plunder *in reprisal.* Thus in 220 and 219 Achaea and Sparta, with an eye on 'public relations', may well have proclaimed a welcome for innocents injured by their enemies who wanted to use Achaean and Spartan land as bases for acts of plunder in reprisal against their injurers.[75] Similarly, in 196 BC the two cities of Miletus and Magnesia, making peace after a war, agreed, besides banning other hostile and malicious acts, not to harbour men with claims for compensation by reprisals against members of the other city. With imaginative and predatory Aetolians themselves just released from various other wars at this time and likely to use any excuse they could dream up for plundering reprisals, this was a wise and tactful clause in the cities' peace treaty.[76] In the same decade Rhodes seems to have referred to her friends' privateers in war in blunter language when she directed that 'those plundering the enemy' should not use the sacred island of Delos as their base but their own harbours. Rhodes, who policed the Hellenistic Aegean till her power was sabotaged by Roman policy, would not wish Delos to be exposed to the enemy's counter-attacks and may have had a low opinion of even the privateers on her own side, some of whom may well have been professional sea-raiders whom she tried to exterminate in peace-time. There is a hint in our record of this Rhodian directive that she regarded privateers as unacceptable visitors on Delos, sacred to Apollo as it was.[77] Meanwhile on Crete a contemporary treaty of alliance between two cities on this island-home of sea-raiders and mercenaries blandly states that 'if by the gods' favour we capture goods from the enemy either in an official expedition or when men go out privately from each city by land or by sea, each side's share shall be in proportion to the number of men from each city and both sides shall take the tithes back to their own cities.' This seems to show that in Crete, a conservative, indeed a backward island, which produced many of the freebooters Rhodes strove to repress, heaven did not only vouchsafe booty to its favourites but also expected a ten per cent cut of the loot ('tithes' of war booty were regularly dedicated to gods as thank-offerings), and from private as well as official expeditions.[78]

Thus the official attitude to privateers varied according as a state was backward or sophisticated. But even Rhodes had to accept that privateers were useful, and mealy-mouthed Achaean or Milesian propaganda and diplomacy could still give privateers a title acceptable to more enlightened public opinion which was now hostile to freebooters and unhappy about the enslavement of Greeks in war. Privateers were too useful in war and in peace for the often conflicting states of the Greek world to abandon. Had Rome not established peace among them, the history of their privateers might have been longer.

16

Septimius Severus and his Generals, AD 193-7

A. J. GRAHAM

Lucius Septimius Severus was proclaimed emperor by his troops in Pannonia on 9 April 193.[1] Within two months he had overthrown the emperor at Rome, Didius Julianus. By the spring of 194 his great eastern rival, Pescennius Niger, had also been defeated. The following year saw his armies campaigning against Parthian vassals far beyond the eastern frontier of the empire. He returned to the West to face the challenge of Clodius Albinus and settled this civil war too by his victory at Lugdunum on 19 February 197. In less than a year from that date he had defeated the Parthians and sacked their capital at Ctesiphon. Even this rapid accumulation of victories does not represent the total of his military achievements, for in his last years he undertook a major campaign in Scotland. In traditional style the official titles proclaimed the victories and conquests of a soldier-emperor: 'twelve times hailed *imperator*, conqueror of the Arabs, conqueror of the Adiabenians, great conqueror of Parthia, great conqueror of Britain'.[2]

It is not surprising that the contemporary historian, Herodian, considered that Septimius Severus' military achievements surpassed those of any predecessor. In a powerful passage (iii, 7, 7–8) he recalls the great wars of Caesar against Pompey, of Augustus against Antony and Pompey's sons, of Marius and of Sulla, only to conclude that none could be compared with those of Septimius Severus for the size of the forces involved, the number of battles, or the distance and speed of the marches. No other, he adds, had overthrown three reigning emperors. When he specifies Septimius Severus' qualities he writes (iii, 8, 8) 'in bravery, endurance and the conduct of military affairs none of the great exemplars

255

surpassed him.' Finally, when describing his death Herodian repeats
the point (iii, 15, 2) : 'his life had been more distinguished, in war,
than that of any other emperor.' Not all modern students have
accepted such a laudatory assessment. One great expert on Roman
military matters went so far as to write :

Severus did not launch his venture until the death of Pertinax, because
he was held back by the consciousness of his own lack of military
ability in the face of the great marshal from the heroic period of the
Marcomannic War. For he was certainly aware of this failing. That
is shown by his decision to remain at a safe distance from the battlefield during the war against Pescennius Niger and by his cowardly
flight at the decisive battle at Lyon.[3]

The implication of such a judgment is that Septimius Severus
won his victories through others. It so happens that we have a
good deal of information about the men chosen by Septimius
Severus to command his armies, and these men, his closest and
greatest associates in the civil war years, have been the subject of
much detailed investigation.[4] The aims of this investigation have
been to elucidate the relations and connections between Septimius
Severus and his most eminent followers, to reveal the sources of his
support, and to seek an answer to the question whether his successful usurpation was the result of a long-planned conspiracy. Inevitably, given the character of our knowledge and the nature of the
events under discussion, no conclusive results have been achieved.[5]
The aim of the present paper is different. The relations between
Septimius Severus and his closest supporters during the civil war
years can help to reveal the actual strategy, policies and purposes
of the usurping emperor at that critical period. These things, though
not always immediately apparent, are not beyond discovery (unlike
the plots and conspiracies of ancient times). Furthermore, it is only
after we have a true picture of these matters that we may hope to
reach a just assessment of Septimius Severus' military achievements
and abilities.

The march on Rome

The first of Septimius Severus' campaigns, the *expeditio felicissima
urbica*,[6] by which he seized the throne from Didius Julianus, was
characterised by speed, by efficient mustering of sufficient military
force for his purposes, and by complete success. Didius Julianus, it
is true, could offer only a feeble military resistance. The total
regular forces in Italy amounted to 11,500 men.[7] The fleets at

Misenum and Ravenna offered in theory perhaps another 15,000.[8] They had been energetically used in the civil wars of 68–70,[9] but Dio makes plain that they were militarily of no use to Didius Julianus (lxxiv, 16, 2–3). The real threats to Septimius Severus came from the great army of Britain under the governor of the province, Clodius Albinus, and the forces in the East under the governor of Syria, Pescennius Niger. The march on Rome was thus merely a preliminary to the more serious warfare. By taking control of Italy, Septimius Severus could make himself the legally established Augustus and brand his rivals as enemies of the Roman people. But the imminent threat from other frontier armies made it essential for him to complete the Italian campaign with no check or delay, much less any kind of failure. There would be no gain in winning control of Italy, if in the meantime he had allowed his rivals to build up an overwhelming strategic advantage. As it was, even though the Italian expedition was a complete success, Pescennius Niger very nearly won complete control of the crossing from Europe to Asia.

Septimius Severus needed, therefore, to strike very fast, but he also needed to assemble sufficient troops to render opposition hopeless. We can calculate his timetable with some assurance. The news of Pertinax' murder and Didius Julianus' accession on 28 March 193 will have reached him by 3 April at the earliest. He was thus probably able to consult only with the commanding officers of the three legions in his own province of Pannonia Superior before he had himself proclaimed emperor at Carnuntum on 9 April.[10] We know that he was at Interamna, some sixty miles from Rome, by 1 June. The march from Carnuntum to Interamna must have required a little over thirty days, so he made the necessary preparations in a short three weeks.[11]

The famous 'legionary' coins issued on his arrival in Rome have been thought[12] to celebrate the units which took part in the march on Rome: namely, all the legions on the Rhine and Danube frontiers (with the curious exception of X Gemina),[13] fifteen in total. Simple calculation, however, shows that of these two certainly, XXX Ulpia in Germania Inferior and XI Claudia in Moesia Inferior, cannot actually have participated in the march. So the coins should rather be interpreted as commemorating the legions which had sworn loyalty to the new emperor before he began his march on Rome.[14] We can only conjecture, therefore, the constituent forces of his army. We may assume, however, that he followed the practice established already by Marcus Aurelius and made up his expeditionary force from detachments of the units on the frontiers.[15] In that case he would have needed contributions from many, or most, of the remaining thirteen legions. At Carnuntum he could have assembled the detachments from XIV Gemina and I Adiutrix in his own province of Pannonia Superior, from II Adiutrix in Pannonia Inferior, II Italica in Noricum and III Italica in Raetia. The detachments from the legions of Moesia Superior, IV Flavia and VII Claudia, could more easily have joined Septimius Severus' army at Poetovio or Aquileia. At the latter meeting-point there could have been added detachments from the legions of Germania Superior, VIII Augusta and XXII Primigenia, and (just possibly) from I Italica in Moesia Inferior, XIII Gemina and V Macedonica in Dacia, and I Minervia in Germania Inferior. In addition we know that the expeditionary force included auxiliary troops, especially cavalry, but we have no evidence to guide conjecture as to the actual numbers or units involved.[16]

Of the important officers in the army we know three. Julius Laetus was sufficiently close to the emperor to provide important advice on one occasion.[17] He was a leading Severan general from 195 onwards, but his position and rank in 193 can only be guessed.[18] L. Valerius Valerianus was probably a cavalry commander, who performed his duties sufficiently well to be given later a key role in the decisive battle at Issus. It is likely that he was serving in his third appointment as an officer at the beginning of an equestrian career, in command of a troop of cavalry in Dacia,[19] when Septimius Severus was proclaimed. Rossius Vitulus was also a knight in command of a troop of cavalry in the Danube area at the time of Septimius Severus' proclamation, and was put in charge of the corn supply for the expeditionary army.[20] This was a most important and testing commission in a large army which had to move very fast, and it is a measure of Rossius Vitulus' success that he was chosen to be paymaster in the war against Pescennius Niger and was again in charge of corn supplies in that against Clodius Albinus. So of the three known subordinates in Septimius Severus' expeditionary force against Rome, two were knights experienced in military affairs but of no distinction.

Throughout the march the emperor was surrounded day and night by a picked bodyguard of 600 men, who never removed their breastplates until they were in Rome.[21] Everyone on the route yielded to him and all the cities opened their gates.[22] Those whom Didius Julianus sent against him simply went over to the usurper or were easily disposed of.[23] The only action which approached a military engagement was the surrounding and disbanding of the Praetorian Guard.[24] Septimius Severus had tricked them into parading before him in ceremonial dress without their armour. At a pre-arranged signal they were swiftly surrounded by the armed frontier troops and could merely submit to the removal of their weapons and banishment from Rome. Septimius Severus had in the meantime taken the precaution of sending picked men to occupy the praetorian camp to obviate the danger that the dismissed praetorians might try to break back into their old quarters and re-form there. This was a well-planned and well-executed military coup, but no fighting was required, and it can thus be said to exemplify in miniature the whole expedition against Rome.

The position of the new emperor throughout the campaign was entirely as one would expect. He was in command, at the head of the strategic planning and tactical operations, living among his soldiers and sharing their hardships. The glory of the victory and the loyalty of the army were his alone.[25]

The military operation was not his sole preoccupation, however. It is likely that he made his agreement with Clodius Albinus, whereby the latter became Caesar, at the earliest possible moment.[26] There have been differing interpretations of this arrangement. To the ancient writers Clodius Albinus was duped by the subtle and deceitful Septimius Severus. He was kept quiet by the honour of the title of Caesar and position as successor to the purple until Septimius Severus had defeated Pescennius Niger. Septimius Severus then made it plain that the succession would pass to his elder son, and Clodius Albinus was duly disposed of at a time of Severus' own choosing.[27] Modern observers argue, to the contrary, that Septimius Severus and Clodius Albinus were true political allies, pointing to the facts that both were of African origin and that Septimius Severus would need a mature successor in times of great danger, when his elder son was only five years old. Septimius Severus' offer is thus seen as genuine and sincere. Support can be found for this interpretation in Septimius Severus' First Parthian War. He would hardly have embarked on this, it is thought, had he been planning to create an open breach with Clodius Albinus. On this line of argument Clodius Albinus deceives Septimius Severus rather than the other way round.[28]

Both these interpretations seem inadequate. Septimius Severus was extremely ambitious to found a dynasty; it is therefore most improbable that he genuinely intended that Clodius Albinus should succeed him. Furthermore, if he merely needed a close connection of mature years as a stop-gap heir while his sons grew older, why did he not choose his brother Geta, whose origin and family connection would seem to make him much better qualified than Clodius Albinus?[29] We must surely allow that the ancients were right in imputing ulterior motives to Septimius Severus.[30] But we cannot allow that they were also right in judging Clodius Albinus to be an innocent dupe.[31] It is perfectly possible to see why the arrangement should also appeal to Clodius Albinus' secret hopes. While the other two contenders for the throne were at war he could be building up his forces; in 193 he was much inferior in military might to both his rivals. When either Septimius Severus or Pescennius Niger had been eliminated, he could hope to challenge the remaining competitor with a sufficiently powerful army. The strongest argument in favour of this interpretation is that that is exactly what happened. Clodius Albinus came very close to winning at Lugdunum and his army is said to have been of equal size to that of Septimius Severus.[32]

For the moment, however, we need only note the advantage for Septimius Severus. He had not only taken Rome; he had also ensured his rear before he embarked on the war against Pescennius Niger.[33]

The war against Pescennius Niger

Pescennius Niger was proclaimed Augustus in Syria at much the same time as Septimius Severus in Pannonia. All the provinces of the East, including Egypt, supported him. On the other hand, Septimius Severus' speed denied him any advantage from the popularity he enjoyed with the urban mob at Rome. It might seem that Niger could have afforded to employ a waiting strategy and expect to win by putting pressure on Rome's corn supply through his control of Egypt, but the Severans' control of the great African corn resources[34] would mean that such a strategy would at best take a long time to be effective. More important, the potential threat from Clodius Albinus meant that both Niger and Septimius Severus needed to seek a quick decision. Each could reasonably hope to win, for the forces available to both emperors were very great.

Since the transport of great armies over long stretches of sea was not feasible,[35] it was of vital importance for both sides to control the short sea-crossing at the Bosporus. Niger showed his appreciation of this by moving very fast into that area and gaining control of Byzantium. With each end of the shortest sea-crossing in his hands, he had an advantage both for attack and for defence. Perinthus, however, which was the next important port westwards and was served by the two great roads from the West, was similarly important strategically. When Niger advanced against that city he met the Severan forces for the first time. Although they lack precision, the ancient writers tell us that Septimius Severus sent off troops to the area,[36] and on the most probable reconstruction of the chronology he did this before he embarked on his march to Rome.[37] The commander he chose was most probably Fabius Cilo, described on one of his career inscriptions as *praepositus vexillationib[us] Illyricianis Perinthi tendentibus.*[38]

Cilo was present in Rome and consul designate on the night of Commodus' murder, 31 December 192, when he was able to perform an important service for Pertinax in arranging for the burial of the corpse of Commodus.[39] If it is correct to assume that Septimius Severus sent him east in command of a force from the Pannonian regions before the march on Rome, he must have slipped away from Italy and joined Severus by April 193. It is an attractive conjecture that Cilo was responsible for smuggling Septimius Severus' family out of Italy to prevent them from falling into the hands of Didius Julianus.[40] The distinguished subsequent career of Cilo during Septimius Severus' rule proves that he was one of the closest of the emperor's advisers and supporters.[41]

The choice of Cilo was not the reward for an exceptionally brilliant earlier career. There is no sign of special distinction or rapid promotion. Nor is there evidence of outstanding military gifts of great military experience. We must therefore conclude that it was for other reasons that Septimius Severus deemed him suitable for such a demanding and important task, reasons which we can now only conjecture. Above all, it may be suggested, Cilo was a man he could trust and a man who represented no threat to the position of Septimius Severus himself. Why he appeared trustworthy we cannot know for certain, though it is a reasonable assumption that he was an established friend or associate of Septimius Severus.[42] He would seem unlikely to pose a threat to the new emperor's position, no doubt, precisely because he was junior to Septimius Severus and lacked special distinction in origins or career. In this connection it is interesting to reflect that Septimius Severus did not employ his brother Geta in commanding troops against Pescennius Niger. Geta was most probably at this time governor of Moesia Inferior, a province close to the Bosporan theatre. Geta, moreover, was senior to Cilo in rank and had had at least as much military experience. Such qualifications, however, would not outweigh Septimius Severus' reluctance to bring into prominence someone from his own family who was at least his equal in rank and probably his senior.[43]

Cilo amply justified Septimius Severus' choice. Niger won some kind of victory over the Severan forces, but he nevertheless failed to take Perinthus and withdrew to Byzantium. The Severan forces had thus succeeded in keeping control of one important harbour on the European side of the short sea-crossing to Asia, and they were sufficiently strong to put Byzantium under siege. We know that part, if not all, of the besieging force consisted of troops from the provinces of Moesia under the leadership of Marius Maximus, who was the legate of the legion I Italica in Moesia Inferior before the war.[44] In that position his superior was Geta, the emperor's brother; yet it was he, and not Geta, who was chosen to lead the Moesian forces at Byzantium.

Marius Maximus was in the relatively junior position of legionary legate; his father had been a knight; his career until that time had shown nothing exceptional. Although we cannot know all the reasons why Septimius Severus chose him to command the Moesian army and direct the siege of Byzantium,[45] we need not doubt that his low rank and lack of special distinction were in his favour.

The emperor left Rome for the eastern war early in July[46] and travelled by the long land route through the Danube provinces to Perinthus, which he made his headquarters.[47] He made arrangements for the assembly of a large army and a large fleet while he was on the way to the Bosporan region.[48] The long delay, some seven months it seems, between the engagements at Perinthus and the next major fighting between Severans and Nigerians can be explained by the difficulty imposed on the Severans by Niger's control of Byzantium. Since Byzantium could not be taken, Niger's position had to be turned by crossing to Asia elsewhere, and the much longer crossing of the Propontis from Perinthus required very full and careful preparations.

For the subsequent stages of the war Septimius Severus decided that he himself would stay at Perinthus[49] and that the direct command of the armies and conduct of the battles should be entrusted to others. In the light of what we know of other emperors and other wars in Roman imperial history, this decision seems surprising. In his own younger days Septimius Severus will have observed how the philosopher-emperor Marcus had deemed it necessary to conduct his campaigns personally and to maintain close contact with the fighting soldiers. In doing so Marcus was simply following a fundamental rule observed by all Roman emperors who took care of their own position : no one but the emperor himself must be the object of the soldiers' loyalty. The importance of this rule is most dramatically revealed in the chaotic conditions of the third century, when the different bodies of troops were all repeatedly proclaiming their own emperors, but the revolt of Avidius Cassius against Marcus and the reported attempts of soldiers to proclaim their governors as emperors during the reign of Commodus prove that such dangers were very real in the period under discussion, even for established emperors. How much more so in a time of civil war! Pescennius Niger, who offers a close comparison, was in personal command of his forces at Perinthus, Byzantium and at the major battles of Nicaea and Issus. He had an important lieutenant, Asellius Aemilianus, but only once, in the fighting near Cyzicus, did he entrust him with command in battle, and then it was presumably because Niger thought that he ought to remain with his forces at the front in Byzantium.[50] Yet Septimius Severus took the risk of allowing others to enjoy the glory of victory and the close personal involvement with the soldiers in battle.

In seeking to explain Septimius Severus' behaviour, we need not take seriously the suggestion of Domaszewski (quoted above, p. 256). Personal fear of battle is a most improbable reason. Septimius Severus took the field not only at Lugdunum, but also in the Second Parthian War and again in Britain; moreover, as we have seen, he led his troops personally in the march on Rome. We must surely assume that, in weighing up the risks in a very insecure situation, he decided that the lesser risk lay in allowing others to command the armies in battle against Niger. It is possible to divine why he should have reached such a conclusion. Had he commanded personally, one serious defeat would almost certainly have meant the end of his hopes of empire; by staying at Perinthus he gave himself the chance to recover from a defeat. He was between his enemies and the vital Pannonian area, as well as between them and Rome. He had a substantial army encamped round Byzantium and there would be more troops which he could call on in emergency along the Danube and Rhine. Furthermore, he was also in control of the sea in the Bosporus area.[51] He could thus hope not only to continue to oppose Niger, if his own forces were defeated, but also to have time and power in reserve if one of his own generals should be encouraged to take advantage of his popularity with the soldiers and seek to be proclaimed emperor himself. In fact, the very presence of Septimius Severus in the strategically vital position of Perinthus would discourage such a move.

We have a clear indication that Septimius Severus was careful to insure against the possibility of defeat. He took trouble to get into his hands the children of Pescennius Niger and Asellius Aemilianus, so that he possessed a powerful bargaining counter if things went against him. And it is clear from the way the battles went that Septimius Severus was well-advised to prepare for the possibility of a defeat. In civil wars, where Roman soldiers fought Roman soldiers, neither side could count on victory, and at both Nicaea and Issus Niger came close to winning. The other danger, of a proclamation by one of his own generals, was not apparent, but it is interesting to observe how carefully Septimius Severus guarded against it.

Once Septimius Severus had determined not to command his army personally, he was faced by a most delicate and important decision in the choice of a general, or generals, to lead his forces into Asia. It would be normal practice in war to choose again a general who had proved himself successful, but Fabius Cilo was replaced as commander of the Illyrian forces,[52] and his successor, Tib. Claudius Candidus, seems to have been in chief command at the first major battle, near Cyzicus (November–December 193), as he certainly was in the second, at Nicaea (December 193–January 194).[53] At the latter battle he had to rally his men by personally forcing the standard-bearers to turn round and face the foe, and it is clear that his own bravery and qualities of leadership were of crucial importance in ensuring Niger's defeat. Yet if we look at Candidus' career down to this time, we seek in vain for evidence to suggest that here was a great general in the making.[54]

Claudius Candidus had served as a young equestrian officer in the later years of Marcus' reign and then passed to the civilian post of procurator of the five per cent tax on inheritances in Gaul. He was adlected to the senate by Commodus and given the rank of ex-praetor. As such he was qualified to command a legion or a province with a garrison of one legion, but we find him in fact occupied during Commodus' reign with purely civil posts of no special distinction in the eastern provinces.[55] Septimius Severus thus chose for a vital command an ex-knight, of merely praetorian rank, who had not held a military command for more than a decade; his choice was brilliantly justified by the event.

Candidus' victory at Nicaea settled the fate of Asia Minor. Pescennius Niger had to leave Byzantium to defend itself and fled south to rebuild his forces and try to protect Syria, the heart of his empire. The main Severan army did not follow closely because they needed to establish full control over the provinces of Asia Minor, by replacing Niger's provincial governors and hunting down his chief supporters in the area. Fabius Cilo was appointed to govern the province of Bithynia and Pontus.[56] Such a post, while the war was still unfinished, might seem a poor reward for his loyalty and earlier success, but the task of pacifying the province, especially while Byzantium remained uncaptured, and the necessity of ensuring safe communications, made it a position of power and responsibility. Even more surprising at first sight is Candidus' new post. Instead of continuing to command the main Severan forces against Niger he was ordered to pursue the supporters of Niger in the province of Asia.[57] Even though such 'mopping-up' activities were no doubt necessary and needed to be successfully carried through, such work cannot be compared in responsibility with the high command against Niger himself.

The man who replaced Candidus in that position was P. Cornelius Anullinus. He was of far higher rank, but also of much more advanced years, than any general Septimius Severus considered hitherto. He came from Iliberris in Spain and had had a long and fairly distinguished senatorial career in the emperor's service, including a legionary command (VII Gemina in Spain) and both praetorian and consular governorships. He was actually in office in the last of these, the proconsulship of Africa, when Septimius Severus seized the empire, and it is likely that he needed to be summoned from Africa in order to take command of the Severan army against Niger.[58] If he held his consulship at the normal age, he must have been born about AD 132, so he was over sixty in 194. As a consular and ex-proconsul of Africa, Anullinus was of high rank, and it may be that this shows that Septimius Severus was now less nervous of his lieutenants; on the other hand, Anullinus' advanced age would make him appear less dangerous as a potential rival. A curious feature of the new appointment is that Anullinus had apparently not had experience of command in war, in spite of his long career, except perhaps in Spain in 171–2.[59] Thus Septimius Severus replaced a general who had proved his ability (Candidus) with a fairly old and rather inexperienced substitute.

It was probably in May 194 that the Severan army under Anullinus' overall command met the Nigerians at Issus.[60] The army of Niger was superior in numbers and had the advantage of position, and we are told that the Severans owed their victory in part to a fortuitous storm of wind and rain which blew in the faces of Niger's men. However, Anullinus had also ordered a cavalry force under the leadership of L. Valerius Valerianus[61] to advance round the Nigerian position and fall on the enemy from the rear. In the event the defeat was utterly decisive : 20,000 of the Nigerians are said to have fallen, and Niger himself was shortly afterwards taken and killed. Once again, therefore, Septimius Severus' choice of general was fully justified by the result.

It is a possible hypothesis that Valerius Valerianus had a large part in the planning of the tactics at Issus. Although we may be sure that he was definitely subordinate to Anullinus, Dio states (lxxv, 7, 1) that the commanders of the Severan forces at Issus were Anullinus and Valerianus. As a relatively junior cavalry officer, who had obviously proved himself in the march on Rome, Valerius Valerianus was the kind of man Septimius Severus liked to choose for responsible roles, and he would have been eminently suitable as an adviser of the more senior but newly-appointed Anullinus.

In military matters only the result counts, and if we are to judge by the result Septimius Severus' direction of the war against Pescennius Niger was a resounding success. Clearly, the matters about which we have no information, such as supply, transport, the provision of adequate troops and their training, were efficiently organised.[62] But it is manifest that his victory depended to a large extent on his well-judged choice of generals, and that choice was all the harder for him because it did not depend solely on questions of military skill. We have seen that he confined himself as a matter of principle to relatively junior and undistinguished men (Anullinus being an apparent rather than a real exception). He also made it a rule to change his generals regularly so that no one man acquired too much glory or too close a relationship with the soldiers. Yet, in spite of greatly adding to the problems of choice in this way, every leader he picked was successful.

Thus a close examination of his choice of generals and his conduct of the war is most revealing. It tells us, for example, what we
need to know about his arrangement with Clodius Albinus. If his
relationship with Clodius Albinus had been a true shared rule, the
most natural choice for his leader in the field would surely have
been his Caesar. There was plenty of time to summon him from
Britain before the main engagements, just as there was time to
summon Cornelius Anullinus from Africa. The absence of Clodius
Albinus from any part in the war shows as clearly as one could
wish that the relationship between Septimius Severus and Albinus
was not a genuine example of an Augustus and his Caesar, an
emperor and his chosen heir.

In general we perceive that Septimius Severus' direction of the
war was determined by considerations other than purely military
ones. His position as a usurping emperor amid many rivals or
potential rivals was extremely precarious. Throughout the war he
was working to defend and strengthen that position against actual
or possible dangers, and his apparently strange and risky treatment
of the high command ensured that the victory won was his alone.

The First Parthian War

For our purposes the interest of the First Parthian War[63] lies in the
emperor's motives and his conduct of the operations. At first sight
it might seem hard to understand that Septimius Severus should
embark on a foreign war when he must have known that the civil
wars were not over, especially as he took steps during the course
of the First Parthian War which quite inevitably produced (or
confirmed) an open breach with Clodius Albinus. It is not difficult
to show, however, that the First Parthian War contributed to
Septimius Severus' final aim : to establish himself firmly as sole
ruler of the Roman Empire and his family as a new dynasty. As
so often with Septimius Severus, we need to be aware of more than
one motive.

His primary motive was the perfectly genuine need to re-establish
the eastern frontier of the Roman empire. It is clear that since
Marcus' Parthian War the Romans had regarded their effective
control of Osrhoene and Mesopotamia as necessary for the security
of Syria and the other eastern provinces. This control was exercised
through client kings and Roman garrisons.[64] The opportunity of
the civil wars had allowed the peoples of this area to throw off

their allegiance to Rome, and the immediate purpose of the war was to re-impose Roman control over the region. Septimius Severus decided that direct rule was necessary, so he made new provinces of part of Osrhoene and of Mesopotamia.[65]

The campaigning necessary for these ends was punitive and demonstrative in nature. The enemies presented no great challenge to organised Roman armies, especially as the Parthians were not themselves involved. Nevertheless the war brought Septimius Severus great additional prestige. He now assumed victory titles for foreign conquests and could boast that he had increased the empire of the Roman people.[66] These were not insignificant matters for a usurping emperor whose earlier victories had been won over Roman armies. The war was also useful in the necessary process of taking over the army of Pescennius Niger and forging strong links of loyalty between these soldiers and their new emperor. It is a most attractive suggestion that it was at this time that Septimius Severus created the three new legions, I–III Parthicae, out of the easterners who had been recently recruited for the civil war. The name of the new legions shows their close connection with Septimius Severus' Parthian Wars, and we know that they were in existence before 196–7.[67] By the means of a foreign war the soldiers of Niger could be accustomed to campaign side by side with their former enemies and win a share of the glory of foreign conquests. Thus the first Parthian expedition was one of the means by which Septimius Severus firmly established his control of the Roman East and its armies.

There is clear confirmation that Septimius Severus was all the time preparing for his struggle with Clodius Albinus in the other measures which we know he took during the actual course of the First Parthian War. His extraordinary 'reverse adoption' into the house of the Antonine emperors, the decision to bring forward his elder son into the public eye as his heir, and the naming of Julia as *Mater Castrorum* were all designed to invest himself and his family with a more securely based imperial dignity, which would have the effect of making any competitor into a pretender or rebel.[68] The implications regarding Clodius Albinus were inescapable. There was no place for his old Caesar in Septimius Severus' view of the future.

Of these measures only Julia's new title is exactly dated (14 April 195), but there is quite unequivocal evidence to prove that the other actions also belong to 195.[69] The conclusion is clear:

Septimius Severus was confident that the First Parthian War would be short and successful, and he was quite ready for his breach with Clodius Albinus to be in the open before the end of 195.

So much for the emperor's motives in the First Parthian War. The overall direction of the war was in Septimius Severus' own hands, and he personally led his troops as far as Nisibis.[70] He then stayed there and sent his army in three separate divisions under three separate generals to attack his different enemies. The generals chosen were Claudius Candidus, Julius Laetus and T. Sextius Lateranus. Claudius Candidus is no surprise; having pacified Asia he had rejoined the main army and was, as before, the commander of the Illyrian troops.[71] This is the first record of Laetus since his action on the march to Rome, but we know that his military ability was outstanding. We cannot be sure that this was his first major command, but he was not, apparently, in overall charge of any of the battles in the war against Pescennius Niger.[72] Of T. Sextius Lateranus' earlier life we know nothing except that he came from an exceptionally ancient and noble Roman family.[73] He was a friend of Septimius Severus and enriched by him. Although he was not the only great aristocrat close to Septimius Severus,[74] it would not be surprising if his very splendid breeding tended to disqualify him from the very highest positions in the Severan army. It would be hazardous to assume that this was his only major command, for new evidence might well overthrow a conclusion based on lack of knowledge, but we may confidently accept that he took no part in the war against Clodius Albinus, for he was ordinary consul in 197.

We also know that Lateranus was not chosen to lead a division when Septimius Severus again divided his army into three in order to invade further territory (the name of which is unfortunately corrupt in our only authority).[75] The three generals chosen for this stage of the First Parthian War were Laetus, Anullinus and Probus. Nothing is known of the last. Anullinus, victor of Issus, is now once more entrusted with a leading position. Septimius Severus follows his principle of changing his commanders; only the brilliant Laetus is allowed to command a division of the army twice, and he, as we have seen, did not have to his credit a victory in the war against Niger. Since the consistently successful Candidus is replaced, we may confidently assume that Septimius Severus is still jealously guarding against the danger that one of his subordinates might acquire too powerful a position with the soldiers, or too splendid a military reputation.

The war against Clodius Albinus

The ancient evidence for the war against Clodius Albinus[76] is so inadequate that it is difficult to reconstruct even the main lines of the strategy.[77] Nevertheless it is a serious error to base one's interpretation on the obviously misleading stereotypes of Herodian. To Herodian, Clodius Albinus was vain and lazy, simple-minded and over-confident, but similar vices are also attributed by him to Pescennius Niger. In his simplified view of history any loser must have had such feeble qualities of character.[78] If we accept such a judgment of Clodius Albinus we are faced with an intolerable paradox : this dilatory and simple fellow brought Septimius Severus to within an ace of losing his whole empire. It is worth speculating how historians would estimate Clodius Albinus' conduct of the war if Septimius Severus had lost the battle of Lugdunum, as he nearly did. All the advantages, in military strength and other resources, in legitimacy and prestige, seem to lie with Severus, yet Albinus so equalised the struggle that it was decided by a single battle, of quite uncertain issue, on ground of Clodius Albinus' own choosing. We shall certainly not come near to the truth of the matter unless we give due weight to that achievement.

The first conclusion which follows from these considerations is that Albinus' troops must have been comparable in number to those available to Septimius Severus. Dio's figures (lxxvi, 6, 1) cannot therefore be simply brushed aside.[79] There is no reason at all to suggest that he was wrong to give the size of the Severan army at Lugdunum as 150,000; the figures would be available and he had no cause to exaggerate them. In that case Albinus' army, which he says was the same size, is most unlikely to have been significantly smaller. Dio may have wished to please Septimius Severus or the successors in the Severan dynasty by exaggerating the numbers of Albinus' soldiers (though his account of Septimius Severus is in fact far from flattering), but the course of the battle is not intelligible if the Severan side had a great numerical advantage. In this connection it is worth remembering that Dio also says (lxxv, 8, 1) that 20,000 of Niger's men were killed at Issus. That suggests that his figures for Lugdunum are of the right order of magnitude.

At the most the garrison in Britain cannot be put at more than 70,000 men.[80] In addition Albinus had the garrison of Spain[81] and the few troops in Gaul. If he was to offer a serious challenge to either Septimius Severus or Pescennius Niger his most pressing need was to add substantially to these forces. It is therefore obvious that his major activity in the years 193–5 must have been recruiting and training new troops.

The main reason why modern observers have tended to accept the ancient picture of the duped and dilatory Clodius Albinus is that he failed to march on Rome while Septimius Severus was in the East.[82] But that argument rests on a major misconception. For Albinus at that time Rome was at best irrelevant, at worst a trap. The winner of the struggle between Septimius Severus and Pescennius Niger would control the forces of the Rhine and Danube frontiers, the whole of the East and Africa. If Clodius Albinus had made Rome his headquarters he would have been vulnerable, first of all, to the strategy of Vespasian in 69; for he would have made himself responsible for feeding the capital city whose corn supplies were in the hands of the enemy. Secondly, if he had made Italy his headquarters, he would also have been vulnerable to the more rapid and aggressive strategy of Vespasian's allies, the commanders of the Danube legions. There was no hope of successfully sheltering in Italy behind the Alps, if your enemy controlled the great majority of the frontier provinces and their armies.

What Albinus needed to do was to win as large a share of the rich and powerful provinces, strong in military resources and military organisation, and this is the strategy he pursued. From his base in the wealthy and populous provinces of Gaul he strove to win control of the military provinces along the Rhine and upper Danube. We know that he met with some success in Germania Inferior,[83] and some check in his attempts on Germania Superior.[84] It also seems probable that he temporarily won control of Noricum.[85] His strategy was therefore to build up his own strength and weaken Septimius Severus by wresting from him strong military provinces. Italy could wait; a march on Rome would have been at best a distraction.

For Septimius Severus, also, it was not Italy so much as strength in the provinces which really mattered. So he did not leave the East until he had secured that part of the empire to his satisfaction. There is thus some probability in the suggestion that he would not wish to return to the West until Byzantium had fallen.[86] We may in principle accept the statement that he arranged for some forces to defend the Alpine passes,[87] for it would be worth his while to protect his position in Italy from a sudden surprise by a small force, but all our analogies suggest that the Alps were not defensible against great armies in the conditions of ancient warfare. Septimius

Severus was well aware that the decision would take place else-where, and he made no attempt to take his main army into Italy. Those forces were needed to repel Albinus' threat to the European frontier provinces, and we may regard Pannonia as the head-quarters of the Severan army for this war. That is where Septimius Severus kept his family.[88]

Of the generals who had proved their worth in his earlier wars we know that Fabius Cilo, Marius Maximus, Claudius Candidus and Julius Laetus were certainly with Septimius Severus at this time. Cilo commanded the detachments who accompanied Sep-timius Severus and Caracalla on their visit to Italy in 196.[89] It is probable that he was then made governor of Pannonia Superior (and hence protector of the emperor's family).[90] Candidus was in charge of the campaigning necessary to win back Noricum to the Severan side.[91] So far we might think that Septimius Severus was following the policy of his earlier civil war and entrusting the direct command of troops to his subordinates. But for the final campaign against Clodius Albinus he decided he must lead the army in person. Dio states the fact and underlines its significance (lxxvi, 6, 1): 'The contest between Severus and Albinus near Lugdunum went as follows. There were 150,000 soldiers on each side and both leaders were present at the battle, since it was a matter of life and death, although Severus had not been present at any previous fight.'

We saw that Septimius Severus kept aloof from the battlefield in the war against Pescennius Niger because it gave him a second chance if he suffered defeat. For that he was willing to risk the danger that one of his own generals might be proclaimed emperor by the soldiers after a victory. From both these points of view the situation now was quite different. It is clear from the size of the armies that victory at Lugdunum would settle the fate of the western empire, including Italy. There was no natural line of defence, like the Bosporus, from which Septimius Severus could safely await the outcome of the battle. Presumably he would have fled, if defeated, via Pannonia to the East, but his situation would have been desperate. He was even without the vital hostages he had carefully collected against Niger; Clodius Albinus had his family by his side.[92] The same factors which made it impossible for Sep-timius Severus to await a defeat made it likely that a victory gained in his absence would have been equally disastrous. For the am-bitious general who exploited the victory to have himself proclaimed emperor would be in the same strong position vis-à-vis Septimius

Severus as Clodius Albinus, if he were to win. We could postulate this on grounds of general probability even if we did not know the story about Laetus at the actual battle. So there was no other place for Septimius Severus to be than at the head of his army in personal command at the decisive battle.

After various minor engagements which we cannot recover in any detail,[93] the Severan forces entered Gaul through Germania Superior and advanced on Lugdunum from the north.[94] Although we have relatively full accounts of the battle (19 February 197)[95] in both Dio (lxxvi, 6) and Herodian (iii, 7, 2–7), they are not sufficiently full or clear to enable one to draw up a complete scheme of the engagement. Septimius Severus was himself with the Praetorian Guard, which he kept in reserve with the intention of going to the assistance of any part of his battle-line which required it. He also organised another reserve force, of cavalry, under the command of Laetus.

When battle was joined the Severan right defeated Albinus' left and pursued them to their camp, but Severus' own left was heavily defeated by the Albinians. The emperor led up the Guard in an attempt to restore the situation, only to come very near to losing his guards and his own life too. Our sources agree that he was dismounted and lost his imperial cloak, but we shall never know whether Dio or Herodian gives the true account of the exact details of those exciting moments. Dio says that the emperor lost his horse and, when he saw his men in flight, tore off his cloak, drew his sword and rushed among the fleeing men with the intention either of shaming them into turning round or of meeting death himself. Herodian states on the contrary that Septimius Severus fled from the stronger Albinian forces, was knocked off his horse, and threw away his purple cloak in order to escape detection. It is tempting to reject Dio's account as pro-Severan propaganda, but Herodian is a most unreliable authority and a lover of the sensational, and in another passage Dio expressly contradicts the emperor's own 'apologetic' account (lxxvi, 7, 3). The deciding factor in both accounts was the appearance of Laetus with his fresh troops, but, according to Dio, Septimius Severus had already successfully rallied his soldiers, whereas in Herodian it is Laetus' troops who save the emperor and turn the battle.

So Septimius Severus won a battle immensely costly in human life. Whether Dio or Herodian gives us the truth, it is beyond question that he came near to defeat, and his barbarous treatment of his rival's corpse presumably reflects the fury of one brought to the very edge of disaster.[96] Nor was the danger only from his nominal enemies. We are told that Laetus hoped to be proclaimed emperor himself and purposely kept his force out of the battle with the intention of intervening at the right moment for his purposes. According to Dio, he did not take part until he saw that the Severans were gaining the upper hand. Herodian and the *Historia Augusta* on the other hand say that Laetus only intervened when Septimius Severus was thought to have fallen.[97]

Thus, Septimius Severus had once again brought a war to a successful conclusion. His general direction and organisation of the war, as well as his overall strategy, must therefore have been sound. The final result of the deciding battle also strictly justifies his tactical dispositions, but the extremely narrow margin of victory is both a tribute to Albinus and a cause for criticism of Septimius Severus.

Conclusion

The results speak for themselves. Since he alone was finally responsible for the conduct of his wars, Septimius Severus cannot be denied great distinction as an organiser of victory. He was splendidly successful in planning general strategy and in choosing subordinates, especially as he did not choose them with purely military considerations in mind. Of all his civil war generals only Laetus turned out to be a bad choice, and Laetus was not a failure, but too successful. After Lugdunum, Laetus completed a great march to Mesopotamia and brilliantly saved Nisibis from the Parthians. He was so highly regarded by the soldiers that they said they would not go on campaign unless he led them. And so Septimius Severus had him killed, from jealousy and, no doubt, for reasons of revenge for what had nearly happened at Lugdunum.[98] All the other Severan generals whose careers we can follow justified the emperor's choice and were rewarded with wealth and high office.[99]

We have seen also that he was always looking beyond the immediate military situation so as to ensure that his victories in war won him his political ends. Subtle and far-sighted in his conceptions, in execution decisive and swift, he was well equipped to emerge the winner from a many-sided and deadly conflict. Yet one hesitates to rank him with the great captains; he was surely no Hannibal. Whatever exactly happened on the field of Lugdunum, he was less than totally successful, and his failure at the siege of Hatra (198 or 199)[100] provides support for the opinion that he was not one of the greatest commanders in the field. If he had immediately exploited the breach in the walls, as his soldiers wished, he could have taken the city. But other considerations led him to sound the retreat; he expected the Arabs to surrender and he wanted to capture the rich and famous religious centre unharmed. But he underestimated the courage and determination of the besieged and his soldiers would not forgive him, so he had to abandon the enterprise.[101] His behaviour was perhaps typical of the man, but it shows that he lacked the single-minded pursuit of victory which characterises an outstanding commander in battle.

These considerations suggest that while there is no justification for a low estimate of Septimius Severus' military achievements, unqualified praise is also inappropriate. Perhaps it would be not unfair to conclude that Septimius Severus was both more than, and less than, a great soldier.

17

Civil War and Society in Southern Etruria

G. D. B. JONES

One of the most important aspects to emerge from Meiggs' study of Ostia[1] was the highlighting of social changes affecting the polyglot population in the first centuries BC and AD. The period was clearly one of great social mobility; yet Ostia, of course, formed a special situation, one that was probably reflected to a large extent in Rome itself. There, in the second period of the later first century BC, the veterans of the legions can be seen as an effective, and sometimes organised, force operating in ways reminiscent of, say, Algerian veterans' associations in metropolitan France. If their influence was perhaps reactionary in political terms, their social effect can hardly have been the same because they carried in many cases both prestige, fortunes and the cachet of social acceptability that reached its height with the distinction accorded to centurions in the early Julio-Claudian period.

If the role of the veterans was a highly fluid one in Rome itself, this does not exclude their deliberate use in a socio-political role elsewhere, in areas where their impact might be considerably heightened by the smaller population in which they appeared. In contrast with Rome and its satellite port, Etruria had a reputation for backwardness fostered to a considerable extent by the continuation of massive feudal estates such as those of Pompey and Domitius Ahenobarbus in the Maremma. While such a generalisation is perhaps commonplace – witness the Etruscan backgrounds of both Agrippa and Maecenas – it loses nothing by a close analysis of the epigraphic material from southern Etruria at the time. Clearly, areas close to Rome were undergoing considerable changes in ownership. Parts of the territory of Veii and Capena, for instance, were proposed for land allotment under the terms of the

277

lex agraria brought forward by the tribune P. Servilius Rullus in 63 BC against considerable opposition from senatorial landowners in the area. Yet a glance at the epigraphically attested names from the territories of Veii, Capena and Falerii at the time shows that non-Etruscan names had hardly begun to make any impression on the mass of the indigenous population. The purpose of this chapter is to show how major social changes were brought into this conservative society by the introduction of veterans in the later first century BC, and to show how this process paved the way to the increasing Romanisation of Etruria. A map of Southern Etruria will be found on p. 288.

The Etruscan matrix

The principal theme of the social history of Etruria concerns the influences at work in diluting and dispersing the indigenous population. The capture of Veii in 396 BC provided Rome with its first permanent settlement in southern Etruria; the Ager Veientanus (along with the Ager Capenas) appears to have been re-distributed to the advantage of settlers who were natives of the region but had fled to Rome during the war. During the next two centuries the steady extension of Rome's influence was marked by the establishment of colonies at Sutrium, Nepet, Cosa and Vulci shown in fig. 1.[2] The early colonies along the Tyrrhenian coast, Ostia, Antium (338 BC) and Tarracina (329 BC), consisted of only three hundred families each receiving not more than seven *iugera* (about four acres) of land. Other *coloniae* may have been larger, like the foundations established after the Punic Wars (but few details are known about the colonies of inland Etruria).[3] The total amount of early Roman colonisation in Etruria, however, is unlikely to have affected the character of the population to a substantial degree.

In the aftermath of the Punic Wars the increase in *ager publicus*, through seizure from towns that had failed to support Rome against Carthage, combined with the unsettled conditions of the period to make large estates cultivated by tenant or slave labour a feature of central and southern Italy. Appian's summary of Roman second-century colonisation contains this important passage :

The rich, getting possession of the greater part of the undistributed lands and being emboldened by the lapse of time to believe that they would never be dispossessed, absorbing any adjacent strips and their poor neighbours' allotments, partly by purchase under persuasion and partly by force, came to cultivate vast tracts instead of single estates, using slaves as labourers and herdsmen in place of free men who might be called away from their work on military service.[4]

It is for such *latifundia* based on a slave economy that Cato's *De agri cultura* (*c.* 175–150 BC) was chiefly written. Appian and Cato were not especially concerned with Etruria and their remarks may have greater relevance to the situation south of Rome. Etruria, however, is specifically mentioned in a much-quoted passage from Plutarch's *Life* of Tiberius Gracchus explaining how he became impressed with the need for agrarian reform :

. . . as Tiberius was passing through Etruria on his way to Numantia he observed the dearth of inhabitants in the country and that those who tilled its soil or tended its flocks were imported barbarian slaves.[5]

In the first century BC Domitius Ahenobarbus and Pompey were able to assemble substantial armies from the freed slaves and tenants of theirestates in Etruria (see below, p. 281).

The growth of an essentially capitalist agricultural economy based on *latifundia* is well substantiated in the literary sources.[6] One should remember, however, that it was a phenomenon that would naturally have attracted literary attention and that there is another side to the picture. Side by side with *latifundia* there were undoubtedly in Etruria large numbers of small settlements that can be documented on the ground. Not only were there official *coloni* such as those from Cosa, but also many settlements that were allocations of property to the disbanded armies of Roman generals, particularly in the last century of the Republic. In addition to these one must take into account the small-holdings of the Etruscan peasantry implied by the prophecy of Vegoia discussed below (p. 280). One of the most valuable results of archaeological survey has been to emphasise the extent of the small-holdings, especially in the late Republican period. In the northern Ager Veientanus, the western Ager Faliscus and the southern Ager Capenas, for instance, there are extensive settlements of the late Republican period. The small farms which compose them are datable from the Campanian black-glaze pottery found on them and in the densest area north of Veii, for instance, examples occur every few hundred yards. This reversal of the picture derived from literary sources shows the danger of any generalisation that fails to take account of the profound regional diversities of Etruria.[7] Whereas large areas of the Maremma may have belonged to the *latifundia* which Tiberius Gracchus would have seen as he travelled

up the Via Aurelia, equally large parts of the interior of Etruria
were probably in the hands of small-holders or deeply entrenched
local families.

The survival of the so-called 'prophecy of Vegoia' preserved in
the *Corpus Agrimensorum Romanorum*[8] tells us a good deal by
implication about the agricultural and social situation in Etruria
in the early years of the first century BC.[9] Recent studies in the
Gracchan reforms had suggested that they left Etruria and Umbria
substantially untouched and that the upper classes therefore retained an undisturbed hold on their *latifundia* and even large areas
of *ager publicus*.[10] The Lex Thoria of 111 BC was an attempt to
consolidate the *status quo* and land allotments in the two subsequent
decades were limited to Gaul and Africa. The agrarian law which
the tribune M. Livius Drusus promulgated in the spring of 91 BC,
however, attacked landowners in Italy. The reaction was strongest
in Etruria and Umbria and, accepting Heurgon's dating to this
year, Vegoia's prophecy forms part of the counter-propaganda to
Drusus' proposed legislation.[11] Events at Rome reveal the group
interests affected. Seneca describes how the tribune was protected
in the city by Marsian supporters of his plans. The consul L.
Marcius Philippus called in the support of Etruscan and Umbrian
landowners ostensibly to complain against Drusus, but in fact to
kill him.[12] They were prompted by the fear that the *ager publicus*
of which they had taken effective control would be taken from
them immediately and that in many cases their private holdings
would suffer.[13] The consul was in fact blatantly appealing to the
interests of the Etruscan and Umbrian landlords.[14] They came to
Rome often with huge *familiae* of tenants and retainers, and the
implications of Vegoia's prophecy illuminate the position of the
lower classes in the Etruscan agricultural tradition[15] and the dualism
of Etruscan society. There was no middle class; the *domini* were
all probably *equites Romani* by this time, while the *servi, familiae*
or *vernae* (the *interpretatio Romana* of the state of the Etruscan
lautni or *etera*) corresponded to the position of *clientes*. There is,
however, one important feature of their position; they had their
own property rights. That is why, in Vegoia's prophecy, they
appear able '*possessionem promovere suam*'.

At the same time, however, military service seems to have been
a regular obligation of the lower classes. Dionysius states that, when
Rome and Veii were fighting in 479 BC, the Etruscans assembled
their πενέστας for the struggle.[16] Zonaras[17] says that two centuries

later the people of Volsinii, after their formal submission to Rome, carried on their campaigns with their οἰκέται. In the middle of the first century BC a passage in the *Bellum Civile* describes how Domitius Ahenobarbus filled ships for the attack on Marseilles from levies amongst his own slaves, freedmen and *coloni*.[18] This is later followed by another passage that attests his use of both *coloni* and his own shepherds.[19] Domitius' estates were in Etruria, since the ships were collected at Igilium and Cosa.[20] This, then, is the way in which a great Etruscan landowner went to war; the heroic picture of a warlord and his army of retainers seems anachronistic in the latter half of the first century BC and demonstrates the conservatism of the Etruscan social system. To a considerable extent this point is made by an analysis of the percentage of Etruscan names attested within a community. Naturally the incidence of a *nomen Etruscum* has to be used carefully. Adoption and manumission have to be allowed for. Even so, although nearly all the epigraphic evidence belongs to the imperial period, when survival of local names would be waning, the percentage of Etruscan *nomina* indicating the local strain represents one-fifth to a quarter of the total known population. With all appropriate *caveats*, in broad terms this nonetheless forms a substantial unit in the society of southern Etruria.[21]

Infusion and dilution

Against this background we can see that the imposition of large units of veterans in the countryside around Rome was a move likely to cause considerable friction. At first, common sense must have dictated that the indigenous should be shielded from abrasive contact with the implanted population so far as possible. Cicero's attack on the agrarian reforms proposed by the tribune P. Servilius Rullus in 63 BC shows that areas of Etruria were proposed for veteran settlement prior to the first triumvirate. That such relatively early veteran groups were settled is clear from the situation at Clusium at this time where *Clusini Novi* existed alongside *Clusini Veteres*.[22] At Arezzo there are hints of a more complicated situation a little later with the conjunction of *Arretini Veteres*, *Arretini Fidentiores* and *Arretino Iulienses*.[23] Such is the evidence for the way a potentially explosive situation might be de-fused, at least in the early years of the second half of the first century. Yet the disruptions of the civil wars, the temptations of re-enlistment, the impatience of the military mind with a change to the slow pace of farming life, all allied with the beguiling proximity of Rome to erode the strength and political value of the veteran implant. This is perhaps most clearly and specifically shown only a few miles from Rome at Veii, where in order to create a town, the *municipium Augustum Veiens*, Octavian was forced to conflate the native with the implanted population : *colonia Veios, prius quam oppugnaretur, ager eius militibus est adsignatus ex lege Iulia, postea deficientibus his ad urbanam civitatem associandos censuerat divus Augustus.*[24] Two relevant points emerge from this important passage. The first is not apparent from the text; it is certain that Octavian's general Agrippa attacked both Veii and the neighbouring town of Sutri for their partiality to the Antonine cause, as a prelude to the confused fighting against L. Antonius in late 41 BC.[25] This shows how a town, perhaps through simple hostility, perhaps through the contrariness that gives politics its abiding interest, espoused the opposite cause to that of the veterans whom Octavian had planted round it. The second point centres on the question of conflation with the intramural population. To balance the *intramurani* attested in the inscription that tells us the formal title of Veii,[26] another mentions *municipes extramurani.*[27] The latter were probably mainly veterans possessing land allotments in the *ager Veientanus* who were united in the main body of the *municipium* because their number had been seriously eroded by the disruptions of the civil war. Such an explanation becomes doubly attractive because it tallies with the probable course of events at the neighbouring town of Sutri, one stage further along the Via Cassia from Rome. An important inscription at Sutri gives the full title of the town as *colonia coniuncta Iulia Sutrina,*[28] suggesting a similar situation to that forced upon Veii by the decline in the number of veterans maintaining their land allotments.

With the rise of Octavian to undisputed power, the need for precautions against local sensibilities diminished in making arrangements for land distribution to veterans; at the same time, such settlements could be used to serve an increasingly overt political role. Veii and its satellite town of Capena serve as informative examples. Although the land reforms proposed in 63 BC were not passed, the idea must have remained in Caesar's mind because eighteen years later he allocated parts of the Ager Veientanus and the Ager Capenas to his veterans.[29] This is one of the principal reasons for thinking that the second town of the Ager Capenas, Lucus Feroniae, became a colony (*colonia Iulia felix Lucofero-*

nensis) at this time. The argument is a complex one that might be challenged in favour of an Augustan date.[30] Yet the debate is in a way pointless; any Caesarian arrangements would have been undone by the ensuing civil wars, leaving Augustus to give the colony its shape as discovered by excavation during the last few years. The *Augusteum* and the aqueduct known as the *Aqua Augusta* show that the major part of the building programme was delayed until the Augustan period. At that time a fragment of Frontinus[31] implies an infusion of Augustan veterans. Where they farmed is also clear. Lucus Feroniae lay at the southern edge of an upraised limestone shelf forming a notable plain on the western side of the Tiber that stood out in contrast to the short, steep and deeply eroded hills of the surrounding volcanic countryside. The *Liber Coloniarum* leaves no doubt that the rehabilitated veterans took the best share, the plain : *id est in planitia ubi miles portionem habuit.*[32] Moreover, a key inscription from the town shows that the colonies were being organised on para-military lines to form a focus of support for Augustus. Lucus Feroniae and Veii have produced almost identical evidence in this respect. The excavations at Lucus Feroniae have shed some light on the kind of men involved. On the western side of the forum a dedicatory inscription to the veteran C. Musanus was discovered in the original 1953 excavations :

C(aio) Musano C(ai) f(ilio) / primo pilo bis/ tr(ibuno) mil(itum), praefecto / stratopedarci, / II viro quiquen(nali) / ex d(ecreto) d(ecurionum) p(ublice).[33]

The inscription is fairly closely datable to the end of the first century BC by the absence of a *cognomen*, by the letter forms, but more particularly by its historical implications. The use of the title *praefectus stratopedarces* makes one think of the commander of a permanent *castra* in a Greek-speaking land, and Egypt is the obvious choice. In this case the reference is probably to the fortress of Alexandria built after 30 BC to hold the legions that Augustus maintained in Egypt.[34] The C. Musanus of the inscription was, therefore, a veteran of the civil wars who was settled at Lucus Feroniae and whose rank gave him an important position in the civil administration. It is hardly a coincidence that Musanus had a very close parallel at Veii in another distinguished veteran, *M. Tarquitius Saturninus pr. pil. leg. XXII trib. milit. leg. III leg. XXII.*[35] The legions in question are the III Cyrenaica and the XXII Deiotariana, which both served in Egypt at the time.

The two veterans were perhaps acquaintances, but whether this indicates a fragment of the dispersal and settlement of legions that had seen service in Egypt until at least 30 BC is beyond absolute proof. Almost certainly, however, the presence of distinguished *primipilares* holding key positions in local government at both Veii and Lucus Feroniae in the Augustan period suggests that at the time, in this politically sensitive area close to Rome, the veteran settlement programme projected the military hierarchy into civil administration. For the Augustan party the advantages were obvious and must have helped weather the crises of the twenties. The system seems to have been abandoned in later years in such places as Anzio and Tarentum in the Neronian settlements of AD 60.[36] At that stage so authoritarian a solution was probably unacceptable in Italy. Yet the system finds an echo in the provinces. Recent excavation at the site of the legionary fortress and colony at Gloucester, in Britain, showed that when the colony came into existence in the later Flavian period, the military buildings were retained for civilian use, and at the same time surely showed a degree of para-military organisation.[37] In effect, a century spans the application of an identical technique to the heartlands of the empire and its extension to the perimeter.

Yet the purpose, politico-military stability, remained the same. The problem in southern Etruria lay in the dissipation of the impact of the veterans on their local society. They drifted away. The process can be documented particularly well around Rome. Earlier in the century, land near Praeneste that had been broken up in grants to Sullan veterans was quickly reformed into large estates.[38] The proximity of the capital naturally accelerated a trend stemming from the disadvantages facing a soldier turned small-scale wine-producer or farmer. Tacitus explains the failure of the colony at Anzio in the late Julio-Claudian period as due to the preference of the veterans for the provinces in which they had served and a reluctance to take wives and rear children to ensure continuity.[39] Entries in the *Liber Coloniarum* suggest that these problems were not uncommon in the last half of the first century BC; settlements at Ostia and Superaequum failed and were broken up for re-sale.[40] The reference to the shortage of veterans at Veii, already discussed on p. 282, showed that the proximity of Rome rendered southern Etruria particularly susceptible to these trends. Many veterans must have drifted away to Rome or elsewhere at the very period when Augustus would have been anxious to continue encouraging support in Italy, particularly amongst those towns whose proximity to Rome made them politically sensitive. A partial solution appears to have emerged from the involvement of a growing number of *liberti* (freedmen) in the sensitive area of the Augustan sevirate. In part this was probably to some extent a subconscious move, fostered by the desire of *arrivistes* to penetrate or ingratiate themselves into accepted establishment circles; on the other hand, it can hardly have been encouraged without the agreement of the emperor, as the cult of the Augustales was so intimately connected with his personal and political reputation. As Chilver wrote, 'emperor worship in the west was mostly corporate expression of loyalty directed from above and, although the sevirate was not a religious institution as such, it can on these lines be envisaged as a typical part of the imperial cult and the propagandist policy of Augustus and his successors.'[41] In the Augusto-Tiberian period several colleges of Augustales are attested in Southern Etruria. Four are attested at Nepet prior to 12 BC and two at Falerii Novi soon after 2 BC.[42] An *Augusteum* of late Augustan or Tiberian date is known at Ferentium,[43] while an altar, statue and games known to have been established at Forum Clodium by AD 18[44] probably imply the establishment of Augustales, as does the dedication of a temple to the imperial family at Pagus Stellatinus in 4–3 BC.[45] Elsewhere in the Julio-Claudian period it was certainly used as an important propaganda vehicle, involving not *liberti* but local or tribal notables who served as Augustales in at least thirty-one of the towns of Cisalpine Gaul. The sevirate was thus geared to involving the representatives of the pre-existing local population. There still remained the question of combining this element with another ill-matched bedfellow, the *liberti*. The problem probably first developed around Rome, where rich *liberti* would arguably have emerged first as a separate financial and social force, potentially to be harnessed to the imperial propaganda machine. The fact that they were trying to put down roots in a society would have made them a more dependable force of support for Augustus as the veterans died off. Yet in a sense it is hard to imagine that they might have made an effective breach in the society of Southern Etruria without he prior inroads already made by the deliberate importation of veterans. Lucus Feroniae, with its wealth of fresh epigraphic material, is again the most relevant source of information. The best known *libertus* of the area was the M. Silius Epaphroditus who built the small amphitheatre at Lucus Feroniae. Historically he is important because the inscriptions in which his name appears show a cross-section of the community at the time and the character of the *seviri Augustales* at Lucus Feroniae. He was known in the first place from the inscription preserved in the Farfa Manuscript that mentioned his construction of an amphitheatre.[46] This was strikingly confirmed during excavation in 1961 by the discovery of the dedicatory inscription of the amphitheatre :

M(anius) Silius Epaphroditus / amphitheatrum / a solo p(ecunia) s(ua) f(ecit) C(oloniae) Jul(iae) Felici / Lucoferon(i)ensium / idemque dedicavit.[47]

Epaphroditus' antecedents lie in the *gens Silia* which gave Rome consuls in AD 13, 20, 28 and 68. He is most likely to have been the *libertus* of P(ublius) Silius P(ubli) f(ilius), who was elected suffect consul in AD 3 and had as colleague L. Volusius L. f. Saturninus, whose uncle (suffect consul in 12 BC) is known to have been a patron of Lucus Feroniae. Epaphroditus, therefore, belongs to the early years of the first century AD and this date agrees well with the masonry style of his amphitheatre. His *floruit* is important because it serves to date a fragmentary inscription listing *seviri Augustales* that was also found in the 1961 excavations. The names of four *Augustales* are given below that of Epaphroditus in the published photograph of the fragmentary inscription :[48]

. . . Au]gus[tales . . ./ M.S]ilius Epap[hroditus . . ./ .] Consius [. . ./ .]L. Vallius [. . ./ . .]L. Cuspius[. . ./ . . .]T. Flavi[us . . . . . .

The names of Epaphroditus and T. Flavius present no problems; they were both *liberti* and the latter may well belong to the family of freedmen *Flavii* attested elsewhere in the Ager Capenas.[49] The middle three names, however, do not appear to be those of *liberti*; their rarity is striking and they almost certainly represent local Capenate or Faliscan nomenclature. *Cuspius*[50] has an Etruscan parallel from Tuder.[51] *Vallius*[52] is not found elsewhere in Etruria, though a *Vallianus* has been identified at nearby Sacrofano.[53] *Consius*[54] is almost as rare; there is an example from Clusium higher up the Tiber valley[55] and another instance from the Ager Capenas itself.

Again there is a close parallel from Veii belonging to the same approximate period. A list of the *centumviri*[56] in AD 26 illustrates the influx of new elements of freedman origin to positions of power amongst the established local families. Names like *C. Iulius Merula* and *Cn. Octavius Sabinus* occur alongside *L. Perpenna Priscus* and *P. Acuvius*, names that proclaim immediately their Etruscan origin and should be compared with those of other local families to be found in the list of *pontifices* from neighbouring Sutri.[57] This inscription, which is Augustan or Tiberian in date, lists forty-seven names at the time. Of these only seventeen share gentile names and of these only eleven can be members of the same branch of a family, such as the Matrinii whose family (apparently from Vicus Matrini to the north, judging from the family tomb)[58] contributed three members. Yet the fact that persons of obvious local origin comprise roughly a third of the total at this time shows the degree to which fresh blood had infiltrated into Sutri, even in the naturally conservative area of religion. The inscription does not contain names of probable freedman origin, but the earlier examples merely herald a notable influx of freedmen into the political life of southern Etruria in the first and second centuries AD. Their presence must have been an important factor in the social and economic life of the area, particularly when retired freedmen from the imperial household were involved. Six apiece are known from both Veii and Capena, and two apiece from Nepet and Caere.

Yet that is a different story. Concerned as we are with the impact of war on society, we can see that the breakdown of an isolated and conservative society really only gained momentum in the period of the civil wars that placed southern Etruria in a politically sensitive zone. Ultimately, persons of freedman origin came to form a startlingly high percentage of the population, as in Latium and Campania.[59] Yet the major breakthrough into Etruscan society was first effected by the veterans implanted in its midst with an increasingly overt socio-political role to play. In describing the evidence from one of the few areas close to the metropolis where the epigraphic evidence permits, I hope to have shown some of the realities underlying generalisations about Augustus' organisation of political support in Italy.

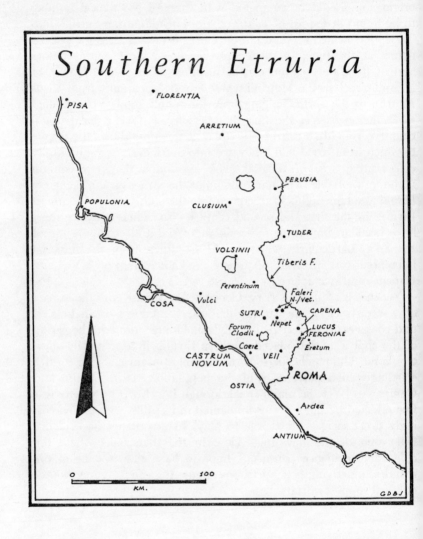

Southern Etruria

PISA

FLORENTIA

ARRETIUM

PERUSIA

POPULONIA

CLUSIUM

TUDER

VOLSINII

Tiberis F.

Ferentinum

Faleri
N./Vet.

COSA

Vulci

SUTRI

CAPENA

Nepet

LUCUS
FERONIAE

Forum
Clodii

Caere

Eretum

CASTRUM
NOVUM

VEII

ROMA

OSTIA

Ardea

ANTIUM

0   100
KM.

GDBJ

Notes

1. The British Government and the Coming of War with Germany, 1939

1. A. J. P. Taylor, *English History 1914–1945* (Oxford, 1965), 450–2, *Beaverbrook* (London, 1972), 395.
2. Public Record Office (PRO), PREMIER 1/331. Crown-copyright records in the PRO are quoted by permission of the Controller of HM Stationery Office.
3. E. L. Woodward and Rohan Butler (eds), *Documents on British Foreign Policy 1919–1939*, Third Series, vol. VII (hereafter DBFP, iii, VII); London, 1954, No. 689.
4. PRO Cab. 23/100 Cabinet 49(39)1.
5. DBFP, iii, VII, Nos. 664, 669.
6. Ibid., No. 696.
7. John Harvey (ed.), *The Diplomatic Diaries of Oliver Harvey 1937–1940* (hereafter 'Harvey's Diaries'), London, 1970, 313.
8. DBFP, iii, VII, Nos. 699, 706, 708.
9. Ibid., Nos. 700, 702.
10. Ibid., No. 708.
11. Ibid., No. 590.
12. Ibid., No. 604.
13. Ibid., Nos. 634, 646.
14. PRO Cab. 23/100 Cabinet 47(39)1.
15. PRO FO 371/22981, C12855/15/18.
16. DBFP, iii, VII, No. 649.
17. Ibid., No. 693.
18. Ibid., No. 654. Ministero degli Affari Esteri, *I Documenti Diplomatici Italiani* (DDI), Rome 1953, series VIII, vol. XIII, No. 571. R. J. Sontag and others (eds), *Documents on German Foreign Policy* (DGFP) 1918–1945, Series D, vol. VII (London and Washington, 1956), No. 539.
19. DBFP, iii, VII, No. 707, DGFP, D, VII, No. 541.
20. DBFP, iii, VII, Nos. 709, 710.
21. Harvey's Diaries, 313–4. Simon's Diary, 'The Last Day Before War' (hereafter 'Simon's "Last Day" '), ff.2–3. The author is

most grateful to the present Lord Simon for access to his father's papers.

22. DBFP, iii, VII, No. 716.
23. Cab. 23/100 Cabinet 48(39)1. Simon's 'Last Day', ff.5–6.
24. D. Dilks (ed.), *The Diaries of Sir Alexander Cadogan 1938–1945* (London, 1971), 212.
25. DBFP, iii, VII, Nos. 718, 727, 728, 739.
26. DDI, viii, XIII, No. 616.
27. DBFP, iii, VII, No. 730.
28. *Hansard*, 5th Series, vol. 351, cols 280–1.
29. Simon's 'Last Day', f.8. Copy diary of Sir Thomas Inskip (Lord Caldecote) deposited in Churchill College, Cambridge (INKP 2), f.38. I am most grateful to the present Lord Caldecote for permission to study this document.
30. Simon's 'Last Day', ff.9–11.
31. INKP 2, ff.37–8.
32. Simon's 'Last Day', ff.11–14. DBFP, iii, VII, No. 740. Copy diary of Euan Wallace deposited in Bodleian Library, Oxford, MS Eng. hist. c.495, ff.18–20.
33. DBFP, iii, VII, No. 741. It is not correct that Chamberlain and Halifax continued to try to defer the delivery of the British ultimatum until 12 noon on the 3rd. They had given that up at the afternoon Cabinet meeting on the 2nd. Cf. A. J. P. Taylor, *The Origins of the Second World War* (London, 1967), 277.
34. Compiled from Lord Birkenhead, *Halifax* (London, 1965), 447; Harvey's Diaries, 315; R. J. Minney, *Private Papers of Hore-Belisha* (London, 1960), 226. INKP 2 f.39. Wallace's diary adds Kingsley Wood to the meeting after dinner, but leaves out Brown and Burgin.
35. Simon's 'Last Day', f.16. R. Rhodes James (ed.), *Chips* (London, 1967), 213.
36. India Office Library, Eur. Mss. D609/11, 230.
37. Cab. 23/100 Cabinet 49(39).
38. *English History 1914–1945*, 452.
39. PRO FO 371/22987 f.175.

2. Great Britain and the Outbreak of War with Japan, 1941

1. W. S. Churchill, *The Second World War*, 6 vols (London, 1948–53), iii, 539. The principal sources used are the archives of the British Foreign Office and of the Cabinet Office at the Public

Record Office, London. Unpublished Crown-copyright material in the Public Record Office, London, is reproduced by permission of the Controller of HM Stationery Office.

2. The clearest examples being the negotiation of the Nazi–Soviet pact in August 1939 and the German attack on Russia in June 1941.

3. P. Calvocoressi and G. Wint, *Total Warfare: Causes and Courses of the Second World War* (London, 1972); nearly one half of the work is devoted to east Asia and the Pacific.

4. See J. MacGregor Burns, *Roosevelt: the Soldier of Freedom 1940–1945* (London, 1971), 66, 119–20, 133; and, for a discussion of isolationism, W. S. Cole, *America First* (Madison, Wis., 1953).

5. See T. A. Wilson, *The First Summit: Roosevelt and Churchill at Placentia Bay, 1941* (London, 1970). 163–7 and 241–7, and C. Hull, *The Memoirs of Cordell Hull*, 2 vols (New York, 1958), ii, 1017–18; for the text of the warning as given by Roosevelt to Admiral Nomura, the Japanese ambassador, see *Foreign Relations of the United States* (hereafter cited as *FRUS*) Japan, *1931–1941*, ii, 556–7. Note also D. Dilks (ed.), *The Diaries of Sir Alexander Cadogan, 1938–1945* (London, 1971), 397–402.

6. See H. Feis, *The Road to Pearl Harbor* (Princeton, NJ, 1950), 173; and note R. Wohlstetter, *Pearl Harbor: Warning and Decision* (Stanford, 1962), ch. 3, for a discussion of problems involved in the translation and utilisation of the 'Magic' code.

7. For a general discussion of the subject, see S. Woodburn Kirby, *The War Against Japan*, 5 vols (London, 1957–70), i, ch i and x; and the more succinct and frank account in S. Woodburn Kirby, *Singapore: the Chain of Disaster* (London, 1971).

8. See 'The Far East : material for a speech by the Secretary of State for Foreign Affairs', 19 July 1940, chiefs of staff committee, C. of S. (40) 557, Cab. 80/15.

9. See 'The situation in the Far East in the event of Japanese intervention against us', memorandum by chiefs of staff, 31 July 1940, C. of S. (40) 592, Cab. 66/10. I am grateful to Mr P. Haggie for originally drawing this reference to my attention.

10. See 'British administration in the Far East, report by the chancellor of the Duchy of Lancaster' (Duff Cooper), 29 October 1941, Cab. 66/20. Duff Cooper stressed the lack of thorough co-ordination among British authorities and, more seriously, between the British, American and Dutch authorities in the Far East.

11. See W. N. Medlicott, *The Economic Blockade*, 2 vols (London, 1953–9), ii, 106–20; and Feis, op. cit., 229.

12. Washington to Foreign Office, 25 July 1941, F6743/1299/23, FO 371/27972.

13. Foreign Office minutes on Commonwealth of Australia to Dominions Office, 25 July 1941, F7168/1299/23, FO 371/27973. The Australian government voiced concern at the possible repercussions of the freezing measures; the view of the Foreign Office was that the risks had to be faced in order to convince the United States of British loyalty.

14. Ministry of Economic Warfare to Washington, 7 September 1941, F9238/1299/23, FO 371/27980.

15. Washington to Foreign Office, 14 September 1941, F9322/1299/23, FO 371/27980.

16. Eden to Bland, 17 September 1941, F9501/1299/23, FO 371/27981.

17. Memorandum by Acheson, 22 September 1941, *FRUS* 1941, iv, 881–4.

18. Minute by Eden, 2 August 1941, F7072/1299/23, FO 371/27973.

19. Washington to Foreign Office, 3 August 1941, with minute by Sterndale Bennett, 3 August 1941, F7220/1299/23, FO 371/27974.

20. Minute by J. C. Sterndale Bennett, 8 August 1941, on 'Measures to counter further Japanese southward moves', report by joint planning staff, 3 August 1941, F8634/299/23, FO 371/27978.

21. Cited *FRUS* 1941, iv, 394. It is interesting to note that Ashley Clarke of the far eastern department of the Foreign Office minuted on 12 August that a public warning to Japan was not desirable, minute on Washington to Foreign Office, 10 August 1941, F7581/210/40, FO 371/28124.

22. Union of South Africa to Dominions Office, 29 August 1941, communicated to Foreign Office, 30 August 1941, F8621/86/23, FO 371/27910.

23. N. Ike (ed.), *Japan's Decision For War: Records of the 1941 Policy Conferences* (Stanford, 1967), 135–6.

24. For the most recent reassessment of the proposed Roosevelt–Konoye meeting, see R. J. C. Butow, 'Backdoor Diplomacy in the Pacific: the proposal for a Konoye–Roosevelt meeting, 1941', *The Journal of American History*, LIX, No. 1 (June 1972), 48–72. Butow's investigation largely vindicates the contemporary reservations of Hull concerning the meeting.

25. Washington to Foreign Office, 9 September 1941, with minutes, F9173/86/23, FO 371/27910.

26. Ibid., minute by Sterndale Bennett, 23 September 1941. Sterndale Bennett quoted an extract from a letter dated 9 September 1941, which he had received from M. E. Dening, a member of the

far eastern department temporarily attached to the Washington embassy: 'My feeling is that there is quite a dangerous tendency in the highest quarters to toy with the idea that something may come of the talks with Japan and that this tendency is violently opposed (though how successfully I do not know) by responsible people below.'

27. Tokyo to Foreign Office, 26 September 1941, F10070/86/23, FO 371/27910.
28. Washington to Foreign Office, 4 October 1941, F10329/86/23, FO 371/27910.
29. Ibid.
30. Minutes, ibid.
31. D. Dilks (ed.), *The Diaries of Sir Alexander Cadogan, 1938–1945* (London, 1971), 409.
32. Grew to Hull, 20 October 1941, *FRUS 1941*, iv, 541–3; and J. C. Grew, *Ten Years in Japan* (New York, 1944), 256–61.
33. Foreign Office to Washington, 18 October 1941, F10885/86/23, FO 371/27910.
34. Washington to Foreign Office, 18 October 1941, F10960/86/23, FO 371/27911.
35. Minute by Churchill, 19 October 1941, ibid.
36. Foreign Office to Washington, 21 October 1941, ibid.
37. Washington to Foreign Office, 22 October 1941, F11204/86/23, FO 371/27911.
38. Tokyo to Foreign Office, 1 November 1941, F11672/86/23, FO 371/27911.
39. Minute by L. H. Foulds (after discussion with A. Clarke), 3 November 1941, ibid.
40. Minute by A. Cadogan, 6 November 1941, ibid.
41. Foreign Office to Tokyo, 8 November and 16 November 1941, ibid.
42. Churchill, op. cit., iii, 528.
43. *FRUS Japan, 1931–1941*, ii, 755–6.
44. *FRUS 1941*, iv, 661–4.
45. Washington to Foreign Office, 18 November 1941, with minutes, F12475/86/23, FO 371/27912.
46. Foreign Office to Washington, 26 November 1941, F12757/86/23 and Tokyo, F12544/86/23, FO 371/27912.
47. See 'The Burma Road', report by chiefs of staff committee, 20 August 1941. C. of S. (41) 481, Cab. 80/29.
48. Churchill, op. cit., iii, 529.
49. *FRUS 1941*, iv, 665.
50. *FRUS Japan, 1931–1941*, ii, 768–70.
51. Washington to Foreign Office, 29 November 1941, F12992/86/23, FO 371/27913.

52. Ibid.
53. Ibid.
54. Ibid.
55. Minutes of chiefs of staff meeting, 29 November 1941, C. of S. (241) 402nd meeting Cab. 79/16.
56. Washington to Foreign Office, 30 November 1941, F13001/86/23, FO 371/27913.
57. Former Naval Person to President, 30 November 1941, F13053/86/23, FO 371/27913.
58. Ike, op. cit., 268–83.
59. Washington to Foreign Office, 1 December 1941, F13114/86/23, FO 371/27913. See also R. A. Esthus, 'President Roosevelt's commitment to Britain to intervene in a Pacific War', *Mississippi Valley Historical Review*, xl (1963–4), 28–38.
60. R. Butler, D. Dakin and M. E. Lambert, *Documents on British Foreign Policy 1919–1939*, ii, IX, 282–3, note.
61. Foreign Office to Washington, 3 December 1941, F13114/86/23, FO 371/27913.
62. Minute by Churchill, 2 December 1941, ibid.
63. Washington to Foreign Office, 4 December 1941, F13219/86/23, FO 371/27914.
64. Washington to Foreign Office, 5 December 1941, F13280/86/23, FO 371/27914.
65. For the text of the appeal, see *FRUS Japan, 1931–1941*, ii, 784–6.
66. Woodburn Kirby, *The War Against Japan*, i, 174–5, 180–2.
67. J. B. Crowley (ed.), *Modern East Asia: Essays in Interpretation* (New York, 1970), 263.
68. Minutes by Eden and Churchill, F9615/1299/23, FO 371/27981.
69. Earl of Avon, *The Eden Memoirs: The Reckoning* (London, 1965), 292–3. For an acute appraisal of the atmosphere and mentality in Malaya in 1941, see I. Simson, *Singapore: Too Little and Too Late* (London, 1970).
70. Dilks, op. cit., 553. When he met Hull at the Quebec conference in August 1943, Cadogan added that he was 'vaguer and wordier than Norman Davis, and rather pig-headed, but quite a nice old thing, I dare say.'
71. Eden to Bland, 17 September 1941, F9501/1299/23, FO 371/27981.
72. Ike, op. cit., xxvi.

3. British Historians and the Beginnings of the Civil
   History of the Second World War

1. See Stationery Office Sectional List 60 (latest edition, revised
   to 1 September 1971) : 'History of the First and Second World
   Wars'.
2. The sale of the published volumes was not regarded, of course,
   as a way of recovering the costs of writing them.
3. In general see *Official Histories: Essays and Bibliographies from
   around the World*, ed. Robin Higham (Manhattan, Kansas,
   Kansas State University Library, 1970), where the British
   histories are discussed on pp. 481–527 by Lt-Commander P. K.
   Kemp (Navy), Sir James Butler (Military History), Sir Arthur
   MacNalty (Medical History), and Sir Keith Hancock (Civil
   Histories).
4. See Jay Luvaas, 'The First British Official Historians' in
   Higham, op. cit., 488–505; Luvaas has some interesting references to the Liddell Hart Papers.
5. See M. M. Postan, D. Hay, J. D. Scott, *Design and Development of Weapons* (London, HMSO, 1964), 256–7, 310–11.
6. See Luvaas, op. cit.
7. *France and Belgium 1914*, ii (London, Macmillan, 1925), 1–19;
   France and Belgium 1915, i (1927), 37–58.
8. Cab. 103/59 in a minute from Col. Daniel to Longhurst for
   Bridges, dated 11 September 1939. Lt-Col. E. Y. Daniel was at
   this time Secretary of the Military History Section and Mr C.
   Longhurst was an Assistant Secretary in the Offices of the War
   Cabinet. It seems likely that Edmonds sent Daniel to get
   Hankey's views.
9. Cab. 103/59.
10. Ibid.
11. See Higham, op. cit., 483, 508–9. Lt-Col. J. S. Yule had been
    transferred from voluntary and part-time work with Edmonds
    to keeping the war diary at Cabinet Office in November 1940.
12. COH, 17th Meeting, 29 April 1940.
13. See above, note 11.
14. COH, 18th Meeting, 31 January 1941.
15. H. 68. These departments are often referred to as 'mushroom
    ministries'.
16. Ibid.
17. Ibid.
18. Ibid.
19. Ibid.
20. COH, 19th Meeting.
21. COH, 53 (a draft of this is in H. 68, parts II and III).

22. COH (U), 1st Meeting, 9 December 1941. COH at its 19th Meeting appointed the following members of the Advisory Committee : Dr E. A. Benians (chairman), Dr G. M. Trevelyan, Professor F. M. Powicke, Professor G. N. Clark, Professor R. H. Tawney, Mr Harold Butler, Mr John Maud, Professor E. H. Carr and Mr C. T. Flower (Deputy Keeper of the Records). Later Professor Lindsay Keir represented Northern Ireland on the Committee and Professor J. D. Mackie, Scotland. 'A lady historian', suggested at one point by Bridges, was not in the end appointed to the Committee.
23. H. 70/2 and H. 68, part III.
24. W. K. Hancock, *Country and Calling* (London, Faber, 1954), 196–7.
25. COH (U), 1st Meeting; for the medical side see MacNalty in Higham, op. cit., 515.
26. COH (U), 2.
27. H. 68, part IV.
28. Cf. *Country and Calling,* 198–9.
29. The War Cabinet considered a paper by the President of the Board of Education on the Civil Histories and approved the arrangements described above on 15 December 1941 : War Cabinet 128 (41). A press release on 18 December attracted attention.
30. Hancock in Higham, op. cit., 520. Some of them were on a part-time basis.
31. Ibid., 521.
32. *Country and Calling,* 204.
33. *Economic History Review,* XIV (1944), 185–90. It is perhaps worthwhile repeating that the printed volumes of the *Munitions History* are in several of the bigger British libraries.
34. *Country and Calling,* 205.
35. *The Times* of 19 December 1969 reported a decision of 1966 to extend official history 'to include selected periods or episodes of peacetime history'; the statement went on : 'suitable subjects had been considered in consultation with the standing group of Privy Councillors, one from each party.' As a result three histories had been commissioned : *Colonial Development 1945–64* (D. J. Morgan), *Environmental Land Use Planning* (J. B. Cullingworth and Gordon E. Cherry), *Nationalization . . . 1945–60* (D. N. Chester). Cf. Higham, op. cit., 527.
36. I have made a nuisance of myself in Cabinet Office in writing this paper, but without straining the charity of Mr C. J. Child and Miss Hilda Merrifield, whom I warmly thank for a great deal of help. I have also consulted and must thank Sir Keith Hancock, Sir James Butler, Sir George Clark and Professor

Margaret Gowing. In now giving these scholars their titles, I should apologise to them and others for treating them less ceremoniously in the body of this essay; nor are they in any way committed to any opinions in the foregoing pages.

4. The IRA and the Origins of SOE

1. G. C. Bolton, *The Passing of the Irish Act of Union* (1965).
2. Tom Corfe, *The Phoenix Park Murders* (1969).
3. Lionel Curtis, *Civitas Dei* (2nd edn, 1950), 487; conversation with Curtis, 1947.
4. *Pace* Correlli Barnett, *The Collapse of British Power* (1972), who argues that the qualitative impact of war casualties was spread evenly over all classes.
5. Even Dod's *Parliamentary Companion*, usually so informative, could say no more of him in 1919 than 'Collins, Michael. (*Cork co., South div.*) A Sinn Feiner who was returned unopposed for West Cork in Dec. 1918.' Collins of course never took his seat at Westminster, nor called himself MP.
6. The author is faced with a professional problem in discussing this correspondence, because he has only seen a few pages of it himself, shown to him by Colonel (as he then was) Hefferon on the afternoon of the lecture.
7. See RUSI, *Civil/Military Relations* (1972), 6–8.
8. Colonels Broy and Neligen were both present at the lecture.
9. According to Colonel Halley (then aged seventy-seven) at the Dublinm eeting, 9 January 1969.
10. Ibid.
11. According to Colonel Neligan, on the same occasion.
12. E.g. *The Observer*, 10 September, 25, and 17 September, 7; and *The Times*, 18 November, 1 e–h and 2 c; all 1972.
13. See Franz Fanon, *The Wretched of the Earth* (1967), 69, quoting Aimé Césaire, *Les Armes Miraculeuses*, 137.
14. See M. Skodvin in Adam Roberts (ed.), *The Strategy of Civilian Defence* (1967), 136sqq.
15. The family of the equally unfortunate W. Bence Jones, the earnest but irredeemably English landlord of Lisselan, Co. Cork, maintain that the system of social isolation used on Boycott would have been named after Bence Jones, to whom it was earlier applied, had his name been more manageable as a verb. And cp. Joyce Marlow, *Captain Boycott* (1973).

---

16. See A. T. Q. Stewart, *The Ulster Crisis* (1967), one of the best books on twentieth-century subversion.
17. The excellence of Frank Pakenham's *Peace by Ordeal* (1935, often reprinted) should not be obscured by its author's later notoriety as the instigator of the *Longford Report* (1972).
18. Compare Colonel Rol-Tanguy, who was prepared to seize Paris with only 600 in August 1944 : A. Dansette, *La Libération de Paris* (1966), 129.
19. The late Captain Henry Harrison drew my attention to this case, outlined in the *Dictionary of National Biography* under Beach, T. M. (the name the double agent died under) and set out in detail in H. Le Caron, *Twenty-five Years in the Secret Service* (1892), published after its author had testified before the Parnell commission of 1888–9.
20. Used, oddly enough, of the Mahdists in the upper Nile valley.
21. V. I. Lenin, *Collected Works* (1961), xvii, 342.
22. See Dr Judith Brown's essay, ch. 6 of this book.
23. M. R. D. Foot, *SOE in France* (1968), 2–4.
24. Joan Bright Astley, *The Inner Circle* (1971), 52 (snapshots of Holland and of Gubbins after 72).
25. Ibid., 32–53; cf. Foot, op. cit., 18.

5. The Success of Social Reform? The Central Control Board (Liquor Traffic) 1915–21

1. G. Kitson Clark, *The Making of Victorian England* (1965 edn), 127.
2. B. Harrison, *Drink and the Victorians. The Temperance Question in England 1815–1872* (1971).
3. On work in progress in this period, see Harrison, op. cit., 20; and A. E. Dingle, 'Drink and Working Class Living Standards in Britain, 1870–1914', *Economic History Review*, XXV (November 1972), 608.
4. F. H. Coller, *A State Trading Adventure* (1925), 138.
5. Henry Carter, *The Control of the Drink Trade* (1918), 90–4.
6. On the 1908 Bill, see N. Longmate, *The Water Drinkers* (1968), 249–56.
7. David Lloyd George, *War Memoirs* (1934), i, 325. Cf. Carter, op. cit., 46–8.
8. Carter, op. cit., 50. Lloyd George, op. cit., i, 326–8, describes the delegation and gives an extract from his reply to them, but does not repeat this wild exaggeration.

9. T. N. Carver, *Government Control of the Liquor Business in Great Britain and the United States* (1919), ch. ii. A. Shadwell, *Drink in 1914–22* (1923), 16.

10. Carver, op. cit., 44–5, 52, 56. Cf. also *Measures Taken in Foreign Countries for the Restriction of the Sale of Intoxicating Liquor* 1914–1916, Cd. 7695, LV.

11. *Brewers' Gazette and Wine and Spirit Trades Chronicle*, 18 March and 15 April 1915.

12. Carter, op. cit., 64–7. Lloyd George proposed doubling the tax on spirits, placing a surtax of from 12s. to 36s. a barrel on heavier gravity beers, and quadrupling the tax on wine. Despite the defeat of these proposals, taxes on alcoholic drinks were increased several times during the war. This had the effect of raising the average price of spirits from 4d. a glass in 1914 to 1s. 2d. by 1920. Beer prices rose from 3d. a pint in 1914 to between 7d. and 9d. a pint in 1920.

13. The Prime Minister, Asquith, was also extremely uneasy about the scheme.
    Lloyd George, op. cit., i, 330–2. Cameron Hazlehurst, *Politicians at War* (1971), i, 210–15.

14. T. Leif Jones, *Why Leave the Straight Road? A Warning to Temperance Reformers* (1915), 4.

15. Carver, op. cit., 44–6. Carter, op. cit., 72–3. M. B. Hammond, *British Labour Conditions and Legislation during the War* (1919), 83.
    Later investigations by Dr H. M. Vernon, on behalf of the Ministry of Munitions, showed fairly conclusively that persistently long hours and the loss of rest periods were the major causes of absenteeism and inefficient work. Indeed, as early as April 1915, the Admiralty had officially urged the discontinuance of Sunday work in shipbuilding and engineering. Ministry of Munitions, *The Health of the Munition Worker* (1917), 22–3, 29–35. *History of the Ministry of Munitions*, vol. 5, part 3 (1920), 95.

16. A. Marwick, *The Deluge. British Society and the First World War* (1967 edn), 58–65, 72–80. Hazlehurst, op. cit., i, 211–12.

17. Carver, op. cit., 69–75.

18. The Board's chairman was Edgar Vincent, Lord D'Abernon (1857–1941), formerly financial adviser to the Egyptian government and governor of the Imperial Ottoman Bank. In 1920 he resigned the chairmanship on being appointed British ambassador in Berlin.
    The other members were: Major Waldorf Astor, chairman of *The Observer* and Conservative MP for Plymouth; E. R. Cross, an associate of Lloyd George in the pre-war Land Cam-

paign; Colonel John Denny, head of a Dumbarton engineering
firm; John Hodge, Labour MP for Gorton and later (January
1917) Minister of Labour; Sir William Lever, the soap magnate; Philip Snowden, prominent ILP member, MP for Black-
burn and later Chancellor of the Exchequer in the first two
Labour governments; Neville Chamberlain, MP for Birmingham and Director of National Service (1917); Mr W. Towle,
manager of the Midland Railway Company's hotels; Sir George
Newman, principal medical officer to the Board of Education;
John Pedder CB from the Home Office; R. Russell Scott CSI
from the Admiralty. Chamberlain resigned early in 1916, and
Scott and Hodge in 1917, whilst Cross was drowned in August
1916. Three new members were appointed in 1916 : W. Waters
Butler of the Midlands brewing firm, the Reverend Henry
Carter of the Wesleyan Temperance Society, and R. S. Meikle-
john CB from the Treasury. In 1917, Mr S. O. Nevile, a
brewer, joined the Board. Newman and Snowden resigned in
1919 and were replaced by Dr H. H. Dale FRS and Will
Thorne, the Labour MP. Major Sir John Baird was appointed
chairman in place of Lord D'Abernon in 1921.
Mr J. C. G. Sykes CB was appointed Secretary to the Board.
See Carter, op. cit., 76.

19. Shadwell, op. cit., 33/5. Carter, op. cit., 130–4. J. A. Fairlie, *British War Administration* (1919), 139.
20. Carver, op. cit., 70–5. Carter, op. cit., 135–70.
21. Carter, op. cit., 197–225. Shadwell, op. cit., 36–43, 56–60.
22. Shadwell, op. cit. The other major study of liquor control in Britain during the war, Henry Carter's *The Control of the Drink Trade* (1918), traced developments only up to 1917. The author was himself a member of the Central Control Board.
23. '. . . in particular the afternoon gap (still with us) was imposed – a lasting memorial of the Great War.' A. J. P. Taylor, *English History 1914–1945* (1965), 37.
24. A. Marwick, op. cit., 65–71.
25. S. J. Hurwitz, *State Intervention in Great Britain* (1949). P. B. Johnson, *Land Fit For Heroes. The Planning of British Reconstruction 1916–19* (1968).
26. As well as drawing on the main printed sources, the author has also made use of some of the minutes, papers and correspondence of the Central Control Board, now deposited at the Public Record Office under Category HO 185. Time allowed only a fairly cursory survey of these records, which deserve more detailed investigation and analysis.
27. CCB, *1st Report*, October 1915, Cd. 8117, 6.
28. CCB, *2nd Report*, May 1916, Cd. 8243, 5–6.

29. CCB, *2nd Report*, 8–9; *3rd Report*, Appendix II, 22–5. See also Carter, op. cit., 168 and Women's Advisory Committee Papers, HO 185/238, 258.

30. *Select Committee on Disinterested Management*, 1927, Cd. 2862, X, 16. Rev. W. Stuart, *Drink Nationalization in England and Its Results* (1927), 29.

31. P. Abrams, 'The Failure of Social Reform 1918–1920', *Past and Present*, no. 24 (1963), 60.

32. Lord D'Abernon, Preface to *Alcohol. Its Action on the Human Organism* (1918), vii.

33. 'Much industrial drinking is done in the belief that work is helped by it.' W. C. Sullivan to Lord D'Abernon, 9 February 1916, HO 185/228.

34. CCB to Under-Secretary, Home Office, 17 October 1921, HO 185/228.

35. One Committee member, Dr W. C. Sullivan, Medical Superintendent of the Rampton Mental Institution, conducted a series of experiments on workers at the Vickers factory at Crayford to determine the effects of alcohol on activity at work. Correspondence with Lord D'Abernon, August 1915–May 1916, HO 185/228.

36. CCB, *Alcohol* (1918), 151–9.

37. *Royal Commission on Licensing 1931–2 XI. Report,* 13–14.

38. CCB, *Alcohol*, 158–9.

39. H. M. Vernon, *The Alcohol Problem* (1928), 82. Lord D'Abernon, Preface to Carter, op. cit., ix.

40. Carter, op. cit., 140. W. C. Sullivan, Report on Alcoholism in Glasgow, 7 October 1916, HO 185/228.

41. P. W. Wilson to Lord D'Abernon, 22 July 1915, HO 185/242.

42. The other members were Major Waldorf Astor, Sir William Lever and William Towle. *History of the Ministry of Munitions*, vol. 5, part 4 (1921), 2.

43. Carter, op. cit., 187. CCB, *3rd Report*, 10–11.

44. *History of the Ministry of Munitions*, vol. 5, part 4 (1921), 19.

45. CCB, *Feeding the Munition Worker* (1916), 7.

46. CCB, *3rd Report*, 12. W. C. Sullivan, Report on Alcoholism in Liverpool, 25 July 1916, HO 185/228.

47. *History of the Ministry of Munitions*, vol. 5, part 4, 11–15.

48. T. L. Heath (Treasury) to Lord D'Abernon, 17 May, 15 July 1918, PRO T. 112.
J. C. G. Sykes (CCB) to Treasury, 8 May 1918, HO 185/242.

49. Lord D'Abernon to Treasury, 11 June 1918, HO 185–242.

50. *History of the Ministry of Munitions*, vol. 5, part 4, 18–19.

51. CCB, Minutes, 19 February 1918, 18 March 1919, HO 185/229.

52. CCB, *3rd Report*, 12.
53. CCB Public House Committee Minutes, 11 September 1915, HO 185/213. Sir Thomas was Clerk to the Lanark County Council.
54. Ibid., 15 October 1915, HO 185/213.
55. Rev. G. Bramwell Evens, *The Truth About Direct Control in Carlisle* (1917), 4.
56. Carter, op. cit., 202–3.
57. Ibid., 200. CCB, *2nd Report*, 13, 21.
58. *Cumberland News*, 13 June 1916.
59. Public House Committee Minutes, 23 August, 11 and 20 September, 1915, 31 March, 4 and 17 April, 6 June 1916.
Treasury, Correspondence with CCB, 17 April and 11 July 1916, T. 112.
60. Carlisle and District Control Area. General Manager's Report to the Board 1918–19 (1920), Cd. 666, XX, 3.
Saunders, a former Clerk to the Liverpool Justices, was the Board's English assessor. He was appointed general manager of the Board's 'present and future undertakings' in June 1916 at a salary of £2,200 per annum.
61. *Select Committee on Disinterested Management*, 1927, Cd. 2862, X, 6–10.
62. 53 pubs were closed between July 1916 and December 1918. General Manager's Report 1917–18 (1919), Cd. 137, XXIV, 12–13.
CCB, *4th Report*, Appendix II.
63. Carter, op. cit., ch. 9. Shadwell, op. cit., 60–80. Arthur Sherwell, *Carlisle and Its Critics* (1923). Rev. Bramwell Evens, op. cit.
64. General Manager's Reports: 1917–18 (1919[137]), XXIV, 10; 1918–19 (1920), Cd. 666, XX, 8; 1919–20 (1921), Cd. 1252, XIV, 10. The total capital involved on 31 December 1918 was £835,000.
65. *Royal Commission on Licensing 1931–2, XI. Report*, 81.
66. A similar committee was set up in the Invergordon and Cromarty State purchase area.
CCB Carlisle Local Committee. Constitution and Correspondence, 17 June 1916, HO 185/8.
Public House Committee Minutes, 2 and 8 December 1915. HO 185/213.
67. CCB Carlisle Local Committee. Minutes 17 May, 18 July, 15 August, 19 September 1917, HO 185/9.
Treasury. Correspondence with CCB, 3 October 1916, 24 February 1917, T. 112.

68. Carlisle Local Committee. Correspondence. 20, 21, 22 February, 12 March 1918, HO 185/8.
69. General Manager's Report 1918–19, op. cit., 10. Sherwell, op. cit., 5.
    Cumberland News, 23 July 1921.
70. General Manager's Report 1918–19, op. cit., 10.
    Carlisle Local Committee Minutes, 15 August 1917, 15 October 1919, HO 185/9.
71. Rev. Wilson Stuart, *The Carlisle and Annan Experiment* (1917). Cf. Sherwell, op. cit.
72. Bramwell Evens, op. cit. Bramwell Evens was later to achieve fame as 'Romany' of the BBC Children's Hour.
73. Carlisle Local Committee Minutes, 17 September, 15 October, 17 December 1919, HO 185/9. Shadwell, op. cit., 123, 142. Carter, op. cit., 219.
74. Carlisle Local Committee Minutes, 17 December 1919, HO 185/9.
75. CCB, *4th Report*, 17.
76. Public House Committee Minutes, 4 July, 5 September 1916, HO 185/213.
77. Ibid., 9 January, 8 February 1917.
78. CCB Minutes, 16 December 1916, HO 185/229.
    Carter, op. cit., Appendix 6, 300–2.
79. CCB Minutes, 2 January 1917, HO 185/229.
80. See above, p. 72.
81. Lloyd George, op. cit., i, 337.
82. Ibid., i, 337–8. Fairlie, op. cit., 138–9.
83. *Advisory Committee on Proposals for the State Purchase of the Licensed Liquor Trade. Report* (1916), Cd. 8283, XII.
84. Lloyd George, op. cit., iii, 1333–4.
85. *State Purchase and Control of the Liquor Trade. Reports of the English, Scotch and Irish Committees* (1918), Cd. 9042, XI, 1.
86. J. H. Thomas, *When Labour Rules*, ch. ix. Hammond, op. cit., 313.
87. J. Rowntree and A. Sherwell, *State Purchase of the Liquor Trade* (1919).
88. Bonar Law told Thomas Jones in 1919 that he had been in favour of State purchase for twenty years. Jones remained sceptical.
    Thomas Jones, *Whitehall Diary* (ed. Keith Middlemas, 1969), i, 88.
89. Ibid., i, 205.
90. Treasury. Correspondence with CCB, 23 May and 12 June 1917, T. 112.
91. Treasury to CCB, 31 December 1918, T. 112.

92. Coller, op. cit., 261.
93. CCB Minutes, 12 November 1918, HO 185/229.
94. See above, p. 77.
95. Treasury. Miscellaneous Letters. Heath to D'Abernon, 17 May 1919, T. 147.
96. CCB Minutes, 6 May 1919, HO 185/229.
97. CCB Press Releases, 1919, HO 185/242.
98. *Hansard*, 5th Series, vol. cxli, 28 April 1921, cols 339–42; cxlii, 31 May 1921, cols 818–19, 840–1.
    Coller, op. cit., 262–3.
99. 11 & 12 Geo. V, c. 42. Shadwell, op. cit., 136–8.
100. Carlisle Local Advisory Committee. Minutes, 17 March 1920, 18 May 1921.
101. The Enfield district was wound up in 1923. Invergordon and Cromarty, Gretna and Carlisle survived until the Conservative government's decision to dispose of them in 1971.
    State Management Districts. Annual Report 1921–2 (1922), Sess. II, Cd. 20, II, 4.
    Hansard, 5th Series, vol. dcccix, January 1971, Written Answers cols 272–3.
102. *Commission of Inquiry on Industrial Unrest. North West Area* (1917), Cd. 8663, 25. Hammond, op. cit., 260–2.
103. Marwick, op. cit., 71.
104. Mass Observation, *The Pub and the People* (1943), 74–6, 78–9.
105. Ibid., 105–7, 208–9.

6.   War and the Colonial Relationship: Britain, India and the War of 1914–18

1. Announcement by E. S. Montagu, Secretary of State for India, 20 August 1917, *Hansard*, 5th Series, vol. xcvii, House of Commons, cols 1695–6.
2. Draft confidential circular to all UP Commissioners and District Officers, 12 February 1918, to be sent on behalf of the Lt-Governor of UP, Sir J. Meston, India Office Library (henceforth IOL), Meston Papers, Mss. EUR.F.136 (15).
3. Speech by Madan Mohan Malaviya in the Imperial Legislative Council, 23 March 1917, *Speeches and Writings of Pandit Madan Mohan Malaviya* (Madras, 1919), 129.
4. Viceroy to Secretary of State, telegram, 18 February 1924, IOL, Reading Papers, Mss. EUR.E.238 (18).

5. Hardinge to Sanderson, 25 July 1912, Cambridge University Library, Hardinge Mss. (92).
6. Chelmsford to Pentland, Governor of Madras, 24 July 1916, IOL, Chelmsford Papers, Mss. EUR.E.264 (17); Government of India's Despatch, No. 17, to the Secretary of State for India, 24 November 1916, National Archives of India (henceforth NAI), Home Pol., A, December 1916, No. 358.
7. Other detailed studies of the background to the 1917 Declaration are available, but none of them deals with the effects of war on Indian society which made it necessary. S. R. Mehrotra describes the build-up of pressure in Britain and India for such a declaration : see his *India and the Commonwealth 1885–1929* (London, 1965), 56–106, and 'The Politics behind the Montagu Declaration of 1917' in C. H. Philips (ed.), *Politics and Society in India* (London, 1963), 71–96. R. Danzig analyses how the Declaration came to be worded as it was by the British Cabinet, the conflicting opinions of which it was the eventual compromise, and the different conceptions of what it actually meant : see his 'The Announcement of August 20th, 1917', *The Journal of Asian Studies*, XXVIII (1968–9), 19–37.
8. These figures are given in the Prime Minister's famous 'Steel Frame' speech which caused such resentment among Indians. The full text is in a telegram from the Secretary of State to the Viceroy, 3 August 1922, Mss. EUR.E.238 (16).
9. *India's Contribution to the Great War* (Calcutta, 1923), 79.
10. Viceroy to Secretary of State, telegram, 5 February 1922; see also Viceroy to Secretary of State, telegram, 7 January 1922, Mss. EUR.E.238 (11).
11. Some studies of the *raj*'s reliance on local men of influence are available. See, for example, C. A. Bayly, 'Local Control in Indian Towns – the case of Allahabad 1880–1920', *Modern Asian Studies*, 5, 4 (1971), 289–311; chapters by T. R. Metcalf in R. E. Frykenberg (ed.), *Land Control and Social Structure in Indian History* (London, 1969), 123–62; F. C. R. Robinson, 'Consultation and Control : The United Provinces' government and its allies, 1860–1906', *Modern Asian Studies*, 5, 4 (1971), 313–36.
12. For the official analysis of India's part in the war see *India's Contribution to the Great War*. It was calculated that up to 31 December 1919, 1,440,437 Indians had been recruited as combatants and non-combatants, a total of 1,381,050 Britons and Indians had been sent overseas, together with 184,350 animals. By the end of 1919–20 India had contributed £1,462 million to the cost of the war, much of this being raised through war loans.
13. Lord Hardinge, *My Indian Years* (London, 1948), 102, 106–7.
14. Hardinge to Sir V. Chirol, 19 December 1914, Hardinge Mss. (93).

15. Hardinge to Crewe, 9 March 1915, Hardinge Mss. (121).
16. Montagu to Reading, 18 January 1922, Mss. EUR.E.238 (4).
17. *Land Revenue Administration Report of the Bombay Presidency, Including Sind, for the Year 1918–19*, 29. *Mamlatdar* was the name used in western India for subordinate Indian civil servant.
18. *Statistical Abstract for British India 1917–18 to 1926–27*, Cmd. 3291, Table No. 297, 628.
19. L. F. Rushbrook Williams, *India in the years 1917–1918* (Calcutta, 1919), 63; C. F. Andrews to Hardinge, 19 December 1914, Hardinge Mss. (63).
20. *Rast Goftar*, 23 June 1918, Report on Indian Papers Published in the Bombay Presidency. For the week ending 29 June 1918. No. 26 of 1918, 15 (IOL).
21. The attitude of Indian Muslims towards the Sultan of Turkey at this time is a moot point and difficult to document with precision. For a discussion of the question see J. M. Brown, *Gandhi's Rise to Power: Indian Politics 1915–1922* (Cambridge, 1972), 136–40.
22. Hardinge to Sir V. Chirol, 17 September 1914, Hardinge Mss. (93); Hardinge to Willingdon, 12 December 1914, Hardinge Mss. (88).
23. See, for example, the warnings of Sir V. Chirol to Hardinge, 24 January 1912, Hardinge Mss. (70).
24. Hardinge to Sir V. Chirol, 13 Mary 1915, Hardinge Mss. (94). British sensitivity to events in the Dardanelles was underlined by Curzon, who later wrote of the 'supreme & hideous disaster' of the evacuation of the Dardanelles, since it was necessarily a fatal undermining of the British position in India (secret paper for Cabinet, 25 November 1915, East Mediterranean folder, Asquith papers box 15).
25. Sir J. Meston to Chelmsford, 11 August 1916, Mss. EUR.F.136 (1). *Maulvi* is a Muslim religious leader, one learned in Muslim law and literature.
26. Hardinge to Crewe, 9 March 1915, Hardinge Mss. (121).
27. Hardinge, *My Indian Years*, 103; see also *India's Contribution to the Great War*.
28. Irwin placed Chelmsford's speech on 3 November 1919 as the starting point of the British pressure for States' reform, Irwin to Wedgwood Benn, 18 January 1930, IOL, Halifax Papers, Mss. EUR.C.152 (6).
    In 1921 the Nizam of Hyderabad complained of press attacks on him from British India and asked for the Viceroy's help. Reading replied with sympathy but said there was nothing he could do to help. Hyderabad to Reading, 7 July 1921, Reading to Hyderabad, 8 August 1921, Mss. EUR.E.238 (23).

29. Hardinge, *My Indian Years*, 116–17.
30. Report on internal political situation from Bombay, 30 September–2 October 1918, NAI, Home Pol., Deposit, October 1918, No. 32.
31. *Report on the Administration of the Bombay Presidency for the Year 1918–19* (Bombay, 1920), xiii; *Land Revenue Administration Report of the Bombay Presidency, Including Sind, for the Year 1920–21*, 36.
32. Ibid., 33–6; *Land Revenue Administration Report of the Bombay Presidency, Including Sind, for the Year 1918–19*, 29.
33. Hardinge to G. B. Allen, 8 June 1915, Hardinge Mss. (94).
34. For a survey of Indian trade during the war see L. F. Rushbrook Williams, *India in 1919* (Calcutta, 1920), 81–98.
35. R. Kumar, 'The Bombay Textile Strike, 1919', *The Indian Economic and Social History Review*, VIII, 1 (March 1971), 1–29.
36. *Report of the XXXII Session of the Indian National Congress. Held at Calcutta on 26th, 28th & 29th December, 1917* (Calcutta, 1918), 27.
37. K. McPherson, 'The Political Development of the Urdu- and Tamil-speaking Muslims of the Madras Presidency 1901 to 1937' (unpublished MA thesis, University of Western Australia, 1968), 92–7.
38. Sir S. Reed to Sir W. Vincent, 22 February 1919, NAI, Home Pol., B, June 1919, Nos. 38–47.
39. Letter dated 4 February 1919 to the Secretary to the Government of India's Finance Department, from businessmen including Jamsetjee Jeejeebhoy, Dinshaw Petit, J. B. Petit, D. J. Tata, Cowasji Jehangir and Purshotamdas Thakurdas, *The Bombay Chronicle*, 8 February 1919, Nehru Memorial Museum & Library, Delhi.
40. See Bayly, *Modern Asian Studies*, 5, 4 (1971), 289–311.
41. See Brown, *Gandhi's Rise to Power*, 113–18.
42. See Kumar, *The Indian Economic and Social History Review*, VIII, 1 (March 1971), 1–29.
43. P. J. Musgrave, 'Landlords and Lords of the Land : Estate Management and Social Control in Uttar Pradesh 1860–1920', *Modern Asian Studies*, 6, 3 (July 1972), 257–75; W. F. Crawley, 'Kisan Sabhas and Agrarian Revolt in the United Provinces 1920 to 1921', *Modern Asian Studies*, 5, 2 (April, 1971), 95–109; P. D. Reeves, 'The Politics of Order "Anti-Non-Co-operation" in the United Provinces, 1921', *The Journal of Asian Studies*, XXV, 2 (February 1966), 261–74.
44. Raja Kushal Singh to Sir J. Meston, 9 December 1916, Mss. EUR.F.136 (4).

45. Sir J. Meston to Sir V. Chirol, 10 September 1916, Mss. EUR.F.136 (4).

46. See enclosure by Nawab Fateh Ali Khan in his letter to Sir J. Meston, 26 December 1913, Mss. EUR.F.136 (6); undated note, some time between 1912 and 1914 probably by T. Morrison, sent by Sir J. Meston to Hardinge, Mss. EUR.F.136 (6). The author of the note commented on the position of the great Muslim aristocracy : 'In the formation of public opinion they are absolutely powerless, though at public meetings they are still occasionally brought from the lumber-room for decorative purposes or because they are believed to have access to Government.'

47. For a more detailed analysis of this see Brown, *Gandhi's Rise to Power*, 29–32, 157–8.

48. Hardinge to Sir W. Wedderburn, 19 December 1910, Hardinge Mss. (81); Hardinge to Curzon, 2 February 1911, Hardinge Mss. (92). Quite what the distinction was between 'Moderates' and 'Extremists' or whether they were two groups of politicians who could really be differentiated by such labels is a moot point : what matters here is the government's perception of the situation.

49. Hardinge to Sir V. Chirol, 27 May 1915, Hardinge Mss. (94); Willingdon to Hardinge, 13 May 1915, Hardinge Mss. (65); Hardinge to Willingdon, 19 May 1915, Hardinge Mss. (89).

50. Speech by Surendranath Bannerjee at 1916 Congress, quoted in M. R. Jayakar, *The Story of My Life. Volume 1. 1873–1922* (Bombay, 1958), 156.

51. Speech of V. S. S. Sastri in the Imperial Legislative Council, 23 March 1917, *The Indian Review*, April 1917, NAI, Sastri Papers, File of extracts from *The Indian Review*, 1915–1946, No. 10.

52. Speech of V. S. S. Sastri, *Report of the Thirty-first Indian National Congress held at Lucknow on the 26th, 28th, 29th and 30th December, 1916* (Allahabad, 1917), 70; Sir S. P. Sinha's Congress Presidential address, 27 December 1915, Appendix IV to Government of India's Despatch, No. 17, to the Secretary of State for India, 24 November 1916, Home Pol., A, December 1916, No. 358.

53. Sir J. Meston to Sir V. Chirol, 10 September 1916, Mss. EUR.F.136 (4); Sir J. Meston to Chelmsford, 7 July 1917; Sir B. Robertson, Chief Commissioner of CP, to Chelmsford, 15 July 1917, Mss. EUR.E.264 (19).

54. Fortnightly report from Madras, 18 December 1916, NAI, Home Pol., Deposit, January 1917, No. 44.
    For the foundation and spread of the Home Rule Leagues

founded by B. G. Tilak and Annie Besant, see H. F. Owen,
'Towards Nation-Wide Agitation and Organisation : The Home
Rule Leagues, 1915–18', in D. A. Low (ed.), *Soundings in
Modern South Asian History* (London, 1968), 159–95; and
Brown, *Gandhi's Rise to Power*, 26–8.
55. Hardinge to G. B. Allen, 19 August 1915, Hardinge Mss. (94).
56. Hardinge to Crewe, 9 October 1915, ibid.
57. For example, Willingdon to Chelmsford, 8 July 1916, Chelmsford to Willingdon, 15 July 1916, Mss. EUR.E.264 (17).
58. Chamberlain to Chelmsford, 27 November 1916, Mss. EUR.E.
264 (2).
59. Government of India's Despatch, No. 17, to the Secretary of
State for India, 24 November 1916, Home Pol., A, December
1916, No. 358; Chelmsford to Chamberlain, 3 January 1917,
Mss. EUR.E.264 (3).
60. Sir J. Meston to Chelmsford, 11 January 1917, Mss. EUR.E.264
(18).

7. Southern Africa and the War of 1914–18

1. The literature on these and subsequent aspects of South Africa's
history is voluminous. For a general discussion see the relevant
sections of E. A. Walker, *A History of Southern Africa* (3rd edn,
1963). Among the many published biographies of participants
in the events, W. K. Hancock, *Smuts, 1. The Sanguine Years,
1870–1919* (1962); *2. The Fields of Force, 1919–1950* (1968);
Oswald Pirow, *James Barry Munik Hertzog* (1957); and
Johannes Meintjes, *General Louis Botha, a Biography* (1970)
are only three of the more recent and illuminating. On
Afrikaner nationalism see also : John Fisher, *The Afrikaners*
(1969) and René de Villiers, 'Afrikaner Nationalism' in Monica
Wilson and Leonard Thompson (eds), *Oxford History of South
Africa*, ii (1971). As these and most of the other works listed in
these notes include references to other published works and to
documentary sources, more detailed bibilographical information
is not given here.
2. Quoted in Fisher, op. cit., 230.
3. Quoted in Hancock, op. cit., i, 381.
4. T. R. H. Davenport, 'The South African Rebellion', *English
Historical Review*, LXXII, 73 (1963).
5. Walker, op. cit., 562.
6. As can be seen from the works cited in n. 2, accounts of the

rebellion vary considerably in detail. The full facts will never emerge; much essential material was never written down and has been lost as the rebels have died. Davenport, op. cit., gives and excellent analysis of the extant source material and its shortcomings drawing from it those conclusions which seem justified.

7. Cf. Fisher, Pirow, Hancock, de Villiers, op. cit.

8. See, for example, Peter Walshe, *The Rise of African Nationalism in South Africa: The African National Congress, 1912–1952* (1972).

9. On the colour bar its development and economic implications, see S. T. van der Horst, *Native Labour in South Africa* (1942), G. V. Doxey, *The Industrial Colour Bar in South Africa* (Cape Town, 1961) and Francis Wilson, *Labour in the South African Gold Mines, 1911–1969*, especially 110–19.

10. Some of the many works on the growth of the iron and steel industry and of South Africa's economy generally are : Monica Cole, *South Africa* (2nd edn, 1961); C. S. Richards, *The Iron and Steel Industry in South Africa* (Johannesburg, 1940); D. Hobart Houghton, 'Economic Development, 1865–1965' in Wilson and Thompson (eds), op. cit.; S. H. Frankel, *Capital Investment in Africa* (1938); and R. Horwitz, *The Political Economy of South Africa* (1967).

11. In this connection, it is interesting to read of the reaction on the part of a Boer commando going into exile to being offered 'fraternal sympathy' by 'natives' – Egyptians who said that their country too was oppressed by the British. Deneys Reitz, who later became a firm supporter of Smuts and Minister of Native Affairs, in recounting this incident goes on to say : '. . . our colour prejudices are so deep-rooted that we did not relish being claimed as fellow patriots in distress by natives; so the incident helped to open our eyes on a great problem.' Reitz, *Trekking On* (1933), 16–17.

12. Millenarianism grew up in many parts of the world and was prevalent throughout Africa. For a discussion of the importance of these cults in central Africa, see R. I. Rotberg, *The Rise of Nationalism in Central Africa; The Making of Malawi and Zambia, 1873–1964* (Cambridge, Massachusetts, 1966), 55–99, and John V. Taylor and Dorothea A. Lehmann, *Christians of the Copperbelt; The Growth of a Church in Northern Rhodesia* (1961). For a discussion of millenarian movements generally and in Melanesia particularly, see P. M. Worsley, *The Trumpet Shall Sound* (2nd edn, 1968).

13. Chilembwe's letter is quoted in full in George Shepperson and Thomas Price, *Independent African, John Chilembwe and the*

Origins, Setting and Significance of the Nyasaland Native Rising of 1915 (1958), 234. This work is the most complete study of Chilembwe, the rising, and its ramifications. Some more recently available material, which tends to confirm the views of Shepperson and Price, has been used in Rotberg, op. cit., 76–92, and in Rotberg's 'Chilembwe's Revolt Reconsidered' in Rotberg (ed.), *Rebellion in Black Africa* (1971). See also Shepperson's article 'The Place of John Chilembwe in Malawi Historiography' in Bridglal Pachai (ed.), *The Early History of Malawi* (1972.

14. See the relevant sections of the works cited in n. 2; also John H. Wellington, *South West Africa and its Human Issues* (1967) and W. R. Louis, *Great Britain and Germany's Lost Colonies, 1914–1919* (1967).

8. The Impact of the War of 1914–18 on the British Political System

1. R. H. Tawney, 'The abolition of economic controls, 1918–1921,' in *Economic History Review*, XIII (1943), 7.

2. See especially Roberta M. Warman, 'The erosion of Foreign Office influence in the making of foreign policy, 1916–1918' in *Historical Journal*, XV, 1 (1972).

3. Mr V. A. H. Wellesley, Steel-Maitland's subordinate at the Foreign Office, believed that 'the economic factor regulates the political atmosphere in all countries and dominates international relations.' But Eyre Crowe as permanent head resisted interference with the consular service in testifying before Lord Cave's committee, and commercial opinion led by *The Economist* was opposed to the promotion of trade by the State.

4. Barry McGill, 'Asquith's predicament, 1914–1918' (in *Journal of Modern History*, 39, 3, 1967), gives the numbers of serving MPs as:

	Unionists	Liberals	Labour
January 1915	139	41	1
„ 1916	125	32	

5. Steel-Maitland papers, Scottish Record Office GD 193/306/1. Undated memo of February 1915. The author gratefully acknowledges permission to quote from these papers, given by the Keeper of the Scottish Record Office. Quotations from the Royal Archives, Windsor, are made by gracious permission of Her Majesty the Queen. For other quotations grateful acknowledgement is due to Lord Selborne, the Bodleian Library, the

University Library Birmingham, the First Beaverbrook Foundation, and the Trustees of the British Museum.

6. McGill, op. cit.
7. *New Statesman*, Saturday 8 May 1915, 97.
8. Selborne papers, 80/285. Description of the personalities in Asquith's Cabinet, c. July 1916.
9. Selborne, writing to Sir Horace Plunkett, 3 November 1916, comments : 'The government, which persistently refused my advice to give a guarantee of the price of wheat during the war, and would never look ahead, is now thoroughly frightened. . . .' (Selborne papers, 83/81.) Poor New World harvests brought a sharp rise in wheat prices in the previous weeks, and Asquith responded by offering to implement the programme of Selborne's committee, which he still chaired after his resignation. In the last days of his ministry Asquith offered Milner the position of Food Controller.
10. Royal Archives, GV K 770/12, memo by Stamfordham of 25 May 1915 noting that at a meeting the previous day there had been 'much haggling and bargaining over various offices' and Asquith resolved to have 'no more such meetings.'
11. Selborne papers, 80/86. 'Note on National Organisation', 27 May 1915.
12. Selborne papers, 80/285, cited above.
13. RA GV K 869/1. Memo by Stamfordham dated 16 October 1915 recording a conversation with Asquith.
14. Steel-Maitland papers, GD 193/306/2. Unsigned typescript of 31 March 1916. This also asserted that, although a general election was 'to be deprecated', it 'must not be assumed that machinery cannot be devised for allowing our soldiers – at any rate those in France – to vote.'
15. Austen Chamberlain papers, AC 19/1/40. 'Memo dictated before a meeting of the Co-ordination Committee of the Cabinet and the Army Council on 15 April 1916 and circulated to Unionist colleagues.' This stated that the unattested married men, if compelled, could only yield 200,000 recruits, and that 'the greatest advantage at this date is to be reaped by a vigorous extension of the practice of diluting labour . . . and in a severer combing out of the badged and starred single men.'
16. Selborne papers, 80/157. Memo by Bonar Law (typescript), 13 April 1916.
17. RA GV K 951/5. Memo by Stamfordham, 17 April 1816 : 'Lord Esher came to see me : he believed that Lord K and Robertson may feel it incumbent upon them to resign. . . . I replied that . . . the question might arise as to what course taken by the Sovereign would be most in consonance with the

opinion of the majority of his people. We agreed that if compulsion is now averted it might only be putting off the evil day . . .'

18. BM Add. Ms 51075. Memo by Lord Robert Cecil following the withdrawal of Asquith's original Military Service Bill which proposed to compel youths and time-expired men.

19. Asquith papers, 28 f.181. Curzon–Asquith, 22 September 1915.

20. Ibid., f.185. Balfour–Asquith, 23 September 1915.

21. Selborne thought this 'almost the worst arrangement possible'. Selborne papers, 80/91. 20 November 1915.)

22. Selborne papers, 80/285. Description of personalities cited above.

23. See correspondence between Lloyd George and Robertson in Asquith papers, 30 ff.255 sqq.

24. The leading narrative is still Lord Beaverbrook's *Politicians and the War, 1914–1916* (1932).

25. At the War Committee of 30 November it was decided to enforce compulsory national service on men up to 60 and advance the military age to 55. Runciman, who was absent, refused to accept 'industrial conscription', but the next day Lloyd George countered this with a demand that Asquith should cease to chair the War Committee. Asquith, however, had already obtained Cabinet approval for a Committee on National Organisation which would effectively remove domestic policy from the purview of the War Committee. See, in addition to the standard authorities, the long memo by Lord Errington on the crisis in RA GV K 1048, a/2.

26. Although much discussion has turned on the motives of the so-called 'three C's' (Curzon, Chamberlain and Cecil) and on the failure of Bonar Law to communicate their views to Asquith adequately, there seems no good reason to doubt their protestations. Stamfordham noted as late as 5 December that they 'came to see me and were most friendly to the P.M. but held that the best solution of the difficulty was for them to resign.' RA GV K 1048 a/1.

27. Chamberlain papers, AC 15/3/6. 'Memo of a conversation between Mr Lloyd George and certain Unionist ex-minsters, December 7 1916' quoted in Beaverbrook, op. cit. (1960 edn), 520–7. That Austen Chamberlain was the real originator of the War Cabinet idea is corroborated in several sources and especially AC 15/3/7, Austen–Neville Chamberlain, 11 December 1916 : 'I told Curzon on Sat. 1st when I first heard of Lloyd George's terms and their rejection . . . I would serve under the proposed Committee if he (Curzon) were added to it . . . I added that I had long held the view that the War Committee

should be the Cabinet, and I would not sit in a *Cabinet* with *no* power under a War Committee with *all* the power. . . . I originally stood alone in this view when the old War Committee was formed.'

28.   For Milner's position see P. A. Lockwood, 'Milner's entry into the War Cabinet, December 1916' in *Historical Journal*, VII, 1 (1964).

29.   RA GV K 1048 a/2. Memo by Lord Errington cited above.

30.   Lloyd George papers, F 74/10/4. 'Proposed Statement' by Professor Adams on the work of the PM's Secretariat, 7 March 1918, 5–6.

31.   Lloyd George papers, F 74/11/2. Typescript by L. S. Amery on 'Future of the Cabinet System', 1.

32.   Ibid., 2.

33.   McGill, op. cit., quoting Geoffrey Howard-Asquith, 10 December 1916 : 'From what I heard Lloyd George would take any reasonable pretext to have a general election but we at the Whips' office are taking care not to give him this pretext.'

34.   The Lloyd George ministry had 60 salaried ministers in the Commons, 23 in the Lords, and 5 in neither House. *Hansard*, 1917, vol. 96, col. 1609.

35.   See e.g. an unsigned and undated paper on the 'Machinery of Parliament' c. July 1917 in Lloyd George papers, F 74/21/1.

36.   *Beatrice Webb's Diaries 1912–24* (ed. Margaret I. Cole, 1952), 82, entry under 22 February 1917. For the composition of the special committees set up under Asquith's and Lloyd George's Reconstruction Committees, see Cd. 9231 (1919), *Report on the Work of the Ministry of Reconstruction*, Appendix 1.

37.   *Beatrice Webb's Diaries*, loc cit.

38.   For the role of the British delegates at the Conference see Cab. 24/4, G. 190, 18.

39.   The committee's terms of reference were 'commercial and industrial policy after the war' in order to maintain industries 'essential to the future safety of the nation', to recover home and foreign trade and secure new markets, develop the resources of the Empire, and prevent its sources of supply from falling under foreign control. See reports in Cd. 8482, 9032–5.

40.   Norman Angell, *The Great Illusion* (1912).

41.   Cab. 27/15. Memo by Carson, 17 October 1917.

42.   J. O. Stubbs, 'Lord Milner and Patriotic Labour, 1914–18,' in *English Historical Review*, LXXXVII (1972).

43.   Steel-Maitland papers, GD 193/99/2/38 b. Milner to Steel-Maitland, 1 November 1916. For Milner's attempt to place Steel-Maitland (his former private secretary) in the War Cabinet Secretariat as an equal to Hankey on the civil side, see John F.

Naylor, 'The establishment of the Cabinet Secretariat', *Historical Journal*, XIV, 4 (1971), 792.

44. Steel-Maitland papers, GD 193/99/2/57. Clauses as amended, August 1917. The programme is summarised in J. O. Stubbs, op. cit., 742, where it is supposed that the proposals 'were merely part of a study programme for the reform-minded in the Unionist Party.' They were, however, clearly intended as a public programme, to be announced by the British Workers' League and approved by the Unionist leaders.
45. Steel-Maitland papers, GD 193/99/2/51. Note appended to letter of 16 November 1917.
46. E.g. *A Constitution for the Socialist Commonwealth* (1920), which advocates an additional Parliament for social affairs.

9. Conscription and Society in Europe before the War of 1914–18

1. H. Kohn, *The Idea of Nationalism* (1945), 244, 254, 257.
2. M. S. Packe, *The Life of John Stuart Mill* (1954), 437, 478, 483.
3. H. Gollwitzer, *Europe in the Age of Imperialism 1880–1914* (1969), 90.
4. General F. von Bernhardi, *Germany and the Next War* (1911), trans. A. H. Powles (25th impression, 1928), 9.
5. N. S. de Bohigas, 'Some Opinions on Exemption from Military Service in Nineteenth-Century Europe', in *Comparative Studies in Society and History*, X, 3 (April 1968), 281, 289.
6. I. S. Bloch, *Is War Now Impossible?* (abridged English edn, 1899), 36, 356.
7. Ibid., 347.
8. Ibid.
9. Cesare Pavese, *The Moon and the Bonfire* (1950), trans. L. Sinclair (1963), 82.
10. See Sir C. R. Markham, *The War between Peru and Chile, 1879–1882* (1882).
11. Franz von Papen, *Memoirs*, trans. B. Connell (1952), 10.
12. A. Vagts, *A History of Militarism, Civil and Military* (revised English edn, 1959), 428sqq., 454.
13. Bernhardi, op. cit., 244.
14. *Encyclopaedia Britannica*, 11th edn, see 'Conscription'.
15. Bernhardi, op. cit., 245–6.

16. K. Demeter, *The German Officer-Corps in Society and State 1650–1945*, trans. A. Malcolm (1965), 28–9.
17. Jerome K. Jerome, *Three Men on the Bummel* (1900), ch. XIV.
18. *Old Diplomacy. The Reminiscences of Lord Hardinge of Penshurst* (1948), 128.
19. Thorstein Veblen, *Imperial Germany and the Industrial Revolution* (1915; London edn 1939), 80–1.
20. Prince Bernhard von Bülow, *Imperial Germany* (revised edn 1916, trans. M. A. Lewenz), 147.
21. Ibid., 154.
22. W. Gorlitz, *The German General Staff*, trans. B. Battershaw (1953), 76.
23. S. Whitman, *German Memories* (1912), 156–7.
24. Papen, op. cit., 10.
25. Engels to Laura Lafargue, 3 February 1892, in *Frederick Engels Paul and Laura Lafargue: Correspondence*, vol. 3, 1891–5 (English edn, Moscow, n.d.), 159.
26. Circular of 25 May 1914, in Demeter, op. cit., 346–7.
27. Gollwitzer, op. cit., 92.
28. Demeter, op. cit., Appendix 23.
29. See Note 14.
30. Bernhardi, op. cit., 170–1.
31. Vagts, op. cit., 207; cf. 219.
32. Paul Lafargue to Engels, 21 May 1891, in *Engels–Lafargue Correspondence*, vol. 2, 1887–90 (1960), 68–9.
33. R. F. Foerster, *The Italian Emigration of Our Times* (1924), 490.
34. M. A. Mügge, *Heinrich von Treitschke* (1915), 60. England still retained a vestigial obligation to serve, by ballot, in the Militia. On the British recruiting system at the end of the nineteenth century, see R. Price, *An Imperial War and the British Working-Class* (1972), 178sqq.
35. A. G. Gardiner, *Pillars of Society* (?1915), 240 (article on Lord Milner).
36. See M. Roberts, 'Queen Christine and the General Crisis of the Seventeenth Century', in *Past and Present*, No. 22 (1962), 40, 55.
37. E. Wangermann, *From Joseph II to the Jacobin Trials* (1959), 69.
38. R. B. Cunninghame Graham, *José Antonio Páez* (1929), 194.
39. See I. Friedlaender, *The Jews of Russia and Poland* (1915).
40. Engels to Laura Lafargue, 25 February 1888; *Correspondence*, vol. 2, 97–8.
41. Engels to P. Lafargue, 7 March 1890; ibid., 367.
42. Vagts, op. cit., 399.

43. Tolstoy, 'Patriotism and Government' (1900), in *Social Evils and their Remedies* (anthology, ed. H. C. Matheson, 2nd edn, 1917), 155.
44. A. Maude, *The Life of Tolstoy* (1910; World's Classics, 1930), vol. 2, 349sqq.
45. Tolstoy, 'Carthago Delenda Est', in *Social Evils and their Remedies*, 224.
46. 'The Only Means', ibid., 58–9.
47. P. Lafargue to Engels, 6 December 1888; *Correspondence*, vol. 2, 171.
48. P. Lafargue to Engels, 23 March 1889; ibid., 208.
49. *Herr Eugen Dühring's Revolution in Science* (1878; English edn, trans. E. Burns, n.d.), 194. The passage expresses a belief that 'this militarism also carries in itself the seed of its own destruction', by 'making the people more and more able at a given moment to make its will prevail.'
50. Engels to P. Lafargue, 25 March 1889; *Correspondence*, vol. 2, 210.
51. Engels to P. Lafargue, late October 1887; ibid., 65–6.
52. F. Bernstein, *Evolutionary Socialism* (English edn, 1961), 169.
53. Such a doubt was expressed, after the outbreak of the Great War, by Jaurès' admirer Margaret Pease; see her *Jean Jaurès* (?1914), 119–21.
54. Engels to P. Lafargue, 5 December 1887; bid., 80.
55. *Daily Chronicle* interview; *Correspondence*, vol. 3, 399.
56. Tolstoy, 'Government', in *Social Evils and their Remedies*, 128–9.
57. Ibid.
58. S. H. Jeyes, 'Foreign Pauper Immigration', in A. White (ed.), *The Destitute Alien in Great Britain* (1892), 192.
59. J. W. Gregory, *Human Migration and the Future* (1928), 86.
60. Mügge, op. cit., 45.
61. Prince Lichnowsky, *Heading for the Abyss* (1927; English edn, 1928), 79.
62. 'Carthago Delenda Est', in op. cit., 125. Cf. 'Letter to a Non-Commissioned Officer' (1899), in *Essays and Letters*, trans. A. Maude (1903), 230–1.
63. *The Note-Books of Anton Tchekov*, trans. S. S. Koteliansky and L. Woolf (1921), 30.
64. Vagts, op. cit., 401.
65. Ibid., 350, 378.

10.   Religion and Nationality in the Mid-Victorian Army

1. *The Queen's Regulations and Orders for the Army*, 1889, II, 142.
2. *The Times*, 7 November 1850.
3. Lord John Russell, *Papal Aggression: Speech . . . in the House of Commons, February 7, 1851* (London, 1851), 42.
4. Lord Stanmore, *Sidney Herbert, Lord Herbert of Lea: a Memoir* (London, 1906), I, 133. I owe this reference to Professor J. B. Conacher.
5. See Appendix I.
6. Ibid.
7. John Devoy, *Recollections of an Irish Rebel . . .* (New York, 1929), 128. For the Fenian troubles of 1865–7 see Leon O'Broin, *Fenian Fever: an Anglo-American Dilemma* (London, 1971).
8. *Diana of the Crossways*, ch. 2.
9. Detailed figures were published in HC 171 (1872), XXXVII, 427; HC 315 (1872), XXXVII, 433; and HC 15 (1878–9), XLIII, 513.
10. E.g. in Sir William Robertson, *From Private to Field-Marshal* (London, 1921), 9.
11. Evelyn Waugh, *Men at Arms* (Penguin edn, 1964), 61.
12. See the *General Annual Return of the British Army*, passim.
13. 2nd Dragoons, Scots Fusilier Guards, 21st, 25th, 26th, 42nd, 71st, 72nd, 73rd, 74th, 75th, 78th, 79th, 90th, 91st, 92nd, 93rd and 99th Foot.
14. The 1st, 25th, 73rd, 75th and 99th Foot, all Lowland regiments.
15. The 2nd Dragoons (39.39 per cent Scots, 51.58 per cent English), the Scots Fusilier Guards (31.28 per cent Scots and 60.02 per cent English in the 1st battalion, 34.34 per cent Scots, 55.01 per cent English in the 2nd).
16. 21st Foot (24.14 per cent Scots, 44.83 per cent English, 31.03 per cent Irish in the 1st battalion, 37.91 per cent Scots, 39.97 per cent English, 22.12 per cent Irish in the 2nd battalion), 26th Foot (40.34 per cent Scots, 30.36 per cent English, 29.30 per cent Irish), 74th Foot (47.91 per cent Scots, 26.43 per cent English, 25.66 per cent Irish), 90th Foot (21.35 per cent Scots, 42.45 per cent English, 36.20 per cent Irish).
17. Their chief successes seem to have been in the 5th Dragoon Guards, the 10th Hussars, the 61st and 73rd Foot, but they also had support in the 2nd, 3rd, 20th, 32nd and 99th Foot according to the War Office records (WO 81/113).
18. 101st (Royal Bengal Fusiliers) 55.22 per cent Irish, 102nd (Royal Madras Fusiliers) 53.79 per cent, 103rd (Royal Bombay

Fusiliers) 58.42 per cent, 104th (Bengal Fusiliers), 46.98 per
cent, 108th (Madras Infantry) 56.21 per cent, 109th (Bombay
Infantry) 35.96 per cent.

19. 89th (Princess Victoria's) 41.65 per cent Irish, 94th Foot 64.73
     per cent, and 100th (Prince of Wales or Royal Canadian) 60.33
     per cent.

20. 18th Foot (Royal Irish) 78.36 per cent Irish in 1st battalion,
     84.66 per cent in 2nd, 27th (Inniskilling) 87.17 per cent, 86th
     (Royal County Down) 87.41 per cent, 87th (Royal Irish
     Fusiliers) 69.82 per cent, 88th (Connaught Rangers) 87.99 per
     cent.

21. 1st Dragoon Guards (Royal Irish) 12.84 per cent, 5th Lancers
     (Royal Irish) 22.11 per cent, 6th Dragoons (Inniskilling) 20.75
     per cent, 8th Hussars (Royal Irish) 17.72 per cent, 83rd Foot
     (County of Dublin) 33.72 per cent.

22. *The Religious Tract Society Reporter*, I (1857), 28.

23. Edwin Hodder, *The Life and Work of the Seventh Earl of
     Shaftesbury, K.G.* (3 vols, London, 1886), ii, 484; iii, 64–5.

24. Among the tributes of 1858 were James P. Grant, *The Christian
     Soldier: Memorials of Major-General Sir Henry Havelock;*
     William Owen, *The Good Soldier: a Memoir of Major-General
     Sir Henry Havelock*; F. S. Williams, *General Havelock and
     Christian Soldiership*; and W. H. Aylen, *The Soldier and the
     Saint: or Two Heroes in One: a Christian Lecture in Memory
     of the late General Havelock.*

25. For two interesting later examples of the genre, see Edwin
     Hodder, *Heroes of Britain in Peace and War* (2 vols, London,
     1878–80), and Henry Morris, *Heroes of Our Indian Empire* (2
     vols, Christian Literature Society for India, London, 1908).

26. Howard N. Cole, *The Story of Aldershot: a History and Guide
     to Town and Camp* (Aldershot, 1951).

27. O. S. Watkins, *Soldiers and Preachers Too* (London, 1906), 159.

28. *Aldershot: a Record of Mrs. Daniell's Work amongst Soldiers,
     and its Sequel*, by her Daughter (London, 1879), 44, 61, 83.

29. Watkins, op. cit., 163–7.

30. Ibid., ch. IX.

31. Robertson, op. cit., 155.

32. For details see the *General Annual Return of the British Army.*

33. 15.6 per cent of those classified as Church of England had
     secured the basic 3rd class certificate in 1878, 16.0 per cent of
     the Presbyterians, 15.3 per cent of the Other Protestants, 11.6
     per cent of the Roman Catholics.

34. Army Temperance Association, *Report* (1893–5), 21. A. C. T.
     White, *The Story of Army Education, 1643–1953* (London,
     1963), 38.

35.　O. S. Watkins, *With Kitchener's Army* (London, 1899), 9.
36.　E.g. the Lieutenant-Colonel of the 15th Lancashire Artillery Volunteers until 1874.
37.　The best life is F. P. Gibbon, *William A. Smith of the Boys' Brigade* (London and Glasgow, 1934).
38.　Austin A. Birch, *The Story of the Boys' Brigade* (London, 1959; 2nd edn 1965).

11.　In the Shadow of Impressment: Friends of a Naval Militia, 1844–74

1.　J. R. Western, *The English Militia in the Eighteenth Century: The Story of a Political Issue, 1660–1802* (London, 1965), 238–40, 264–71.
2.　J. K. Dunlop, *The Development of the British Army, 1899–1914* (London, 1938), 268–73.
3.　J. W. Fortescue, *A History of the British Army* (13 vols, London, 1899–1930), xi, 99–103; cf. ibid., xiii, 24, 525 for the author's opinion of Parliament's 'unutterable meanness' on the subject.
4.　Ibid., xiii, 525–30.
5.　For a trenchant summary see A. J. Marder, *British Naval Policy, 1880–1905* (London, 1940), ch. v.
6.　See C. J. Bartlett, *Great Britain and Sea Power, 1815–1853* (Oxford, 1963), especially 110, 154, 162, 230. It was assumed that the French would call up 40,000 seamen in a fortnight – a view supported by the realistic calculations of a commission of the National Legislative Assembly set up late in 1849 : *Enquête Parlementaire sur la situation et l'organisation des services de la marine militaire* (2 vols, Paris, 1851), i, 243sqq. This mine of information was well known to English publicists, including Cobden, who, however, in *The Three Panics* (1862), concentrated on a seductive comparison of standing navies without regard to relative mobilisation potentials, for him merely a matter of demand and supply – a naïve notion easily controverted by the Registrar-General of Seamen among others : see J. H. Brown's (anonymous) *Some Observations on manning the fleet* (1847), of which there is a copy in the Naval Historical Library at Earl's Court.
7.　A Temple Patterson, 'Captain Cowper Coles and Palmerston's "Folly"', *The Mariner's Mirror*, 51 (1965), 19–25; Bartlett, op. cit., 168–70, 183–95; Marder, op. cit., 71.

8. Bartlett, op. cit., especially 52, 139, 232–3, 273, 306–10.
9. See his evidence in the Manning Commission Report, P[arlia-mentary] P[apers] 1859, sess. 1 (2469), VI, 51–8; cf. C. S. Parker, *Life and Letters of Sir James Graham* (2 vols, London, 1907), i, 160 and ii, 361–2.
10. The statutes are 5 and 6 Wm. IV, c. 24 and 16, and 17 Vict., c. 69. On manning during the Crimean War see, besides the 1859 Commission, the cross-examinations by the House of Commons Select Committee on the Board of Admiralty, PP 1861 (438), V.
11. PP 1859, sess. 2 (45), XVII, 158. His (anonymous) *Impressment of seamen, and a few remarks on corporal punishment* (London, 1834) found favour with King William IV : see his *Letters and Papers*, ed. R. Vesey Hamilton (3 vols, London, Navy Record Soc., 1901–3), iii, 130–1.
12. PP 1859/1 (2469), VI. 147. Denman was also questioned at length by the Select Committee of 1861 [PP 1861 (438), VI, 512sqq.], still upholding his earlier opinions.
13. Prince Albert, apparently, first suggested the expatriation of militia units in 1854 : Spencer Walpole, *A History of England*, v (1886), 126n.
14. *Observations on the naval resources of France and England and plan for a reserve of trained seamen*, dated 17 October 1852, in PP (1859/2) XVII, 191–203. Cf. his *Plan for the more efficient manning the navy*, dated 1 May 1852 and containing many of the concrete proposals put forward by the Parker Committee (copy in Naval Historical Library). Between these dates Pennell abandoned the idea of a naval ballot in favour of a small 'Royal Naval Reserve' consisting of ex-servicemen.
15. 'Manning the Navy', PP 1859/2 (45), XVII, 132–3 : evidently a revision of some 'Memoranda on Naval Affairs' printed for private circulation in 1846; I have not yet traced a copy. J. H. Brown, with the incomparable knowledge gained as Registrar of Seamen since 1835, was equally clear that the execution of press warrants would again cause bloodshed, and he doubted the co-operation of magistrates and police, especially as it would be more necessary to arrest men ashore now that, with the construction of docks, less time was spent on board after tying up; in any case, most seamen had relatives with votes. PP 1859/1 (2469), VI, 213.
16. Ibid., 147. The Manning Commission favoured only a voluntary and self-supporting pension fund for seamen, but admitted that none of the suggestions made to them had been 'so strongly and so ably advocated as the re-establishment of a compulsory merchant seamen's fund, free indeed from those objections

which caused the old fund [of 1747] to become insolvent [the Winding up Act of 1851], but still a compulsory fund' (ibid., xiii).

17. PP 1859/2 (45), XVII, 132.
18. PP 1861 (438), V, 390; *A militia our only naval reserve* (2nd edn, 1860), vi.
19. *A Letter to the Right Hon. XXXXXXX containing hints of a plan for a militia on a new and better footing* . . . (London, 1758; *A View of the Naval Force of Great Britain* (London 1791), 22–4.
20. PP 1859/2 (45), XVII, 137–8; Captain A. J. Griffiths, *Impressment fully considered with a view to its gradual abolition* (London, 1826), 11; cf. Bartlett, op. cit., 89.
21. Ibid., 241, 306; *The Times*, 17 November 1851; PP 1859/2 (45), XVII, 157–60.
22. Ibid., 137–8, 148–9.
23. Ibid., 138 and (for protections) 55; 43 Geo. III, c. 50, s. vii provided 'That no Seamen or Seafaring Man shall hereafter be enrolled in the Militia of Great Britain, either as a substitute or volunteer.'
24. PP 1859/2 (45), XVII, 35. In *The Nautical Magazine*, XXI (1852), 233–44, Sheringham objected to the ballot as a kind of impressment. On his career, see G. S. Ritchie, *The Admiralty Chart* (London, 1967), 161, 197, 247.
25. PP 1859/2 (45), XVII, 31–2. In 1844 Hall had laid before government a scheme for adapting merchant steamers to war purposes.
26. Ibid., 22–3.
27. For Hastings (but, regrettably, not Bowles) see *DNB*; cf. C. Lloyd, 'The Origins of H.M.S. *Excellent*' in *Mariner's Mirror*, 41 (1955), 193–7. Bowles had been promoted to captain in 1807 and his name can be followed in the Navy List until 1869. He began to publish in 1830, but his interest in manning dates from 1844, when he took to addressing his Board colleagues on paper, 'a more satisfactory way than discussing important subjects in desultory conversation' [PP 1861 (438), V, 386]. Many of his papers were collected in *Pamphlets on Naval Subjects* (London, 1854).
28. A copy was appended to his *A militia our only naval reserve* (London, 1856, 2nd edn 1860). The Hastings–Bowles memorandum is printed in PP 1859/2 (45), XVII, 127–8.
29. Ibid., 125–6.
30. *On the impressment of British seamen* (London, 1874), 30 and note.
31. Bartlett, op. cit., 222.

32. *A plan for the formation of a maritime militia and sea fencible force, in a letter to the Right Hon. the Earl of Derby* (London, 1852). Though the *Letter* is dated 6 December 1852, there was a second edition before the year was out.
33. PP 1852–3 (1628), LX, 28; 26 and 27 Vict., c. 5 repealed 16 and 17 Vict., c. 73, s. 5.
34. PP 1852–3 (1628), LX, 28–9.
35. PP 1859/1 (2469), VI, xi; Captain Griffiths (op. cit., 11–18, see note 20 above) had anticipated these objections as early as 1826.
36. PP 1861 (438), V, 400; *A militia our only naval reserve,* vi.
37. PP 1859/1 (2469), VI, 109–10.
38. Ibid., 147–58.
39. See R. Taylor's useful but undocumented articles on 'Manning the Royal Navy : the Reform of the Recruiting System, 1852–1862', *Mariner's Mirror* 44 (1958), 302–13, and 45 (1959), 46–58. Cf. Bartlett, op. cit., 305–9. The Admiralty Regulations of 1 October 1856 for the Coastguard Service and RNVC are printed in PP 1859/1 (2469), VI, 401–5.
40. Ibid., xiv-xix. The RNR was created under 22 and Vict., c. 40. The additional twelve school-ships were ruled out as too expensive and as likely to benefit private shipping more than the navy; nor was action taken to restore even a contributory pension scheme for the merchant marine. Cf. the critical report of the Admiralty/Board of Trade Committee on the working of the RNR regulations in PP 1870 (C. 46), XII.
41. PP 1859/1 (2469), VI, 152.
42. Wages, billeting, bounty and conduct money at £3,500 represented a cut of 50 per cent on the vote for 1872–3. At the outset £50,000 a year had been voted, but this fell to £20,000 in 1856–7 and to £10,000 in 1858–9, rising to nearly £40,000 in 1860–1, by which year a total of £205,280 had been spent (Bowles, *A militia our only naval reserve,* appendix to Preface, 9–10).
43. PP 1859/1 (2469), VI, 86–146. Recruitment figures, ibid., 32–3, and for 1863–6 in PP 1866 (506), XLVI (Admiralty return dated 8 August), are as follows :

1854	2692	1863	905
1855	517	1864	1209
1856	339	1865	1470
1857	1031	1866 (7 months)	691
1858	1675 (6 months)		

44. Cf. *Papers and Addresses by Lord Brassey* (2 vols, ed. S. Eardley-Wilmot, London, 1894), ii, 23–5.
45. PP 1859/1 (2469), VI, 143.

46. *Journal of the Royal United Service Institution*, XVII (1874), 26. On the recommendation of the captains of the district ships at Leith and Greenock, 2,000 Scots Volunteeers were retained after the English entry had been stopped, but there were linguistic difficulties : PP 1870 (C. 46), XII, 34–5.

47. *Papers and Addresses by Lord Brassey*, ii, 23–4, 77–9. Cf. Lord Frederick Kerr at the RUSI, 21 April 1873 : *Journal*, XVII (1874), 23.

48. 'On Manning the Navy', *The Nautical Magazine*, XXVII (1858), 548–9.

49. T. W. Fleming, *A marine militia the country's best national defence* (London, 1846), 12–16. He was frank enough to acknowledge that 'gentlemen could afford yachts of a much larger tonnage, and likewise have them more strongly manned'.

50. Brassey, ii, 153–62. Cf. *The Nautical Magazine*, XLII (1873), 215–6 : 'Yachting men . . . all gentlemen by birth and education.'

51. Clagette Blake, *Charles Elliot, R.N., 1801–1875* (London, 1960), 117–8.

12. The French Revolution and the Nationalisation of Honour

1. Notably by Mrs J. Macdonald in *Rousseau and the French Revolution 1762–91* (London, 1965).

2. On the circulation of *Du Contrat social*, see R. R. Palmer, *The Age of the Democratic Revolution* (Princeton, 1959), vol. I, 120.

3. *De l'Esprit des lois*, iv, 2.

4. Ibid., iii, 7.

5. Ibid.

6. Ibid.

7. Ibid., iv, 2.

8. Ibid., iv, 5.

9. Ibid., v, 2.

10. Ibid., v, 3.

11. Ibid., iv, 5.

12. Ibid., iii, 5.

13. *Du Contrat social*, ii, 6.

14. Ibid., i, 7.

15. *De l'Esprit des lois*, iv, 4.

16. See Michael Lewis, *Napoleon and his British Captives* (London, 1962), ch. II.

17. Yves Florenne, *Le Président de Brosses* (Paris, 1964), 282.
18. Robert Forster, *The House of Saulx-Tavanes* (Baltimore and London, 1971), 219–21.
19. The abbé Berthe, *Maximilien Robespierre, 'Les Droits et l'État des Bâtards'*, Lazare Carnot, *'Le Pouvoir de l'Habitude'* (Arras, 1971), 150–1.
20. *Respectueuses représentations des militaires de France au roi*, in vol. iv of *Recueil de Pièces intéressantes pour servir à l'Histoire de la Révolution de France*, a collection of several hundred of these pamphlets in the John Rylands Library (R 65600 and 80465).
21. Ibid. Remonstrance of the Parlement of Nancy, vol. i.
22. Ibid., vol. viii, *La Nation aux Militaires français*.
23. Archives Nationales, H. 38.
24. Archives Nationales, B^a 15.
25. Ibid.
26. *Moniteur*, 14–15 January 1791.
27. *Moniteur*, 19 August 1790.
28. *Oeuvres de Maximilien Robespierre* (ed. Bouloiseau, Lefebvre and Soboul), vi, 634.
29. Ibid., vii, 476.
30. Ibid., viii, 38.
31. *Moniteur*, 18–21 May 1790.
32. Robespierre, 5 February 1794, in *Oeuvres*, x, 357.
33. General Herlaut, *Le Colonel Bouchotte* (Paris, 1946), ii, 137.
34. Quoted in *Mémoires sur Carnot par son fils* (Paris, 1861), 466 note 1.
35. *Oeuvres*, x, 342.
36. Ibid., 180, 444.
37. Ibid., v, 245.
38. Ibid., v, 265.
39. Ibid., 293.
40. *Moniteur*, 29 Mary 1794.
41. *Moniteur*, 26 May 1793. This seems to have been almost universally disregarded, but it did result in the execution of the crew of a British merchantman captured in the Mediterranean. Archives Nationales, BB^4 42, ff.215–18.

13.   War Transport and 'Counter-revolution' in France in
      1793: the Case of the Winter Company and the
      Financier Jean-Jacques de Beaune

  1.   The only other study of this episode is a somewhat tendentious
       article by M. Arnaud de Lestapis, 'Gentilshommes Charretiers'
       in *La Revue des Deux Mondes* (September 1953, 151–66). The
       chief French MS sources used in the present article are the
       records of the Revolutionary Tribunal : W4, 169; 20; 173; 277;
       279 and 234; the Register of the Committee of General Security,
       October 1792–August 1793, AFII* 288; the T series of seques-
       trated papers; the BB³ series of the Ministry of Justice and the
       F⁷ series of police dossiers – all at the Archives Nationales in
       Paris.

  2.   F. Foiret, *Une Corporation Parisienne pendant la Révolution*
       (Les Notaires) (Paris, 1912), 133.

  3.   AN (Archives Nationales) F⁷ 4775.

  4.   *The Royal Criterion: or a narrative of the transactions, relative
       to the loans made in London by the Prince of Wales, Duke of
       York, Duke of Clarence and their advisers; negotiated upon the
       Continent* (London, 1814), 28.

  5.   William Lecky, *History of England in the Eighteenth Century*,
       v, 92 (London, 1887). The papers of the committee of enquiry
       into the Prince's debts are in the PRO (HO 73).

  6.   A. Britsch, *Lettres de L. P. J. d'Orléans duc de Chartres à
       Nathaniel Parker Forth* (1778–1785) (Paris, 1926), x–xiii.

  7.   PRO Gifts and Deposits. Documents of unknown ownership.
       Bundle 2 No. 4. The late Professor Beatrice Hyslop kindly drew
       my attention to this source.

  8.   In reality Orleans had been driven into temporary exile by
       Lafayette, who suspected him of complicity in a plot to oust
       Louis XVI from the throne in the October Days of 1789.

  9.   A printed notarial copy of the bond in English and in French
       is in AN W324.

 10.   Confidence in the new *assignats* was undermined almost imme-
       diately owing to mistakes in the first impression. J. Bouchary,
       Les Faux-Monnayeurs sous la Révolution Français (Paris, 1946),
       102.

 11.   This prospectus and the French translation of the notarial copy
       of de Beaune's bond was the work of an abbé called Desfrançais,
       who paid for this complicity in February 1794 by being sent to
       the guillotine along with Brichard and de Beaune.

 12.   Undated MS petition of the Winter Company to the Committee
       of Public Safety, AN W4(169). Internal evidence suggests that
       this petition was drawn up between 13 and 18 May 1793.

13. Ibid.
14. See C. Poisson, *Les Fournisseurs aux armées sous la Révolution français* (Paris, 1932).
15. G. Lefebvre, La Convention (Les Cours de Sorbonne), I, 159.
16. Poisson, op. cit., passim.
17. F. Bornard, *Cambon et la Révolution français* (Paris, 1905), 199–201.
18. De Beaune's testimony before the Contracts Commission, 19 July 1793, AN AFII* 19, f.149.
19. AN T521¹.
20. Each *conducteur en chef* undertook to recruit 25 men; each *conducteur en second* 15; and each subaltern 10. Between 13 February and 23 March these officers had engaged to raise 2,380 drivers. 'État des officiers qui ont signé des soumissions pour fournir des charretiers', AN W4(169).
21. Petition of Winter Company to the Convention (?18 May 1793). Ibid.
22. AN T521¹, 'État des employés au dépot d'équipages d'artillerie du citoyen Winter et Cie à Bercy.'
23. AN BB³71. Denunciation of Winter Company.
24. Ibid.
25. AN W4(169).
26. AN AFII*288.
27. F. A. Aulard, *Actes du comité de Salut Public*, IV, 123.
28. AN W4(169).
29. Ibid.
30. Interrogation 18 May 1793. AN W4(169).
31. Interrogation 14 May 1793. AN W(277) and F⁷4365.
32. Interrogation 14 May 1793. AN W4(169).
33. Interrogation 15 May 1793. AN W4(169).
34. Ibid.
35. AN W4(169); W277; W279.
36. AN W4(169).
37. AN AFII* 19, ff.143–50.
38. Aulard, op. cit., IV, 296.
39. Ibid.
40. Minutes of the War Contracts Commission, 18 July 1793. AN AFII* 19, ff.143/4.
41. *Moniteur* (réimpression), XVII, 214–33.
42. *Procès-verbal de la Convention Nationale*, XVII, 222–31.
43. *Procès-verbal de la Convention Nationale*, XXVIII, 317–22.
44. AN F⁷4775.
45. AN W324.
46. Ibid.

14. Rebellion and Revolution in Early Modern England

1. J. H. Elliott, 'Revolution and Continuity in early modern Europe', *Past and Present*, no. 42 (1969), 35–56.

2. Aristotle, *Politics* (trans. B. Jowett, Oxford, 1905), Bk v, ch. i. When this article was already in typescript I read, too late to take it into account, John Dunn, *Modern Revolutions* (Cambridge, 1972). This remarkable work is essential reading for anyone interested in rebellions and revolutions.

3. E. Hall, *Chronicle* (ed. H. Ellis, London, 1809), 694sqq. H. Ellis, *Original Letters* (Third Series, London, 1846), I, 359–81; II, 3–12. *Letters and Papers of Henry VIII* (ed. J. S. Brewer *et al.*, London, 1862–1910; hereafter *Letters and Papers*), IV, i, nos. 1200, 1235, 1241, 1243, 1260–7, 1272, 1292, 1295, 1299, 1305–6, 1311, 1318–21, 1323–5, 1329–32, 1343, 1345, 1567; IV, iii, App. nos. 34, 36; *Addenda*, I, i, no. 457.

4. *Letters and Papers*, IV, ii, nos. 4012, 4043–5, 4058, 4085, 4129, 4145, 4173, 4188–92, 4236, 4239, 4276, 4296, 4300–1, 4306, 4310, 4331, 4414.

5. M. E. James, 'Obedience and Dissent in Henrician England : the Lincolnshire Rebellion, 1536', *Past and Present*, no. 48 (1970), 3–78. The standard work on the Pilgrimage is M. H. and Ruth Dodds, *The Pilgrimage of Grace, 1536–37* (2 vols, Cambridge, 1915). See also : A. G. Dickens, 'Secular and Religious Motivation in the Pilgrimage of Grace', *Studies in Church History* (ed. C. J. Cuming, vol. IV, Cambridge, 1967), 39–64; C. S. L. Davies, 'The Pilgrimage of Grace Reconsidered', *Past and Present*, no. 41 (1968), 54–76; Christopher Haigh, *The Last Days of the Lancashire Monasteries and the Pilgrimage of Grace* (Manchester, 1969); R. B. Smith, *Land and Politics in the England of Henry VIII* (Oxford, 1970); Margaret Bowker 'Lincolnshire, 1536 : heresy, schism or religious discontent?', *Studies in Church History* (ed. Derek Baker, vol IX, Cambridge, 1972), 195–212.

6. *Letters and Papers*, XI, no. 768 (ii).

7. Ibid., XII, i, no. 976.

8. Ibid., XI, no. 1244. I have modernised the spelling of all quotations.

9. M. E. James, 'The First Earl of Cumberland (1493–1542) and the Decline of Northern Feudalism', *Northern History*, I (1966), 43–69.

10. James, *Past and Present*, no. 48, 3–78.

11. Quoted in Dodds, op. cit., I, 300–6.

12. *Letters and Papers*, XI, nos. 1182, 1246. See Bowker, op. cit., passim.

13. BM Harleian MS 1576, ff.251–9.
14. Alexander Neville, *Norfolk Furies and their Foyle* (trans. Richard Woods, London, 1623).
15. BM Harleian MS 304, f.75.
16. This point is not easily documented in a short space; but it emerges from Sotherton's narrative of the revolt in Harleian 1576.
17. The articles of the pilgrims are in *Letters and Papers*, XI, nos. 705, 1246. Those of Ket's rebels are in BM Harleian MS 304, f.75, and are printed in A. F. Bland, P. A. Brown, R. H. Tawney, *English Economic History: select documents* (London, 1914), 247. The articles of the south-western rebels survive in several versions. Easily accessible is the set in Cranmer's Answer to the rebels, printed in T. Cranmer, *Works* (ed. J. E. Cox, Parker Society, 1844–6), ii, 163–87.
18. D. M. Loades, *Two Tudor Conspiracies* (Cambridge, 1965), 18–23. J. Proctor, *The History of Wyatt's Rebellion* (1st edn, 1555); reproduced in A. F. Pollard (ed.), *Tudor Tracts, 1532–1588* (London, n.d.), 212.
19. Loades, op. cit., ch. viii for Dudley's conspiracy.
20. Quoted in J. C. Davis, 'The Levellers and Democracy', *Past and Present*, no. 40 (1968), 178. See also R. Howell and D. E. Brewster, 'Reconsidering the Levellers : the evidence of the moderate', *Past and Present*, no. 46 (1970).
21. H. N. Brailsford, *The Levellers and the English Revolution* (London, 1961), ch. xxvii. Also, 'An Agreement of the Free People of England' in W. Haller and G. Davies, *The Leveller Tracts* (New York, 1944), 318–28.
22. C. Russell, 'The Theory of Treason in the Trial of Strafford', *English Historical Review*, LXXX (1965), 30–50. P. Zagorin, *The Court and the Country* (London, 1969), 217–26. It could be held that there were precedents for Strafford's trial in the fourteenth century, when 'accroaching the royal power' was a form of treason. This charge was used by the Lords Appellant; and rather similar charges were brought in 1450 against Suffolk. But after 1450 this use of treason charges against royal favourites or ministers disappeared. Although the commons claimed that when they accused Strafford they were defending the law of the realm, they would seem to have been acting against the received constitution of the previous two centuries. On the Appellants see Richard H. Jones, *The Royal Policy of Richard II* (Oxford, 1968), ch. v.
23. Quoted in Zagorin, op. cit., 260.
24. Quoted ibid., 269.
25. See Zagorin, op. cit., chs viii and ix. For a similar view to my

330   *War and Society*

own of the events of 1640–2 see Lawrence Stone, *The Causes of the English Revolution, 1529–1642* (London, 1972), 48–54, published when the present article was in an early draft. For a contrary view see Conrad Russell, *The Crisis of Parliaments* (Oxford, 1971), 330–48.

26. See James, *Past and Present*, no. 48, and Davies, ibid., no. 41. While James sees the Pilgrimage as part of the late medieval tradition of protest, Davies emphasises its potentialities for a more profound conflict. But these two views are complementary rather than contradictory, as I have tried to show. A rather different view of mid-Tudor rebellions is given in Loades, *Two Tudor Conspiracies*.

27. Quoted in J. E. Oxley, *The Reformation in Essex* (Manchester, 1965), 116.

28. M. E. James, *Change and Continuity in the Tudor North* (Borthwick Papers, no. 27; York, 1965), 16–26. Id., 'The First Earl of Cumberland', *Northern History*, I (1966), 43–69. Davies, 'Pilgrimage of Grace', *Past and Present*, no. 41, 74–6.

29. See M. L. Bush, 'The Tudors and the Royal Race', *History*, LV (1970), 37–48.

30. *Letters and Papers*, XI, no. 1244. The author was probably Sir Thomas Tempest.

31. Ibid., no. 1086. Quoted in Dodds, op. cit., i, 300–6.

32. Ibid., XII, i, no. 1021.

33. E.g. R. Crowley, *The Way to Wealth* (London, 1550).

34. W. Cobbett, *State Trials* (London, 1809), vol. i, 861.

35. Quoted in Rachel Reid, 'The Rebellion of the Earls, 1569', *Transactions of the Royal Historical Society*, new series, XX (1906), 192.

36. See Stone, *Causes of the English Revolution*, 117–45, on the evolution of political opposition under the early Stuarts.

37. Ibid., 93–4.

38. W. M. Lamont, 'Puritanism as History and Historiography', *Past and Present*, no. 44 (1969).

39. See, for example, A. M. Everitt, *The Local Community and the Great Rebellion* (Historical Association, London, 1969).

40. W. Haller, *Foxe's Book of Martyrs and the Elect Nation* (London, 1963), ch. vii. Lamont, op. cit.

41. Valerie Pearl, *London and the Outbreak of the Puritan Revolution* (Oxford, 1961), chs iv–vi.

42. On peasants, townsmen and revolution see Dunn, *Modern Revolutions*, 7–8, and K. Marx, *Pre-Capitalist Economic Formations* (ed. E. J. Hobsbawm, London, 1964), 127–9.

15. Privateers in the Ancient Greek World

Privateers in the ancient Greek world enjoy no monograph to themselves, but are sometimes the subject of valuable remarks in works on other subjects, for example :

Fr Becker, *Der Seeraub im Mittelmeer in den ersten 2 Jahrhunderten nach Alexanders Tod,* Diss. Greifswald 1923.

H. A. Ormerod, *Piracy in the Ancient World* (Liverpool and London, 1924).

E. Ziebarth, *Beiträge zur Geschichte des Seeraubs und Seehandels im alten Griechenland* (Hamburg, 1929).

M. Rostovtzeff, *Social and Economic History of the Hellenistic World.*

P. Ducrey, op. cit., in note 17 below, especially ch. 5.

Ormerod's and Rostovtzeff's works are referred to respectively as *Piracy* and as *SEHHW* in these notes. Ancient sources cited below in abbreviated form are :

Hdt. = Herodotus
Thuc. = Thucydides
Xen. H. = Xenophon, *Hellenica*
Dem. = Demosthenes
Pb. = Polybius; (Walbank = F. W. Walbank, *A Historical Commentary on Polybius* (vol. I, Oxford, 1957; vol. II, 1967).
DS = Diodorus Siculus
Plut. = Plutarch

All passages in these and in most other ancient authors referred to here can be consulted in the translations of the Loeb Classical Library. Inscriptions : IG = Inscriptiones Graecae; SIG³ = W. Dittenberger, Sylloge Inscriptionum Graecarum (3rd edn, Leipzig, 1915–24); OGIS = idem, Orientis Graecae Inscriptiones Selectae (Leipzig, 1903–5); Inscr. Cret. = M. Guarducci, Inscriptiones Creticae (1935–50).

The limits of length necessarily imposed on contributions to this volume make inevitable only brief discussion and reference to ancient sources and modern literature in these notes.

1. Transliterated they are *lēstēs*, literally 'plunderer' – e.g. Aristophanes, *Acharnians,* 1077 (land); (Dem.), XII, 2 (sea); IG I², 87, line 7 (undefined but both elements would be concerned) – and *peiratēs*, literally 'attacker', e.g. Pb., IV, 3, 8 and 6, 1 (land and sea respectively).

2. Cf. L. Oppenheim, *International Law* (7th edn, ed. H. Lauterpacht, London, 1952), vol. II, 138; K. R. Andrews, *Elizabethan Privateering 1585–1603* (Cambridge, 1964), 3–5.

3. E.g. Thuc., T, 5, 2 and VII, 26, 2; Plut., *Pompey,* 25, 1; DS, XX, 83, 3. This makes it hard to decide if privateers or freebooters are meant in some texts.

4. E.g. Thuc., I, 13 and VI, 4, 5; Hdt., I, 166, II, 152 and III, 57–9.
5. Hdt., VI, 88–90; cf. V, 34, 3, VIII, 32 and IX, 31, 5.
6. The raiders envisaged in Teos' curse need only be freebooters preying on Teos; SIG³ 37/38 B 18–23.
7. Thuc., II, 67, 4 and 69; V, 56, 3 and 115, 2; cf. II, 26 and 32.
8. Thuc., VIII, 98, 1; Andocides, I, 101; Dem., XXIV, 128; cf. DS, XII, 81, 4.
9. E.g. Xen. B., III, 2, 29–30 and perhaps IV, 8, 35 and V, 4, 42; but cf. use of the word *lēstēs* in Xen. *Hipparchicus*, 7, 7. Probably also DS, XV, 3, 1 and 95, 1–2.
10. Xen. H., V, 1, 1 and 1, 29; cf. VI, 2, 1.
11. Aeschines, II, 12; (Dem.), XII, 2 and 6; Dem., XVIII, 145 (cf. 230 and 241).
12. Arrian, III, 2 (cf. II, 1); Dittenberger, OGIS I, 8 (especially lines 59sqq.); Q. Curtius Rufus, IV, 8, 15.
13. W. W. Tarn, *Antigonos Gonatas* (Oxford, 1913), 85–8. The mysterious kidnappers threatening Athens' harvest and country-folk in 265–4 BC seem almost certainly Gonatas' privateers; cf. V. Ch. Petrakos in *Archaiologikon Deltion*, 22 (1967), 38–52.
14. E.g. Livy, XXXI, 22, 4–8; XXXIV, 32, 15–20 and 36; 2–3; XXXVII, 11 and 13, 12 and perhaps 27–8, 5; SIG³ 582.
15. Strabo, 668; Plut., *Pompey*, 24, 1; Ormerod, *Piracy*, ch. VI; E. Maróti, *Diodotus Tryphon et la piraterie*, Acta Antiqua Academiae Scientiarum Hungaricae, Tomus X (1962), 187–94.
16. Ormerod, *Piracy*, 250–2; E. Maróti, 'Die Rölle der Seeräuber unter den Anhängern des Sextus Pompeius', in H. J. Diesner *et al.*, *Sozialökonomische Verhältnisse im Alten Orient und im Klassischen Altertum* (Berlin, 1961), 208–16.
17. Cf. H. D. Westlake, 'Seaborne Raids in Periclean Strategy', *Classical Quarterly*, 39 (1945); *Essays on the Greek Historians and Greek History* (Manchester, 1969), ch. 5; Rostovtzeff, *SEHHW*, I, 192–206; P. Ducrey, *Le traitement des prisonniers de guerre dans la Grèce antique* (Paris, 1968), chs 2, 3, 6 and 7; M. I. Finley, *Klio*, 40 (1962), 51–9; a typical incident where profit overcomes massacre, DS, XIV, 53.
18. Rostovtzeff, *SEHHW*, I, 196–9; Tarn, loc. cit. in note 13 above; R. Flacelière, *Les Aitoliens à Delphes* (Paris, 1937), 202sqq., 213sqq.; J. A. O. Larsen, *Greek Federal States* (Oxford, 1968), 209–12.
19. Pb., IX, 27, 10–11 with Walbank's note; Livy, XXVI, 40, 13–18.
20. M. Holleaux, in *Revue des Études Grecques*, 33 (1920), 223–47; Livy, XXXI, 22.

21. Thuc., IV, 41; V, 35, 6–7 and 56; VII, 26; VIII, 38 and 40 (slaves on Chios).
22. Cf. Dem., LII, 5; L. Casson, *Ships and Seamanship in the Ancient World* (Princeton, 1971), chs 6, iv (especially 128sq.) and 8, 157–63.
23. Aetolians: Polyaenus, IV, 6, 18. Sicilians: Livy, XXVII, 12, 1–6; 15, 8; 16, 9.
24. Cf. note 8 above and Lysias, XX, 28.
25. Cf. note 20 above and F. W. Walbank, *Philip V of Macedon* (Cambridge, 1940 and Archon Books, 1967), 108–15.
26. Pb., IX, 27, 10–11; Hyperides, I, col. 2, 2; G. T. Griffith, *The Mercenaries of the Hellenistic World* (Cambridge, 1935 and Groningen, 1968), ch. X.
27. Pb., IV, 29, 7: 20 talents a year for 30 *lembi* (an Illyrian *lembus* had 50 men, Pb., II, 3, 1) would strictly be under regulars' rates; for the latter see Griffith, op. cit. in note 26 above, 303–5.
28. Cf. the analogies of Xen., *Anabasis*, VII, 2, 31–4 and 3, 1–14.
29. All loot the privateer's: Pb., VIII, 24, 13; cf. Roman privateers in the First Punic War, Zonaras, 8, 397A. Share for employer: Dem., XXIV, 128–9 (if not rhetorical fantasy); Pb., XIII, 8, 2; probably also Xen. H., III, 4, 19; Aeneas Tacticus, 24; Philip's Aetolian in 204 presumably, cf. note 20 above; Pb., XXI, 26, 7–18. If the Athenian laws of Dem., XXIV, 11–12, about booty belonging to the State, covered not just regular troops (cf. Lysias, XX, 24) but also irregulars, it helps to explain why Athenian citizen privateers serving Classical Athens are not recorded (Meidias was not one; Dem., XXI, 173).
30. Thuc., III, 51 and IV, 67; Aeneas Tacticus, 24; Polyaenus, II, 35 and V, 19; Pb., VIII, 24–30.
31. Cf. Aristotle, *Constitution of Athens*, 19; Pb., XVIII, 5, 1–2 is suggestive, although about raiders in service.
32. DS, XIV, III, 1, corn at 100 times a normal peace-time price, in a siege; DS, XX, 82–4, foraging for besiegers; Arrian, II, 1 (cf. III, 2).
33. Cf. Pb., VIII, 25, 8 for gifts to sentries; Thuc., VII, 85, 3, regulars.
34. Lysias, XXIV, 13; cf. Aristophanes, *Wasps*, 300–1; Glotz, *Ancient Greece at Work* (London, 1926), 286. Ransoms: Dem., LIII, 7; Diogenes Laertius, III, 19–20; DS, XIV, 102, 2 and XV, 47, 7 with Xen. H., VI, 2, 33–6 (and these are flat-rates in mass ransoms, therefore cheaper).
35. Larsen, 'Roman Greece', in T. Frank, *Economic Survey of Ancient Rome*, IV, 412sqq.; Petrakos, op. cit., in note 13 above, 39, lines 19sqq.

36. Pb., XXI, 26, 7–18.
37. Dem., XXIV, 11–12.
38. Xen., *Anab.*, VII, 8, 6; W. K. Pritchett, *Hesperia* 25 (1956), 255sqq., 258sqq.; cf. *Hellenica Oxyrhynchia*, XII, 4.
39. Equal shares : Appian, *Civil Wars*, I, 116. Extra for leaders : Homer, *Odyssey*, 229–34; Xen., *Anab.*, VII, 8, 20–23.
40. Cf. Plut., *Aratus*, 6.
41. Examples and analogies : Plut., *Philopoemen*, 4 (not on estates); Xen., *Anab.*, VII, 8, 23 (cf. V, 3, 4–13); Pb., XIII, 1 (cf. Rostovtzeff, *SEHHW*, II, 1146–7); Athenaeus, 130D; M. I. Finley, *Political Science Quarterly* (1953), 249–68.
42. Cf. note 18 above; Inscr. Cret., III, Hierapytna no. 4, lines 53–6; Thuc., I, 5.
43. Pb., VIII, 24; Livy, XXV, 8; Aeneas Tacticus, 24; cf. Xen. H., II, 1, 30.
44. Cf. note 29 above and SIG³ 582.
45. Pb., XVIII, 4, 7–5, 4. Privateering as well as mercenary service will be included. Even from Philip V this cannot all be malicious rhetorical distortion.
46. Against own land; e.g. DS, XII, 81; Xen. H., III, 2, 29–30; DS, XV, 45. Random : e.g. Hdt., III, 57–9; Xen. H., III, 2, 11; Plut. *Aratus*, 6 (some random raids seem implied).
47. Tarn, *Antigonos Gonatas*, 88; Livy, XXVI, 40, 17; Thuc., VIII, 40; Athenaeus, 265d sqq.
48. The robber-chief with soldiers to hire to raiding exiles in 251 BC at Argos is indicative; Plut., *Aratus* 6. Cf. Griffith, op. cit. note 26 above, 262–3. Another group that could plunder for the benefit of a belligerent was the body of camp-followers and traders who travelled with and often supplied armies in the field (e.g. DS, XIV, 79, 1–2 and XX, 82–3), sometimes buying and selling soldiers' booty, sometimes looting for sale themselves; some stateless, some citizens perhaps, but the ancient writers rarely bother with them. Between these men, traders primarily, and the raiders discussed in the text, there would not always be a clear distinction.
49. DS. XX, 110, 4.
50. Livy, XXVI, 40, 17; Cilicians, after Mithridates took them up, numbered 30,000 in 67 BC if we may trust Plut., *Pompey* 28, 2 and Appian, *Mithridatic Wars*, 96 *ad fin.*
51. 430 BC (Thuc., II 69), facing 6 Athenian warships. 332 BC if Arrian, III, 2 is right against Curtius Rufus, IV, 5, 19. 190 BC (Livy, XXXVII, 27–8, 5), perhaps Antiochus' irregulars.
52. Aeneas Tacticus, 24; but Polyaenus, III, 14 gives him helpers.
53. Thuc., IV, 67 and IV, 9.
54. E.g. complaints over wrongful capture, investment in ventures,

class and occupation of privateers (especially citizens), overall economic effects of privateering as distinct from looting and disruption by regular forces.

55. Cf. W. H. D. Rouse, *Greek Votive Offerings* (Cambridge, 1902), 55sq., 118sqq.

56. Cf. Xen. H., I, 6, 14–15; Kiechle, *Historia*, VII (1958), 129–56, paints too rosy a picture of this change of mind and of its effects.

57. Xen., *Agesilaus*, xi, 1; Plut., *Alcibiades*, 29; E. Schlesinger, *Die griechische Asylie*, Diss. Giessen 1933. These immunities were not always respected in practice.

58. There is room here for only a brief statement of this view, which runs counter to that of Ormerod, *Piracy*, 96–8 and 142.

59. Cf. *Odyssey*, XIV, 199–285; XVI, 418–30.

60. *Odyssey*, XIV, 80–8; XV, 390–484.

61. *Works and Days*, 320sq.

62. Cf. Xenophanes of Colophon, fr. 11 Diels-Kranz *Fgte. d. Vorsokratiker*; Hdt., I, 166, VI, 17; Justin, XLIII, 3, 5.

63. Digest, XLVII, 22, 4; cf. L. Beauchet, *Histoire du Droit privé de la République Athénienne* (Paris, 1897), vol. IV, 364sqq. Space does not permit discussion of the many questions relating to this text which the present writer hopes to deal with in full detail elsewhere. Presumably, it would lapse into obsolescence (*de facto*) after c. 482 BC.

64. From 482 if Nepos, *Themistocles*, 2, 2 is reliable.

65. Thuc., I, 5.

66. Plato, *Gorgias*, 484A sqq.

67. The writer hopes to discuss in detail elsewhere the inconclusive evidence of (Dem.), VII, 2–4; Dem., XXIII, 60–1; XXIV, 11sqq.; LI, 13–15, etc., which limited space excludes here, but which may contain more rhetoric than actual law.

68. Flacelière, loc. cit. in note 18 above; Larsen, op. cit. in note 18, 211; well put by Ducrey, op. cit. in note 17 above, 44, note 3; for the legal background, Schlesinger, op. cit. in note 57 above.

69. Cf. Cicero, *De Republica*, III, 9; SIG³ 539A, line 6.

70. Cf. E. Maróti, *Klio*, 40 (1962), 124–7.

71. Cf. M. I. Finley, 'The Problem of the Unity of Greek Law', Atti del I Congresso Internazionale della Società Italiana di Storia del Diritto (Florence, 1966), 129–42.

72. IG I² 53, lines 7–8; ibid., 87, 7–8. The word translated 'raider' here is *lēstēs*. The verb that is derived from this word is translated 'raid', and either or both of these simple words are used in the texts cited in this paragraph. If it were objected that Athens' language in these treaties is not neutral in tone, that still does not weaken the argument based on the proclamations

of 416 and 389 (se below, note 73), and the objection has its own weaknesses.

73. 416 : Thuc., V, 115, 2; no talk of reprisals despite several years of raids against Sparta sponsored by Athens, though it is significant that only those on Sparta's side were invited : 'they proclaimed that anyone who wished on their side could raid Athenians.'

389 : Xen. H., V, 1, 1; by agreement with the Spartan government a Spartan officer invited 'anyone who wished to raid Attica'.

341–40 : (Dem.), XII, 2; if we may trust the statement of their victim, the Thasians harboured 'those of the raiders who wished, though the treaty stated explicitly that this was to be regarded as a hostile act'. Ibid., 13 : 'you must admit to sending out raiders' may be a reference to the same clause. Despite possible distortion and the doubtful authorship of this letter the absence of words and phrases to do with reprisals is noteworthy.

74. E.g. Pb., XXII, 4 and XXXII, 7.

75. *Supplementum Epigraphicum Graecum*, XVIII, 243. J. Bousquet, *Bulletin de Correspondance Hellénique*, 83 (1959), 172–4; line 1 : *laphuron kēruttein* seems equivalent to *sulān* and *rusiazein* used in lines 8–9, and close to Polybius' *to laphuron epikēruttein*. But the *laphuropōlion* in the fourth-century Arcadian text IG, V, ii, 6, and the reference to *laphuron* in SIG³ 535, line 13, may not concern plunder in reprisals, but plunder in warfare in general.

76. SIG³ 588, lines 47–50.

77. SIG³ 582.

78. Inscription cited in note 42 above; tithes : Rouse, op. cit. in note 55 above. 'Tithes' may have been a courtesy title more often than not; Thuc., III, 50, 2 is the only certain case of an exact tenth for the gods.

16. Septimius Severus and His Generals, AD 193–7

1. A. R. Birley, *Septimius Severus* (London, 1971), 158. In what follows I shall refer, where appropriate, to this recent and fully-documented account (by the author's name alone), which absolves me from the need to provide again the full apparatus of references to ancient sources. I also refer to the following works by the author's name or by the abbreviation indicated :

G. Alföldy, 'Septimius Severus under der Senat', *Bonner Jahr-bücher*, CLXVIII (1968), 112–60.

J. Hasebroek, *Untersuchungen zur Geschichte des Kaisers Septimius Severus* (Heidelberg, 1921).

ILS : H. Dessau (ed.), *Inscriptiones Latinae Selectae* (3rd edn, Berlin, 1962).

H-G. Pflaum, *Les carrières procuratoriennes equestres sous le haut-empire romain* (Paris, 1960).

Dio : *Cassii Dionis Cocceiani Historiarum Romanarum Quae Supersunt*, ed. U. P. Boissevain. (I cite the books of Dio according to the new numbering proposed by Boissevain.)

Hdn : Herodian, *Ab excessu divi Marci*, ed. C. R. Whittaker (Loeb Classical Library, London, 1969). I cite the historical notes by Whittaker's name alone.

SHA : *Scriptores Historiae Augustae.*

2. E.g. *The Inscriptions of Roman Tripolitania*, ed. J. M. Reynolds and J. B. Ward Perkins (London, 1952), 428 : 'Imperator Caesar Lucius Septimius [Severus Pius] Pert[inax Aug(ustus) Arabicus Adiabenicus Parthicus maximus Britannicus] max[imus . . .] . . . . . imperator duodecies.' On the question of the numbers of imperial salutations, see the convincing discussion by A. A. Boyce, *American Journal of Archaeology*, LIII (1949), 337–44.

3. A von Domaszewski, *Rheinisches Museum für Philologie*, LIII (1898), 639.

4. See especially A. R. Birley, *Bonner Jahrbücher*, CLXIX (1969), 247–80; Alföldy (note 1 above); J. B. Leaning, , 'A prosopographical investigation into the politics of the reign of Septimius Severus and Caracalla' (unpublished MA thesis, University of Manchester, 1968); J. Fitz, *Acta of the fifth international congress of Greek and Latin epigraphy, Cambridge 1967* (Oxford, 1971), 425–9; *Alba Regia*, X (1969), 69–86.

5. Cf. my chapter entitled 'The limitations of prosopography in Roman imperial history (with special reference to the Severan period)', to appear in *Aufstieg und Niedergang der römischen Welt, II Prinzipat*, ed. H. Temporini (Berlin, 1973), where I subject these speculations to detailed examination.

6. For the title see the inscription of Rossius Vitulus, Pflaum 224. The wording in the inscription of Valerius Valerianus, though not quite certain, was similar; see n. 19 below. For the events and sources see Birley, 158–67.

7. M. Durry, *Les cohortes prétoriennes* (Paris, 1938), 88 n. 4.

8. Chester G. Starr, *The Roman Imperial Navy* (New York, 1941), 16sq.

9. Cf. Starr, 180–5.

10. Contrast Birley, 158, who implies that he had time to consult much more widely before his proclamation.

11. On all the distances and calculations compare Hasebroek, 17–19; R. O. Fink, A. S. Hoey and W. F. Snyder, *Yale Classical Studies*, VII (1940), 130 n. 567; C. W. J. Eliot, *Phoenix*, IX (1955), 76–80; Whittaker, 204 n.l, 214 n.l. Birley (158) rightly points out that Eliot's calculations for the speed of the message from Rome to Carnuntum are much too long. We know from other examples that really urgent messages could be carried at the rate of up to 125 Roman miles a day (at least up to distances of 1,000 Roman miles). See the recent calculations by K. Wellesley, *Journal of Roman Studies*, LVII (1967), 25–7 with n. 15. However, 1 April (as Birley, loc. cit.) implies an impossibly fast journey. To achieve this date Birley has to make the unsupported and unnecessary conjecture that Septimius Severus moved to the south-western border of his province.

12. Cf. Hasebroek, 23sq. and, more recently, Birley, 167 (by implication).

13. An unsolved problem. Since Birley's explanation cannot be correct, the absence of this legion from the coins presumably implies some temporary displeasure on the emperor's part; see, e.g., Hasebroek, 23. But it is impossible that one of the legions in his own province could have long refused to take the oath of loyalty, and the legion received honorary titles from Septimius Severus; cf. Whittaker, 206 n.l. It is tempting to conclude that coins of X Gemina were struck but have not survived, but the experts discount that possibility; cf. H. Mattingly and E. A. Sydenham, *The Roman Imperial Coinage*, iv, 1 (London, 1936), 65.

14. I owe to Mr J. B. Leaning the original observation that not all the legions commemorated on the coins could have taken part in the march. The interpretation I propose seems the best way to account for the remaining absentees from the legions of the West. We know that their absence was not due to hostility to Septimius Severus, because III Augusta in Numidia was loyal to him from the beginning and continued so throughout. That disposes of the inherently unlikely notion that VII Gemina in Spain and the three British legions were absent because they were hostile to Septimius Severus already at this date; cf. Hasebroek, 23sq. The distance alone would have prevented the legions in Spain and Africa from informing Septimius Severus of their loyalty before he left Carnuntum, even if (which is by no means certain) he had been able to get messages to them. A message to Britain and back to Carnuntum within the time available is feasible if we assume the fastest possible rate, but the sea-crossing was an unpredictable factor and the oath of loyalty would have had to be administered to the three legions

separately at their different headquarters. So here again the factors of time and distance may be the whole explanation. Nevertheless, one could speculate that Clodius Albinus delayed administering the oath until he knew that Septimius Severus had kept his word and duly had him proclaimed Caesar by the senate at Rome.

15. On the general practice see R. E. Smith, *Historia*, XXI (1972), 483, 486. The statement of the *Historia Augusta* (*SHA Sept. Sev.*, v. 3) that Septimius Severus left troops behind to guard the provinces (cf. Hdn, ii, 14, 6) accords with what one would expect. Apart from the necessity of guarding against external enemies, he could not remove all the troops from the European provinces loyal to him in face of the threat from Pescennius Niger and even, perhaps, from Clodius Albinus.

16. See Dio, lxxv, 1, 3 for the presence of cavalry.

17. *SHA Did. Julianus*, viii, 1.

18. The problems of identification which affect Laetus are convincingly handled by Birley, 345sq., whose conclusion I accept : namely, that there was one distinguished general of Severus called Julius Laetus, a senator. However, the statement that he commanded the advance guard of the Severan expedition to Rome (Hasebroek, 34, followed by Birley, 160) goes beyond the evidence.

19. Cf. Birley, 160, who makes an unwarranted assumption when he says that Valerius Valerianus was 'given command over the cavalry'. The career of Valerius Valerianus (whom we may confidently identify with the Valerianus at Issus; Dio, lxxv, 7) is known from an inscription, *Année Epigraphique*, 1966, 495, the text of which is still not satisfactorily established. See J. Fitz, *Latomus*, xxviii (1969), 126–40, who has at least demonstrated convincingly that earlier editors underestimated the length of the lines. His own text, though not always correct or persuasive in detail, must be more nearly right than that in *Année Epigraphique*. This means that the conclusion that Valerianus commanded units of *peregrini* in the march on Rome (Birley, 160 n.) must now be abandoned. Birley is surely right in suggesting that Valerianus was procurator of Cyprus after the civil wars (loc. cit.), which allows the natural assumption that the office which preceded his activity in the civil wars was 'praef-(ecto) a[lae I Hispan(orum)] Campagonum in Dac[ia]'; see Fitz, 140.

20. For the career see Pflaum 224. According to his reconstruction Rossius Vitulus was an equestrian officer of long experience, who was in command of the 'ala praet(oria) c(ivium) R(omanorum)' in the Danube area in 193.

21. Birley, 163 n.l.
22. Ibid., loc. cit.
23. Birley, 161sq.
24. Birley, 164sq.
25. Hasebroek's suggestion that Laetus might have had 'den Oberbefehl' in the expedition against Rome (34 n. 5) goes against the evidence and has no inherent probability.
26. Birley, 159.
27. Cf. Dio, lxxiv, 15, 1–2; lxxvi, 4, 1; Hdn, ii, 15, 1–5; iii, 5, 1–2.
28. This interpretation is argued most clearly by J. B. Leaning in his unpublished MA thesis, 'A prosopographical investigation into the politics of the reigns of Septimius Severus and Caracalla' (University of Manchester, 1968). However, Birley too argues that Clodius Albinus and Septimius Severus were fellow-members of the same conspiracy against Commodus; *Bonner Jahrbücher*, CLXIX (1969), 247–80. Alföldy (118), although he does not assume that there was any genuine alliance between Septimius Severus and Clodius Albinus, argues that the formal break between them was precipitated by Clodius Albinus.
29. On the career of P. Septimius Geta see Birley, 302sq.; *Bonner Jahrbücher*, CLXIX (1969), 261–4. The *Historia Augusta* hints at disagreements between the emperor and his brother; see *Sept. Sev.*, viii, 10 and x, 3. On both occasions Septimius Severus is said to have disappointed his brother's ambitions.
30. As Alföldy, 118.
31. As Alföldy rightly emphasises, loc. cit.
32. See the section on the war against Clodius Albinus below.
33. Birley, 172–88. D. Magie gives a very good summary account of the war with copious source material : *Roman Rule in Asia Minor* (Princeton, 1950), i, 669–72, ii, 1538–41.
34. Cf. *SHA Sept. Sev.*, viii, 7. See Birley, 171 and 177 (emphasis on Africa in the coinage).
35. This fundamental truth of ancient warfare is not shaken by Herodian's statement (iii, 1, 1) that Niger ordered his provincial governors to guard the ports. If true, we may either regard the measure as a matter of minor security or apply it only to the relevant ports in Asia Minor, but it is part of a passage obviously false in its general tendency.
36. *SHA Sept. Sev.*, viii, 12; cf. Hdn, ii, 14, 6.
37. See Hasebroek, 55sq. The passage Dio lxxiv, 15, 2 proves that Niger had taken control of Byzantium before Septimius Severus reached Rome.
38. *Année Epigraphique*, 1926, 79, but more correctly in *Journal of Roman Studies*, XIV (1924), 185. Hasebroek (55), writing before the inscription was known, assumed that Cilo led vexil-

lations from the Moesian army. Birley (160) and Whittaker (241 n. 2) follow him in the assumption that the first Severan troops in the Byzantine area came from the most adjacent garrisons in Moesia. That may well be so, but Cilo was not in command of them. The Illyrian army and Moesian army are formally distinguished on the inscriptions : see *ILS* 1140 and 2935 (at Lugdunum Claudius Candidus led the *exercitus Illyricus*, Marius Maximus the *exercitus Mysiacus*). The emphasis on Perinthus in Cilo's inscriptions (in addition to *Année Epigraphique*, 1926, 79, see *ILS* 1141) suggests that the leading Severan general at Perinthus was Cilo, not Marius Maximus. Thus Whittaker's suggestion, that Cilo brought up the Illyrian detachments by sea would appear to be excluded on chronological grounds, if for no other reason.

39. Birley, 145.
40. Hinted by Birley, 159. Herodian (iii, 2, 4) records the fact that Septimius Severus' children were smuggled out of Rome, while Dio (lxxviii, 4, 2) describes Cilo as Caracalla's *tropheus* (i.e. tutor or foster-father) and benefactor.
41. For Cilo's career see Alföldy, 141sq.; Birley, 342.
42. Cf. the suggestions of Birley, *Bonner Jahrbücher*, CLXIX (1969), 275, and Fitz, *Acta of the fifth international congress of Greek and Latin epigraphy, Cambridge 1967* (Oxford, 1971), 426; *Alba Regia*, X (1969), 72.
43. See n. 29 above.
44. *ILS* 2935. On Marius Maximus see Alföldy, 146sq.; Birley, Appendix II.
45. Birley, 174–5. The common assumption that Marius Maximus directed the siege of Byzantium seems likely to be correct.
46. *SHA Sept. Sev.*, viii, 8; cf. Hdn, ii, 14, 5. Hasebroek, 52, attempts too great precision.
47. Birley, 172, 175.
48. Hdn, ii, 14, 6–7.
49. The evidence for Septimius Severus' stay at Perinthus was collected by Hasebroek, 56, 62. The coins of Perinthus prove that the emperor stayed in the city twice (the second time, it may be assumed, on the way back from the East in 195–6); that he greatly honoured the city; and that his forces crossed from there. Together with this evidence we have the negative indication that Septimius Severus was not present at any of the battles against Niger's forces (Dio, lxxvi, 6, 1). This makes quite a strong case, but a more precise indication has been sought in the passages Jordanes, *Getica*, 84 and *SHA Max.*, i, 5 to iii, 6. If trustworthy, these show that Septimius Severus celebrated the birthday of his son in Thrace. The son was Geta according

to the *Historia Augusta* (not Caracalla, as Domaszewski proposed, arguing that he was the son in Jordanes' mind, whereas the Geta of the *Historia Augusta* must be false. See *Die Personennamen bei den Scriptores Historiae Augustae, Sitzungsberichte der Heidelberger Akademie der dissenschaften, philosophisch-historische Klasse*, 1918 Abh. 13, 93sq. It is a measure of Domazewski's authority that this extraordinarily dogmatic and perverse argument has been widely accepted; see, e.g., Hasebroek, 62; M. Fluss, *Paulys Realencylopädie* s.v. Severus 13, 1957; Birley, 177). If we press this rather dubious evidence, Septimius Severus was in Thrace on 7 March – for Geta's birthday see T. D. Barnes, *Journal of Theological Studies*, XIX 1968), 522–5 – but Perinthus is not named in the passages in question. Nevertheless, taken together, evidence and probability suggest that Hasebroek was right.

50. Cf. Birley, 175. The passage Dio, lxxv, 6, 3–4 shows that Niger commanded at Byzantium and Perinthus; see also *SHA Sept. Sev.*, viii, 13, 16. Herodian (iii, 2, 2) appears to assign a greater role to Aemilianus, but the wording is mere embroidery, for he too only gives Aemilianus command at Cyzicus.

51. The large fleet which had been required to enable the Severan army to cross the Propontis was now, we may assume, largely occupied in the siege of Byzantium; cf. Dio, lxxv, 11, 2 and 3; 12, 1–2; and especially 13.

52. Apart from his specific commands he was a *comes* of the emperor in the eastern expedition; see n. 41 above.

53. Dio states (lxxv, 6, 5) that Candidus was in command at Nicaea, and according to *SHA Sept. Sev.*, viii, 16–17 the same generals ('*iisdem ducibus*') were in command of the Severan forces at Cyzicus and Nicaea. The plural, however, allows a small element of doubt as to the chief commander at the first battle.

54. For Candidus' career see *ILS* 1140; Pflaum 203; Birley, 339sq.; G. Alföldy, *Fasti Hispanienses* (Wiesbaden, 1969), 43–5.

55. This seemed so surprising to J. Fitz that he proposed to insert into Candidus' career the completely unattested command of the legion X Gemina in the period 190/1–193 : *Latomus*, XXV (1966), 831–46; repeated without any indication that it is hypothetical in *Acta of the fifth international congress of Greek and Latin epigraphy*, 427, and *Alba Regia*, X (1969), 73. The suggestion is convincingly rejected by Alföldy, ibid.

56. See n. 41 above.

57. See n. 54 above.

58. For Anullinus' career see Alföldy, *Fasti Hispanienses*, 122sq.; Birley, 341. It seems much more likely that his year as proconsul of Africa was 193–4, as B. E. Thomasson, *Die Statthalter der*

römischen Provinzen Nordafrikas van Augustus bis Diokletian (Lund, 1960), 100, rather than 192–3, as Alföldy, op. cit. above. In the latter case he should surely have been relieved before Septimius Severus became 'cos. des. II' (*ILS* 413).

59. As Alföldy suggests, op. cit. above.
60. Birley, 178.
61. See above n. 19.
62. Our only information is that Rossius Vitulus was in charge of the war chest; see above n. 20.
63. Birley 181–5; D. Magie, *Roman Rule in Asia Minor*, i, 672–3; ii, 1542–4. The war was certainly called Parthian, even though there was no fighting against the Parthians themselves; see, for instance, *ILS* 1140 and *Année Epigraphique* 1957, 123. On the appearance and non-appearance of *Parthicus* in Septimius Severus' victory titles see Birley, 182; Hasebroek, 80sq.
64. See D. Oates, *Studies in the ancient history of Northern Iraq* (London, 1968), 69–73.
65. Magie (op. cit., ii, 1543sq.) seems to have the best solution for the apparently conflicting evidence about Osrhoene. The passage Dio, lxxv, 3, 2 shows that Mesopotamia was made a province and put under an equestrian prefect already in 195. Indirect confirmation comes from the inscription *ILS* 1353, as brilliantly interpreted by Pflaum, 229. Since Pacatianus was *praefectus* of one of the new Parthian legions before the war against Clodius Albinus, the decision to put these legions under *equites*, which cannot be separated from the decision to put Mesopotamia under an *eques*, must have been taken by 195.
66. Cf. Dio, loc. cit. n. 65 above and lxxv, 2, 4. Notice also the wording on the famous arch at Rome; *ILS* 425.
67. See n. 65 above and R. E. Smith, *Historia*, XXI (1972), 485sq. with n. 28.
68. Birley, 182, 183 n.l, 184–6.
69. Ibid.
70. Dio, lxxv, 2, 1–3.
71. *ILS* 1140; see n. 54 above.
72. Note however the slight doubt about Cyzicus; see n. 53 above. For his outstanding gifts see Dio, lxxvi, 9, 2.
73. On the family and career of Lateranus see Alföldy, 152.
74. See Birley, 183.
75. Dio, lxxv, 3, 2.
76. Birley, 189–95.
77. The life of Clodius Albinus in the *Historia Augusta* is completely worthless.
78. On Niger see ii, 8, 9; 9, 1; 14, 6; iii, 4, 7, though elsewhere he praises him for other qualities; ii, 7, 4–5. His own narrative

frequently refutes these generalisations; e.g. iii, 2, 1; 4, 1. On Albinus see iii, 15, 3; iii, 7, 1; cf. Whittaker's note *ad loc.*

79. As they are by Birley, 194.

80. At the most the auxiliary troops in Britain might have numbered as many as 50,000; see S. S. Frere, *Britannia* (London, 1967), 160–2. To these we need to add the three legions.

81. It has long been known that Spain belonged to the empire of Albinus. Not only did its governor Novius Rufus (see Alföldy, *Fasti Hispanienses*, 42sq.) figure among the supporters of Albinus put to death by Septimius Severus (*SHA Sept. Sev.*, xiii, 7), but Candidus had a special command against rebels in Spain which can only be attributed to the aftermath of the war against Albinus (*ILS* 1140; see n. 54 above). However, the legion in Spain, VII Gemina, received honorary titles (*pia felix*; *ILS* 1155, hence also *ILS* 1145) from Septimius Severus, which can hardly have been bestowed for anything other than its behaviour in the civil wars; see E. Ritterling, *Paulys Realencylopädie* s.v. legio, 1314sq., 1637. Hence some conclude that the legion remained loyal to the Septimius Severus even though its governor and his province supported Albinus (Ritterling, 1314sq.; Alföldy, 120; Birley, 190sq.). That seems to pass beyond the limits of credibility. We must rather suppose that the legion showed enthusiastic loyalty to its new emperor immediately after Lugdunum (cf. Ritterling, 1637), or even that it deserted to him during the battle. Septimius Severus did not cashier or degrade any unit which opposed him in the civil wars except the old Praetorian Guard and, probably, Cohors XIII Urbana at Lugdunum (cf. *Paulys Realencyclopädie*, Suppl. X [1965], 1129sq.). It is possible that Legio II Italica in Noricum provides an illuminating parallel for VII Gemina in Spain (see n. 85 below).

82. Even Alföldy, whose interpretation seems to me otherwise very sound; 118. It is a mistake, as so often, to trust Herodian (ii, 15, 2).

83. Dio, lxxvi, 6, 2; see Hasebroek, 96; Birley, 190.

84. *ILS* 419; see Hasebroek and Birley, loc. cit.

85. Claudius Candidus pursued rebels in Asia, Noricum and Spain (*ILS* 1140). Since we know that Asia had belonged to Niger's empire, and Spain to Albinus', it would be logical to suppose that Noricum too belonged for a time to a rival of Septimius Severus. It is interesting to observe that, as in the case of Spain (see n. 81 above), although the province of Noricum was rebellious, its legion, II Italica, received the honorary title of *fidelis* at the time of the civil wars (Ritterling, *Paulys Realencyclopädie* s.v. legio 1313sq.).

86. As Birley, 186.
87. Hdn, iii, 6, 10. The theory that the 'general' mentioned was Julius Pacatianus, and that he commanded one of the Parthian legions at the same time as he was procurator of the Cottian Alps (e.g. Birley, 191), is open to formal objections; Pflaum, 229 (607sq.). However, Pflaum shows, as we should expect, that governorships in the Alps were specially important positions at this time; see also 226.
88. See *SHA Sept. Sev.*, x, 7 ('*a Pannoniacis auguribus*') and *ILS* 1143, which shows that Caracalla was in Pannonia and separated from his father immediately after the Lugdunum campaign; Hasebroek, 94, 100; Birley, 193.
89. Birley, 191.
90. Birley, 193. Cf. n. 40 above.
91. See n. 85 above.
92. *SHA Sept. Sev.*, xi, 9.
93. Birley, 190sq., 194.
94. Birley, 193 n. 3, is too pessimistic. The route is well-established if we combine the engagement of Tinurtium recorded in *SHA Sept. Sev.*, xi, 1 (see Hasebroek, 97) with the knowledge that the army came from Pannonia.
95. The date is given by *SHA Sept. Sev.*, xi, 7. Normally it would be very incautious to accept an exact date in the *Historia Augusta*, but the appearance of the same date as a special day to be commemorated in the municipal *feriale* at Theveste may be taken to confirm it; see W. F. Snyder, *Yale Classical Studies*, VII (1940), 297–317, especially 306sq.
96. Dio, lxxvi, 7, 3; *SHA Sept. Sev.*, xi, 7–9.
97. Dio, lxxvi, 6, 8; Hdn, iii, 7, 4; *SHA Sept. Sev.*, xi, 2. It is possible to regard this story as propaganda put out by Septimius Severus to justify himself for later killing Laetus (as Birley, 203), though our sources do not usually unite to repeat Severan propaganda. In any case, the mere fact that the tale had verisimilitude shows the potential danger to Septimius Severus at Lugdunum.
98. See Birley, 345sq.
99. Cft. *Epitome de Caesaribus*, xx, 6 and the full account by Fitz, *Alba Regia*, X (1969), 83–5.
100. See Birley, 203–5, who chooses spring and autumn 198 as the dates of the two attempts to take the city.
101. Dio, lxxvi, 11, 1 to 13, 1.

17. Civil War and Society in Southern Etruria

Apart from the conventional abbreviations for classical authors, the following are here also used :

AHR	American Historical Review.
Am. J. Phil.	American Journal of Philology.
Bull. Comm.	Bullettino Communale di Roma.
Bull. Pal. Ital.	Bullettino di Paletnologia Italiana.
CIE	Corpus Inscriptionum Etruscarum.
CIL	Corpus Inscriptionum Latinarum.
JRS	Journal of Roman Studies.
Mon. Ant.	Monumenti Antichi.
Not. Scav.	Notizie degli Scavi di antichità.
PBSR	Papers of the British School at Rome.
RE	Pauly-Wissowa-Kroll, Real-Encyclopädie der classischen Altertumswissenschaft.
Röm. Mitt.	Mitteilungen d. deutsch. Arch. Inst. Römische Abteilung.
ZGLE	W. Schulze, Zur Geschichte der Lateinischen Eigennamen.

1. R. Meiggs, *Roman Ostia*, 214sqq.
2. For the historical picture see *CAH*, VII, ch. XV, vii (esp. 517) and XVII, viii (cf. G. de Sanctis, *Storia dei Romani*, II, 149sqq); D. A. Bullough, 'Movements of Populations in Etruria since the Beginning of the Roman Republic', CIBA Foundation Symposium, 93–109. Also H. H. Scullard, *Etruria and Rome*, passim, and W. V. Harris, *Rome in Etruria and Umbria*.
3. e.g. for Sutri see *PBSR*, XXVI (1958), 68, n. 4.
4. Appian, *Bellum Civile*, 1, 7.
5. Plut. Ti. Gracch, 8. One should remember that this description is derived from a βιβλίον by Gaius Gracchus and may reflect a propagandist view. See E. Badian, *Historia*, XI, 2 (1962), 201.
6. For discussions of the subject, see E. Badian, *Historia*, XI, 2 (1962), 209–14, with its accompanying bibliography, 233–45.
7. G. D. B. Jones, *PBSR*, XXX (1962), 121sqq.
8. K. Lachmann, *Die Schriften der Römischen Feldmesser*, I, 350–1.
9. J. Heurgon, 'The Date of Vegoia's Prophecy', *JRS*, XLIX (1959), 41sqq.
10. J. Carcopino, 'Les lois agraires des Gracques et la guerre sociale', *Bull. Assoc. Guillaume Budé* (Jan. 1929), 16sqq. Cf. Bernardi, 'La Guerra Sociale e le lotte dei partiti in Roma', *Nuova Rivista Storica*, XXVIII–XIX (1944–5), 67sqq.

11. J. Heurgon, loc. cit. For the most recent discussion of this incident, see E. Badian, *Historia*, XI, 2 (1962), 225–6, where further references are given.

12. Appian, I, 36.

13. Ibid., loc. cit.

14. Pliny, NH, II, 149 describes ominous portents from Etruria that were publicised by the consul.

15. S. Mazzarino, 'Sociologia del Mondo Etrusco e Problemi della Tarda Etruscità', *Historia*, VI (1957), 98–122.

16. Dion, 9, 5; cf. Livy, II, 44; VI, 12; IX, 36.

17. 8, 7.

18. Caes., *Bellum Civile*, I, 34. For a fuller discussion of the passage see R. M. Haywood, *Am. J. Phil.*, LIV (1933), 145–53, where he traces some evidence of serfdom in Cicero's day.

19. Caes. B.C., I, 56.

20. *CIL*, I, 1344 offers further evidence that he possessed estates in the region.

21. Some of the relevant figures compiled from *CIL*, XI are: Falerii 50:243 = 19%; Nepet 19:99 = 19%; Sutri 28:101 = 28%; Viterbium 13:174 = 17%.

22. Pliny, *Nat. Hist.*, III, 52.

23. Ibid., loc. cit.

24. *Lib. Col.*, 220, L.

25. For the history of this episode see now G. D. B. Jones, 'Southern Etruria 50–40 BC', *Latomus*, XXII (1963), 773sqq.
    It has been suggested that Sutri received a colony of Antonian veterans after Philippi and was re-colonised after Actium, see L. Gabba, 'Sulle colonie triumvirale di Antonio in Italia', *La Parola del Passato*, VIII (1953), 103.

26. *CIL*, XI, 3797; cf. 3799.

27. *CIL*, XI, 3798; cf. PBSR, XXIX (1961), 59–60.

28. *CIL*, XI, 3524.

29. Cic., *Ad Fam.*, IX, 17, 2.

30. G. D. B. Jones, 'Capena and the Ager Capenas', PBSR, XXX (1962), 194sqq.; for the suggestion of an Augustan foundation, W. V. Harris, *Rome in Etruria and Umbria*, 224.
    For a provisional description of the site see R. Bartoccini, *Estratto dagli Atti del VII Congresso Internazionale di Archeologia Classica* (1958), 5.
    Id., 'L'Anfiteatro di Lucus Feroniae e il suo fondatore', *Rendiconti della Pontificia Accademia Romana di Archeologia*, XXXIII, 1 sqq.
    G. D. B. Jones, op. cit., 191sqq.

31. *de controv. agr.* A. 164 (= K. Lachmann, *Die Schriften der Römischen Feldmesser*, I, 47, 1, 17). Cf. *CIL*, VI, 2584. *d.m.*

348   *War and Society*

P. Octavio P. fil. Vol. Marcellino Luco Feroniae veterano Augustorum.

32. *Lib. Col.*, 216, L.
33. *Not. Scav.* (1953), 15, fig. 4. Cf. *Année Epigraphique* (1954), n. 163, 46.
34. The argument is taken from R. Bartoccini, op. cit. (n. 30 above).
35. *CIL*, XI, 3801, 3802.
36. *Non enim ut olim universae legiones deducebantur cum tribunis et centurionibus et sui cuiusque ordinis militibus ut consensu et caritate rem publicam efficerent, sed ignoti inter se diversis manipulis sine rectore, sine adfectibus mutuis, quasi ex alio genere mortalium repente in unum collecti, numerus magis quam colonia.* Tac., *Ann.*, XIV, 27, 4;
    cf. Appian, *Bellum Civile*, II, 120; Hyg. Grom. B. 226 (= K. Lachmann, *Die Schriften der Römischer Feldmesser*, 176, 11, 11–13).
37. H. Hurst, *Ant. J.*, LII (1972), 24sqq.
38. Cicero, *de leg. agr.*, II, 28, 78; cf. Kornemann, 'Bauernstand', *ap. PW.*, Supp. 4, 103, following Kromayer, *Neue Jahrb*, XVII 1914), 160sqq. For the background see R. E. Smith, *Service in the Post-Marian army.*
39. *Veterani Tarentum et Antium adscripti non tamen infrequentiae* (= depopulation) *locorum subvenere, dilapsis pluribus in provincia in quibus stipendia expleverent; neque coniugiis suscipiendis neque alendis liberis sueti orbas sine posteris domos relinquebant.* Tac., *Ann.*, XIV, 27, 3. For the overall trends see P. A. Brunt, 'The Army and Land in the Roman Revolution', *JRS* LII (1962), 67ff.
40. *Lib. Col.*, 76, 243.
41. G. Chilver, *Cisalpine Gaul.*
42. *CIL*, XI, 3200, 3258, 3083.
43. *CIL*, XI, 7431.
44. *CIL*, XI, 3303.
45. *CIL*, XI, 3040.
46. *M. Silio Epaphrodito patrono sevirum Aug. magistro iuvenum iterum iuvenes Lucoferonenses patrono ob marita quod amphithe(a)tru(m) col. Iul. Felici Luco Fer. s.p.f. dedicavitque, l.d.d.d.h.c.i.r.* Codex Vaticanus 6808 (= *CIL*, XI, 3938).
47. R. Bartoccini, 'L'Anfiteatro di Lucus Feroniae e il suo Fondatore', *Rend. Pont. Acc. Rom.*, XXXIII (1961), 1sqq.
48. Ibid., 10, fig. 8.
49. *CIL*, XI, 3932.
50. *ZGLE*, 162.
51. *CIL*, XI, 4689.
52. *ZGLE*, 376, 425.

53. *CIL*, XI, 3800.
54. *ZGLE*, 158, 468.
55. *CIL*, XI, 2317 = CIE 854.
56. *CIL*, XI, 3805.
57. *CIL*, XI 3254.
58. *CIL*, XI, 3331.
59. M. Bang, 'Die Herkunft der Röm. Sklaven', *Röm. Mitt.*, XXV (1910), 223sqq.; XXVII (1912), 180sqq. What the list of *liberti* signifies in proportion to the total population is not easy to assess, because the *total* population remains largely guesswork. Yet even in an agricultural area like the Ager Capenas, the *liberti* account for a startlingly high 46 per cent of all the names recorded in the region (172). For Rome proper, where obviously different considerations hold, Frank concluded that nearly 90 per cent of the population in the city was of foreign extraction (*Economic History of Rome*, 213sqq.; cf. 'Race Mixture in the Roman Empire', *AHR* XXI [1916], 689sqq.). While this estimate is probably exaggerated, the newly-excavated cemetery beneath St Peter's gives a figure of over 50 per cent for people ultimately of slave and, overwhelmingly, of 'oriental' origin (*Esplorazioni sotto la Confessione di San Pietro in Vaticano*, Vatican, 1951; cf. J. M. C. Toynbee and J. B. Ward-Perkins, *The Shrine of St. Peter and the Vatican Excavations*, 105sqq.).